Across the Pacific

Liners from Australia and New Zealand to North America

Aorangi (Vancouver Maritime Museum)

Across the Pacific

Liners from Australia and New Zealand to North America

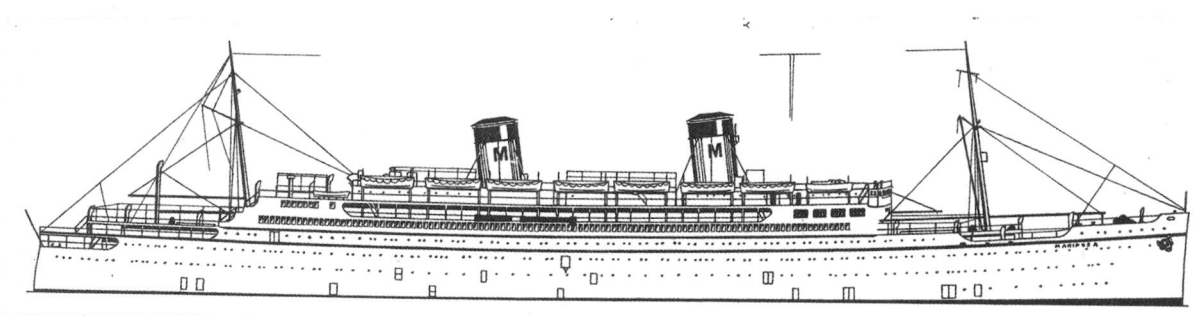

Mariposa

Peter Plowman

ROSENBERG

First published in Australia in 2010
by Rosenberg Publishing Pty Ltd
PO Box 6125, Dural Delivery Centre NSW 2158
Phone: 61 2 9654 1502 Fax: 61 2 9654 1338
Email: rosenbergpub@smartchat.net.au
Web: www.rosenbergpub.com.au

Copyright © Chiswick Publications Pty Ltd 2010

All rights reserved. No part of this publication may be reproduced, stored in a retrieval system, or transmitted, in any form or by any means, electronic, mechanical, photocopying, recording or otherwise, without the prior permission of the publisher in writing.

National Library of Australia Cataloguing-in-Publication data:

Author: Plowman, Peter.

Title: Across the Paciific : liners from Australia and New Zealand to North America / Peter Plowman.

Edition: 1st ed.

ISBN: 9781877058967 (pbk.)

Notes: Includes index.

Subjects: Ocean liners—Pacific Ocean.

Dewey Number: 623.82432

Cover: Stan Stefaniak painting of *Aorangi* and *Tahiti* off Sydney Heads

Printed in China by Everbest Printing Co Limited

CONTENTS

	Introduction	6
	Acknowledgments	8
1	Early Days	9
2	Early San Francisco Services	19
3	The A and A Line	29
4	The Pacific Mail Years	39
5	Oceanic and the Union Line	55
6	The All Red Route	66
7	Changes	79
8	The *Sierra* Trio	84
9	The Vancouver Route 1901 – 1914	93
10	Reviving the San Francisco Service	108
11	The First World War	120
12	The Post-War Years	129
13	The Second *Aorangi*	141
14	From San Francisco to Wellington	153
15	Disaster on Sydney Harbour	163
16	Times of Change	169
17	*Mariposa* and *Monterey*	183
18	1934 to 1939	195
19	The Second World War	209
20	Post-War Problems	224
21	Reviving the Vancouver Service	234
22	Orient-Pacific Line	245
23	The New *Mariposa* and *Monterey*	249
24	Aground and Sunk	258
25	Under new colours	265
	Index	272

Introduction

For just over a hundred years there was a regular passenger liner service across the Pacific connecting Australia and New Zealand with North America, the main terminal ports being San Francisco and Vancouver. This book describes the rather chaotic development of these services into a reliable and successful trade that flourished into the 1970s before the advent of the jumbo jet led to a rather rapid decline and eventual termination of the trans-Pacific passenger liner.

The possibility of establishing a steamship service across the Pacific from North America to Australia and New Zealand was raised in newspapers from time to time during the first half of the nineteenth century, but in the meantime the connection was maintained by an occasional sailing ship. It was the discovery of gold in Australia that finally gave the impetus for serious consideration of such a service.

In 1853 the first steamships made the long voyage across the Pacific from California to Australia, though this did not herald the start of a regular service. It was not until 1870 that the first attempt was made to operate a regular steamship service from North America to New Zealand and Australia, when the North Pacific Transportation Company began offering departures from San Francisco on the 10th of each month for Honolulu, Auckland, Sydney and Melbourne. This service lasted only a year, but then a new company was formed, the California, New Zealand & Australia Mail Steamship Co, the principals being Ben Holloday and William H Webb, and the company became better known as the Webb Line. They obtained three large paddle steamers for the service, which operated for two years before collapsing.

Despite this failure interest continued in developing a steamship service from San Francisco to Sydney, and during 1873 the Californian & Australian Steamship Company was formed, with financial backing from both British and American sources. They planned to operate five chartered ships on the route, but this lasted only a year.

In 1875, the Pacific Mail Steamship Company was given a ten-year mail contract to operate the Pacific route. Founded in 1848, Pacific Mail was already a well established company, operating regular services from San Francisco to Hong Kong and Japan. The contract with Pacific Mail ran its full ten years, expiring on 1 October 1885, but when it came up for renewal the company withdrew from the South Pacific trade.

A new contract was then signed for a joint service to be operated by the Oceanic Steamship Company, of America, and the Union Steam Ship Company of New Zealand, both well-established operators. They provided a successful service across the Pacific between San Francisco and Auckland and Sydney for the next fifteen years.

Although a regular steamship service was now operating between Australia, New Zealand and the United States, there were many British people attracted to the idea of an "All Red Route", or an all British route. This would entail the use of a Canadian Pacific steamer across the Atlantic from Britain to ports in eastern Canada, then being transported by train to the west coast port of Vancouver, to join another British steamer across the Pacific to New Zealand and Australia.

In 1893, an Australian, James Huddart, formed the Canadian-Australian Royal Mail Line, to operate the Pacific sector of the "All Red Route", and a regular service was commenced using two vessels, soon increased to three. However, in January 1898 James Huddart went bankrupt, and the New Zealand Shipping Company took over the Canadian-Australasian Royal Steamship Company and its ships, and the service continued without interruption. In 1901 the Union Steam Ship Company of New Zealand bought a half share in the service, and in future all ships used on the service to Vancouver would be owned and operated by them.

On 14 June 1900 Hawaii became a Territory of the United States, which meant that the Union Steam Ship Company vessels operating to San Francisco could no longer carry passengers on the sector between California and Hawaii. As a result, the New Zealand company withdrew from the San Francisco trade, leaving it entirely to the American-owned Oceanic Steamship Company. They decided to replace the two aging vessels they had been operating on the route with three new, larger vessels, which entered service during 1900 as *Sierra*, *Sonoma* and *Ventura*.

This trio became very popular on the South Pacific trade, but in 1907 an economic downturn in the United States, and heavy losses being incurred on the service, forced the Oceanic Steamship Company to withdraw from the San Francisco trade. The three vessels were laid up in San Francisco, leaving Australia and New Zealand with no direct connection to the United States. However, on the positive side, the service to Vancouver had been expanded over the past few years, and was proving very successful. A notable addition to the ships serving Vancouver was the *Niagara*, which entered service in 1913.

In 1908, The Union Steam Ship Company began a new service from Wellington to Tahiti, to connect with a service being operated by the Oceanic Steamship Company from San Francisco to Tahiti. This arrangement remained in place just over a year, but at the end of 1910 the Union Line decided to extend their service from Tahiti to San Francisco, once again providing a through service. At the end of 1911, the Union Line placed a recently purchased large vessel, renamed *Tahiti*, on the trade. In 1912, the Oceanic Steamship Company decided to resume their service from San Francisco and Honolulu to Sydney, so once again there were two companies providing a link between Australia and New Zealand and the United States.

When Great Britain went to war against Germany in August 1914, both Australia and New Zealand also declared war. Within months several of the Union Line ships that had been operating across the Pacific were taken for military duty. The Vancouver service was maintained by *Niagara* and *Makura* throughout the war, while various vessels were used to maintain the Union Line San Francisco route. Even after the United States came into the war in 1917, two Oceanic ships continued to trade to the South Pacific on a regular basis.

After the war ended, the San Francisco service took some time to be fully restored, but the Vancouver service was not as badly affected. By 1922 both services were operating fully, and in 1925 the Oceanic Steamship Company was purchased by the Matson Line, but the service to the South Pacific continued without change for the next few years. In 1925, the brand new *Aorangi* joined *Niagara* on the Vancouver route.

On 15 August 1930, the *Tahiti* suffered a major accident at sea, and sank two days later. The Union Line was quickly able to secure a replacement, the P&O liner *Razmak*, which was renamed *Monowai* and began operating on the San Francisco trade in 1931. Meanwhile, in August 1931 the Union Steamship Company of New Zealand reached an agreement with the Canadian Pacific Railway Company to form a new joint company, Canadian-Australasian Line Limited, in which each company would own a half share in both *Aorangi* and *Niagara* on the Vancouver trade.

During 1932, the Oceanic Steamship Company, as a subsidiary of the Matson Line, introduced two brand new liners on the trans-Pacific trade, *Mariposa* and *Monterey*, which immediately rendered all existing ships on the Pacific obsolete. The two American liners quickly became very popular on the San Francisco trade, so much so that the Union Line withdrew *Monowai* from the service. At the end of 1936 the New Zealand firm withdrew altogether from the San Francisco route, leaving it to the two American liners.

When Britain and Germany went to war again in 1939, both *Niagara* and *Aorangi* were left on the Vancouver trade, while *Mariposa* and *Monterey* continued the service from San Francisco, as the United States was still neutral. However, in June 1940 *Niagara* was sunk after hitting a mine off the New Zealand coast, being replaced by a magnificent liner, *Awatea*, built in 1936. *Aorangi* was taken for war service in July 1941, and *Awatea* was requisitioned two months later, and the Vancouver service ceased for the duration of the war.

Mariposa and *Monterey* remained on the San Francisco trade until 7 December 1941, when the United States came into the war. Both liners subsequently served as troop transports, and there was no connection at all between Australia and New Zealand and North America for the rest of the war.

When the war ended Matson Line planned to restore *Mariposa* and *Monterey* to the South Pacific trade, but due to the enormous cost of refitting them this was abandoned, and neither ship returned to the service. Instead, Matson Line operated a variety of war-built former troopships on the route for about eighteen months before abandoning it.

Aorangi had survived the war as well, and after a lengthy refit resumed the service from Sydney and Auckland to Vancouver in August 1948. For the next five years *Aorangi* struggled to survive operating a one-ship service, but in June 1953 the old liner was withdrawn, and the Vancouver service was terminated. To fill the gap on trans-Pacific services, the British Orient Line began scheduling occasional voyages from Sydney and Auckland to both Vancouver and San Francisco, with the P&O Line joining them a few years later. However, these were never on a regular basis, and often formed part of a voyage between Britain and the South Pacific.

In 1957 the Matson Line resumed the trade from San Francisco to the South Pacific when they placed a new *Mariposa* and *Monterey* on the route. Rebuilt from cargo ships, the new liners were smaller than their pre-war namesakes, but for over a decade enjoyed considerable success on the trade. However, in 1971 Matson sold the entire operation to Pacific Far East Line, who kept *Mariposa* and *Monterey* on the Pacific trade until 1977, when both ships were withdrawn, thus bringing to an end the era of regular passenger liner services between North America and the South Pacific.

Acknowledgments

For many years I have been keeping records on passenger ships that have operated to Australia and New Zealand from overseas ports with a view to eventually using the information in books. The material contained in this volume has come from many sources, including newspapers, maritime magazines and various published works.

My inspiration to write this book came some years ago, when I found that there was very little material available on the services operated across the Pacific. I felt it was a story worth telling, but did not realise the extent and scope of the project I had set myself.

As with all my books, I hoped to include a wide variety of photographs to accompany the text, many drawn from my own collection. However, there were gaps that needed filling, if possible with previously unpublished photographic and brochure material.

Illustrations included in this book were taken by a number of photographers, and where their names are known to me I have attributed them, while those photographs with no attribution have been in my collection for many years. This includes pictures from the collection of the late Fred Roderick, now held by the New South Wales Branch of the World Ship Society, from the vast collection of the late Bob Tompkins, as well as material I received many years ago from the late Vic Scrivens. The late Robert W "Bobby" Brookes, who lived in Launceston, sent me a large amount of material shortly before he passed away, knowing that one day I would be able to use it in various books.

The Whitehead Collection is held by the Victoria Branch of the World Ship Society, and I am extremely grateful to the Branch President, John Bone, for granting me permission to use a number of photographs from that collection in this book. I am sure they will be greatly appreciated by readers. Fortunately, the entire Whitehead Collection has been scanned by John Asome, and I particularly thank Glen Stuart for taking the time to locate the photographs I requested and send them to me.

Other valuable photographs and information for the book have been provided by Dallas Hogan, John Mathieson, David Robinson, John Bennett, Ross Gillett, Jim Freeman, David Cooper, Vic Young and Bob McDougall, to whom I express my warmest appreciation.

I was very fortunate to meet up with Ken Hall, who showed me the brochures that had been collected by his father in the 1920s and 30s, among them some amazing material produced by Canadian-Australasian Line, including the interior pictures of *Niagara* and *Aorangi* which are reproduced in this book.

I am also very grateful to my friend Tony Ralph, from Auckland, who lent me a variety of brochures produced by the Matson Line, enabling me to include the wonderful interior illustrations of the first *Mariposa* and *Monterey*.

In my quest to find interesting photographs of vessels in foreign locations, I was able to purchase a number of illustrations held by the Vancouver Maritime Museum, to whom I express my thanks.

On a visit to Wellington, New Zealand, I spent many enjoyable hours going through the shipping photographs at the Alexander Turnbull Library, where I was greatly assisted by Joan McCracken, who pointed me to the location of some of the best pictures to be found in this book.

I had always hoped to include some colour photographs in this book, and have been able to obtain copies of a selection of very interesting paintings.

I am very grateful to Laureen Sadlier at the Museum of Wellington City and Sea, who enabled me to go through the entire series of ship paintings by J E Hobbs, from which I selected nine to be included in this book.

Thanks are also expressed to John Bradley for giving me permission to reproduce his painting "When Steam Ruled", depicting the Matson liner *Monterey* passing under the Sydney Harbour Bridge. Prints of this painting are available from the artist over the internet.

I have been most fortunate in obtaining a variety of colour slides, taken by the late Fred Roderick, the late Ron Knight, Stephen Berry and John Mathieson.

The wonderful painting that appears on the cover, and another in the colour inserts, were done specially for this book by my good friend, Stan Stefaniak, who is a superb maritime artist. This is my third book to feature one of his paintings on the cover, and I am pleased to have another opportunity to bring his work to a wider audience.

To all these people who so generously helped me with this book I extend my sincere thanks.

Any errors, omissions or misinterpretations included in this book are entirely my own responsibility.

Chapter One

Early Days

The possibility of establishing a steamship service across the Pacific from Australia and New Zealand to North America had been raised in newspapers from time to time during the first half of the nineteenth century, but in the meantime the connection was maintained by an occasional sailing ship. It was the discovery of gold in Australia that finally gave the impetus for serious consideration of such a service.

The discovery of gold in California in January 1848 had resulted in a rush to the area by people hoping to make their fortune, but for the vast majority this had not happened. When reports began reaching America in 1851 of large gold finds in Australia that far exceeded those in California, it created an unprecedented demand for passages that could not be met by the available sailing ships. Those ships that did make the voyage often were left stranded in Melbourne or Geelong when their crew deserted en masse to join the rush to the gold fields around Ballarat and Bendigo.

Crossing the Pacific presented serious problems for the early steamships, primarily lack of available coaling stations. The rather primitive engines installed in these vessels required large amounts of coal to keep the boilers producing steam, but good quality coal was not available as a natural resource in any of the Pacific islands. This meant that the vessel had to load much more coal than would be required for a trip across the Atlantic, and the only place the extra coal could be stored was in the cargo holds, which consequently reduced the amount of cargo that could be carried. This meant a reduction in income for the shipowner, combined with the extra expense of having to carry more coal than the ship had been designed to hold in its bunkers, so in every aspect the prospect of sending a steamship across the Pacific was not economic.

It was not until 1853 that the first steamships made the long voyage across the Pacific from California to Australia, though this did not herald the start of a regular service. In fact, the earliest steamers to make the voyage were owned by speculators who wanted to make money by filling the ship with prospectors for the voyage out, then selling the vessel in Australia.

The first vessel to be sent in this manner was the tiny 368 gross ton iron-hulled screw steamer *Conside*, which was only 105 ft/32m long and 27 ft/8.2m wide, and powered by a two-cylinder geared oscillating steam engine. It had been built in Britain in 1848 by Thomas Dunn Marshall at South Shields for Joseph Clay to operate on the coal trade to Hamburg, and is considered to be the first specially built steam powered collier. In 1851 *Conside* must have been fitted with passenger accommodation, as it made a voyage from Le Havre in France around Cape Horn to San Francisco, carrying gold seekers from Europe.

Late in 1851, advertisements began appearing in San Francisco newspapers that *Conside* would be making a voyage to Sydney, though the departure date was delayed several times. On 23 November the following advertisement appeared in the *Daily Alta*:

STEAMER FOR SYDNEY
Lying alongside Pacific Wharf.
In consequence of an unavoidable detention the departure of the splendid steam packet CONSIDE, 700 tons burthen, Capt Appleby, has been postponed until Saturday, 29th inst, on which day she will be positively dispatched. She has received her coal on board, and completed her fitting up for passengers, who are invited to go on board and judge for themselves of the accommodation offered by this opportunity.

In fact it was not until 6 December 1851 that *Conside* departed San Francisco on the voyage to Australia, again carrying gold seekers. Because of the great distance involved, and the lack of suitable coaling ports, the vessel took 70 days to cross the Pacific, though only 16 days were under steam, the rest being made under sail, the vessel having been rigged as a barque. It is not known if the vessel stopped anywhere on the voyage. *Conside* arrived in Sydney on 14 February 1852.

On 16 February the *Sydney Morning Herald* stated "her lengthy passage may be attributed to a succession of calms and baffling winds, as she only steamed sixteen days during the run; she brought several passengers, but no cargo".

Soon after arriving in Sydney, *Conside* was offered for sale by auction, but was not sold. The vessel was then put into Mort's Dock to have the bottom cleaned and repainted, while at the same time the machinery was overhauled, a new propeller fitted, and the rig changed from barque to schooner. After this work was completed, *Conside* became the first propeller-powered steamer to be placed in service between Sydney and Melbourne.

Just before midnight on 14 September 1852 the vessel, on its fifth voyage from Sydney, with 180 passengers on board, was approaching Port Phillip Heads when Captain Appleby was apparently misled by the lights of the schooner *Portland*, which had been wrecked on Lonsdale Reef only a few hours earlier. The *Conside* ran aground on Lonsdale Reef at full speed, and almost immediately 19 passengers panicked and rushed into one of the lifeboats, released only one of the falls, and were thrown into the sea, with only five being rescued. The second officer was able to reach the shore and summon help, and early on the morning of 15 September the steamer *Maitland* rescued the survivors. Two days after going aground, the *Conside* slipped off the rocks and sank, and the wreck is now a popular diving site.

The first complete crossing of the Pacific by a vessel under steam power only was made in 1853 by the American vessel *Monumental City*. A 768 gross ton wooden-hulled single-screw vessel, *Monumental City* was built in Baltimore by Murray & Hazelhurst Ltd for Allan A Chapman, Robert Kirkland, Isaac Norris and Peter Strobel, who wanted to establish a shipping service between Baltimore and San Francisco.

Launched on 14 November 1850, *Monumental City* was completed in 1851, and was described as having a flush promenade deck and accommodation for about 250 passengers in first and second class. The vessel was 174 ft/53.3m long with a beam of 30 2ft/9.1m, and powered by a two-cylinder oscillating engine giving a speed of 12 knots.

Taking advantage of the California gold rush, *Monumental City* was sent to the Pacific to operate a service between Panama and San Francisco, operating under the banner of the Empire City Line, and early in 1852 it also made one return voyage from San Francisco to San Juan del Sur on behalf of shipowner Cornelius Vanderbilt.

Monumental City departed San Francisco on 17 February 1853 for Australia, taking twenty days to reach Otaheite in Tahiti where coal bunkers were available. The vessel remained there fifteen days taking on coal, then left for Sydney, but had to divert to Tongataboo, where it arrived on 6 April for repairs to the rudder. While in Tongataboo, the vessel took on board Captain Creswell and fifteen passengers from the wrecked sailing ship *Rapid*. Leaving on 9 April, *Monumental City* arrived in Sydney on 23 April, having taken 65 days to cross the Pacific.

It was reported that on arrival *Monumental City* was carrying 16 cabins passengers, these being the *Rapid* survivors, and 124 men in steerage. The report continued: "She is a very fine steamer, magnificently fitted up, her accommodation for passengers being very superior. It is very probable after her arrival in Melbourne she will be employed in the trade between that port, Adelaide and Sydney." The cargo brought to Sydney by the vessel was listed as "100,000 cigars, 11 boxes merchandise, 1 case Colt's pistols."

Monumental City stayed nearly two weeks in Sydney, and was advertised as carrying passengers to Melbourne, departing on 4 May, but due to "unavoidable circumstances" did not leave Sydney until 5 May, arriving in Melbourne on 8 May. On its first northbound voyage *Monumental City* was wrecked on 15 May 1853 after running aground on Tullaberga Island near Mallacoota Inlet and Gabo Island, on the coast of Victoria. Out of the 86 passengers and crew on board, 33 lost their lives in the disaster. At the time of the tragedy there was no lighthouse on Gabo Island, and to rectify this situation a temporary six metre high tower with a four metre diameter lantern attached was erected there in December 1853.

The next steamship to arrive in Australia from America was to enjoy more success. The 682 gross ton paddle steamer *New Orleans* had been built in 1848 in New York, and from early in 1850 had been operating a service between Panama and San Francisco, carrying gold prospectors who had been taken by ship from ports along the eastern seaboard of North America to Chagres, in Panama. After disembarking there, the travellers would board canoes, locally called cayugas, which carried them forty miles up the Chagres River to a town called Gorgona, where a track began to the west coast, the travellers either walking or riding horses or mules. Although this section was only twenty miles long, it involved climbing over hills and took up to ten hours to complete. At Panama the travellers boarded another ship for the final leg to California. This overland route was also used by other travellers who wanted to avoid the dangerous passage around Cape Horn to get from the Atlantic to the Pacific on their way to Peru or Chile.

In 1849 the Panama Railroad Company was formed in New York, with the aim of building a railroad connection from Gorgona to the west coast of Panama. Work commenced on this project in January 1850, but the great difficulty experienced

Monumental City, the first steamer to cross the Pacific

in getting workers and materials up the Chagres River to Gorgona proved insurmountable. It was decided that the only practical solution was to build a railroad right across the isthmus, with the eastern starting point being in a mangrove swamp eight miles east of Chagres. Initially this eastern terminus was called Aspinwall, but the name was later changed to Colon. This 47-mile railroad was completed in October 1854, the travelling time from coast to coast being reduced to less than four hours, and in much greater comfort.

On 10 March 1853, *New Orleans* departed San Francisco on a voyage to Australia with 110 passengers on board. Voyaging by way of Nukahiva, Tahiti and Tongatabu, the *New Orleans* stopped first at Brisbane before arriving in Sydney on 14 May, after a 64 day voyage. Time spent in port was 22½ days, including almost nine days in Brisbane, so the actual travelling time was just over 41½ days.

The month following its arrival in Sydney, *New Orleans* was offered for sale. A description of the ship stated there was accommodation for 160 passengers in the saloon, 60 in the ladies cabin, and 400 in steerage, but they would not have all been supplied with bunks. *New Orleans* was bought by the Sydney & Melbourne Steam Packet Co, by whom it was renamed *Governor General*, to distance it from its American background. The vessel spent six years plying along the east coast of Australia, then in January 1861 was sent to Hong Kong and sold for service on the Yangtse River, becoming the third foreign vessel to reach Hankow.

Up to this time there had been no attempt to send a steamship across the Pacific from Australia to North America, this trade being maintained by sailing ships on a very irregular basis. For example, on 25 April 1853 the following advertisement appeared in the *Sydney Morning Herald*:

FOR SAN FRANCISCO DIRECT
The splendid clipper barque SPEED, A1, 600 tons burthen, Thomas Cannell, commander, is (by the request of numerous parties who arrived in this ship, and are desirous of returning by the same vessel) again laid on, and, having all her deadweight engaged, will have immediate dispatch. Intending passengers are invited to inspect her splendid 'tween decks, 7 feet in height, so that they may make immediate arrangements for proceeding by this unusually eligible opportunity. For light freight, or passage, apply to Captain Cannell; or to
SHEPPARD AND ALGER, Packet Offices,
480 George Street.

In April 1852 a special meeting had been held at the London head office of the Royal Mail Steam Packet Co, to which several directors from the Pacific Steam Navigation Company were invited. Both these firms had developed a network of services from Britain to the West Indies, Central America and South America, but the object of the meeting was the establishment of a connecting service across the Pacific from Panama to New Zealand and Australia.

As a direct result of this meeting, on 9 October 1852 the Australasian Pacific Mail Steam Packet Co was incorporated by Royal Charter, and orders were immediately placed for the construction of six steamships to be used on the new service, which would ultimately offer monthly departures from each end. As soon as each ship was completed in Britain, it would be sent on a special voyage from Southampton to Australia via Cape Town.

One of the reasons behind this new venture was the building of a railway across the isthmus of Panama, which would greatly expedite the transfer of passengers and mail. The Royal Mail Line had taken a financial interest in the Panama Railroad, which was completed in February 1855.

The plan was that passengers and mail would be carried from Britain to Colon on the east coast of Panama on one of the Royal Mail Line vessels then operating to the West Indies. After being transported across the narrow isthmus to the west coast, they would join one of the new vessels for the voyage to Tahiti, Wellington and Sydney, on which five of the new 1,700 gross tons steamers, to be named *Kangaroo*, *Emeu*, *Dinornis*, *Black Swan* and *Menura*, would operate, this sector being managed by the Pacific Steam Navigation Co. The sixth vessel, *Pelican*, would be smaller, about 1,100 gross tons, and provide a feeder service between Sydney and Melbourne.

The departure from Southampton of the first ship, *Kangaroo*, was originally scheduled for August 1853, but it was not launched until 20 August, and two days later the second ship, *Emeu*, was launched. The date for the departure of *Kangaroo* from Britain was put back to October 1853, but this failed to happen, and soon it was being advertised that the first vessel to leave would be the *Emeu*, on 21 February 1854. The vessel was described as providing accommodation for 80 first class and 130 second class passengers, and although it arrived in Southampton from the Clyde, where it had been built, on 7 February, the departure date was put back to 30 March. Then, quite suddenly, the entire operation was abandoned, as the British Government had refused to offer a mail contract to the company, and the price of obtaining coal at Tahiti had increased enormously.

Kangaroo and *Emeu* were chartered out to the Admiralty for six months as troop transports for the Crimean War, then sold. *Dinornis*, *Black Swan* and *Menura* were sold immediately they were completed, while work on the sixth vessel, *Pelican*, never started. *Emeu*, which was bought by the Cunard Line, was later sold to the P&O, and under their ownership made several voyages to Australia in 1859 and 1860.

The possibility of establishing a regular steamship service across the Pacific moved closer to reality in March 1853, when the New York and Australian Navigation Company was established in New York. They announced that a service would be established using five paddlesteamers on a route from Sydney to Panama, where passengers and cargo would be transported overland to the east coast and join another steamer for the passage to New York. However, the American terminal would become San Francisco when the trans-continental railway was completed.

The new company was able to purchase a paddle-steamer then under construction by William H Brown at New York, which had been laid down as the *Adriatic* in the hope that it would be bought by the Collins Line, which at that time was the major American operator on the trans-Atlantic trade. The vessel was renamed *Golden Age* prior to completion, following which it made a voyage across the Atlantic to New York.

Golden Age had a wooden hull, the lower frames being oak while the top-frames were locust-wood and cedar. The entire hull was double-diagonally braced with iron bars. Power was provided by an American-built beam engine in which an upright cylinder, said at the time to be the largest yet installed in a ship, worked direct to one end of a massive, stoutly braced beam, which swung in heavy trunnions above the deckhouse. The idea behind these engines was to save space and fuel.

Good quality accommodation for 200 first class, 200 second class and 800 third class passengers was installed, with particular attention having been paid to ventilation inside the ship, which was a problem in early steamships. In first class there were three saloons, panelled in rose, satin and zebra woods, two having crimson and gold plush furnishings, while the upper saloon had white and gold furnishings. Five hundred tons of cargo could be carried, and the bunkers could hold 1,200 tons of coal.

Having boarded a full complement of passengers, *Golden Age* departed Liverpool on 28 November 1853 on a voyage to Australia via South Africa, but the trip had barely commenced when the vessel collided with the North Wall on the Birkenhead shore of the River Mersey, and had to return for dry docking and repairs.

Departing again on 5 December, *Golden Age* called at the Cape Verde Islands and Cape Town for bunkers, arriving in Melbourne on 14 February 1854 and Sydney on 23 February. For the next three months the vessel was employed on the coastal trade between Sydney and Melbourne.

Despite a report appearing in the *Sydney Shipping Gazette* that the vessel "was originally intended to trade between Panama and Sydney, but it is now intended that she shall ply between San Francisco and Sydney", The *Golden Age* departed Melbourne on 5 May 1854 for Sydney, where more passengers and cargo were taken on board, then on 11 May 1854 the vessel departed, bound for Tahiti and Panama. On board were only 100 passengers, mail, and some general cargo.

Golden Age arrived in Tahiti in 13 days 6 hours, departing on 30 May and taking 19 days to reach Panama, on 17 June, having consumed 2,600 tons of coal on the entire 9,862 mile voyage. However, the high price paid for poor quality coal obtained at Tahiti resulted in the voyage showing a considerable loss of £20,000, although the mails sent overland across Panama and placed on another steamer arrived in London in just 65 days.

At the conclusion of the voyage to Panama, the commander of the *Golden Age*, Lieutenant Porter, suggested to the owners of the New York &

Golden Age

Australian Navigation Co that "Until coal can be provided in New Zealand at a moderate cost the Panama route must be abandoned, except a mail contract of 10/- a mile be entered into".

Lieutenant Porter also stated that the route would only be a success if it was operated in two stages, each operated by two steamers meeting up in Tahiti. To suit the stormy weather encountered on the Australian coast and in the Tasman Sea, it would require two substantial vessels for the sector to Tahiti, while two vessels of much lighter construction and better suited to the tropics would provide the link to Panama.

This suggestion was not taken up, and the losses suffered on the voyage were sufficient to cause the company to abandon plans to establish a regular service. *Golden Age* never returned to Australia, but was sold to the Pacific Mail Steamship Co, and spent twenty-one years serving them before being sold to a Japanese company, Mitsubishi Shoji Kaisha, and renamed *Hiroshima Maru*.

The railway line across Panama was completed on 25 January 1855, and in October 1856 the Royal Mail Line again proposed the establishment of a "line of auxiliary screw steamships from Panama to New Zealand", with monthly departures and a passage time from Britain of 55 days, but nothing more was heard of this scheme.

In 1857 the Intercolonial Royal Mail Steam Packet Co was formed in New Zealand to operate a regular service across the Tasman Sea to Australia, and commenced operations in November 1858, eventually having three vessels on the trade, *Lord Ashley*, *Lord Worsley* and *Prince Alfred*. Over the next few years the New Zealand Government tried to obtain better shipping services from Britain, but when nothing had been achieved by 1863, the Government decided to proceed on their own by inviting tenders for a monthly mail service from New Zealand to Panama. In December 1863, the contract was awarded to the Intercolonial Royal Mail Steam Packet Co. Soon after the New South Wales Government approached the New Zealand Government with regard to the service being extended to include Australia, and the subsidy would be shared by the two governments.

Under this new arrangement there would be monthly departures from Sydney, with a call at Wellington on the way to Panama. There passengers and mail would be transported across the isthmus on the newly opened railroad, and join a Royal Mail Line ship at Colon for the voyage across the Atlantic to Southampton. The entire trip was scheduled to take 60 days.

As a result, the Intercolonial Royal Mail Steam Packet Co was reorganised, and a new company registered as the Panama, New Zealand and Australia Royal Mail Co, with a capital of £375,000, some of which was provided by the Royal Mail Steam Packet Co. Four iron-hulled steamers were ordered from different British shipyards, to enable the new service to commence in 1866. Accommodation would be provided for 100 first class and 60 second class passengers, and the ships would have a service speed of 10 knots.

The first of the new ships to be completed was the 1,561 gross ton *Kaikoura*, which was built by Charles Lungley & Co, at Deptford on the River Thames, being launched on 12 June 1865 and departing London on 28 February 1866 and Plymouth on 8 March for Sydney via Cape Town. The vessel was 272 feet long with a beam of 34 feet, fitted with accommodation for 100 first, 60 second and about 50 steerage passengers, and at a service speed of 10½ knots consumed 28 tons of coal every 24 hours.

Drawing of *Kaikoura* with sails set.

The outward voyage by *Kaikoura* was not without incident as two of the three blades of the propeller were lost, the first on 30 March in the vicinity of St Helena and the second four days later. As the vessel was fully-rigged it was able to proceed under sail into Cape Town, where a temporary replacement propeller was fitted while a new one was manufactured in Britain to be fitted later. *Kaikoura* arrived in Melbourne on 7 May and Sydney five days later. On 10 May the following report appeared in the *Sydney Morning Herald*:

> The Kaikoura, the first of the ocean line of steamers in these waters of the Panama, New Zealand, and Australian Royal Mail Company, which was telegraphed off the Otway on Saturday afternoon, at half-past 4 o'clock, came up the bay yesterday, and anchored off the Sandridge Railway Pier shortly before 1 p.m. The Kaikoura, although by no means pretentious in appearance, is a fine vessel of beautiful lines and brig rigged. The registered tonnage of this smart steamer is 1,501 tons; and her engines are of 300 horse-power nominal. She carries 1200 tons of coal, and can steam thirteen knots easily on a consumption of twenty-eight tons per day. Her cylinders are eighty inches, with a three feet six inch stroke. On her trial trip she steamed thirteen knots and a half per hour with her expansion valves opened. She is also built in watertight compartments, and has proved herself a remarkably rapid vessel, under steam or canvas. Her saloon accommodation is of a first-class order, and aims at a judicious combination of comfort and economy in providing for upwards of 100 saloon and 40 second-class passengers. She has a spacious spar-deck, which forms a splendid promenade. Her pantry is fitted up with a due regard to creature comforts, and contains a steam hot chest, steam boiler, and a steam tea and coffee percolator for the use of the saloon. Below there is a capacious ice-house, capable of containing sufficient ice for the entire voyage from Wellington to Panama, and from the Isthmus to these colonies. Her provedore arrangements are spoken of as being complete, and the saloon table is alleged to be equal to that of any first-class hotel in London. On deck the Kaikoura is supplied with all the latest and most efficient improvements in the shape of steam winches. She has also a steam capstan for lifting the anchor, and carries patent reefing topsails. She has a top gallant forecastle for the housing of the crew.

Advertisements had been appearing in local newspapers since 21 April advising that *Kaikoura* would depart Sydney on 1 June, but due to the late arrive this was put back two weeks. Fares from Sydney to Southampton were shown as £95 to £105 saloon, £65 second cabin, while Sydney to Panama was £55 to £60 saloon and £35 second cabin.

On 15 June 1866 *Kaikoura* departed Sydney, on the first ever trans-Pacific mail service, preceding Pacific Mail's first North America to the Orient voyage by almost six months. On board were six saloon and seven second-cabin passengers for Wellington, and eighteen saloon and seven second-cabin passengers for Panama. Cargo comprised three packages for Wellington and eleven for Panama. Departing Wellington on 15 June, *Kaikoura* arrived at Panama on 21 July. After completing the overland connection, passengers left Colon on 23 July, arriving at Southampton on 14 August.

The second vessel, *Rakaia*, was built by Randolph

Ruahine

Elder & Co, at Govan on the Clyde, and launched on 31 January 1866, being an almost exact sister to *Kaikoura*. *Rakaia* departed Milford Haven for a positioning voyage to Panama, with calls at St. Vincent and Rio de Janeiro for coal.

The third vessel, the 1,504 gross ton *Ruahine*, was built on the River Thames by J & W Dudgeon Co. It is possible this vessel was ordered by other interests and bought while under construction, as it was fitted with twin propellers. *Ruahine* provided accommodation for 100 first class, 40 second class and 65 steerage passengers, but had a smaller cargo capacity due to the two sets of machinery required to power the twin propellers. On trials *Ruahine* achieved a top speed of 13.8 knots, and departed London on 31 March 1866 for Australia, reaching Melbourne on 12 June and Sydney on 18 June. On 13 June *The Argus* reported:

> The Panama, New Zealand, and Australian Royal Mail Company's screw steamship Ruahine, which was telegraphed off Cape Otway on Monday afternoon about 4 o'clock, arrived at the heads the same evening at 11, where she anchored for the night, and came up the bay yesterday morning. The Ruahine is the second of the line of ocean steamers intended to perform the Transpacific mail service between Wellington, NZ, and Panama, and her arrival in anticipation of the April mails from Europe has been eagerly expected. This magnificent steamer, like her forerunner the Kaikoura, is brig rigged, and is a handsome specimen of vessels of her class. She has a sharp entrance, and a fine clear run fore and aft, and her passenger accommodation is something extensive, her maindeck berths being fitted up for seventy first-class passengers, forty second-class, and seventy third-class. Her saloon, seventy-seven feet in length, is luxuriously furnished, and is fitted up with a piano, library, and plunge and shower baths, and contains almost every comfort and convenience for voyagers by the Panama route. The Ruahine is registered at 1,610 tons, and her load displacement is stated to be 2,440 tons, her coal bunkers carrying 1,200 tons of fuel, an amount in excess of her requirements, even with full steam during the entire voyage. The steamer is propelled by twin screws, which can be driven together or separately, according as the vessel *may* have the wind, and the motive power is supplied by two pairs of engines, of the combined nominal horse-power of 400. The engines have two pairs of annular cylinders, with a two-foot stroke, and drive two three-bladed screws, having a diameter of ten feet and a half, and a pitch of 18 feet 6 inches. By working the screws separately the vessel can be turned round as if on a pivot. The boilers are heated by ten furnaces, and are fitted with Davison's patent surface condensers. The engines are made by the builders of the steamer, Messrs. J and W Dudgeon, of Millwall. The Ruahine left London on April 6th, and called at Plymouth, leaving that port on the 8th. Her commander, Captain T S Beal, is of some eminence in his profession, having commanded the Queen of the South, the Harbinger, the Hellespont, and other large steam vessels. At the termination of the voyage highly laudatory addresses were presented to Captain Beal and his officers by the passengers. The new screw for the P and NZ Company's steamer Kaikoura has been brought out by the Company's steamer Ruahine, and will be forwarded to Wellington with all possible dispatch.

Meanwhile, *Rakaia* had been making its positioning voyage to Panama. Off the River Plate estuary the vessel encountered extremely bad weather, being forced to heave to for forty-eight hours. While passing through the Straits of Magellan another storm forced the ship to seek safe anchorage in Borgia Bay for a day. *Rakaia* finally arrived in Panama on 17 June, having completed the 19,000 mile voyage in just under three months, with forty-six days actual steaming.

On 2 June 1866 the Royal Mail Line steamer *Atrato* had departed Southampton on a regular voyage to St Thomas in the West Indies, where passengers and mail were transferred to the feeder vessel *Danube* for the short passage to Colon. After crossing the isthmus, the passengers and mail joined the *Rakaia*, which left Colon on 24 June, arriving in Wellington 28 days later to an enthusiastic welcome. After several days in port the vessel then continued on to Sydney, arriving on 1 August. Next day the Sydney *Morning Herald* reported on the arrival of *Rakaia* as follows:

> This beautiful ship, the third belonging to the Panama and New Zealand Company, arrived yesterday morning, at 9 o'clock bringing the English mails of June 2nd. She sailed from Panama on the 24th of June, and arrived at Wellington on 22nd of July, the voyage being accomplished in twenty-eight days, during the first twelve of which she encountered fair weather; but after passing Pitcairn's Island a series of heavy gales were encountered, which caused the slight delay in her passage from Panama. At Wellington the ship was received with a perfect ovation. She left on the 25th ultimo, and has met with very heavy gales at W and SW; but for which, and the fact of having run short of coal, owing to the loss of four of the company's colliers, and consequent short

supply at Wellington, she would have been here on the 29th ultimo. She was within 300 miles of this port on the 30th ultimo, proving under ordinary circumstances how easily the service can be performed; and be it remembered that this, the first ship, has had to labour under disadvantages that will not occur again,- hurried to sea from England; arrived at Panama; dispatched thence without any rest, or time to make the few repairs or adjustments that are so essential after so long a voyage, and the passage completed, to the satisfaction of all on board. At Wellington she is again dispatched with a short supply of coal. The Rakaia is a brig-rigged vessel of 1,500 tons, 265 feet in length, 32 feet beam, and 28 feet depth of hold; her internal arrangements are a counterpart of the Kaikoura and Ruahine, but the saloon displays a far higher style and finish, the ornamentation being elaborate in the extreme, and affords accommodation for 140 first-class passengers, the cabins, it is needless to say, being fitted with every conceivable appliance that can in any way conduce to the comfort of those on board. The engines are by the same firm as the ship, and bear the reputation of being the finest set yet turned out. They are patent compound geared engines of 350 horse-power, nominal working up to 1,500 indicated. The two smaller engines are high pressure, with 43-inch cylinders. These first use the steam, it then expands into the compressure cylinders of 79 inches diameter, and having a 4-feet 3-inch stroke, this combined power is given off on a drum fitted with internal gearing, causing the 4-bladed propeller, which is 15 feet in diameter, with a 17 feet pitch, to revolve 2½ times for every stroke of the engines. The engines are supplied with superheaters and surface condensers, patented by Messrs. Davidson. Steam is generated in two cylindrical tubular boilers, 13 feet in diameter, and 16 feet in length. This noble ship is commanded by Captain SH Wright, late of the Calcutta.

Ruahine took the second departure from Sydney for Panama at the start of August 1866, thus becoming the first twin-screw ocean steamship to enter regular commercial service. It was followed by *Rakaia* on 2 September, carrying only 23 passengers and a small amount of cargo, comprising 15 cases and one box, as well as 1,000 sovereigns in safe keeping. *Kaikoura* took the October departure and *Ruahine* left in November, thus establishing a regular timetable of departures from Sydney at the beginning of each month.

In order to ensure a regular service, the 1,122 gross ton *Prince Alfred* was taken off the trans-Tasman trade and left Sydney on 5 October for Panama to be held in reserve there in case of any breakdowns or other problems affecting one of the four regular vessels. For the positioning voyage *Prince Alfred* mostly was under sail, only using the engine when necessary.

The fourth vessel, *Mataura*, was launched at the Millwall Shipbuilding & Graving Dock Co yard on 17 February 1866. It was larger than the three previous vessels, being 1,786 gross tons, 302 feet long with a beam of 35 feet. *Mataura* departed London on 9 July 1866, but had a disastrous delivery voyage, not arriving in Sydney until 6 November. Next day the *Sydney Morning Herald* reported:

Mataura arrived Sydney on 6 November after a most protracted voyage from London and was advertised to sail for Panama on 1 December. She left London on 23 July and on 4 September the driving wheel was seriously damaged. She arrived Cape Town on the 15th after spending ten days under sail alone while the engineers worked on the damaged machinery. Repairs to the engines kept her at Cape Town until the 23rd but after only three days at sea a further breakdown disabled the machinery for another three days. When nearing the Australian coast on 21 October the engines again broke down resulting in the ship being under sail only for yet another four days.

The arrival of this fine steamer has completed the line of vessels intended by the Panama and New Zealand Co to run the mail between this port and Panama, and although her passage from England has not been as rapid as the steamers preceding her; she is, nevertheless, equally as fine a ship.

The proportions of the Mataura exceed in every respect those of the company's steamers which have yet been in this port, and her lines, although equally fine and symmetrical as those of her predecessors, the Kaikoura and the Ruahine, are more suggestive of strength than fleetness. Like them, she is brig-rigged, and fitted up with steam winches and all the latest mechanical improvements. Her length overall is 305 feet, and between perpendiculars 285 feet, her beam being thirty-five and a half feet, with a depth of hold of twenty-seven feet. Her builders are the Millwall Ironworks Shipbuilding Company, and it is but justice to state that they have succeeded in launching a first-class vessel, and have been unsparing in their attention to useful details. Her saloon is a noble apartment, fitted up in superb style, and when lit up at night is almost Oriental in its appearance. There is a well stored library, a piano, plunge and shower baths, and accommodation for 130 first class passengers, and in the second cabin there is accommodation for 75 passengers. There is a washing and drying machine on

Mataura

board, and the pantry is supplied with a steam hot chest, steam boiler, steam percolator for tea and coffee, and various other arrangements conducive to the comfort of passengers. Her engines are by the same builders as the ship, and consist of three inverted cylinders 70 inches in diameter, with three feet length of stroke, and are nominally of 450 horsepower but will work up to 2,300, driving the ship at a speed of 13½ knots; she has surface condensers with 1,410 tubes in each, the consumption of fuel being 36 tons per twenty-four hours, and in fact all the most recent improvements have been supplied. Nor must we forget to mention that the comfort of the passengers, and the various arrangements connected therewith have been entrusted to Mr Owen, the purser, a gentleman whose long experience has justly fitted him to take the office. Her commander, Captain George E Bird, who has acquired no mean reputation in his profession, having commanded the screw steamship Golden Fleece, and also the company's steamer Ruahine, on the West India station, is highly spoken of, and, together with his officers, was complimented at the pleasant termination of the passage.

The trans-Pacific fleet was now complete, but with *Mataura* being at the yard of M'Arthur & Co for a continuation of repairs to the machinery, on 23 November it was announced that the December sailing would be taken by *Tararua*. It would depart on 2 December and connect at Wellington with *Rakaia*, which would turn around and return to Panama, while passengers and cargo for Sydney would be carried there on *Tararua*. *Mataura* was ready in time to take the January departure.

The 6,500 mile haul across the Pacific between Wellington and Panama meant the ships had to load a huge amount of coal, but if bad weather was encountered there was the possibility of the bunkers running out before the ship reached port. On its second southbound voyage from Panama, in December 1866, *Kaikoura* called at the tiny island of Rapa, also known as Opara, 2,080 miles from Wellington and 4,365 miles from Panama, and took soundings to evaluate the island as a possible intermediate coaling station. Rapa was stated to have one of the finest harbours in the world, though the native population was only about 500. It was decided to establish a bunker supply at Rapa, with coal being delivered there by sailing ships, which then anchored in the harbour until their cargo had been exhausted.

Considering the enormous distance travelled, the service suffered surprisingly few mishaps, and became noted for its reliability. On its first voyage, *Mataura* was held up three days at Panama due to the late arrival in Colon of the Royal Mail Line steamer from Britain, and also took on board some very poor quality coal in Panama, which caused it to run short on the way to Wellington, and have to raise sail. *Mataura* eventually arrived in Sydney on 18 April 1867, over two weeks late.

Bad weather also caused unavoidable delays and damage. *Ruahine*, which arrived in Sydney on 1 June 1867, lost a boat overboard in heavy weather, while one month later *Rakaia* lost its jib boom, topgallant masts and several sails in a gale off New Zealand.

Kaikoura arrived several days late in Sydney on 4 September 1867, having been delayed through an accident on the Colon–Panama Railroad and then making a passage of seven days from Wellington to Sydney through adverse weather. The following item appeared in the Wellington Daily Times on Wednesday, 28 August:

Wellington, Tuesday

The RNZ and ARMCo's ss Kaikoura, Captain Machin, arrived at Port Nicholson this morning, at 9am. She left Panama on July 25th, at 2.32pm. Called at Pitcairn Island and delivered Mail on the 10th August, and sighted Opara on the 13th; since then she had head winds. She sighted land about Castle Point on the 26th, at 3am, Pencarrow Heads at 11.30pm same day, and lay on and off till this morning.

The next southbound steamer, Ruahine, was the first to call at Rapa, taking on bunkers from the barque Midas, and most subsequent southbound voyages included a bunkering call at the island. On 4 November 1867, the Sydney Morning Herald reported:

The Rakaia brought from Oparo [*sic*] one of the natives who wished to visit Sydney, a powerful athletic man, who made himself very useful, and became a great favourite amongst the crew,: the man had been reading his bible (in native language) and was observed to be in a melancholy state of mind during the afternoon of the 24th instant; at 11 o'clock pm, he was seen to take a lighted lamp away, which soon after fell on deck, and after a lapse of a few seconds one of the watch went to pick it up, and see what had happened [to] the native, when he could not be found. Search was made, and after ten minutes, not finding him, the ship was put round and steered on the opposite course for the lapse of time the man had been in the water, viz., ten minutes, when the engines were stopped and then immediately the man's voice was heard, a boat was lowered and pulled in the direction of the voice, but instead of trying to save himself he evaded the boat by diving underneath it; at last he was secured and has been left at Wellington, to be sent back in the Ruahine.

The main problem encountered by the Line was the lack of cargo, the only regular income being derived from the Government subsidies, the mails and occasional quantities of bullion. When *Kaikoura* arrived in Sydney 1 May 1867 it carried 420 bags of coffee from Costa Rica, which reports at the time described as the first of what was hoped would be a continuing and expanding business. This does not appear to have happened, and although imports exceeded exports by a ratio of about two to one there was insufficient cargo in either direction to justify the continuation of the service. Also, despite their extensive accommodation, the ships only averaged about thirty passengers per voyage.

After two years of struggling to make the service a financial success, the Panama, New Zealand and Australia Royal Mail Co gave up the fight, and over a period of four months the vessels were withdrawn as they arrived back in Sydney. The first to be withdrawn was *Mataura*, which left Sydney for the last time on 2 September 1868, and on its final southbound voyage lost two seamen overboard in heavy weather between Panama and Wellington.

Kaikoura followed on 2 October, but when it returned to Sydney with 19 passengers from Panama and ten from Wellington it was placed in quarantine due to smallpox on board. *Ruahine* made its final departure from Sydney for Panama on 2 November and *Rakaia* made the last sailing on 2 December. *Rakaia* left Panama on 25 January 1869, and its return to Sydney terminated the service.

The four ships all returned to England, the first to leave being *Mataura* on 15 January 1869, carrying 56 passengers and 1,700 packages of cargo for London, voyaging via Wellington and Rio de Janiero. Next to leave for London, on 22 March, was *Ruahine*, on the same route, carrying 69 passengers from Sydney which increased to 140 upon departure from Wellington. The two remaining ships, *Rakaia* and *Kaikoura*, were both dispatched for London under sail only on 20 April and 23 May respectively.

On arrival in Britain the four steamers were all laid up for several years. The mortgage for *Kaikoura*, *Rakaia* and *Ruahine* was held by the Royal Mail Line, who took over the three ships in 1872, and renamed them *Tiber*, *Ebro* and *Liffey* respectively. They were re-engined with compound machinery at Southampton by Day, Summers & Co, and joined the Royal Mail Atlantic services. *Tiber* was wrecked 10 February 1882 at Porto Plata, Haiti, *Liffey* was also wrecked, on 22 August 1874, 27 miles west of Santa Maria, Uruguay, on passage from Southampton to Montevideo. *Ebro* was sold to foreign owners after some years in the RMSP fleet, and its fate is unknown.

The fate of *Mataura* also remains a mystery. Upon arrival in England the vessel appears to have been renamed *Babel* at some stage before being "sold foreign" in the early 1870s. *Prince Alfred*, which spent two years at Panama as reserve ship, was laid up there until being sold to Canadian owners in 1871.

Chapter Two

Early San Francisco Services

Following the collapse of the Panama, New Zealand and Australia Royal Mail Co, no further attempts were made to develop a service to New Zealand and Australia from Panama, as on 10 May 1869 the railway between the east and west coast of the United States was completed when the lines being built from the east coast and west coast were linked at Promontory, Utah.

The transcontinental railroad offered the totally new option of a service from San Francisco to the South Pacific, with passengers being able to cross the Atlantic to New York on one of the prime steamers of the day, then go right across the United States to San Francisco by train in considerable comfort.

The potential of this route was of particular interest to the New South Wales Government, as an alternative to the existing services being offered from Britain. At that time passengers would join a ship at London or Southampton and be taken through the Mediterranean to Egypt, where they would cross the desert by train to the Red Sea, and join another ship for the passage to Point de Galle in Ceylon. Here they would be transferred to another ship for the final leg to Australia.

At that time there were a number of sailing ships providing a service from Australia to San Francisco. For example, on 15 May 1869 the following sailings were advertised in the *Sydney Morning Herald*:

FOR SAN FRANCISCO – to sail from NEWCASTLE about 20th instant – The fine AI American clipper ship, CENTURION, 874 tons register, R G Darbey, commander, will be dispatched as above. Has room for a limited number of passengers, for which immediate application is necessary to
R TOWNS and CO

TO PASSENGERS FOR SAN FRANCISCO
The unrivalled and favourite clipper ship QUEEN OF THE COLONIES, 1346 tons register, Thomas Jones commander, will sail from Sydney direct for SAN FRANCISCO, on TUESDAY, 1st June. Intending passengers are invited to inspect the very superior and comfortable accommodation which this vessel affords for all classes. Stewards attendance being included and a liberal dietary scale.
   Saloon...........................£35
   Families according to agreement
   Second Cabin..................£25
   Steerage.........................£18
An experienced surgeon accompanies this ship, and a cow provided for benefit of cabin passengers.
In order to secure passages early application should be made to Captain JONES, on board at Circular Quay; or WILLIS, MERRY, and LLOYD, 100 New Pitt St

SAN FRANCISCO MONTHLY LINE OF PACKETS – A vessel, fitted for passengers, leaves direct each month. California never offered greater inducement to all classes. Intending emigrants can obtain every information, and secure passages by applying to
H H HALL, U S Consul, 21 Bridge Street

FOR SAN FRANCISCO direct – The AI American clipper ship M J SMITH, 850 tons, D Smith, commander, will be dispatched on or about TUESDAY, the 18th instant. Parties are invited to inspect the saloon accommodations, which have been admitted to be of a superior description. The intermediate will be fitted with every comfort, having the attendance of a steward, and provided with a very liberal dietary scale. This ship will be the first to leave belonging to the MONTHLY LINE of PACKETS. Early application is necessary to secure passages, as a great many are already engaged.
Apply to H H HALL, U S Consul, 21 Bridge Street

SAN FRANCISCO direct – The AI American clipper ship MAUD HELEN, 1000 tons, J A Thomas commander, will be dispatched on SATURDAY, the 29th instant. The second cabin accommodations cannot be surpassed, having enclosed state rooms, steward's attendance and a most liberal dietary scale. The intermediate will be fitted with every comfort for the accommodation of families.
Early application is necessary to secure passages by this favourite ship.
 Apply H H HALL, U S Consul, 21 Bridge Street

Hayden Hezekiah Hall, who would play a prominent role in the establishment of steamship services between Sydney and San Francisco, was an American with a rather dubious reputation. Born in 1825 at Hartford, Connecticut, about 1846 he began building steamers on Lake Ontario, but from 1848 to 1850 he was in China operating a shipping service and in 1852 was running several steamers among the Philippine Islands.

Leaving Manila on 2 January 1854, in one of his own vessels, the paddle steamer *General Urbistondo*, on 23 March Hall arrived at Sydney, and shortly after the *General Urbistondo* was offered for sale. When no buyer came forward, Hall renamed the vessel *Ben Bolt*, after a famous Australian bushranger, and placed it in the trade from Sydney to the Hunter River.

Hall became known in Sydney as "the handsome American" and in 1855 rented James Paterson's wharf and store at Morpeth. Declared bankrupt in December 1855, he was discharged on 8 March 1856 and left for New York where in January 1857 he married, and later that year returned to Australia with his new wife.

In September 1857 Hall opened the American Stores in West Maitland, but on 11 December 1862 was again declared bankrupt, being discharged the following March and again returning to America.

By 1864 Hall was back in Sydney as a partner in the firm of Samuel Hebblewhite & Co. He floated the Mineral Oil Company to manufacture kerosene from Hartley shale and persuaded Ebenezer Vickery that his land at the Illawarra, south of Sydney, would yield oil. Hall left Sydney in July 1866 to have Vickery's shale samples tested at Yale University but the results were negative. On 1 November 1866 Hebblewhite & Co went bankrupt, and Hall terminated his partnership.

In December 1866 Hall was appointed the United States commercial agent in Sydney, though he preferred to refer to himself as the US Consul, and returned to Sydney in February 1867. Hall had reported to the Secretary of State in Washington that earlier consuls had developed a bad reputation with the New South Wales government "owing to their ungentlemanly conduct". In 1867 Hall encouraged the migration to California of some 300 labourers and their families by issuing under his official seal worthless certificates of employment on the Central Pacific Railroad. The migrants' destitute condition on their arrival in the United States resulted in inquiries in Washington and London, and the New South Wales Premier, Henry Parkes, published a caution regarding dealings with Hall in the *Government Gazette* on 21 July 1868.

Hall became a strong advocate of improving the shipping connection between Sydney and San Francisco. To this end he had managed to organise a monthly service by sailing ships, but this could not be operated to an exact timetable. The first proposal to operate a steamship service from San Francisco to Sydney came from the newly formed Atlantic & Pacific Corporation, but it did not have the financial resources to continue, and the scheme was abandoned. It was then that H H Hall became involved in the development of a steamship service.

During 1868 and 1869 Hall tried to interest three American shipping companies in opening a steamship line between San Francisco and Sydney, and when this failed he decided to strike out on his own. Initially he was able to interest the New Zealand Government in providing a subsidy for a service using chartered Australian vessels from Sydney and Auckland to Honolulu, where passengers and mail would be trans-shipped to an American flag vessel for the voyage to San Francisco.

On 6 January 1870 Hall signed a mail contract with the New Zealand Government. To operate the service, Hall arranged the charter of two vessels owned by the Australasian Steam Navigation Co, *Wonga Wonga* and *City of Melbourne*, both of which were engaged in the Australian coastal trades.

The 1,002 gross ton *Wonga Wonga* had been built in Glasgow, being launched on 15 May 1854, and lengthened in 1868. *City of Melbourne* was smaller, at just 838 gross tons, having been launched on 13 August 1862, also in Glasgow. Both vessels had iron hulls, could carry passengers and cargo, and were powered by compound engines giving a service speed of 10 knots, though sails were also carried to provide additional speed with a following wind.

The first advertisement for the new service appeared in *The Sydney Morning Herald* of 17 January, 1870:

SAN FRANCISCO AND OVERLAND TO ENGLAND – THE CALIFORNIAN, NEW ZEALAND, and AUSTRALIAN LINE OF MAIL STEAM PACKETS, under contract for a monthly MAIL SERVICE. – The splendid steamship Wonga Wonga, 1,500 tons, TS Beal, commander, will be despatched from Sydney on the 26th March, at 4p.m., via Auckland and Honolulu (Sandwich Islands), carrying an experienced surgeon. Superior accommodation for saloon, cabin, and intermediate passengers. A good table, with attendance, can be relied upon in each department. Saloon passengers are provided with every requisite – wines and spirits extra. Bedding, etc, is not provided in the cabin or intermediate. Parties proceeding to the United States of America or Europe should avail themselves of this line which has decided advantages over all others, having cabin beds, and avoid the disagreeable of a long sea voyage; the whole journey may be considered a pleasure trip. Immediate application for passages should be made to avoid disappointment, as many berths are already engaged, to HH HALL, US Consul, 21, Bridge Street.

In British newspapers the new service was advertised as the North Pacific Transportation Co, offering departures from San Francisco on the 10th of each month for Honolulu, Auckland, Sydney and Melbourne, and through bookings were available from British ports via New York and the transcontinental railway, with the sector between San Francisco and Honolulu being operated by the American flag steamers *Idaho* and *Ajax*, owned by John Holloday & Co.

The 1,077 gross ton, wooden-hulled *Idaho* had been built in Maine in 1867 for the Anchor Line, being transferred to the North Pacific Transportation Co in 1869 and placed on the Honolulu trade. The 1,354 gross ton *Ajax* had been on the Honolulu trade since being built at New York in 1866, originally for the California Steam Navigation Co, also being transferred to the North Pacific Transportation Co in 1869.

The New Zealand Government had pressured the New South Wales Government to assist with the subsidy, and in March 1870 the New South Wales Government agreed to contribute £7,500 towards the cost of the service until the end of December 1870, and a further £2,500 up to March 1871.

The first sailing on the new service was taken as advertised by *Wonga Wonga* from Sydney on 26 March 1870, carrying 52 cabin passengers, including Mr and Mrs H H Hall, 39 saloon passengers and 70 in steerage. *Wonga Wonga* left Auckland on 9 April and arrived in Honolulu on 19 April, where passengers and mail transferred to *Idaho* for the final leg to San Francisco.

At the same time passengers and cargo brought to Honolulu by *Idaho* transferred to *Wonga Wonga*, which departed on 21 April, arriving back in Sydney on 17 May.

City of Melbourne made its first departure on the new service from Sydney on 27 April, with 39 saloon and 70 steerage passengers on board. At Honolulu they were transferred to *Ajax* for the final leg to San Francisco. The new service was subsequently advertised as the American-Australian Mail Line, but was usually known as "the Hall Line".

Wonga Wonga and *City of Melbourne* managed to maintain a schedule of monthly departures from Sydney to Honolulu over the next year, with the occasional misfortune. A continual problem was the poor quality of the coal that was taken on board in Honolulu, which frequently affected the speed and consumption of the vessels.

On 27 May, 1870 between Honolulu and Auckland, a steerage passenger on *City of Melbourne* was lost overboard. The report did not name him but described him as being well known in Adelaide business circles and added that he had shown some signs of insanity in the days immediately preceding his disappearance.

The same ship also experienced a major engine breakdown on its next southbound trip. On 4 August the cross head on the after cylinder broke when the vessel was in position 10.59°S 170.57°W, and it arrived at Auckland ten days late. Repairs there took a further four days, making the vessel two weeks late arriving in Sydney.

When *Wonga Wonga* arrived in Sydney on 20 September 1870, it was reported that on 4 September, and with all sail set, the fore and main topmasts came down bringing the lower mast heads

City of Melbourne (WSS Vic)

with them. The ship was hove to for some hours whilst the damage was cleared.

When nearing Honolulu northbound on 24 September 1870, *City of Melbourne* encountered an exceptionally severe storm with the starboard quarter boat lost overboard and the one on the port side damaged.

Arriving in Sydney on 17 November 1870, *Wonga Wonga* reported that when 1,100 miles from Auckland, the forward cylinder broke, completely disabling that engine.

Referring to the January 1871 northbound voyage by *City of Melbourne*, the *Otago Witness* reported on Saturday 28 January that among the passengers to join the ship at Auckland was Mr Julius Vogel, the Prime Minister of New Zealand, and his family:

Auckland. Jan. 11
Mr Vogel, with his family, were passengers, per City of Melbourne, for San Francisco, on Saturday. He only arrived on the previous Thursday and was much hurried. In the same vessel with Mr Vogel went Mr H H Hall to arrange for a mail line between San Francisco and Sydney, calling at the Fiji Islands. Mr Hall promised support by the Governments of Victoria, NSW, and Queensland, and is to have the City of Melbourne, City of Adelaide, and Wonga Wonga from the A.S.N. Company to carry out the contract. Captain Troughton, manger of the Australasian Navigation Company is also in Auckland on business connected with the traffic of the company's steamers to Auckland.

As *Wonga Wonga* was approaching Sydney early on the morning of 23 March 1871 at the end of a southbound voyage, the ship's officers sighted a sailing ship in distress. It turned out to be the barque *Day Spring*, which had loaded 600 tons of coal in Newcastle and left there on 21 March for Melbourne. *Day Spring* ran into a severe gale off the New South Wales coast, and was close to sinking when *Wonga Wonga* hove into sight, and rescued the entire crew before their vessel sank.

The New South Wales Government had agreed to contribute towards the cost of the service until the end of March 1871, but their subsidy was not extended beyond that date. As a result, at the end of April 1871 the New Zealand Government terminated their contract with HH Hall, and instead wanted an American organisation, John Holloday & Co, to operate the entire service, but with no subsidy. The last departure for Honolulu under the original arrangement was taken by *Wonga Wonga* from Sydney on 1 April 1871.

However, in February 1871 Hall had renewed his charter of *Wonga Wonga* and *City of Melbourne*. Hall decided to inaugurate a service right through from Sydney to San Francisco on the one ship, for which he had to charter a third vessel, *City of Adelaide*, which had been launched on 22 December 1863 and delivered the following year, and was a sister of *City of Melbourne*.

Prior to starting the new service *City of Melbourne* was given an extensive overhaul at the ASN yard in Sydney, then drydocked, when the hull of the vessel was thoroughly cleaned and repainted, and a new propeller fitted. The following advertisement began appearing regularly in the *Sydney Morning Herald*:

The splendid SS CITY OF MELBOURNE, 1,500 tons, H Grainger, commander, will be dispatched from SYDNEY on Thursday, the 4th May, at 4pm, via FIJI and HONOLULU, thence to SAN FRANCISCO, WITHOUT CHANGE OF STEAMER.
Superior accommodation for Saloon, Second cabin, and intermediate passengers. A good table, with attendance, may be relied on, as hundreds can testify who have travelled by the line during the past thirteen months, who admit the route's superiority over all others.
Saloon passengers are provided with every requisite, wines and spirits excepted. Parties proceeding to the United States of America or Europe should avail themselves of this line; as the New Zealand coast is now avoided, pleasant weather and smooth seas can be depended on. The longest time at sea without landing will be twelve days, thereby making the voyage a perfect pleasure trip, cheaper and quicker than by any other route.
Special arrangements will be made with families. 20 per cent will be allowed on return tickets, available for twelve months. To avoid disappointment, immediate application should be made for berths, as only a limited number of passengers will be taken. For full particulars apply to Messrs M METCALFE and CO, Bridge Street; or at Head Office, Grafton Wharf,
HH HALL, US Consul.

Refloated on 1 May 1871, *City of Melbourne* ran successful trials in Sydney Harbour two days later, and departed as scheduled, making a fast voyage to Fiji and on to Honolulu. The *Honolulu Advertiser* carried the following reports:

May 27 – The City of Melbourne, which sails today at noon for San Francisco, is the pioneer of the new through line from Sydney. She is a pretty fast boat, and was thoroughly overhauled during her last stay at Sydney. Her trial trip, made the day before sailing, was pronounced to be highly satisfactory, her speed being eleven knots. The passengers represent the passage up to have been most pleasant, the temperature and the weather being delightful, and the ship satisfactory in all respects. She brought twenty passengers to Fiji, one for Honolulu, and fifty-two for San Francisco. It is anticipated that she will make the passage hence to San Francisco in eight days, arriving there on the 5th of June. Leaving there on the 20th she will be due here on the 28th. The object of the delay in San Francisco is to alternate the arrival of the Australian mail by this line with those carried by the P&O ships.

May 31 – The City of Melbourne sailed for San Francisco at 2pm on Saturday, taking from here a few passengers and about 200 tons of freight, mostly sugar. Judging from the time made on the passage from Sydney by this vessel, it is fair to suppose that she will make one of the quickest passages to San Francisco ever made.

Maintaining a four-weekly schedule, City of Melbourne was followed on 1 June by Wonga Wonga. The next departure was taken by City of Adelaide from Sydney on Saturday, 1 July, while City of Melbourne made another trip, leaving Sydney on 2 August.

One passenger who travelled on the *City of Melbourne* later wrote a damning article, stating that rats, both dead and alive, were a problem in second class, where there were only four passengers occupying the twenty-seven bunks available, while there was only one women in the ladies cabin, which could accommodate fifteen.

H H Hall lost heavily on each trip, and by July 1871 he had withdrawn from the arrangement. The final departure from Sydney was taken by *Wonga Wonga* on 1 September, but in San Francisco United States officials refused to allow the vessel to load the southbound mails. *City of Adelaide* had been advertised to depart Sydney 23 September, but after 15 September all advertising ceased and the voyage was cancelled, with all three ships being handed back to the Australasian Steam Navigation Company. On 30 November 1871 Hall was again declared bankrupt, but in January 1872 he sought in vain a United States subsidy, mentioning his "past services in opening up the Pacific by a mail line … and holding it at great loss".

Instead of returning their ships to the Australian coastal trades, the Australasian Steam Navigation Co decided to retain them on the trans-Pacific trade on their own account. The route would be direct from Sydney to Honolulu, where passengers and mail would again be transferred to one of the John Holloday ships to be carried to San Francisco. However, by the time the ASN Co embarked on this scheme, new competition had appeared on the route.

Following the withdrawal of the New Zealand subsidy from the H H Hall operation, and their subsequent request to John Holloday & Co to take over the route, a new company had been formed in America, the California, New Zealand & Australia Mail Steamship Co, the principals being Ben Holloday and William H Webb, and the company became better known as the Webb Line. They planned to establish a through service from San Francisco to Honolulu, New Zealand and Sydney using three large paddle steamers, *Nevada*, *Nebraska* and *Dakota*, that had originally been built in New York as Civil War transports.

The *Nevada* had been named *Paou Shan* when launched on 18 March 1865 as a speculative venture by the builder, Thomas W Dearborn. First sold to Thomas Dexter, the vessel was bought from him by William Webb on 9 November 1866, prior to completion, and the name changed to *Nevada*. A wooden-hulled side-wheel steamer, 281 ft long, *Nevada* was 2,143 gross tons, with three decks and two masts.

Nevada sailed from New York on her trial trip on 9 May 1867 and made three voyages from New York to San Juan de Nicaragua for the North American Steamship Company in 1867. She was then operated by them on the San Francisco-Panama run from December 1867 through October 1868 and then, when the North American Steamship Co could not cover its debt to William Webb, ownership of the *Nevada*, and North American's other ships, reverted to him, and he turned *Nevada* over to the California, New Zealand & Australia Steamship Company.

The first advertisements for this line, which appeared in the *Alta California* newspaper, stated:

UNITED STATES, NEW ZEALAND and AUSTRALIAN STEAMSHIP Co. under contract with the UNITED STATES and NEW ZEALAND GOVERNMENTS.
The first vessel of this line will be despatched as under:
The **NEVADA**, 2,146 tons register,
J.H. Blethen, Esq., Commander,
will leave SAN FRANCISCO on 31st March next, and will reach AUCKLAND on or about 25th April, WELLINGTON the 28th, LYTTELTON the 29th, and PORT CHALMERS on the 30th. Will leave PORT CHALMERS on the 6th May (calling at LYTTELTON and WELLINGTON), and leave AUCKLAND on the 12th for SAN FRANCISCO calling at HONOLULU.

H WEBB, President.

However, on 12 March 1871 another advertisement stated that the *Nevada* of the Australian Mail Steamship Line would leave San Francisco on 8 April for Auckland, Wellington, Lyttelton and Port Chalmers in New Zealand, and also would connect with a steamer going to Sydney.

Nevada departed San Francisco on 8 April 1871, and left Honolulu on 18 April, arriving in Auckland on 4 May. Passengers and mail destined for Sydney were transferred to the small steamer *James Paterson* for the onward voyage to Sydney.

Nevada arrived at Wellington on 7 May and Lyttelton the next day, the voyage terminating at Port Chalmers on 9 May. *Nevada* left Port Chalmers on 13 May at the start of the voyage back to San Francisco, calling again at Lyttelton and Wellington before departing Auckland on 19 May.

A letter written in Auckland on 21 May by a correspondent of the newspaper *Alta California* stated that whole towns turned out in New Zealand when Captain James H Blethen sailed "the magnificent Steamer *Nevada*" into port: "In Auckland, after the signal had been run up that she was making for the harbor true to her time almost to an hour – the excitement was intense, and thousands crowded on the wharf awaiting her arrival". A luncheon was held in Auckland where the Governor of the Colony, 150 merchants and the townspeople honoured Captain Blethen, Mr. Webb, Jr, the American Consul and the Defence Minister.

The second voyage was taken by the 2,143 gross ton *Nebraska*, which was also built in New York, in 1865 by Henry Steers, for the Aspinwall Line, but purchased in 1867 by Webb, who incorporated a number of improvements in the vessel. In January 1868 *Nebraska* made the long voyage around South America to California, and began operating between San Francisco and Panama.

A description of the accommodation stated that "running along the centre of the deck are 20 state rooms, each having a close and Venetian door, and a window. On the main deck is the grand saloon, 90 feet by 28 feet wide by 8 feet high. On each side of this saloon is a row of staterooms, opening on the deck and accommodating 80 passengers, with 2 bridal chambers on the forward part. The berth deck is occupied by the third class passengers and will accommodate 620. Abaft this there are well ventilated staterooms for second class passengers."

On 6 May 1871 *Nebraska* departed San Francisco on the second voyage by the company, and after calling at Honolulu and Auckland the ship crossed the Tasman Sea to Sydney, where it arrived on 5 June. Next day the *Sydney Morning Herald* reported:

The steamship *Nebraska*, the first of the Webb's line of mail vessels, arrived in port at 8.30pm yesterday, after a most rapid passage right through from San Francisco, and through the courtesy of the purser, Mr Craig, we are in receipt of California papers to the date of sailing. The *Nebraska* left San Francisco at noon, May 6th, arrived at Honolulu 7am on the 14th, seven days nineteen hours out; landed 70 tons freight, mails, and 113 passengers; shipped 350 tons coal, 543 kegs sugar, 50 cases bitters, and 3 passengers; left 11.30am 15th; arrived at Auckland at 7am 31st, twenty-three days from San Francisco, twenty-eight hours within contract time; landed mails and freight, and shipped 150 tons coal, mails and 21 passengers, and left at 9.30am June 1.

The *Nebraska* is 270 feet long, has a breadth of 40 feet, and a 26 foot depth. She is brig-rigged, and is classed A1 at Lloyds, being an extra mark. She is a trifle wider and deeper than the *Nevada*, the pioneer vessel of the Webb line to Australia and New Zealand, but in tonnage and most other respects is her twin. The Dacatoh, also to be put on this line, is almost identical in built. The engines are of 2000 horsepower, vertical beam, with cylinder 81 inches diameter, 12 feet stroke, fitted with patent surface-condensers. There are two large tubular boilers, just refitted with new tubes. The vessel will make 12 knots easily, at a consumption of 31 tons of coal per diem. The coal bunkers have a capacity of 750 tons, allowing ample margin for contingencies, as she can coal at Honolulu and Auckland. The vessel draws 16 feet of water with all her coal, etc, on board.

The *Nebraska* has three decks, independent of her hurricane deck. She has been very thoroughly overhauled, and is as dry and smells as sweet as any vessel can do. The number of passengers allowed to her, after Government inspection, is 140 first-class, 229 second-class, and 506

Nebraska

third-class or steerage. The passenger accommodations have, however, been rearranged, and much greater room allowed. In the first cabin, main saloon, there are 10 inside and 5 outside rooms, with three berths to each. Two passengers only will be allotted to each. On the hurricane deck are 14 passenger cabins besides those of the ship's officers. On the lower deck there are also four large double-berthed rooms, for ladies or family accommodation. Each of these has an extra berth, removable at pleasure, intended to serve as a child's cot. The main saloon is fitted with every modern convenience and luxury. It can be heated by steam, when necessary.

There is every convenience for first-class passengers, in the shape of a barber's shop, baths, etc. The pantry also affords the accommodations of a first-class hotel. In the second class, there are four berths to each cabin, the two lower ones being removed for stowing away baggage etc. The ladies cabins are separated by a lattice screen. This department is wonderfully airy and roomy, and equal to the first-class accommodation on most vessels. The steerage is admirably arranged. The upper steerage for ladies and families will accommodate 45, and there are also in the lower steerage cabins for 30 ladies partitioned off. There is ample accommodation for 300 third-class passengers. The deck is roomy, clean and cool, and is fitted with all the conveniences which could possibly be desired.

Every precaution has been taken for the safety of the passengers. There are eight boats and a life-raft capable of holding 300 or more persons. The *Nebraska* was originally built for the Aspinwall line by Henry Steers, of New York, after which she was bought by Mr Webb, who replanked and double-strapped her throughout. She left New York on the 8th of January, 1868, and arrived in San Francisco soon after, when she was immediately placed on the Panama route. Great attention has been paid to ventilation and light in all parts of the vessel, and ample room is afforded for passengers to enjoy themselves on deck in fine weather, and also in smoking and card saloons, and ladies' drawing room on upper–deck in rainy or hot weather.

From the following it will be seen that Mr Webb, the owner of the *Nebraska*, has not forgotten New Zealand or Australia in the appointment of officers to his vessels. In the *Nebraska*, Mr Francis Ross, the chief officer, is a native of Tasmania, and is well known both there, and in Sydney and Melbourne, when in command of the brigs Jane and Pet, and lately captain of the barque Maud Ellen. He is spoken of very highly by the passengers on the present trip. Mr Hugh Craig, the purser, is a native of Sydney, but has been residing in San Francisco for some years. The *Nebraska* will be thrown open to the public on Friday.

Nebraska departed Sydney on 9 June on the return voyage. However, both *Nebraska* and *Nevada* only returned as far as Honolulu, from where subsequent voyages began every four weeks. A connection to the mainland was carried out by two smaller wooden-hulled paddle steamers, the *Moses Taylor* and *Mohongo*.

Nevada continued to serve New Zealand ports only, while *Nebraska* made a trip to Auckland and back to Honolulu before making its second voyage to Australia, departing Honolulu on 26 August. On this voyage *Nebraska*, which could make up to 17 knots in good sea conditions, steamed from Honolulu to Auckland in 14 days 16 hours, arriving there on 13 September, and continued to Sydney in 4 days 11 hours, arriving on 18 September. Next day *Nebraska* left for Melbourne, "to give Victorians an opportunity to inspect this magnificent vessel". This took the shipping community by surprise as she had been expected to go to Melbourne before coming to Sydney. The vessel returned to Sydney to commence its voyage back to Honolulu.

Their size, combined with superior passenger amenities, made *Nevada* and *Nebraska* far more popular than the three Australian ships being operated between Sydney and Honolulu by the Australasian Steam Navigation Co, and late in 1871 they withdrew from the Pacific trade, the last departure from San Francisco being that of the *City of Adelaide* on 31 October 1871. In January 1872 the ASN reported having incurred a loss of £5,000 on the route in the previous year.

Nebraska and *Nevada* then operated between Honolulu and Sydney via Auckland until *Nebraska* departed Sydney 20 January, 1872. *Nevada* arrived in Sydney for the first time on 19 October 1871 and on arrival reported that at 11.45pm on the 15th it had been in collision with a barque showing no lights, in which the barque's spanker boom scraped down the port side of the mail steamer, but neither ship stopped. An inspection the following morning revealed some damage to the bow and it was assumed that the barque had been struck on its port quarter. *Nevada* had been advertised to continue on to Melbourne but this was cancelled to allow the damage to be repaired in Sydney.

The sailing ship the *Nevada* collided with was the barque *A H Badger*, which sank soon after the collision. The crew managed to evacuate the ship in lifeboats and was fortunate to be picked up by a passing ship and brought to Sydney, where the story of the incident was widely reported. The fact that the *Nevada* did not stop to render assistance was the subject of numerous unfavourable articles in the press on both sides of the Tasman, and it was said the captain of the *Nevada* did not dare allow himself to be seen on the streets of Sydney. The Admiralty Court later awarded a judgment against the *Nevada* amounting to £1,600.

During December 1871 and January 1872 advertisements for the California, New Zealand & Australia Mail Steamship Co listed a planned departure by a vessel named *Colorado*, a wooden-hulled paddle steamer owned by the Pacific Mail Steamship Co, but then its name was removed.

Neither *Nebraska* nor *Nevada* returned to Australia

after *Nebraska* departed Sydney on 20 January, 1872, and Auckland became the southern terminal until the service ended. From February 1872 the company advertised a connecting ship from Sydney sailing about seven days before the mail steamer was scheduled to leave Auckland. *City of Melbourne*, *Wonga Wonga* and *Alexandra* of the ASN Co filled this role until 25 October 1872, when *Wonga Wonga* departed Sydney to connect with *Nevada* departing Auckland on 2 November, following which the provision of a connecting steamer ceased.

On Saturday, 17 February 1872, the *Otago Witness* reported:

Port Chalmers Arrived Nevada, U.S. p.s., 2,143 tons, Blethen, from Honolulu, 21st January, via Auckland and East Coast ports.

The United States mail steamer Nevada, the pioneer of the fleet, has visited our Port – this time with less ostentation than on her first visit to our shores. On her arrival at noon on Wednesday, she was literally besieged by labourers and workmen of all classes, in order to give her prompt despatch. The barque Eleanor and the brigantine Stranger were shortly afterwards placed alongside with a supply of coal, and work at once begun. The mails being in readiness were quickly placed on board the Harbour Company's steamer Peninsula, and brought to Dunedin. The Nevada left Honolulu on the 21st ult; called at the Island of Anne on the 30th and remained there for 2½ hours. On the 1st instant she met the Nebraska, bound for Honolulu and exchanged papers. Arrived at Auckland on the 7th with 30 passengers, 545 pks freight and 270 bags of mails. Left Auckland on the 9th, landed mails at Napier on the 10th, and reached Wellington on the 11th; left there at 8 am on the 12th and arrived at Lyttelton at 3am on the 13th; took in a large quantity of wool for America, and sailed at 1am for Dunedin. Since her last visit to this port she appears to be none the worse for the buffeting she has had, and comes into harbour clean and tidy. Captain Blethen, who is accompanied by his old chief officer and second mate, is still in command, and the veteran barber is still at his post.

On 31 August 1872 the *Otago Witness* carried the following report:

Auckland August, 23.
The Nevada arrived this morning. No sickness on board. Her passage occupied 16 days nine hours. She was retained for nine days at Honolulu, owing to a breakdown in her machinery. She brings 35 passengers and 60 tons of cargo. The Nevada remains in quarantine until the expiration of the extreme period required, since she left Honolulu, for the development of small-pox.

In August 1872 the New South Wales Government had called for tenders to be submitted to operate a service between Sydney and San Francisco. Three routes were to be considered, one from Sydney direct to Honolulu and San Francisco, another including a call at Auckland as well, while the third was from Sydney to Kandavu in Fiji, Honolulu and San Francisco. On this latter route, there would be a connecting service provided from Kandavu to New Zealand. Four tenders were received, including one from the Australasian Steam Navigation Co, and another from German interests, along with two separate submissions by H H Hall, but none was accepted.

With only two ships available the service being operated by the California, New Zealand & Australia Mail Steamship Co became somewhat erratic during 1872 until the third vessel that had originally been designated for the Pacific service, the 2,135 gross ton *Dakota*, became available. *Dakota* had been built by William H Webb at Greenport in New York in 1865 for the North American Steamship Company, and operated on the east coast of North America. On 10 August 1872 *Dakota* departed New York on a voyage to San Francisco from where it departed on 6 December for Honolulu and Auckland.

On 16 November 1872 the *Otago Witness* carried the following report, though the name of the ship presented them with some difficulty:

Auckland, Nov. 7
The Dacotah is expected to make the passage from California in 22 days arriving here on November 28th. She will bring a large number of passengers including Chiaini's Italian Circus, consisting of 50 performers and 50 trained horses.

The *Otago Witness* carried the following reports on the voyage of the *Dakota*:

Auckland, 1 January
The ps Dakota arrived today via San Francisco, Dec 6th, and Honolulu Dec 15th. Passengers:
For Lyttelton:
Circus Troupe (45)
Mr John Anderson
Miss Hastings
For Dunedin: Mrs Blair
For Wellington: Mr J.R. Broomhead
besides 29 for Australia

2 January
The Dakota sails for the South tonight, among her passengers being Mrs Blair and Mrs Fenn for Dunedin. Her passengers from San Francisco are highly pleased with their vessel and the voyage.

The *Dakota* reached Port Chalmers on 11 January, prompting this comment in the *Otago Witness* the same day:

At last one of the San Francisco steamers, the Dakota, has

performed the passage from California to New Zealand within the contract time. Not much to boast about in one steamer performing the voyage within contract time during the space of eighteen months. We shall therefore refrain from rejoicing.

The *Dakota* departed Port Chalmers on 16 January at the start of its voyage back to San Francisco, and on 22 January left Auckland for Honolulu, a connecting service from Sydney being provided by the *Hero*, owned by Gibbs Bright & Co, on 15 January.

By this time *Nevada* and *Nebraska* were both in rather poor condition, and numerous complaints were being made about both the ships and the service. On 7 January 1873 a critical editorial appeared in the *Sydney Morning Herald*, which said in part:

The late trip of the *Nevada* will not do much to raise the reputation of the line to which she belongs. There are reports of a powerful American company having been formed to purchase the vessels to continue the service, but 'leading capitalists' in New York and San Francisco will be of no avail unless the ships are seaworthy. The people of New Zealand have had great faith in Mr Vogel's diplomacy, and have endured the discomforts of it with much long-suffering; but there are signs now that their patience is nearly exhausted. They are beginning to count up what it has cost them, and what they have had for the money. They are paying £40,000 a year, which is double what they ever paid towards the Suez line, and in return they have had only a dilatory and irregular mail service, with constant promises of a better state of things, and a constant postponement of performance. And now there is the additional drawback to the line that the mails and passengers have a fair prospect of going to the bottom. A statement signed by the passengers asserts that the *Nevada* is totally unseaworthy, and has been for some time running without a certificate – that her boiler-tubes give out every twenty-four hours, and that when rolling in a heavy seaway the vessel leaks so much as to require constant work at the pumps. We venture to say that there is no other subsidised steam line in the world in which vessels are employed of which such statements can be made. It is abundantly clear that that these old wooden steamships are not suitable for the service, and that the experiment of employing them has been a failure. It is an expensive experiment too, and if New Zealand does not soon get tired of paying so much, Mr Webb will get tired of receiving so little. Although the sums paid is out of all proportion to the service rendered it is too small to leave a profit with such vessels on such a line. The freight traffic has naturally been small while the business has been confined to New Zealand, and has missed the great trade of Australia. The passenger traffic has never been very great, and is now likely to become less. Mr Webb, who admits to great losses, has been hanging on, hoping to get a subsidy from Washington. But it is already known in Washington that the New South Wales Government has advertised for tenders for the service to be performed by first-class iron screw steamships, and it is probably now known by telegraph that three tenders for this service have been received, one of which will, in all probability, be accepted. Knowing this, Congress is not likely to vote away the public money. If, unsustained by Washington, Mr Webb withdraws, New Zealand will not renew the service single handed. Its interest is clearly to become a co-partner in the Sydney line; and if the colony were only clear of its entanglements, there would hardly be two opinions on the subject. Mr Vogel himself must see that it is quite impossible now to get any adequate Australian support towards the project for which he has fought so hard. Mr Vogel comes to the Congress with his hands tied to a certain extent by the Webb contract, although the non-performance of the terms of that contract would release him, if he chooses to press them. If he can arrange with Mr Webb to cancel the agreement, it is quite clear now that he can secure for New Zealand a fortnightly mail for less than it is paying at present for a monthly line; and that each fortnight the mail will be delivered more punctually and more promptly than it is at present.

The *Otago Witness* on 1 February 1873 stated:

Hurrah for the San Francisco steamer! Only six days late! No wonder the Government journals brag of it. Talking about steamers, and the class of vessels that are sometimes allowed to run, reminds me of an anecdote told of a Yankee steamboat captain whose opinion was asked as to a certain river-boat that a friend had some idea of buying - "Wall," said he, "I reckon she may do for passengers, but I wouldn't trust treasure in her."

The *Nevada* did not return to the South Pacific, the service being maintained by *Nebraska* and *Dakota*, but they only made one round trip each from Honolulu. The first of these voyages was taken by *Dakota*, departing on 15 February, and the *Otago Witness* reported on 15 March 1873:

Arrivals – March 10 – Dakotah, US ps mail steamer, Ingersoll, from Honolulu 15th ult, via Auckland, 5th inst., Napier 7th, Wellington 8th, and Lyttelton 9th inst. with European and American miles. Her mails were brought up to Dunedin by the 1.30 pm train. Left Honolulu with 198 bags of English mails for NZ and 28 bags for Australia and 28 tons freight from San Francisco and 283 tons from Honolulu and 19 passengers from San Francisco and 2 from Honolulu. At the latter place she connected with the steamer Moses Taylor for California on the 18th. She was brought up to the railway Pier by Mr Pilot Kelly. Mr C.J. Robertson is her purser. Passengers: Mrs Blackadder, Miss Millan, Mrs McGuce and son, Mr and Mrs Seaby and child, Miss McKay, Messrs Sidey, Blythe, Carney, Tuckfield, Perry, Bridge, Atkinson, C.C. Bowen, H.P. Barbour, G. Clarkson, W. Holden, L. Shepherd, and M. Dagg. For Melbourne — Mr and Mrs

J. Brown, Messrs Charles Cobbath, C. L. Horth, George McCormick, and D. McGlashan.

The *Dakota* departed Port Chalmers on 15 March on the return voyage to Honolulu. However, when the United States Government decided against awarding a subsidy to the California, New Zealand & Australia Mail Steamship Co, it left Webb with no option but to pull out of the trade.

The final voyage was taken by *Nebraska*, which departed Port Chalmers on 13 April on its last northward trip, and was due to depart Auckland on 19 April 1873. It had again been arranged for the *Hero* to connect with this sailing, departing Sydney on 9 April, but that day the following notice appeared in Sydney newspapers:

CALIFORNIA, NEW ZEALAND AND AUSTRALIAMAIL STEAMSHIP COMPANY
SPECIAL NOTICE TO PASSENGERS
S.S. NEBRASKA
A TELEGRAM was received by us yesterday morning, from which it would appear doubtful whether or not the ABOVEMENTIONED STEAMER returns to HONOLULU and SAN FRANCISCO from AUCKLAND. We are, therefore, prepared to return PASSAGE MONEY IN FULL to all PASSENGERS; BUT; SHOULD THEY THINK FIT to go on, they must understand that they will do so at their OWN RISK.
WILLIAM LAIDLEY and CO, as Agents.

Such an alarming announcement appearing on the morning of *Hero*'s sailing day must have been a devastating experience for all the passengers booked to join the *Nebraska*, and most decided not to take the voyage to Auckland. However, *Nebraska* actually did depart Auckland on 19 April for Honolulu and San Francisco. The *Otago Witness* reported on 3 May 1873:

> The Nebraska left on her final voyage with a better list of passengers than for some time past, taking, besides Chinese, nearly 60 for San Francisco. The Sydney and Melbourne passengers would have added 30 to the number, but under the impression there would be no mail boat to Francisco they took the Suez route instead of coming on to Auckland. It is astonishing how little general interest people display her with reference to the closing of the line. No one seems to care, although Auckland, as a terminus of the steamers, might be expected to feel their loss more acutely than other ports.

This voyage brought to an end the operation of the California, New Zealand & Australia Mail Steamship Co, and later that year *Nevada*, *Nebraska* and *Dakota* were all sold to the Pacific Mail Steamship Company.

Chapter Three

The A and A Line

Despite the failure of the California, New Zealand & Australia Mail Steamship Co, interest continued in developing a steamship service across the Pacific from Sydney to San Francisco, and during 1873 H H Hall tried again. Although he had continued to refer to himself as "U S Consul", the United States Government had terminated all contact with him following the collapse of his company.

In May 1872 his assets were released from bankruptcy, and on 19 November that year Hall tendered privately to the New South Wales and New Zealand governments for a permanent monthly mail service with passengers between Sydney and San Francisco.

Hall formed the Californian & Australian Steamship Company, with financial backing from both British and American sources. The new venture was awarded a six-year mail contract by the New South Wales Government and the New Zealand Government, with Hall as managing director of the Australasian and American Mail Steam Ship Co, although some members of the New South Wales Legislative Assembly claimed that the Premier, Henry Parkes, had been bribed into a dubious contract.

The company stated its intention to build new ships for the service, but in the interim would operate chartered vessels flying the British flag. Arrangements were completed for the charter of five vessels to establish the service. Two were chartered from the New York, London & China Steamship Co, these being the 2,254 gross ton sister ships *Mongol* and the *Tartar*, both built at the Dobie & Co shipyard in Govan, Scotland. *Tartar* had been launched on 19 April 1873, while *Mongol* was launched on 12 August the same year, and both vessels entered service in eastern waters by the end of the year.

The smallest of the five vessels was the 1,994 gross ton *Cyphrenes*, launched on 8 February 1872 as a speculative venture to their own account by A Stephen & Sons, Dundee, which left London on 8 January 1874 for Sydney. The largest of the group, the 3,034 gross ton *Mikado*, had been built by Aitkin & Mansel at Whiteinch for D R Macgregor & Co, of Leith in Scotland, being launched on 15 April 1873. It was already operating in eastern waters, as was the 2,167 gross ton *Macgregor*, built by J Key and Sons at Kinghorn in Glasgow, being launched on 9 March 1872 and also owned by Donald MacGregor & Co, which arrived in Sydney at the end of 1873 to inaugurate the new service.

Hall placed the following advertisement in local newspapers on 28 October 1873:

OVERLAND ROUTE TO EUROPE,
via SAN FRANCISCO AND NEW YORK
CALIFORNIAN AND AUSTRALIAN
STEAMSHIP CO

Under contract with the New South Wales and New Zealand Governments for the conveyance of her Majesty's Mails. The SS ship Macgregor, 2,500 tons, the first of the chartered vessels for the temporary service, will leave this port for SAN FRANCISCO, (calling at KANDAVU and HONOLULU), on SATURDAY, the 20th December next at 12 o'clock noon. For freight and passage apply at the office, Grafton Wharf,
HH Hall, Managing Director

The inclusion of a stop at Kandavu was no doubt done in the hope that a subsidy could be obtained from the Fijian Government. Kandavu was a small island south of Suva, but it had a very large, safe harbour in which large ships could anchor. *Macgregor* arrived in Sydney on 14 December 1873 and the following day the *Sydney Morning Herald* described the vessel in some detail:

The Macgregor, The first of the chartered boats to run the new mail service between this port and San Francisco arrived yesterday from Batavia, via Melbourne, the passage from the latter port having occupied fifty-three hours, not a bad performance for a steamer with a very foul bottom. The appearance of this ship is peculiar, for her extraordinary length in proportion to her beam, and the extensive midship deck-house, which has been added since first intended for the tea trade between China and England, and now serves for accommodation for passengers; she is, however, a fine wholesome looking craft, with good lines where it is necessary to combine speed with cargo capacity.

The ship is propelled by a powerful screw, driven by a pair of compound engines of 300-horse power nominal, steam being generated in four boilers with three furnaces each, and with a consumption of 25 tons of fuel per day will drive the vessel at the rate of 11 knots per hour. The most notable feature in the Macgregor is the mechanism by which she is steered, and which is quite new in these colonies; it is a compound of hydraulic and steam power, the cylinder and machinery being on deck and immediately abaft the rudder-head, the steering-wheel being in a small house on the fore part of the midship deck-house.

The fore deck is fitted up with sheep and pig pens, etc, all very completely arranged. She carries a Chinese crew with the exception of the officers and engineers, the four masts are of iron, fitted with fore and aft canvas, together with two square sails on the fore and main masts, which with a smart breeze adds 1½ knots to her speed.

On 18 December 1873, two days before *Macgregor* sailed, the name of the company was changed to the Australasian and American Mail Steamship Company, usually abbreviated to the A & A Line. The first northbound sailing was taken by the *Macgregor* from Sydney on 20 December 1873, and the same day the *Sydney Morning Herald* could not resist the opportunity of expressing the competitive atmosphere that existed between New South Wales and the southern colonies:

The RMS Macgregor affords the latest instance of the superior advantages which this port has as a depot for mail steamers in the South Pacific. This vessel, as already stated in our columns, arrived here on Sunday last, and on Monday morning commenced to discharge a cargo of some 700 tons, principally dead weight in small packages. She had a clear hold that evening, and was next morning placed in dock, where she was cleaned, painted, and floated again within twenty-four hours. She then commenced to coal, and yesterday morning had 2,200 tons aboard. Decks were washed, stores for the round voyage aboard, and everything ready for the receipt of passengers last evening, and at noon today the pioneer ship of the service which New South Wales inaugurated on her own responsibility when her sister colonies ignored her position, together with the natural and acquired facilities of her capital, take the first mails from these shores under the new contract. At no other port in the Australian colonies could the Macgregor have been docked.

The *Macgregor* went first to Kandavau, where it met up with the *Governor Blackall*, which had been chartered from the Australasian Steam Navigation Company to operate the connecting service between Kandavau and Auckland. *Governor Blackall* was a 487 gross ton steamship built in 1871 by Mort's Dock and Engineering Company, at Balmain in Sydney Harbour. After transferring mails and passengers destined for San Francisco to the *Macgregor*, *Governor Blackall* returned to Auckland. A report that appeared in the *Sydney Morning Herald* on 13 January 1874 stated:

The Governor Blackall arrived at Auckland on the morning of the 5th inst, after a magnificent passage of four days and twelve hours from Kandavau. The RMS Macgregor, from Sydney, arrived off Kandavau on the evening of the 28th December, remained under easy steam until next morning at daylight, when she entered harbour. She encountered very heavy SE gales on the passage, but made a good average passage of 8½ knots. The transshipment of the New Zealand mail and passengers was completed by 10am on the 29th, and the Macgregor proceeded on her voyage the same day. Captain Saunders, of the Blackall, speaks highly of the anchorage in West Bay, Kandavau, where he brought up; the anchorage is good, and the harbour easy of access. HMS Pearl was in port. The Blackall left Kandavau for Auckland on the 30th December, and encountered a violent hurricane 100 miles south of the island, but no damage was sustained.

After a stop at Honolulu, *Macgregor* arrived off San Francisco late on Saturday, 23 January 1874, and tried to attract the attention of a local pilot by blowing its whistle and sending up rockets, but no pilot boat came out, so the captain of the *Macgregor* decided to enter the port in the dark without one, in which he was successful.

It had been planned that the second eastbound voyage would be taken by *Mikado*, departing Sydney on 12 January 1874, which was later put back to 17 January, but the vessel did not arrive in Sydney in time. Hall approached the Australasian Steam Navigation Co, and was able to charter *City of Melbourne* for one return trip. *City of Melbourne* had just completed a major refit and had new compound engines installed. A report in the *Sydney Morning Herald* on Monday, 12 January stated:

The City of Melbourne, which was withdrawn from active service over twelve months ago, owing to some defects in her machinery, made a trial trip on Saturday with new compound engines, which were fitted at the Company's works; and although it was pretty generally understood that she would be a smart ship, no one had the slightest idea that she would prove herself to be the fastest steamer in the Australian colonies. The machinery was fitted by Mr George Davidson, the Company's superintending engineer, and it must be very gratifying to that gentleman, as well as to everyone interested, that the trial trip on Saturday was so great a success.

The old engines, which were the four piston-rod steeple class of the ordinary type, were taken out, and foundations necessary for the new ones substantially built. The compound engines were then carefully set up and completed in a most satisfactory manner. They carry a working pressure of 60lbs, the high pressure cylinder being 40 inches in diameter, low pressure cylinder 71 inches, stroke 36 inches, driving a screw 13 feet in diameter, and 21 feet pitch, making 74 revolutions. The saving in coal too is another very important item, as she previously consumed about 30 tons per day, whereas now with increased speed she only disposes of 15 tons, indicating 970-horsepower. She has two boilers, double ended, with separate combustion chambers. They were brought out from England in pieces and riveted together with the powerful steam riveting machine belonging to the Company. Each boiler is fitted with two superheaters, making four in all.

The hull of the vessel while laid up was also thoroughly overhauled, and the cabin, before she is again placed in commission, will be redecorated. In fact she is now in every respect a new ship.

On Saturday morning, shortly before 11 o'clock, she left her moorings in Darling Harbour, under the command of Captain Moore – Captain Munro, the Company's marine superintendent and several gentlemen who took an interest in the trial being also on board. She proceeded down the harbour under very easy steam, Mr Davidson being anxious to see that everything worked properly, and on clearing the Heads the ship Aborgoldie, bound to London, was sighted about 6 miles to the eastward, with every stitch set to a fair NE breeze. The City steamed alongside and her passengers cheered the homeward bound vessel, and wished her a bon voyage. The steamer's head was then turned to the northward, to try her against the wind, and when off Cape Three Points the Morpeth, (steamship), from the Hunter River, was met with coming at a good speed, with her fore and aft canvas drawing well. The City of Melbourne rounded to about half a mile after her, and although a stern chase is generally a long one, it was not so in this instance. The Morpeth is a very fast ship, but the City soon overhauled her without the aid of canvas, and beat her to the Heads by half an hour. The speed of the vessel throughout the day's trial was 13½ knots, but owing to the engines being on their first trial, Mr Davidson considered the pressure of 50lbs, which was carried, to be sufficient. The measured mile was done in 4 minutes 20 seconds, and after making a trip or two she will, no doubt, attain a speed of 14 knots. When under full steam the vibration was scarcely perceptible, and the trial was in every respect an unqualified success.

Shortly after 1 o'clock Captain Munro invited the visitors down to the saloon, where an excellent luncheon was laid out for them; and after dinner success to the City of Melbourne, and the health of Captain Munro, were drunk by the company. Captain Brown, of the Wentworth, will probably take command of the City of Melbourne, and Mr Cromack will superintend in the engine room.

City of Melbourne departed Sydney on 14 January 1874, leaving San Francisco on 28 February and returning to Sydney on 7 April.

Mikado, which finally arrived in Sydney on 24 January, was almost brand new, having commenced its maiden voyage on 31 August 1873 from Liverpool to Hong Kong, making the fastest passage to China up to that time. The vessel had accommodation for 108 saloon, 87 second cabin and 668 fore cabin passengers. *Mikado* had been constructed for charter to the Pacific Mail Company, but the contract was cancelled by mutual consent as the American company was not permitted under United States law to use a British registered ship. *Mikado* had made a voyage from Hong Kong to Dunedin, in New Zealand, and on arriving in Sydney went into drydock. On 3 February *Mikado* left Sydney on its first northbound voyage, going via New Zealand ports.

Tartar arrived in Sydney on 7 February from Hong Kong via Melbourne, and took the next sailing of the new service on 14 February. *Tartar* went first to Kandavu where the passengers, mails and cargo for San Francisco were transshipped on 23 February to *Mikado*, which called at Kandavu after visiting New Zealand ports. *Tartar* then waited for *Macgregor* to arrive.

Macgregor had departed San Francisco on 31 January 1874 to open the southbound service, but, after transferring mails and passengers bound for New Zealand to the *Tartar*, ran aground on a reef off Kandavu early on the morning of 26 February. *Tartar* was still at Kandavu, and the same afternoon attempted to pull *Macgregor* free, but without success. All the passengers, mails and cargo bound for Sydney on *Macgregor* were transferred to *Tartar*, which proceeded to Auckland, then arrived back in Sydney very early on 10 March. Late editions of the *Sydney Morning Herald* carried the first report on the grounding of the *Macgregor*:

Tartar

The following report of the running on a reef of the steamer Macgregor has been kindly prepared by Captain J S Ferries of the Tartar:

The Tartar left her moorings at Sydney on the 14th of February, at 12.30pm; came to anchor at Watson's Bay, awaiting the arrival of the Rangatira with mails and passengers from Melbourne; was detained there till the 15th February, the Rangatira having been detained by adverse winds; at 9.30am weighed and proceeded on our voyage. Experienced strong head winds and heavy cross seas all the passage. Arrived off Kandavu at 8pm 22nd February, and lay off till daylight. Took pilot on board at 8am and went into harbour. At 9am made fast alongside the Mikado. Transferred mails, passengers, and cargo. At 4.30pm on the 23rd the Mikado weighed and proceeded on her voyage to San Francisco.

On the 25th the Macgregor arrived from San Francisco and came alongside at 2pm to transfer mails and passengers. At 11.45pm the Macgregor cast off, the pilot stating that he could take both steamers to sea that night by the Star of the South (steamship) leading the way. All the steamers proceeded slowly towards the entrance of the harbour. The leading steamer failing to find the passage as the moon had gone down, judged it advisable to anchor till daylight.

At 5.15am on the morning of the 26th, the Macgregor got under way, in charge of Pilot Frost, the Tartar weighing and following slowly in her wake. At 6.15am the Macgregor struck on the shoal inside the reef; the Tartar came near to the stern of the Macgregor and anchored. At the request of Captain Grainger passed a hawser to tow him off. After a trial of several hours, during which time we parted all our best hawsers, it was thought expedient to lighten the Macgregor forward, and await the night tide. This was accomplished by the Star of the South going alongside the Macgregor, and receiving from 80 to 90 tons of cargo from her for transshipment to Auckland. The Tartar then made fast to the Macgregor with stream chains and best hawsers; after a three hours trial it was thought advisable to remove aft a portion of coal remaining forward in the Macgregor, and make another trial on the day tide of the 27th. This was done and likewise proved unsuccessful. It was then considered inexpedient to make any further trial to get the Macgregor off until she was thoroughly lightened forward. We found after consultation, that this would occupy too much time, and it was thought advisable to transfer all mails and passengers to the Tartar. This was accomplished, and the Tartar went outside the reef without a pilot at 7pm. At 8.30 proceeded on our voyage to Sydney, by way of Auckland.

Captain Grainger expressed himself as fully confident that on removing all his coal and cargo aft, his ship will float off the shoal, and he will then proceed to Sydney without delay. The sole blame of the mishap is attributable to Pilot Frost, as, with ordinary caution, no danger need

Drawing of *Macgregor* aground

be incurred in entering the harbour of Kandavu by day. When the lights, now placid, are in position, it will be equally safe by night.

On the passage down the Tartar experienced ESE winds, with heavy cross sea. At 2.30pm of March 3rd was abreast of the Poor Knights. Anchored off Rangitoto Reef at 10.45pm on 3rd March. Time of passage from Kandavu four days and two hours.

Tartar departed Sydney again for San Francisco on 14 March. The next of the chartered vessels to arrive in Australia was *Cyphrenes*, which made a voyage from Britain with emigrants, stopping at Melbourne on 22 March, and next day the following description of the vessel appeared in *The Argus*:

The dimensions of the steamer are as follows: Length over all, 312 feet; beam, 35 feet; and depth of hold, 25 feet, giving her a gross measurement of close on 3,000 tons. Being rigged as a fore-and-aft schooner, she has, for so large a vessel, quite a scanty look aloft, spars and yards, and the usual top hamper of square-rigged vessels being conspicuous by their absence. This is an unmistakable indication that the strong point of the Cyphrenes is steaming, and that she does not depend greatly on her spread of canvas. She is propelled by a screw driven by powerful compound engines made by Elder & co, of Glasgow. They are direct acting; and are of 250 horse-power nominal, and have inverted cylinders, and on a consumption of from 20 to 22 tons coal per diem a speed of 10 knots can be obtained, and under favourable circumstances of 11 knots. There are two boilers, each having four furnaces. In addition to the larger machinery, there is also a handy donkey engine for discharging and taking in cargo, and not the least useful piece of mechanism on board is the blast-engine for securing a current of fresh air to the stokehole. The steamer is specially constructed so as to secure unlimited ventilation throughout, and both passengers and cargo have been amply cared for in this respect. The saloon of the Cyphrenes is not very much unlike that of the Tartar, and at present there is only accommodation for 36 passengers, for whom every comfort and convenience is furnished. There is available space, however, for the erection of more first-class cabins, and also for the accommodation of about 100 second-class passengers. The space of the long flush deck of the Cyphrenes is only broken by the captain's cabin over the saloon companion aft; by an extensive house amidships, where the officers quarters, donkey-engine house, cooking gallery, carpenter's stores, boatswain's lockers, etc, are situated; and by a house forward, where the crew is lodged. Over the house amidships is the chart room, in front of which is the wheel, the steering gear being Davis's patent. The steamer is well provided with boats, amongst them being a handy little steam launch.

Cyphrenes arrived in Sydney on 27 March, and departed on 11 April on its first voyage to San Francisco. Among the passengers on this trip were four Frenchmen who had arrived in Newcastle on 27 March aboard the barque *P C E* after escaping from imprisonment in New Caledonia. Altogether six men had stowed away on the sailing ship in Noumea, and made themselves known to the captain once the ship was well out to sea on its voyage to Australia, claiming they had been exiled to New Caledonia.

The escapees had participated in an uprising known as the Paris Commune, and included Henri Rochefort, a former member of the Government of the National Defence in France, Paschal Grousset, ex-Minister of Foreign Affairs, Francis Joarde, ex-Minister of Finance, Olivier Pain, ex Secretary of Foreign Affairs, and Caven Grant Achille, ex-Commandant of the National Guard. On April 10 the *Sydney Morning Herald* carried the following comment, rather reminiscent of the early days of Australian settlement by Europeans:

Considerable excitement was caused in Newcastle on the morning of 27th ultimo by the announcement that the P C E barque, from New Caledonia, had brought a number of escaped prisoners from the convict settlement at that place. The arrival of these fugitives will also justify the apprehension which has already been expressed, that the Australian colonies have something to fear from the establishment of a large penal settlement in such close neighbourhood. Some time since, representations were made to the French Government on the subject, and assurances were given that the surveillance would be so complete as to prevent the possibility of escape. New Caledonia is being made the receptacle for the worst class of French prisoners. It is stated that a transport ship will leave the citadel of St Martin-de-Re every three months with fresh batches of prisoners for Noumea. This circumstance, in connection with the escape of the Communist prisoners, will no doubt lead to further correspondence upon the subject between England and France.

The last of the chartered ships to be delivered was *Mongol*. On 13 November 1873, the following advertisement appeared in the London newspaper, *The Times*:

The Australasian and American Mail Steam Ship Company's new Clyde-built steamer Mongol, 100 A1, 2,252 tons register, 400hp nominal, Captain Flamank, will be dispatched for Otago, Canterbury, Wellington and Auckland, from South West India Dock, on December 12th. The steamer has magnificent accommodation for saloon and second-class passengers, and will carry a surgeon.

Mongol left London on 12 December 1873 on its delivery voyage, going via South Africa to New Zealand, and the *Wellington Independent* reported on 14 March 1874:

Mongol at Port Chalmers (De Maus photo)

The SS Mongol sailed from Wellington on Thursday, the 12th inst, with the San Francisco mail. She would call at Napier, and then at Auckland. The mails would be transferred at Kandavau to the SS Tartar, from Sydney, which would carry them on to California. The commencement of this service has been marked, unfortunately, by the stranding of the pioneer vessel of the fleet, the Macgregor, which was run upon a bank inside the reef of Kandavau Harbour, while coming out in charge of a pilot on her voyage from San Francisco and Fiji to New Zealand. The Tartar, bound for Sydney with the branch mails, was following the Macgregor, but was stopped in time to prevent her touching the bank also. Every effort was made to tow the Macgregor off by the Tartar, but without effect, although the stranded ship had been lightened. The Tartar, therefore, took on board the Macgregor's mails, which she brought on to Auckland, then proceeding on to Sydney. She returns from that port with the outward mails of the present month, and will receive the Mongol's mails at Fiji. The home-coming steamer of the line is the City of Melbourne, which will proceed on to Sydney, the Mongol receiving her New Zealand mails at Kandavau, and returning with them to this colony.

However, this arrangement did not go quite to plan, as the *Mongol* left Fiji before the *City of Melbourne* arrived there. The voyage report of the *City of Melbourne* which appeared in the *Sydney Morning Herald* on 10 April stated:

Following the disaster of the steamship Macgregor at Kandavu, which was an unfortunate commencement of the Australasian and American Mail steamship service, the splendid trip made by the City of Melbourne will be hailed with delight by all who have the welfare of the new line at heart. This finely appointed ship, which is owned by the Australasian Steam Navigation Company, and was chartered by the A&AMSS Company, has made the quickest and most successful voyage ever achieved in the Pacific waters. The fine new compound engine which was put into her just previously to her departure from Sydney for San Francisco was of a character to justify the highest expectations. Considering the pretty model of the vessel, and the well known ability of Captain Brown, her commander, there was abundant reason for the belief that she would make an average, under favourable circumstances, of eleven or twelve knots an hour. It will suffice to state that these expectations have been fully realised. Although retarded by violent headwinds, she made the trip to San Francisco in thirty days; and if she had been allowed to make a direct return trip to Sydney, without any detention at Honolulu or any other port, or any detour to Auckland, she would undoubtedly have made it in twenty-six days. As the case stands, she has accomplished a feat which places her ahead of colonial steamships in regard to fastness and efficient management. This is the more gratifying, by reason of the fact that the success of the new Australasian and American mail service greatly depended on the satisfactory achievements of the pioneer steamships of the line. Although it is well known that the service will not be conducted on the most punctual and reliable basis until the new steamers which are now in the course of construction shall have been put on, and that while the chartered steamers are employed, unexpected contingencies may arise which will possibly produce inconvenience and delay, yet the nature of the service is such that any series of mishaps and disappointments at the outset cannot well fail to seriously damage the reputation of the line.

Thus viewed, the very rapid voyage of the City of Melbourne, and the punctual delivery of her mails at both Auckland and Sydney, will go a long way towards repairing any mischief that may have been done by the failure of the Macgregor to come to time.

The City of Melbourne left San Francisco on the morning of the 7th of March, and after a splendid run of eight days, reached Honolulu on the morning of the 15th. Thirty-three persons comprised the passenger list, and more than half of the number were only booked for Honolulu.

Nothing but the usual trifles of shipboard life marked the voyage thus far. As the City of Melbourne steamed her way to the commodious pier at Honolulu, it was found that a large crowd of natives and other residents were awaiting her arrival. The women were all dressed in their Sunday clothes, and presented in nearly every instance a very neat appearance, and the men were likewise very cleanly attired. The excitement attendant on the election of a new king had just been allayed. Lunalilo reposed in his grave, and Kalakaua was the choice of the House of Representatives.

Such was the condition of things there when the City of Melbourne left, after taking in a sufficient quantity of coal, on the 16th. Rapid progress was made by the steamer to Loma Islands, which were sighted on the 24th, and afterwards to the Kandavu harbour, Fiji, which was entered on the morning of the 26th, after a magnificent run of nineteen days from San Francisco. As Kandavu is the place provided for the transfer of the New Zealand mails and passengers to a branch steamer, those on board who were bound for that colony were eagerly on the watch for a first sight of the connecting steamship. Unfortunately, disappointment awaited them. A few minutes after the pilot came on board, it was known that, in consequence of the disaster which had befallen the Macgregor, the arrangements had temporarily broken through, and that the Mongol, after waiting six days overtime for the City of Melbourne, had started for New Zealand the previous afternoon. The great question of the moment, therefore, was, how were the New Zealand mails and passengers to be forwarded?

The remarkable success of the City of Melbourne, as a fast sailer, attended her to Auckland, at which port she arrived at noon on the 1st instant. There, in consequence of a tedious and quite unnecessary delay caused by the tardy manner in which coal was put on board, she was detained until daylight the following morning. Her run from Auckland is the fastest on record, the time being four days and fourteen hours. The next fastest time was made by the Hero, in four days and eighteen hours.

Meanwhile, at Kandavu the *Macgregor* had been refloated with the assistance of HMS *Pearl*, but had suffered far more damage than originally thought, as a report published in the *Sydney Morning Herald* on 10 April stated:

In reference to the steamship Macgregor, full particulars of the disaster to which have already appeared in the Sydney newspapers – it will be sufficient to state that she was safely got off the reef but that the injuries sustained by her are of a serious nature that no sufficient repairs to bring her to Auckland could be made in less than a month, and that then she will require to be completely overhauled, some thirty feet of her bottom having been broken on the reefs, and several plates battered through. Orders were sent by the Mongol for the necessary timber and other material to coffer dam the holes, and after this shall have been done, the steamer will have to be taken to Sydney, or some port in New Zealand, and thoroughly repaired, the cost of doing which will, it is estimated, amount to several thousand pounds.

Macgregor did not get away from Kandavu until 29 April, arriving in Sydney on 8 May, and the next day a full report on the refloating of the vessel appeared in the *Sydney Morning Herald*:

We have much pleasure in recording the safe arrival in port of this fine vessel. The particulars of her getting ashore on a reef at Kandavau have already appeared; the dangerous position of the ship, and the small chance that existed of her ever again being again floated, was the current topic for some time, but Captain Grainger's indomitable perseverance has overcome all difficulties, and he has the proud satisfaction of knowing that in spite of the apparent odds against him, he has brought his vessel from the Fijis to Sydney with safety.

The Macgregor got ashore on the 26th February, and every means were used at that time with the assistance of other steamers to drag her off, but without success. Abandoned to his own resources Captain Grainger at once set to work on his own account. The whole of the cargo and coals were thrown overboard, but this had no effect in floating her, previous to which sails properly constructed were in readiness to sweep under the ship's bottom over the damaged portion. HMS Pearl then came to his assistance, Commodore Goodenough being most kind in placing at Captain Grainger's disposal his gear and crew.

The successful method used by which the Macgregor was floated being as follows: The Pearl laid out 160 fathoms of her bower chain, and from her stern passed on board of the Macgregor 115 fathoms of the second bower, which was then hove taut. The result was that the weight of the chain connecting the sterns of the two ships, together with the swell of the ocean, setting into the harbour, and acting on the heavy hull of the Pearl, drew the Macgregor off without the assistance of steam. Once again afloat, sails were passed under the bottom, and the pumps set to work, but were unable to overcome the leak, until Captain Grainger, with considerable ingenuity, contrived to manufacture a Californian pump. This had the desired effect in reducing the water in the hold until the canvas took on the outside, and thus the leaks were stopped to a great extent. A cofferdam was then built inside the ship over the fractured parts and securely battened down and shored off to the beams of the main deck; the fore compartment was then filled with 100,000 cocoanuts, and the main deck hatches put on, and again the whole was shored off to the upper deck; and in this state the ship has reached port.

Captain Grainger speaks most highly of the conduct of his crew, who, in the hour of difficulty and danger, never deserted him – but from first to last worked with a will. The Macgregor was coaled by the Cyphrenes, and took in a sufficient quantity of ballast to render her safe, the stone being hewn from the rocks by the seamen. She took her departure from Kandavau on the 29th ultimo, had variable winds, but fortunately moderate weather throughout the passage, making Cape Hawks at daylight yesterday. The pumps have been going all the trip and have kept the hold comparatively dry.

The *Macgregor* was placed in the Fitzroy Dock where it was found that the keel had been so badly damaged it necessitated the renewal of 30 plates. Repairs were carried out by Mort & Co, and while this work was in progress the opportunity was taken to totally rebuild the passenger accommodation.

Mongol, having made a round voyage from Kandavu to New Zealand ports and back, had arrived in Sydney on 5 May 1874 from Auckland via Kandavu with mails and passengers transferred from *Mikado*, which had terminated its southbound passage at the Fijian port. *Mongol* had been advertised to sail for San Francisco on 9 May, but instead was taken back by its owners and left for Hong Kong on 16 May.

With *Macgregor* not available the A & A Line again turned to the ASN Co for assistance, and chartered the *City of Adelaide* to take the departure from Sydney on 9 May, under the command of Captain Brown. The departure report listed the numbers on board, showing there were only three passengers bound for Kandavau, two getting off at Honolulu, and 26 saloon and 13 steerage passengers destined for San Francisco. In addition, 6 steerage passengers would be going on to New York, while 21 saloon passengers and one from steerage would also be making the overland trip to New York and connecting with a steamer to take them to Liverpool. A report published on 11 May stated:

The ASN chartered steamer City of Adelaide took her departure from Smith's Wharf punctually to her advertised time, 2pm on Saturday. The arrangements on board are perfect, and the ship scrupulously clean and neat. The steamer cleared the Heads for Kandavu with a light westerly wind and smooth sea.

Instead of going all the way to San Francisco, *City of Adelaide* went to Kandavu, where the passengers and mail were transferred to the waiting *Cyphrenes*, which then left for Honolulu and San Francisco. *City of Adelaide* subsequently made two round trips from Kandavu to New Zealand ports, and on 2 July, the *Timaru Herald* reported:

The City of Adelaide left at 2pm, for Lyttelton, and ought to arrive there tomorrow morning, and reach Port Chalmers on Friday morning. She will leave Port Chalmers on her return voyage, carrying the outward San Francisco mails, on Friday afternoon, reaching Lyttelton on Saturday morning, and, without delay, sail for Wellington, where she should arrive early on Saturday afternoon; she will then proceed to Napier without delay, arriving there on Monday, and at once leave for Auckland, which should be reached on Wednesday, July 8. The City of Adelaide will leave Auckland for Kandavau late on the 8th, with the San Francisco mails, and will be thus two days late. She is expected to connect with the Macgregor at Kandavau, which it is believed will proceed through to San Francisco.

City of Adelaide returned to Sydney on 24 July, and a report on its voyages over the past eleven weeks appeared in the *Sydney Morning Herald* on 25 July 1874, which graphically illustrated the complicated nature of the service being operated:

The City of Adelaide (Captain J W Brown) being chartered by the A & A Mail Company, started from Smith's Wharf punctually at 2pm on the 9th May, with mails, passengers, and cargo, to be transshipped into the Cyphrenes at Kandavu, the passage to which port was made in 7 days 23 hours through fine steaming weather. At 9am on Tuesday, May 19, the steamer Tartar, from San Francisco, and Cyphrenes, from New Zealand, arrived. The Tartar leaving same day for Sydney, and the Cyphrenes, after receiving coal, mails, etc, on 20th May proceeded on her voyage to San Francisco, and the City of Adelaide towards New Zealand, and after a run of 4 days 13 hours, with moderate weather, arrived at Auckland on the 24th May, where she discharged a portion of mail etc, received a quantity of coal, and left again at midnight on the 25th, with heavy westerly gale, thunder and lightning, and very heavy rain. After going round the coast, with thick rainy weather and strong head wind, arrived at Napier at midnight on the 27th, remaining there two hours, then proceeded on to Wellington, with fresh head wind and misty weather, arriving there about 4am on 29th, where mails etc were again discharged, leaving in a few hours and proceeded to Lyttelton, where, after a run of fine weather, she arrived at 8am on the 30th May, and, after discharging mails etc, left at 10am same day for the terminus of the line, Dunedin, where she arrived at 6am on the 31st May, and mails, passengers cargo etc, were landed.

Everything having been made ready, the City of Adelaide started on her return trip at 6pm on the 2nd June, arriving at Lyttelton on the 3rd, and after a stay of two hours, started for Wellington, where she arrived on the 4th, and after staying a few hours to receive coal, left for Napier, reaching there at noon on the 5th, and after one hour and a half's delay, proceeded towards Auckland, arriving there at 3am on the 7th June. This passage along the coast has been marked by the usual amount of wind, rain and sea. After coaling and receiving mails, she proceeded on her voyage at 2pm on the 8th June, when, after a run of four days and thirteen hours, with tolerable moderate weather, she arrived at Kandavu on the 13th June. At 4pm on the same day the Tartar arrived from Sydney. She received New Zealand cargo that had been taken through on a previous voyage, and transshipped the New Zealand mail and passengers. She then left at 10am on the 14th for San Francisco. The City of Adelaide now waited the arrival of the Mikado which came into port on Sunday, June 21, and after receiving a portion of her cargo with the mails and passengers, proceeded at 7am, 22nd, for Auckland, leaving the Mikado still in port, and after a run of four days fourteen and a half hours through moderate weather arrived at Auckland about midnight June 26th, and after discharging cargo, mails etc, left again at 6pm 27th, for the coast, the weather becoming very bad, breeze increasing to a heavy head gale, with high sea and thick weather, through which we arrived at Napier at 11pm, 29th, and after a few hours detention left for Wellington, weather more moderate, arriving there daylight 31st, leaving in a few hours for Lyttelton, where, remaining three hours to discharge mails and cargo, proceeded to Dunedin, arriving there at noon July 2nd, and in consequence of the mails being two days behind contract time through ship being sent south of Wellington and returned back in a few hours, leaving Dunedin same day at 4pm for Lyttelton, arriving there on the 4th, and after a stay of three hours left for Wellington, where we arrived on the 5th, and, staying three hours, proceeded to Napier, reaching it on the 5th, remaining there two hours, then made the best of our way to Auckland through very thick, heavy, dirty weather, arriving there at noon July 8th, and, after receiving coals, cargo, mails, and passengers, started a.m. 9th, en route for Kandavu, where we arrived after a fine passage of 4 days 13 hours at 8am, July 14th, the Cyphrenes entering the harbour at the same time. The MacGregor arrived at daylight on 15th, after a passage of very heavy weather. The mails, passengers and cargo were immediately transshipped, and the MacGregor sailed about noon for San Francisco. The cargo was then taken from the Cyphrenes with all dispatch, the mails and passengers received on board, and both vessels started for their respective destinations at 7am, 16th July; since leaving Kandavu experienced moderate and fresh southerly breezes with squally weather and high SE swell, passing Lord Howe Island at 9am, 22nd, the weather since which has been light and fine from SE, and arrived at Sydney Heads at 2am on the 24th, making the passage in 8 days.

By the middle of 1874 the Australasian & American Mail Steamship Co was in serious financial trouble, but encountered further problems over the next few months. *Tartar*, under the command of Captain J A Ferries, departed Sydney on 6 June on its second voyage to San Francisco, meeting up with *City of Adelaide* at Kandavu to collect the New Zealand passengers and mail. Heading for Honolulu, at 2.45am on 22 June, *Tartar* grounded on an uncharted coral reef, refloating itself two days later and being able to continue its voyage. The voyage report stated:

Left Sydney Heads at 2pm on June 6; arrived at Kandavu at 3pm on the 12th, and left for Honolulu at 12 noon on the 14th, after receiving the New Zealand mails and passengers from the steamship City of Adelaide. The line was crossed on the evening of June 18 and fine weather was experienced until Sunday, the 21st, when the weather became thick, with heavy rain, and it was impossible to obtain noon observations. On the morning of the 22nd, at 3am, the Tartar struck upon a coral reef, and it was found by Monday's observations that the ship had been set forty miles to the eastward by an easterly current, whereas westerly currents only are supposed to prevail in that latitude. It was found necessary to lighten the ship immediately, and the work of discharging coal, etc, was continued until the ship floated on the morning of the 24th. The ship made no water either then or since. The centre of the shoal, none of which shows above water, was found by accurate observations to be in latitude 6.25N and longitude 162.22W. The shoal appears to be of considerable extent, and is of a horseshoe shape. A current was found setting across it ENE at the rate of from three and one-half to four knots per hour. The commander of the Tartar takes this opportunity of publicly thanking his passengers, of all classes, for the valuable assistance they rendered in lightening the ship, and of complimenting them upon the self-possession they displayed. Thence to Honolulu experienced fresh trades and fine weather, the current being more uncertain than usual. Arrived in Honolulu at 8.45pm of the 28th of June, bearing again for San Francisco at 1.50am of the 30th. Experienced light airs and calms to port; passed the Farralones at .30pm 8th July, receiving pilot on board at 8.30pm, and anchored off Market Street wharf at 10.30pm.

Macgregor came out of drydock in Sydney on 6 June, and rejoined the service with a departure on 4 July, due to the late arrival of *Mikado*, which berthed in Sydney on 1 July after a protracted southbound voyage. *Mikado* had been delayed four days at San Francisco owing to the late arrival of the English mails, and then experienced boiler trouble between Honolulu and Kandavu necessitating the steamer being hove to for 53 hours followed by a three day stay in Fiji to effect repairs. *Cyphrenes* departed San Francisco on Sunday, 21 June on its voyage back to New Zealand and Sydney, but then the company's San Francisco agents arrested three of its ships for debt.

Although the A & A Line continued advertising that *Cyphrenes* would leave Sydney for San Francisco on 29 August, the departure of *Mikado* on 1 August was to be their last sailing from Sydney. Faced with financial collapse, H H Hall left Sydney on the *Mikado* in a desperate attempt to save the situation, but six weeks later the company and his own assets in New South Wales were sequestrated.

Tartar left San Francisco for Sydney on the afternoon of 28 July. The vessel reached Honolulu in seven days 17½ hours, making it the fastest passage between the two ports up to that time. *Tartar* entered the harbour at Kandavu on the morning of 19 August, but on finding no ship there to take the New Zealand mails, left after a few hours for Auckland, where it arrived at 10pm on 23 August. Bad weather delayed the unloading of the mails and cargo, and *Tartar* did not leave until 6pm on 25 August. After rounding North Cape the vessel ran into atrocious weather, with, according to the voyage report, "terrific squalls accompanied by thunder, lightning and hail; the ship was hove-to at different times, on account of the very high sea; all storm sails blown away and otherwise damaged". The weather did not moderate until the night of 31 August, and the ship finally reached Sydney at midday on 2 September.

This was the final voyage to be operated by the A and A Line, as shortly after *Tartar* arrived back in Sydney the vessel was taken back by its owners when charter fees were not paid. *Tartar* departed Sydney on 19 September for Hong Kong.

H H Hall went to London to try and raise funds to save his operation, but when this failed he advised the New South Wales and New Zealand governments on 24 February 1875 that his company could not pay the penalties they had imposed for non-fulfilment of the contract he had signed.

With the collapse of the Australian and American Mail Steamship Company, the New South Wales Government paid the Australasian Steam Navigation Co £1,000 for *City of Melbourne* to take the 29 August 1874 departure from Sydney, originally scheduled for *Cyphrenes*. On Tuesday, 1 September, the *Sydney Morning Herald* reported:

> The ASN Co's steamer City of Melbourne took her departure on Saturday punctually at noon, being under charter for the conveyance of the English mails via San Francisco. But short notice was afforded the company to provide a boat, but their resources were equal to the task, and the Melbourne was slipped, cleaned, and coaled, and ready to start on her voyage of some 7,000 miles at the appointed time. Judging from the ample display of livestock placed on board by the providores, her passengers will have no cause to cavil on the score of supply, and they will, doubtless, have a most enjoyable run across the Pacific. Captain Brown is in command, Mr Tait chief officer, and Mr Cromack chief engineer, together with a picked crew in every department. She cleared the Sydney Heads with a fair wind, and a rapid passage may be anticipated.

The New South Wales Government contract for the trans-Pacific service was then passed on to the Australasian Steam Navigation Co, who took over the charters of *Cyphrenes*, *Macgregor* and *Mikado*, and placed *City of Melbourne* and *City of Adelaide* alongside them to provide a regular service, with a departure every four weeks, still operating as the A and A Line. This was only intended to be a temporary arrangement, but it was extended to the end of 1874, and then to June 1875. In January 1875 it was advertised in the Melbourne newspaper *The Argus* that:

> Under contract with the NSW Government for the conveying of His Majesty's Mails, the SS City of Melbourne, J W Brown, commander, will be dispatched from Sydney for San Francisco, via Auckland and Honolulu on Saturday 16th January 1875. Passengers and cargo.

Early in 1875 the New South Wales Government called for tenders to replace this temporary arrangement. As the Australasian Steam Navigation Company had operated the service with regularity for the past year, the directors thought no other company would be interested in the trade so did not submit a tender. Instead they wrote to the New South Wales Government advising they were not prepared to tender for the service as advertised by the Government, but would be prepared to operate a service from Sydney to San Francisco via either Auckland or Kandavu, but not both, at a reduced subsidy.

Unbeknown to the directors of the ASN, a tender was submitted by an American operator, the Pacific Mail Steamship Company, which was a well established shipping company, and was prepared to accept a lower subsidy than was then being paid to the Australasian Steam Navigation Co for the sector from Honolulu to New Zealand and Australia.

Chapter Four

The Pacific Mail Years

In 1847 a group of New York City merchants had acquired the right to transport mail under contract from the United States Government from Panama to California, and The Pacific Mail Steamship Company had been founded on 18 April 1848 as a joint stock company. The company initially believed it would also be transporting agricultural goods from California to the East Coast, but just as operations began, gold was discovered in California, and business boomed almost from the start. During the California Gold Rush in 1849, the company was a key mover of goods and people and played a key role in the growth of San Francisco.

In 1867 the company expanded, launching a scheduled trans-Pacific steamship service with a route from San Francisco to Hong Kong and Yokohama, later extending to Shanghai. Initially wooden-hulled paddle steamers fitted with beam engines were used, but when these proved unsuited for such a service they were replaced by propeller-driven steamers, and the service had prospered. The Pacific Mail had then obtained a postal subsidy from the United States Government for the service between San Francisco and Honolulu.

In April 1875, H H Hall joined The Pacific Mail Steamship Co, and no doubt played a leading role in their making a tender for the South Pacific service. In July 1875 the New South Wales Government and the New Zealand Government signed a ten-year contract with The Pacific Mail Steamship Co to operate from San Francisco to New Zealand ports and Sydney, the annual subsidy of £89,950 being almost £15,000 less than was currently being paid to the ASN.

Under the contract Pacific Mail would provide five screw steamers from San Francisco to Honolulu and Kandavu, in Fiji. From there alternate ships would either steam directly to Sydney, or to Auckland, Wellington, Lyttelton and Port Chalmers.

When the through vessel was destined for Sydney, passengers and mail for New Zealand would be transshipped to a feeder vessel at Kandavu, with a similar arrangement for Sydney when the through vessel was bound for New Zealand. In Britain the new service was advertised as the "Australian Overland Mail Service". Gilchrist, Watt & Co was appointed Sydney agent for Pacific Mail, whose service was due to start in October 1875.

Despite the new agreement, the ASN continued to operate the service to San Francisco on monthly extensions of their contract. The chartered *Cyphrenes* made the departure from San Francisco in September 1875 to Auckland and Sydney, its arrival in Auckland being reported in *The Southern Cross* on Monday, 11 October 1875:

Port of Auckland - Arrivals - October 9
Cyphrenes, R.M.S.S., 1,280 tons, Thomas Wood, from San Francisco, via Honolulu.
Passengers: - From San Francisco to Auckland - Saloon:
Balfour Hon. A.J. and servant
Duncan Misses (2)
Livesay Mr C
Lyttelton Hon. S.G.
McKellar Mr John
Petherbridge Captain C.
Thompson Mr and Mrs William
and 18 in steerage.

The Cyphrenes left the wharf at San Francisco at 11.20 a.m. Monday, 13th September (Auckland time, 14th September). Cleared the Golden Gate at 12.30 p.m., wind fresh from W.S.W. Passed Farallone islands at 3 p.m. Arrived off Honolulu at 9 p.m. on the 22nd September, 8 days 9 hours from San Francisco; entered Honolulu harbour at 11 p.m. Left Honolulu at 4.30 p.m. on the 23rd, cleared harbour at 5 p.m. The Equator was crossed on the 29th September, in long. 165° W; On the 2nd October passed Upolu (Navigator's islands), put a gentleman passenger (bound there) on board a cutter called the Mary, flying the British flag. On the 4th October passed Eoa and Tongatabu. The meridian was crossed on Thursday 7th October, in latitude 28° S. Sighted the great Barrier Reef on the 8th October. Sighted Tiritiri at midnight and entered the harbour at 7 a.m. on the 9th being 24 days and 18 hours from San Francisco, and 15 days 14 hours from Honolulu. Mr H. Adams, purser. the Cyphrenes left again for Sydney early yesterday with passengers (listed) from San Francisco

plus 30 in steerage and 7 plus 9 in steerage for Melbourne and from Auckland:
Saloon:
Marks Mr E
Oatem Mr J
Short Mr G
Steerage
Arnold Mr and Mrs and child
Bott Mr G.
Morrish Mr W.
Riber Mr J.W.
Waterworth Mr and Mrs

Pacific Mail officially took over the service in October 1875, but the new ships were not ready when the service was due to commence, and a variety of vessels was used during the period to June 1876. The first departure for Pacific Mail was taken by the chartered *Vasco da Gama*, a 2,912 gross ton iron-hulled steamship built in 1873 and owned by the China Transpacific Steamship Company. *Vasco da Gama* did not carry any mail when it departed San Francisco on 10 October 1875, while *City of Melbourne*, operating for the ASN, left the same port two days later. On Friday, 5 November the *Timaru Herald* reported:

Auckland, Thursday Morning.
Arrived, City of Melbourne, with the English and American mails from San Francisco, making the passage in 22 days 18 hours, or three days under contract time. The RMS Vasco de Gama, the new line steamer, left San Francisco for Auckland and Sydney two days before the City of Melbourne, which overtook her in Honolulu. Thomas Henderson, of Auckland, is a passenger by the Vasco de Gama. Passengers for Auckland – Messrs Mullins, B. Tonks, Horsby, Rattray, Stevenson (mail agent), and 24 steerage, besides 21 saloon and 45 steerage for Sydney. The Vasco de Gama left Honolulu seven hours before the City of Melbourne. She has a large cargo and 70 passengers, and is expected to arrive hourly. She brings a box of salmon ova for Napier.

On 13 November the *Sydney Morning Herald* reported on the arrival of *Vasco da Gama* in Sydney the previous day:

This, the pioneer vessel under the new contract for conveying mails for England via San Francisco, arrived yesterday afternoon from the latter port via Auckland, and is, without doubt, one of the finest ships that has ever entered Port Jackson Heads. She is an iron screw steamer of the highest class, and was built by Messrs Henderson and Colbourn at Renfrew in November 1873, under special survey for the China Trans-Pacific Company to run between China and San Francisco. She is 370 feet long and 37½ feet in the beam, and her gross tonnage 2,912. The total deadweight carrying capacity is 3,000 tons. She has compound engines of 550 horse power nominal, with cylinder boilers. The vessel is barque rigged, and her expanse of canvas under full sail is equal to that of a 1,000 ton sailing ship.
There is first class passenger accommodation for 70 persons, second class accommodation for 30, and steerage for about 100. The saloon is in the after end, and is built and fitted in the style of the first-class P&O steamers. Each stateroom has large 2-feet square ports with 15 inch deadlights. The length of the saloon is 80 feet, and it has a single tier of state-rooms on either side. There are five large skylights, which give ample light and ventilation. The fittings are very elegant, and are composed of four woods, viz, the panels of satinwood, with the surroundings of rosewood, English oak and Hungarian walnut. There are an ample supply of baths etc, and hot and cold water is constantly laid on. The 2nd and 3rd class accommodation is well ventilated and roomy, and there is every convenience that can reasonably be expected.

Vasco da Gama departed Sydney on 19 November on the return voyage to San Francisco, this being the only trip this vessel would make on the route.
On 26 November 1875, the *Timaru Herald* reported:

The price of passage through from San Francisco to Sydney or to Port Chalmers in NZ, a distance over 7,000 miles, will be 200 dols or £40 – the cheapest rate on any ocean route in the world. Passengers will be allowed two stoppages – one at the Fijis, and again at Honolulu; and can, if they choose, remain over a month at each point. The route taken by these steamers on leaving San Francisco will by via Honolulu and Kandavu, in the Fiji Group. From Kandavu, the service will fork – the mails, passengers and freight being transferred at Kandavu from the branch boat. It is expected that the London mails will then be regularly delivered in Auckland and Sydney in forty days, or ten days less than the present average time of the Suez route.

The second Pacific Mail departure from San Francisco was taken by one of their own ships, *Colima*. Built in 1873 at Chester, Pennsylvania, the iron-hulled, 2,905 gross ton *Colima* had been operating on the coastal trades, but departed San Francisco on 10 November 1875 carrying mail as well as passengers. After leaving Honolulu on Friday, 19 November, and over the next week the ship covered between 260 and 270 miles a day in variable weather.
However, at 10.10am on 26 November the forward arm of the crank shaft to the main engine broke, and *Colima* came to a stop. Sails were raised, and the vessel began moving very slowly through the water while the engineers completed repairs. The ship spent all day of 27 November under sail, managing only 40 miles in the 24 hour period, but the next day was much better, with 86 miles being covered.

Colima

On 29 November the engineers were finally able to secure the spare crank shaft in place, but during the day only 63 miles were achieved. With the engine running again the ship was able to resume its usual cruising speed of about 11 knots to Auckland. After leaving Auckland on 18 December, *Colima* continued to Sydney, arriving at 11.50pm on 25 December. The vessel had to enter the Fitzroy Dock at Cockatoo Island for extensive repairs. On 27 December the following item appeared in the *Sydney Morning Herald*:

> This vessel, to be employed under the new mail contract between this port and San Francisco, arrived at midnight on Saturday, her detention having been caused by the breaking down of the low pressure engine, which took place shortly after leaving Honolulu, causing a detention of nine days. The crank shaft which gave out was manufactured at the Lancefield forge, on the Clyde, and the crank was defective to the extent of three-quarters of its entire strength. It broke, as a matter of course, on the first heavy strain, and then broke the piston and cylinder cover, fortunately doing no other damage. The engineer, Mr Forsaith, deserves the greatest credit for the manner in which he has dealt with such a difficulty, and enabled the vessel to steam with one cylinder and a broken shaft for so great a distance. The wonder is that so defective a forge was not detected as inefficient at the outset, since the whole interior was sapped as a pear would be that appeared sound outside, but was entirely rotten within. The vessel has actually performed 12,000 miles with this defective crank before it broke. Fortunately the talent was at hand to repair the mischief when it occurred.
>
> The Colima is a fine ship of 2900 tons and 450 horsepower. Her passenger accommodation fore and aft is decidedly the most complete we have ever had the opportunity of inspecting, the fittings being simply superb. There are three decks, viz main, saloon and spar. The gangway leads up to the saloon deck, down the centre of which is carried a deck house, the after part being appropriated to first class passengers, and the forward part to the officers and steerage passengers. The principal saloon is fitted in a most elaborate manner, the sleeping apartments being placed on either side; a wide space, however, being left to pass between the cabins and the bulwarks. An elegantly furnished boudoir, with piano etc, is also connected, while immediately at the stern is a very comfortable smoking room.
>
> Descending from the spar deck by means of a spacious and beautifully designed companion way, the dining room is reached, fitted with the same regard to comfort and elegance that marks the arrangements throughout the ship. The spar deck affords a fine promenade, on the sides of which are carried the boats, ten in number, each being fitted with water beakers, biscuit lockers etc, ready for lowering at a moments notice, the officers and crew being properly told off to each boat, practice being carried on at certain intervals. Altogether the Colima is a most compact and well furnished ship.
>
> With respect to her passage we learn that she left San Francisco, November 10, 11.20am; arrived at Honolulu, November 18, 9 pm; left Honolulu, November 19, 10.20am; arrived at Auckland, December 13, 4.15pm; left Auckland, December 18, 2.30pm; arrived at Sydney, December 25, 12 m.

Shortly after the *Colima* arrived in Sydney a letter signed by one of the passengers, Mr Young, was circulated in Sydney, and published in the *Sydney Morning Herald*. Mr Young criticised the master and the ship, claiming that they had almost run out of drinking water, the broken crank shaft had been the result of shoddy workmanship, and the ship had very poor sailing ability. A reply from Captain Shackford of the *Colima* was printed in the same newspaper on 2 January 1876, which said in part:

The ship made, under sail alone, 700 miles, while the engine was being repaired, averaging during a moderate breeze 6¼ knots per hour, and in a strong breeze.

The condensing apparatus can produce 2500 gallons water per day; but we had an ample supply of drinking water independently of condensed water. None of the latter was used for drinking purposes, and on arrival in Sydney we had twenty-three days drinking water on board.

Before my ship left San Francisco she was most carefully examined, and every point of her machinery overhauled. A crank-shaft was found to be suspicious, and was at once detached from the engine, and another shaft, which I have reason to believe was forged in the Clyde, was put on board and fitted, the old crank shaft being left on board in case of need, and was used after the first broke, until it also gave way at the suspicious spot. Meantime, the shaft with which the vessel had left San Francisco had been repaired on board, and it took the ship to Auckland, where it was further strengthened, and then brought the ship to Sydney.

The shaft that was put in in San Francisco was tested in the usual way, but no defect was discovered. There was no external fracture whatever, and the defect proved to be in the texture of the iron in its inner part, being a defect which I believe there is no means known to engineers for detecting short of absolute fracture.

Mr Young states he was told by the best authorities on board that both crank shafts were made in America, and imputes a want of veracity to these authorities. Courtesy generally recognises the captain as the best authority in his department on board ship, and the chief engineer in his; and neither of us made such a statement to Mr Young. It is quite possible that we told him that the engines were made in America, as they were.

Due to the problems affecting the southbound voyage by *Colima*, Pacific Mail was forced to find an alternative vessel to take the northbound departure from Sydney scheduled for 20 December by *Colima*. At short notice *City of Melbourne* was chartered from the ASN Co and departed on 20 December 1875, carrying passengers only. Clearly there was some confusion as to the route the ship should follow, as in a voyage report published on 10 March in the *Sydney Morning Herald* it was stated:

The City of Melbourne, after having been hurriedly chartered and fitted out for the San Francisco mail service, cast off her moorings at 11pm, December 20th, 1875, proceeded down the harbour, and at midnight cleared the Heads, the weather being light and fine from the SE, but gradually increased, veering to the eastward into a very strong breeze, with heavy head sea, which lasted until passing the Three Kings, when it became more moderate, and she arrived at Auckland on Sunday, 26th December, at 11 am. The postal authorities were communicated with as quickly as possible, and by 8pm a telegram was received from Wellington with instructions to proceed to Kandavau and pick up the New Zealand mails (that had left by the Cyphrenes) and convey them to San Francisco. The postmaster deemed it prudent to make a supplementary mail, so advertised the City of Melbourne to sail at noon on Monday 27, at which hour she left the wharf and proceeded on her voyage, when, after a run of four days, she arrived at Kandavau, December 31, and found the Cyphrenes had left for Levuka, but a letter remained stating she would return next day, so dropped anchor waiting her arrival.

Cyphrenes was apparently rather fortunate to be able to reach Fiji at all, as on 11 December the *Auckland Star* carried the following report involving a near disaster when the vessel was approaching Bluff:

The mail steamer Cyphrenes had a narrow escape of running ashore yesterday morning at daylight, when steering straight for the lighthouse, situated at the gaol, near the Bluff. Fortunately the Rangatira hove in sight in time to assist. The Cyphrenes followed her round the Bluff. The authorities should at once see the lighthouse removed to the proper site before any casualty ensues. The site on which it is erected was chosen by general Government agents against the express opinions given by captains of vessels who visit the port.

The *City of Melbourne* report continued:

At 11am, January 1, 1876, the Cyphrenes came alongside, transferred mails, cargo, and passengers, and after weighing anchor at 2pm, the City started on her voyage, passing through the Fiji Group, which was cleared by noon on January 2. The weather after this became unsettled, the wind veering to the NE, blowing fresh with heavy and rough seas. Increased to a strong gale, with very high sea; found the westerly and easterly currents as usual, running about one knot per hour. The NE trades continued to blow fresh until arrival at Honolulu, when the ship was made fast to the wharf at 7am, 12th January. After receiving coals, cargo and passengers, left port at 7pm; the NE trades, which are a head wind, blew very strong, causing a high head sea that lasted for six days. The wind then veered round to the N and NW, blowing a smart gale, with heavy beam seas and hard hail squalls – at times the hail was six inches deep on deck; this lasted until nearing the coast, when it became more moderate. The Farallones light was sighted at 4am, 21st, and the harbour entered at 9am same day, making the round passage from Sydney, including all stoppages and head weather, thirty days and nine hours.

At the time Pacific Mail won the South Pacific contract, they had three ships under construction at the Chester, Pennsylvania, shipyard of John Roach & Son. The vessels had iron hulls, three masts and a single funnel, and were just over 3,000 gross tons, with a length of 339 ft/103.3m and a 40 ft/12.2m

City of San Francisco (Alexander Turnbull Library)

beam. They were powered by a compound inverted steam engine driving a single propeller for a service speed of 14 knots.

The first of the trio was named *City of San Francisco* when launched on 6 May 1875, being completed five months later then making the long voyage around South America to California. *City of San Francisco* departed San Francisco on 8 December 1875 on its first voyage to the South Pacific. On Tuesday, 4 January 1876, the *Timaru Herald* reported:

Auckland, Monday
The City of San Francisco has arrived. She left on Dec. the 10th. She brings 43 cabin and 23 steerage passengers. The mails were sent on per Mikado, which left a day before. She sighted the Mikado at six o'clock yesterday morning astern. She will therefore arrive in the morning. The whole time occupied from San Francisco was 21 days 21 hours. This was the fastest time on record.

City of San Francisco arrived in Sydney on the late evening of 6 January 1876, and two days later the *Sydney Morning Herald* reported:

The first of the Pacific Mail Co line of steamers, built specially to carry the mails between the colony and San Francisco, arrived on Thursday night. She is truly a splendid vessel, and fully bears out the glowing accounts that have reached us. The public will now have an opportunity of judging of the fine class of steamers the company intend employing in the service. So many first-class vessels have lately visited our port that it would almost appear invidious to draw comparisons, but in strict justice it is only fair to state that, whether in the form of hull or elaborate adornment of interior, it would be difficult to conceive any thing more perfect.

The City of San Francisco was built at Chester (US), by the well-known firm, Messrs John Roach & Sons, who have turned out many of the finest steamers afloat. She is 356 feet long, with a beam of 43 feet, and has three decks – viz main, spar and hurricane – on the same principle as the Colima, and, like the latter vessel, is similar in general appearance and arrangements. The dining saloon is placed on the main deck, from the after-part of which runs an alleyway with enclosed cabins on either side. These apartments are fitted with every conceivable convenience, and elaborately furnished. Mention may especially be made of four large cabins, known as the bridal chambers.

On the spar deck is a large, well ventilated withdrawing saloon, furnished with lounges, piano etc; and above this again, and immediately under the hurricane deck, is an elegantly arranged boudoir. These several apartments are reached by broad massive staircases formed of solid rosewood. The furniture throughout is of crimson velvet, and richly carpeted. The panelling is formed of highly polished American woods of the finest kinds, relieved by large mirrors, forming a general effect very difficult to describe.

The after portion of the ship affords accommodation for 150 first-class passengers, which will convey some slight idea of the size. The comforts carried out for the second and third class passengers are of the same spacious character, but of course not so elaborate in ornamentation. The accommodation for the officers is on the spar deck, running forward from the upper saloon. The hurricane deck forms a fine promenade, right fore and aft, on the fore-part of which is placed the wheelhouse, with its steam-steering machinery. The fore part of the main deck is allotted to cattle and sheep pens, windlass etc.

The vessel is propelled by a four-bladed screw, driven by compound direct-acting engines of 600 hp nominal, which will give a mean speed of 12 knots without any extraordinary pressure, on a consumption of 50 tons of fuel per day, which is borne out by the fact of the splendid run from San Francisco, although only using one half the boiler power. The vessel is rigged as a barque, and shows a large spread of canvas. There are also ten large hydrants distributed about the decks, and immediately connected with the main engine; steam winches are placed at the various hatchways, and every modern appliance has been brought to bear to economise labours.

In short, the vessel appears perfect in every particular, and no expense has been spared by the company to make her a credit to the service.

The next departure from San Francisco was taken by *City of Melbourne*. At that time North America was suffering one of its worst ever winters, and the mail from Britain was five days late arriving by train in San Francisco, so *City of Melbourne* did not leave until 7 February, again encountering very bad weather, as the voyage report states:

City of Melbourne cast off her moorings, clearing the Golden Gate at noon, the wind light and fair; but from the unsettled state of the weather at this season, the general appearance of the atmosphere, and a falling barometer, all gave indications that the placidity of the misnamed Pacific Ocean was to be aroused; and when little more than twelve hours from port, the wind, after veering about from one bow to the other, finally settled at West, and increased to a severe gale, with a very high sea. The ship being deeply laden with coals, as she always is on leaving port, laboured and tumbled about tremendously, shipping heavy seas, wetting every place fore and aft; this last forty-eight hours, and then moderated down to fine weather; eventually catching the trades, and making, as the little vessel always does, a good average passage, arriving at Honolulu at 1.15pm on 15th, being eight days one hour.

Departing Honolulu at 4am on 16 March, *City of Melbourne* steamed directly to Auckland, where it arrived on 1 March. On 2 March the *Timaru Herald* reported:

San Francisco Mail – This mail arrived at Auckland yesterday morning at 7 a.m. by the steamer City of Melbourne. She left San Francisco at 11am on the 7th February, (Auckland time) and Honolulu at 4 a.m. on the 16th making the passage in 22 days 20 hours, including 15 hours' detention at Honolulu. She experienced a heavy westerly gale on the day after leaving San Francisco, which lasted 47 hours. She brings two saloon passengers for Auckland, Mr Sinclair and Dr. Mahaber, and seven for Sydney; 32 in steerage.

Departure was delayed twelve hours due to extremely bad weather, but on the morning of 2 March *City of Melbourne* left Auckland and made a fast passage across the Tasman Sea, reaching Sydney on 7 March 1876. This was the twelfth and last voyage across the Pacific by *City of Melbourne*.

Meanwhile trans-Pacific voyages had continued to be operated by the Australasian Steam Navigation Co, the last round trip for them being taken by the chartered *Mikado*, which arrived back in Sydney on 7 January 1876, and it marked the end of the Australasian Steam Navigation Co interest in both the trans-Pacific and trans-Tasman services, as subsequently the company only operated ships on the Australian coastal trades.

On 2 January the following item had appeared in the *Sydney Morning Herald* regarding the *Mikado*:

The A and A mail steamer Mikado, which left San Francisco on the 9th ultimo, will be due in Sydney on or about the 8th instant, judging from the punctuality with which this steamer has hitherto made her passages. The new steamer for the mail line (City of San Francisco) would likely have left San Francisco about the same time; but as the latter vessel has to touch at Kandavu, and thence to Auckland, her arrival in this port would be about two days later.

The next departure from Sydney for Pacific Mail was taken by *Mikado* on 12 January, and on Friday, 21 January, the *Timaru Herald* reported:

Auckland, Wednesday evening.
The Mikado arrived from Sydney, to take the outward San Francisco mails. She left under contract with the Pacific Mail Company, on the 12th. She is expected to leave Auckland to contract time, but the voyage was protracted by continued easterly winds. For the February service the City of San Francisco will leave Port Chalmers, and either the Zealandia or Granada from Sydney. The Mikado remains in the service till all the other vessels are on the station and probably will then be kept at Sydney as a spare vessel in case of accident. Blondin is a passenger by the Mikado.

Meanwhile, in September 1875 H H Hall had returned to Sydney, probably on behalf of Pacific Mail, but he left again in March 1876, never to return. In May 1876 his assets in New South Wales were released from sequestration, but the financial affairs involving his A and A Line were never settled. For some years afterwards Hall promoted the building of a railway and canal in Mexico, and during the 1880s his name was in New York directories as 'manager' and later 'president' of unspecified companies. His last known address was a New York office in 1888, after which he disappears from history.

Pacific Mail was forced to operate their service under some rather strange conditions, as set out in the contract they signed. To maintain a regular schedule of departures from San Francisco and Sydney every four weeks only three vessels were required, but New South Wales, which was the main contributor to the subsidy, had insisted that a spare vessel always be available in Sydney in case of breakdowns, requiring Pacific Mail to allocate four ships to the service.

A vessel would depart San Francisco once a month, call at Honolulu, then head south to Kandavau, and on to Sydney, where the vessel would have to remain for about forty days to ensure a spare ship was available.

On leaving Sydney the vessel would return to Kandavau, to meet up with the next ship coming from San Francisco. Passengers and mail destined for New Zealand would be transferred to the vessel that had come from Sydney, and it would then head south to Auckland, Wellington, Lyttelton and Port Chalmers, turn around and visit the same ports northbound, and call at Kandavau again.

This time the vessel would take on board the mail, passengers and cargo from the ship that had arrived from Sydney, then continue to Honolulu and San Francisco, the entire round trip taking three months to complete. The schedule depended on three vessels being at Kandavau at the same time, and any delays caused by weather or breakdowns would throw this into disarray.

With only one of the three new vessels having entered service, the next vessel sent to Australia by Pacific Mail was *Granada*, a 2,572 gross ton steamship built in 1873 by Harlan & Hollingsworth at Wilmington, Delaware. This vessel was usually employed on the coastal trades, but was brought in to make one round trip on the Pacific service. *Granada* had been scheduled to leave San Francisco on 3 January 1876, but did not depart until 9 January, passing through Honolulu on 17 January.

City of San Francisco departed Sydney on 14 January on its return voyage, arriving at Kandavau on 21 January, where it stayed four and a half days awaiting the arrival of *Granada*. When that vessel failed to arrive, *City of San Francisco* continued its voyage, arriving in Auckland on 29 January, and going on to visit other New Zealand ports. The fact that the ship had not collected the British mail at Kandavu from *Granada* resulted in the following item appearing in the Wellington *Evening Star* on 7 February:

That unhappy arrangement made by Sir Julius Vogel, the San Francisco mail contract, has no one to say a word in its favour. Even the Southern Cross, the special and peculiar organ of Vogel, has come down upon it. The arrival of the City of San Francisco without mail, and with only a solitary passenger on board has been too much for the Cross, which remarks: "Supposing, as is believed to be likely, the ss Grenada comes on here from Kandavu, it simply places the City of San Francisco in the light of a coasting steamer, trading between various ports of New Zealand ports, at an enormous expense to the colony, and without the colony reaping any advantage. It is getting time that the costly coastal service was discontinued, as our own steamers are better suited for such a service than a large ocean going steamer, which merely lies out in the stream and does not even come alongside the wharves in the different ports. ... In the emphatic words of Mr J.S. Macfarlane, 'When a three thousand ton steamer brings only one passenger, two letters, and a bunch of bananas, it's just damnable for those who will have to pay the piper.' What remains to be done is to enforce the penalties against the contractors and bring the abortive arrangement to an end...Surely £45,000 a year was not too much to pay for such a result."

Granada did not reach Kandavau until 30 January, and finding *City of San Francisco* had already left for New Zealand, quickly continued its voyage, arriving in Sydney on 5 February. Next day the *Sydney Morning Herald* reported:

This fine steamer arrived on Saturday night from San Francisco via Honolulu and Kandavau, having made a

Granada (De Maus photo)

splendid passage of 26 days 7 hours, duly discharging the European and American mails within an hour. She did not proceed to Auckland, and, as no steamer was at Kandavau, brought on to this port the New Zealand portion of the mails. The Granada is a sister ship to the Company's steamer Colima, and, like that vessel, is fitted and furnished in the most elaborate manner, and came into port a perfect pattern of cleanliness and good order.

For several weeks the Pacific Mail had been advertising a departure from Sydney by *Colima* on 11 February, which was in the Fitzroy Dock undergoing extensive repairs. When *Colima* was refloated on 1 February, the *Sydney Morning Herald* stated "The hull has been thoroughly overhauled, cleaned and repainted. The propeller, fastenings etc are now in excellent order." However, there was still a lot of work left to be done, so *Granada* had to be turned around very quickly in Sydney.

Granada left on 11 February in place of *Colima*, arriving at Kandavau on 18 February. There *Granada* met up with *City of San Francisco*, which had left Port Chalmers on 9 February and called at Lyttelton, Wellington and Auckland en route to Fiji. All the passengers and mail on *Granada* destined for San Francisco were transferred to *City of San Francisco*, which then continued its voyage north, while *Granada* departed for New Zealand.

Towards the end of 1875 Pacific Mail had begun seeking a suitable vessel to charter as the fourth ship required to maintain the service. Instead, they arranged the charter of two vessels then under construction in Scotland at the John Elder shipyard, which later became the Fairfield Shipbuilding & Engineering Co Ltd. These two vessels were being built for a consortium comprising J F Ure, J Jamieson, and Sir William Pearce, who owned the John Elder shipyard, for a planned service from Britain to Australia and New Zealand via South Africa, for which they were to be named *Zealandia* and *Nova Cambria*, the latter a reference to New South Wales. The charter became effective on 1 December 1875.

The first chartered vessel was named *Zealandia* when launched on 18 October 1875, closely followed by the second vessel, though its name was changed to *Australia* when it was launched on 15 November. These iron-hulled vessels were slightly smaller than the American pair, with a length of 377 ft/114.9m and 37 ft/11.4m beam. They had four masts that were barquentine rigged, a single funnel, and were powered by compound steam engines driving a single propeller for a service speed of 13 knots. Accommodation was provided for 170 first class, 30 second class and 100 third class passengers. On completion, both vessels made a voyage from Britain to Australia via South Africa.

Zealandia embarked passengers at Plymouth, departing on 19 December 1875 on its long voyage, meeting strong southerly gales for the first few days. A stop was made at St Vincent to take on coal, with the vessel leaving there on 30 December and voyaging non-stop to Melbourne, where it arrived on the afternoon of 6 February 1876, then continued to Sydney, berthing there on 9 February. On the voyage the vessel consumed 32 tons of coal per day and maintained an average speed of between 11½ and 12 knots. Next day the *Sydney Morning Herald* reported:

> This magnificent vessel, being the second steamer built specially for the mail service between this port and San Francisco, arrived here last evening from Plymouth, via Melbourne. Her speed on this maiden passage has stamped her as a vessel of no ordinary power; and although no extra pressure was brought to bear, the run

Zealandia

to Port Phillip was accomplished in 43 days 14 hours. In appearance outside she at once attracts attention. Her lines appear perfection, and one can hardly conceive anything finer, even in a clipper yacht. She is fitted with four masts, being square rigged on the two forward masts.

On deck and below many improvements have been carried out comparative with other steamers. A spacious poop, which is gained from the main deck, extends in front of the funnel nearly to the 'house' in which the steering apparatus is placed under cover, almost at the bow of the ship. In the latitudes which the Zealandia will have to traverse, such an elevated and commodious space will form a splendid promenade. Immediately under this, on each side of a central corridor, there is a series of deck staterooms, each containing a bed, a couch, and the requisite accommodation for washing and dressing. Being flush with the deck, these will form very comfortable sleeping and sitting apartments. Descending by another staircase to the grand saloon, it is found to be very tastefully and appropriately decorated. The main feature and absolute novelty, however, is the large and lofty central skylight, which ascends in a somewhat pyramidal form to a great height, and which imparts an idea of light and air rarely, if ever, found on board the most luxuriously appointed vessels. A careful inspection shows everywhere a liberal provision for the wants of passengers. The arrangements for cooking etc are very complete, and in sanitary matters, the bathrooms and lavatories are all that could be desired. Her passenger accommodation is equal to the berthing of 164 in the saloon, from 24 to 30 in the second cabin, and from 85 to 100 in the third cabin or steerage.

Considering the enormous power requisite to drive such a vessel through the water, the engine-room does not occupy so much space as might be expected, but the machinery, though massive, is compactly arranged, and hence the saving of room. The engines are compound of 2400 horse-power indicated. They are direct acting, surface condensing, and have three cylinders, one high pressure and two low pressure, the former being 45 inches and the latter 63 inches each, with a four foot 3 inch stroke. The three cylinders have three holders on the crank shafts, which gives the vessel a very easy, smooth, and equable motion. There are two immense boilers, with six furnaces to each, and the stokehole is well ventilated. The screw is four-bladed, and 17 feet in diameter, with 25 feet pitch, number of revolutions at full speed 65. Steam is in great request on board, and there are a dozen or more separate little engines for various purposes. The steering is done by hydraulic gear. The steamer is amply supplied with boats etc for saving life and property in case of fire or other accident.

Shortly after arriving in Sydney *Zealandia* entered drydock for cleaning and overhaul in preparation for its first trip across the Pacific, which was scheduled to depart on 7 April.

Having completed its repairs, *Colima* took the departure from Sydney on 12 March. At Kandavau, *Colima* met up with *Mikado*, which had left San Francisco on 29 February, and called at Honolulu on 9 March before arriving at Kandavau early on 21 March. *Granada*, which had returned to Kandavau from New Zealand, was already at anchor, both ships awaiting the arrival of *Colima* that afternoon. What happened next was included in the *Mikado*'s voyage report published in the *Sydney Morning Herald* on 7 April:

At 2.30pm Colima arrived, and went alongside RMS Granada to transship her New South Wales mails, passengers and cargo, and at 5pm Granada, in getting under weigh, fouled Colima's anchor, and after endeavouring for some time to clear she was obliged to bring up for the night to do so, and both vessels were occupied for a considerable time clearing their anchors and chains. At daylight on the 22nd, Granada steamed outwards for San Francisco, and at the same time Mikado hauled alongside Colima, and, having transshipped mail, passengers and cargo, sailed at 5pm for Australia.

After this one trip to the South Pacific, *Granada* returned to the coastal service to Panama until being wrecked on the Mexican coast on 22 June 1889. *Colima* left Kandavau on 22 March on the round trip to New Zealand ports, while *Mikado* arrived in Sydney on the morning of 29 March, and the voyage report in the *Sydney Morning Herald* next day stated:

Experienced hard gales with high sea and unpleasant weather for the first three days after leaving San Francisco; and afterwards, as far as Honolulu, moderate winds and unsettled weather; and from thence to Sydney a pleasant passage throughout. Owing to the measles having prevailed on board, more or less since leaving San Francisco, the ship was quarantined at Honolulu and Kandavau, which caused some loss of time at the former port, but none of consequence at the latter; the great delay, or loss of a good twenty-four hours at Kandavau being in consequence of the late arrival of RMS Colima from Sydney, and the accident which happened when the Granada was about to leave.

This was the last round trip to be operated by *Mikado*, which was handed back to its owners after returning to Sydney, subsequently trading from Calcutta to the Far East.

Unfortunately it was not long before *Colima* was in trouble again. On 6 April the *Sydney Morning Herald* carried this report from New Zealand:

The PMS Co's steamer Colima, which left Sydney on the 12th March, was unable to enter Otago harbour on account of the rough weather. The captain turned her head for Lyttelton, but, having lost the blades of her screw, she had to be towed into port.

The following telegrams were received yesterday:

"From Mr R Driver, Dunedin, to Gilchrist, Watt and Co – The Colima was off the Otago Heads yesterday. The bar is too rough for the pilots to bring her in. The captain wishing time to work the engine-room, turned for Lyttelton. Just heard that she broke down twenty miles south of Lyttelton. The screw is gone. I do not know the extent of the injury, or if cannot go through I advise sending the Zealandia."

"Christchurch. From Wilson, Lawbell, and Co, to Gilchrist, Watt and Co: The Colima's screw blades are all gone. Will you send the Zealandia or some other steamer to Auckland. Advise us immediately what action we shall take. We will tow her into Lyttelton tonight."

The *Southern Cross* reported on Wednesday 26 April:

The breakdown of the Colima and the cost of repairs will run into a little fortune. To begin with, it will cost about £500 to tow her from Lyttelton to Port Chalmers, where she is to be docked. The mishap and its consequences will cost at least £2,000.

At that time *Zealandia* was in Sydney preparing for its first voyage to San Francisco, scheduled to depart on 7 April for Kandavau, where its passengers and mail for Honolulu and San Francisco were due to be transferred to *Colima*. At the same time the *City of San Francisco*, southbound from San Francisco, was due to transfer its mail and passengers for New Zealand to *Zealandia*, which would do the trip to New Zealand ports. Any change to this routine had to be approved by both the New South Wales and New Zealand Governments. This resulted in the following exchange of telegrams with Sir Julius Vogel, Prime Minister of New Zealand, also reported in the *Sydney Morning Herald* on 6 April:

"From Gilchrist, Watt and Co to Sir Julius Vogel: Consequent on the Colima's accident, we ask this Government to authorise, subject to your sanction, Zealandia leaving this (7th) via Auckland for San Francisco, and City of San Francisco inwards diverging to Auckland with the New Zealand mails. If approved by Mr Driver, Dunedin, we will arrange for the coast conveyance. Trusting to the consideration of both Governments in this emergency, waiting your reply."

"From Sir Julius Vogel to Gilchrist, Watt, and Co: April 5. If the Sydney Government agree, we will concur, subject to your paying all expenses of coastal services. We also think you should arrange not to use the Colima when repaired; however repaired, she will be unfit for the mail service."

"Sir Julius Vogel to Postmaster-General, Sydney: The Colima is broken down. The best plan is to allow the Sydney boat to call at Auckland this month. Reply as soon as possible. If you meet agents in this way, I think they should undertake not to employ the Colima as a mail boat. When repaired she will not be suitable."

"From Gilchrist, Watt, and Co to Mr Driver, Dunedin: We have telegraphed to Wellington asking permission for the Zealandia, leaving here on the 7th, to call at Auckland and City of San Francisco inwards diverging there with New Zealand mails. If conceded we will arrange coast conveyance both ways. Ask the postmaster at Wellington for instructions. Advise agencies with regard to your arrangements."

"From Gilchrist, Watt, and Co to Wilson, Lawbell, and Co: We are communicating with your postmaster. Mr Driver, at Dunedin, will advise what Captain Shackford intends to do with the ship."

The outcome of all these messages was a last minute change in the route to be followed by *Zealandia*, which left Sydney on time on 7 April, but proceeded directly to Auckland, where the New Zealand passengers and mail were offloaded. *Zealandia* then proceeded directly to Honolulu, there being no requirement to stop at Kandavau. Meanwhile, the southbound *City of San Francisco* also bypassed Kandavau, steaming directly to Auckland, then continuing to Sydney.

Despite the demand by the New Zealand Prime Minister that *Colima* not be used to carry mail in future, once a new propeller had been fitted to the ship at Lyttelton, it left New Zealand waters in early May, bound for Kandavau.

Meanwhile, the second ship built in Britain, *Australia*, had completed its delivery voyage to Sydney. Departing Plymouth on 20 January, the vessel had arrived in St Vincent on 28 January, leaving the next day and steaming non-stop to Melbourne, arriving on the evening of 7 March. *Australia* reached Sydney on 9 March, having completed the entire voyage in 49 days, the quickest time to date. *Australia* also entered drydock for overhaul and cleaning prior to making its first departure for San Francisco.

Australia departed Sydney on 6 May on its first trans-Pacific voyage, and on arrival in Kandavau on the 15th transferred passengers, mail and cargo from Sydney to the *Colima*, which took them to San Francisco.

By the time *Colima* returned to the California port, the single round trip it completed had lasted over seven months, much of that time spent idle or undergoing repairs. *Colima* returned to the coastal trade between San Francisco and Panama on which it operated for the next twenty years before sinking in a storm on 27 May 1895 off Manzanillo, Mexico, with the loss of 187 lives.

The second of the vessels being built at Chester for Pacific Mail had been launched on 5 June 1875, and named *City of New York*. This vessel departed San Francisco on 26 April 1876, and arrived at Kandavu on 17 May and transferred the New Zealand mails,

Officers on the open bridge of *City of New York* (Alexander Turnbull Library)

passengers and cargo to *Australia*. On 23 May 1876, the *Sydney Morning Herald* carried this report received from Wellington:

> The P M Co's steamer Australia, with the New Zealand portion of the European and American mail, via San Francisco, transshipped from the City of New York, arrived at Auckland yesterday. The Australia experienced very rough weather to Kandavau, by which the purser's cabin was swept away. The City of New York left San Francisco on April 26, and Kandavau on the 17th May, for Sydney. Passengers for Sydney – Sir Daniel Cooper and son, Mr Rolleston, Mr Kirby, Mr Malder and wife (scenic artist), Mr Roberts (the billiards champion), Lemand von Halke, Mr Makie and wife, Mr Mahew and wife, and six in steerage. It is understood that Sir Daniel Cooper's mission to Australia is to advocate the abandonment of Kandavau as a port of call in connection with the Californian mail service.

City of New York had continued its voyage to Sydney, arriving on 24 May. It is perhaps indicative of the lack of patronage the service was suffering that on board the ship when it reached Sydney there were only 11 First class, 6 Second Cabin and 7 steerage passengers. *City of New York* remained in Sydney for over a month, not departing until 30 June on the return trip.

On 25 May 1876, the *Sydney Morning Herald* published details from a letter sent from Kandavau aboard *City of New York* by Captain Cargill of the *Australia* to Gilchrist, Watt, & Co:

> "I beg to inform you that the Australia arrived here today after a tedious passage of eight days nineteen hours, having encountered strong northerly gales for the first three days, and then fresh head winds and high seas for the remainder of the passage. We got alongside the Colima at 2pm and left at 5pm. We were unable to put any ice on board, as Captain Shackford would not wait, being anxious to get out before dark. The Colima had 65 saloon passengers from New Zealand, these, with our 85, would make her pretty crowded. The City of New York has just hauled alongside, and I find has about 70 tons of cargo for us, which we will get on board as soon as possible." From an abstract of the vessel's log it would appear that the ship had a very hard time, and shipped much water, and the smoking-room and officer's cabins were flooded.

Also on 25 May the *Sydney Morning Herald* published an item captioned "From Sydney to Fiji – by a roving correspondent", written by a passenger on the *Australia* on the voyage to Kandavau:

> The passengers from Sydney by the steamship Australia built up their expectations for the voyage on the passage made out from London. Than that passage nothing could have been more prosperous. But it is not given to ships or to men to be uniformly fortunate. Here we are at Kandavau, after a passage of nine days which we had hoped to accomplish in six, and which, according to schedule, ought to have been accomplished in seven.
>
> The Australia left Port Jackson with a smooth sea, but very soon lost it. During the first night the wind rose, and the vessel rolled considerably. She had on board 2,300 tons of coal, and drew on an even keel twenty feet of water. She was only ten inches deeper than when she

left England, and considerably within the limits allowed by the Board of Trade or Mr Plimsoll's line. But it soon became evident that she was too deep to make it prudent to drive her at full speed through the sea that was beginning to rise. Captain Cargill slackened the pace, and as the wind freshened to a gale he turned her head to the sea, and just kept sufficient way on to make her steer. Her open bulwarks let off easily enough the water that came on deck, but by the same token they let the water in, and the decks were consequently continually wet. The occupants of the deck cabins, who rejoiced in their superior ventilation found that they were subject to one drawback from there being no interior communication between the cabins and the saloon. To pass from one to the other it was necessary to run the gauntlet, and more than one adventurer got a ducking. The lower cabins are much quieter and more accessible, but though ventilation was evidently made a special study by the builders, the system adopted becomes a failure when all the inlets for fresh air have to be closed in consequence of the rain or the sea. After the gale had abated there was a stiff head wind for several days, and which then only veered sufficiently to allow some of the fore and aft canvas being occasionally used. A lumpy sea got up, which made it impossible to drive the ship at full speed without taking much more water over her bows than was at all convenient. The consequence is that she has been under-driven the whole journey, never having exceeded 250 miles in the twenty-four hours, and her ordinary pace being from nine and a half to ten knots an hour. She has not, therefore, had a fair term of what her average performances may be expected to be. On the voyage out from England her side-ports were open nearly all the way. On this trip they have been strictly closed, there not having been an hour during which they could have been opened with safety. It added to the discomfort.

On 17 August 1876, the following report of the full voyage completed by *Australia* appeared in the *Sydney Morning Herald*:

The RMS Australia left Sydney, Saturday, 6th May, at 4pm; experienced very bad weather to Kandavu, which in consequence was not reached till 2pm on the 15th; transshipped mails and passengers for San Francisco to Colima, and on the 17th, after receiving New Zealand mails from City of New York, proceeded to New Zealand ports, arrived at Auckland midnight of 21st, left again on the 22nd, and arrived at Napier at 6.40pm 23rd, but owing to thick weather could not communicate with the shore; proceeded at 7.30pm, encountered strong NE gale with thick weather at the entrance of the Straits, reached Wellington on the 25th at 10.50am, and left at 4pm same day; arrived at Lyttelton 7.05am on the 26th, and left at 5.30pm; had a stiff W gale along the coast, and entered Port Chalmers Heads at 2pm on the 27th. On the 31st May received mail and passengers outside the Heads, and owing to heavy sea experienced some difficulty. Sailed at 6.45pm same day for Lyttelton, arriving at 11.15am, 1st June; left at 5.20pm; arrived at Wellington 10am, 2nd June, left again at 3.30pm; anchored off Napier at 11.45am, 3rd June; received mails and passengers and proceeded to Auckland, arriving there at 4am, 5th June. Took in some coal, received mails, and proceeded, having on board 59 passengers. Arrived at Kandavu, (having experienced moderate weather), at 3pm, 9th June. Received mails and 62 passengers from City of San Francisco, and at 0.10am on the 10th cast off and proceeded. Experienced moderate winds and weather, arriving off Honolulu at 3am, 20th June, and got alongside the wharf at 7am; at 3.15 cast off and proceeded. Had fine weather till the 26th, when a heavy head sea and strong breeze followed by hazy weather was experienced. Entered the Golden Gate at 5pm, and landed mails at San Francisco 28th at 6.40. July 19th (Sydney time 20th), 9am received mails, 9.55 cast off from PMSS Co's Wharf; 11.15 discharged pilot and proceeded; arrived off Honolulu 3.02pm on the 27th; 7.40 made fast alongside the wharf; at 5.30pm proceeded, experiencing fine weather till the 5th, when squally weather with southerly swell was met with, lasting till the Fiji Group was reached; anchored in Kandavu harbour at 7.55am, 9th August. Transhipped New Zealand mails and passengers, and proceeded for Sydney at 2.30pm; experienced fine weather; passed Lord Howe Island at 6.10am on the 15th, and entered Sydney Heads on the 16th at 8pm, and was anchored on the Quarantine Ground.

The third ship to be built in America for Pacific Mail was launched as *City of Sydney* on 5 August 1875, and made its initial departure San Francisco on 21 June 1876, arriving in Sydney on 20 July. Next day the *Sydney Morning Herald* reported:

This fine vessel, which completes the fleet built specially for the Pacific Mail Company, to perform the service between this port and San Francisco, arrived yesterday morning. She is a sister vessel to the City of San Francisco and New York, and is fitted in every particular the same as those splendid boats. Indeed, it would prove a task to improve upon such admirable arrangements, as will be seen from the subjoined report. She had very pleasant weather until making the Australian coast, when rather a rough welcome was accorded the passengers in the shape of a SE gale. The City of Sydney left San Francisco on 21st June at 12.45pm, with 441 bags of mail, 46 cabin passengers and 48 steerage, and 294 tons of cargo. On 24th June, at 9.15am, spoke barque Edward May, of Boston, from Philadelphia for San Francisco Arrived at Honolulu on 29th, at 8.30am; discharged and received mails, passengers and cargo, and left at 3.50pm same day; detention 7 hours 20 minutes. Arrived at Kandavu, Fiji, on 11th instant, at 10.35am. Met at this port the company's steamer City of New York, bound for Auckland, NZ, to which were transferred 275 bags mails, with passengers and cargo, and left same day at 5.45pm; detention 7 hours 10 minutes. 134 days out. Fine smooth sea and weather from Honolulu to Kandavu; from Kandavu to Sydney, 11th to 14th fine; thence succession of heavy gales, with high running sea to port. She brings 161 bags mails for Sydney, 132 for Melbourne, 13 for Queensland, 5 for South Australia, 6 for West Australia, 1 for Tasmania. Whole time from San Francisco to Sydney, 27 days 10 hours and 30 minutes.

In the same issue of the *Sydney Morning Herald* the following also appeared in the shipping news section:

THE PACIFIC MAIL STEAMERS
Messrs Gilchrist, Watt & Co have favoured us with the following extracts received from Captain Cargill:
"SS Australia, Honolulu, 20th June 1876
We arrived off here this morning, at 2 o'clock, after a fair run of 11 days, having experienced fresh north-east winds throughout. We got alongside the wharf at 7am, and will leave again about 3pm. We will have some 30 first-class and a few steerage passengers."
The same firm have obliged us by furnishing an extract from Captain Cavarly's letter of 24th instant:
"SS City of New York, Kandavu, 11th July 1876
The SS City of New York arrived safely at Kandavu at 4.30pm, July 6th, after a very pleasant and quick passage of 6 days 1 hour 15 minutes from Sydney. The health of the passengers was excellent, and the sea quite smooth throughout the passage. The SS City of San Francisco arrived at Kandavu at 9am next day, July 7th. We transferred passengers, mails, and baggage to her, and she sailed for Honolulu and San Francisco at 1.30pm same date."

The *City of San Francisco* had departed its namesake port on 25 May on its second voyage across the Pacific. Passing through Honolulu on 2 June, the vessel arrived at Kandavau on 9 June, and in Auckland on 17 June. Two days later the Auckland newspaper, *The Press*, reported:

The City of San Francisco arrived this morning. She connects with the Zealandia at Kandavau on the 13th. The latter left San Francisco on 25th May.
Passengers – C Ferguson, W Crake, Hendle and Manning.
Third class – Messrs Ross, Elliott, Michael, Casey.
For Wellington – Captain Bower and wife;
third class Mr Burke wife and sister.
For Lyttleton – second class : Miss McCadam.
For Port Chalmers-Cabin: Rev Coleman Creigh and Messrs Clows, Hall and Cuff.
Cargo – For Wellington, 100 cases goods 25 bales hops;
for Lyttleton, 2 samples, 25 bales hops;
for Port Chalmers, 25 pieces redwood timber, 50 cases salmon, 1 sample.

The third class passengers for Wellington, Mr Burke, wife and sister, have been identified as James Bourke, his wife Mary (nee Crotty) and his sister Lucy Bourke, migrating from Tipperary, Ireland, having travelled via New York. The same day *The Press* also carried the following voyage reports:

The Zealandia arrived at Kandavau from Auckland on the 16th April, and at Honolulu on the 26th, and was alongside the wharf at San Francisco on the 5th May at 7:40am too late for the despatch of mails by that morning's train. She had head winds all the way from Auckland. Left San Francisco May 24th and arrived at Honolulu on June 1st; left same day and arrived at Kandavau on the 11th. Had fine weather to the 9th, after which fresh winds with fog and squalls to Kandavau. Transhipped the mails on board the City of San Francisco, which sailed on 13th, and arrived at Auckland at 4am. After second day from Kandavau had strong SE winds to Auckland. The New Zealand mails consist of 265 bags, the Sydney 166 bags. Passengers for New Zealand, ten in cabin, eight in steerage. During the morning of the 13th the sorting-room which contained the bags of letters was flooded, owing to the carelessness of some one who had been using the bathroom adjoining. The bags were removed at once and opened, the letters dried and transferred to dry bags. The letters did not sustain any very material damage. The Zealandia, whilst lying alongside the wharf at San Francisco on May 14th, received considerable damage by being run into by the City of Panama; about 14ft from the main deck down towards the water line on the starboard side, she had her plates twisted and split. The damage was made sufficiently good to enable her to sail on the 24th. The Australia left Kandavau with mails for San Francisco on the evening of the 9th June. The City of San Francisco left Auckland for the south at 10 this morning.

City of San Francisco called at Napier on 18 June, as reported next day in the Wellington newspaper, *The Evening Post*:

The RMSS City of San Francisco arrived at Napier last evening at six o'clock, making a very quick run of 31 hours from Auckland. She left again at 9 p m for the port, and should arrive here before dark this evening. We understand she will not be brought along-side. She proceeds South two hours after arrival.

On 20 June *The Evening Post* could not resist a dig at its competition when it reported:

The RMSS City of San Francisco delivered the inward English Mail (from London, May 4) in this port at 8.30 pm yesterday, having been delayed by head winds on the run down from Napier, which occupied 23½ hours, averaging only 8¼ knots per hour. Her previous run from Auckland to Napier, 31 hours (not 19 as stated in error by our morning contemporary, which would have involved a continued speed of 20 knots per hour) was, however, a very good one, averaging 12½ knots. We may remark here that the new boats will have their work cut out to beat the performance of the ill-fated Mongol while employed on the temporary service. That steamer made the run from Wellington to Napier in 14 hours, 20 minutes, averaging 14 knots, and from Auckland to Kandavu in 3 days, 17 hours, or at the rate of 13 knots per hour.

On 21 June *The Press* carried a report on the arrival of *City of San Francisco* in Lyttelton, where the vessel only went to anchorage:

This magnificent steamer arrived yesterday (20th June 1876) at 2:30pm. The ss Moa was waiting with steam up and directly the signal was made that the mail boat was inside the heads, she started to meet her with agents, reporters and visitors on board. The Customs steam launch was first to reach the vessel and with commendable promptitude the mails were at once placed in that vessel, in order that the 3:20pm train might be caught to carry up the Christchurch portion to town. In spite however of the efforts used, the launch arrived a minute late but the mails were forwarded by the 3:30pm goods train, so that few minutes were lost. After discharging her inward cargo and taking on board a few passengers, the City of San Francisco sailed for her destination at 4 pm. The steamer was beautifully clean throughout, and as on her first visit was much admired. We append a report of the trip from Sydney furnished us by the purser.

The ss City of San Francisco, J S Waddell, commander left Sydney June 2nd 3.5 pm, fine weather up to 9th, when heavy squall, accompanied with rain, lightning and thunder set in, lasting three hours; 8am anchored in Kandavau; 2pm ss Australia came in, and left at 12 midnight; 12th HBM frigate Pearl came in; 4 pm Zealandia came in transferred mails, freight and passengers; 5:30 pm Pearl left for Sydney; 13th 1:45am sailed from Kandavau in company with Zealandia; 16th strong breeze, very heavy sea; 17th at 3:15am arrived Auckland; left same day at 11am, arrived off Napier 18th at 6pm; left at 9:30pm after delivering receiving mails and passengers; 19th very heavy weather, strong head winds, squally, very high sea; arrived Wellington at 9pm; did not leave until 11pm owing to our being detained forty minutes by pilot, arrived Lyttelton, at 2:30pm.

City of San Francisco continued south to Port Chalmers, where it arrived on 21 June, and left a week later on the voyage back up the New Zealand east coast and on to Kandavau and San Francisco. *City of San Francisco* arrived back in Lyttelton on 29 June, and the same day the following advertisement appeared in the local newspapers:

THE SHORTEST AND MOST DIRECT
ROUTE TO GREAT BRITAIN AND
EUROPE VIA
SAN FRANCISCO AND NEW YORK.

THE PACIFIC MAIL STEAMSHIP
COMPANY
(Under contract with the NSW and NZ
Governments for the conveyance of H.M
Mails).
The magnificent steam-ship,
City of San Francisco,
3400 tons,
J J Wardell, Commander,
is appointed to sail from LYTTELTON
for SAN FRANCISCO,
calling at
Wellington, Napier, Auckland, Kandavu,
THIS DAY
At 4pm sharp.
A steamer will be in attendance upon
arrival of 2:30 pm train from Christchurch,
to convey passengers off.
Passengers must obtain tickets before
going on board.

WILSON, SAWTELL & CO
Agents,
Lyttleton and Christchurch

The local newspaper reported:

This fine steamer was signalled at 2:30pm yesterday and arrived at 3pm. Quite a crowd of people went off to her in the SS Moa. The outward San Francisco mail consisted of twenty-two bags, an usually large one. The City of San Francisco left Port Chalmers at 8:30pm on Wednesday, and had strong NE gale in her teeth during the run up, arriving as above. She sailed north at 5:30pm last night.

On its northbound voyage *Australia* had departed Sydney on 22 September, arriving at Kandavau on the 28th, where passengers and mail for San Francisco were transferred to *City of Sydney*, arriving the same day from New Zealand. *Australia* then waited at Kandavau until 4 October, when *City of New York* arrived from San Francisco, and transferred the New Zealand passengers and mail to *Australia*, which departed the same day. *Australia* arrived in Auckland on 8 October, having made the fastest run to date, three days and thirteen hours. The vessel then continued to Napier, Wellington, Lyttelton and Port Chalmers, where the mails were delivered on 12 October, 42 hours ahead of contract time.

On the voyage north *Australia* called at the same ports, among the passengers joining the ship at Wellington being the Prime Minister, Sir Julius Vogel, accompanied by his wife and daughter, who were bound for San Francisco. Leaving Auckland on 23 October, *Australia* was back at Kandavau on four days later, and took on the mails and passengers from *City of New York*, which had arrived from Sydney. *Australia* reached Honolulu on 6 November, and berthed in San Francisco at 1.30am on 15 November.

The December northbound voyage from Sydney was taken by *City of Sydney*, which departed on the 15th for Kandavau, where it was due to meet up with the northbound *Zealandia*, to which ship the passengers and mail for North America would be transferred, then wait for the southbound *Australia*, to take on its passengers and mail destined for New Zealand.

The new steamers soon gained a good reputation with travellers, and maintained the service with few major interruptions, but the convoluted routine of transhipping mail and passengers at Kandavau was a constant cause of discomfort and disruption to the schedule when a ship was running late. Pacific Mail wanted to change the route, and had not been allowed to do so, but an unfortunate incident involving the *Australia* ending up changing this.

The southbound voyage by *Australia* did not go according to plan, as the voyage report shows:

> At 9am 6th December (Australian time) cast off the PMSS Co's wharf, San Francisco. While proceeding down the bay the Oakland ferry steamer Capitol ran into the Australia, damaging starboard bow, whereby she had to put back for repairs. At 9.30am next day cast off again from wharf. Moderate variable winds prevailed to Honolulu, at which port she arrived at 7pm, 15th; left again at noon following day; experienced light steady trade winds during the entire run to Kandavau; 6.30am of the 26th arrived at Kandavau. In consequence of sickness on board, she was not permitted to transship New Zealand portion of mails and passengers to company's steamer City of Sydney.

What had happened during the voyage was one of the crew members had become sick, and it was thought to be smallpox. Since this was highly contagious, *Australia* was placed in quarantine, and no one was allowed to leave the ship. Faced with an unprecedented situation, the two captains came to the conclusion that the only alternative was for both *Australia* and *City of Sydney* to proceed to Auckland, so the New Zealand-bound passengers on board *Australia* could be disembarked and placed in quarantine, and the mails could be fumigated and distributed. The voyage report for *Australia* stated:

> 2pm same date, left Kandavau for New Zealand; at 3.50pm of the 27th ultimo, John Morgan, one of the ship's company, died of variola, or varialoid; 5.30pm same date, committed his body to the deep; 6.30am 30th December, arrived in Auckland, landed cabin and steerage passengers in quarantine.

On 1 January 1877, the *Sydney Morning Herald* carried the following report sent from Auckland on 30 December, though some details were incorrect:

> The RMS steamships Australia and City of Sydney arrived this morning. The Australia has been placed in quarantine, a passenger having died from smallpox when on the voyage between San Francisco and Kandavau. The City of Sydney will therefore proceed to Sydney to take her place, as soon as the mails from the Australia have been transshipped. The Australia will also proceed to Sydney after she has landed the New Zealand mails and passengers at the quarantine station. The Australia brings

Australia

139 bags mail, 28 cabin and 46 steerage passengers.

Australia departed Auckland at 6.30am on 31 December, followed by *City of Sydney* at noon the same day. *Australia* arrived in Sydney on the morning of 4 January, and went to anchor in Spring Cove in quarantine. On board were 18 cabin and 42 steerage passengers. *City of Sydney* did not reach Sydney until the morning of 5 January, having on board only one cabin and four steerage passengers from New Zealand.

By now the entire Pacific Mail schedule had been disrupted, with the northbound voyage of *City of Sydney* being terminated, so there would be no vessel in San Francisco to take the southbound departure from San Francisco in February. *Australia* was due to depart Sydney on 12 January, but would not have received a clean bill of health by then, so that departure was taken over by *City of Sydney*, while *Australia* was rescheduled to take the departure on 9 February.

Meanwhile, *City of New York* had departed San Francisco on 4 January on a southbound voyage, which was scheduled to go to Kandavau and then Sydney as before. However, the disruption to the schedule caused by the *Australia* situation changed this, and also the route to be followed by *City of Sydney* on the northbound voyage. On 11 January it was advertised that *City of Sydney* would go from Sydney directly to Auckland, then Kandavau, Honolulu and San Francisco. *City of New York*, after leaving Kandavau, steamed south to Auckland, arriving on 28 January, leaving the next day for Sydney, where it arrived on 2 February. The connecting services for both ships from Auckland to New Zealand ports were operated by a coastal steamer.

From this time on the Pacific Mail ships followed this route, which eliminated the transhipping at Kandavau, and speeded up the entire voyage. *Australia* departed Sydney on 9 February, followed by *City of New York* on 9 March, *Zealandia* on 6 April, and *City of Sydney* on 4 May. These four ships maintained this service with few further interruptions for the next nine years.

When *City of Sydney* arrived in Sydney 8 April 1877 it was about ten days late, having had the low-pressure cylinder disabled when approaching Honolulu. When it was discovered that repairs if carried out there would take up to a month, it was decided to continue the voyage on one cylinder only.

In July 1877 the furnace crowns in one of the two boilers of *Australia* collapsed, resulting in the vessel completing the southbound voyage with only 50% of normal steam available, arriving in Sydney on 8 August, about a week late.

On 5 March 1878 J F Ure and J Jamieson sold their shares in the ships to Sir William Pearce, who took over sole ownership of the pair, but the charter arrangement continued as before.

In 1880 the stipulation that a reserve ship be kept in Sydney was removed, although at the same time there was a reduction in the subsidy provided by New South Wales. This enabled Pacific Mail to maintain the service with just three ships, with *Zealandia* and *Australia* remaining permanently on the route, being partnered by either *City of New York* or *City of Sydney*.

On 11 January 1879, *City of Sydney* suffered a major engine breakdown 400 miles out from Auckland, resulting in the vessel being under sail alone for three days while temporary repairs were carried out at sea. *City of Sydney* arrived in Auckland on 16 January, and passengers and mails were transferred to *Wakatipu* of the Union Steamship Company for the Tasman crossing, arriving in Sydney on 23 January. *City of Sydney* arrived in Sydney on 9 February following repairs in Auckland.

On 15 March 1880, while in port at San Francisco, *City of Sydney* suffered a fire which was extinguished before any serious damage occurred and the departure for Australia was not affected. Later the same year, *City of New York* experienced a gale of exceptional violence when approaching Honolulu on 23-24 December. Two seamen were lost overboard, a boat was washed away from its davits and additional damage caused to the deckhouses. The captain reported very disagreeable weather upon arrival in Honolulu.

While the residents of Auckland were able to receive their mails from Britain and Europe immediately the vessel from San Francisco berthed, there were complaints from those living in other cities, especially Christchurch, about the time it took for them to receive their mail. In 1882, the Union Steam Ship Company decided to build a fast ship to improve this service. Rather than operating from Auckland, it was to depart from Onehunga on Manakua Harbour, and call at New Plymouth, Nelson, Wellington, Lyttelton and Dunedin, with the voyage from Onehunga to Lyttelton being completed in just thirty-six hours. Named *Takapuna*, the vessel left Onehunga on 19 November 1883 to open the new service, but in 1886 both Lyttelton and Dunedin were dropped from the service.

The contract with Pacific Mail ran its full ten years, expiring on 1 October 1885. When it came up for renewal the company decided not to put in a tender, and withdrew from the South Pacific trade. The final departure from Sydney by one of the Pacific Mail ships was taken by *City of Sydney*, which left on 5 November 1885.

Chapter Five

Oceanic and the Union Line

Following the withdrawal of the Pacific Mail Steamship Company from the trade between San Francisco, New Zealand and Australia, the New Zealand and New South Wales Governments called for tenders from companies interested in continuing the Pacific service, but one stipulation was that a British company had to be involved in it as a joint venture with an American company.

Until a new contract was organised, *Australia* and *Zealandia* continued to provide a service under a temporary subsidy, and Sir William Pearce was hopeful of gaining a new contract. However, when a new contract was organised it was for a joint service supplied by the Oceanic Steamship Company, of America, and the Union Steam Ship Company of New Zealand, both well-established operators.

The Oceanic Steamship Company had its beginnings in 1879, when brothers John and Adolph Spreckels started their own shipping company primarily to transport sugar from Hawaii to the mainland, on behalf of their father, Claus Spreckels, who was known as "the sugar king" in California. In 1876 Claus Spreckels had voyaged to Hawaii, and the following year purchased half the entire sugar crop of the islands to be sent to his sugar mills in California.

Starting with a single sailing ship, suitably named *Claud Spreckels*, the Spreckels' brothers quickly built up a fleet of six sailing ships, and the venture thrived. On 22 December 1881 the Oceanic Steamship Company was incorporated in California. In 1882 the company chartered its first steamship, which proved much more reliable than the sailing vessels, so two new steamships were ordered from the William Cramp & Sons shipyard in Philadelphia.

The first of the new vessels was named *Mariposa* when launched on 7 March 1883, and on trials achieved a top speed of 15.5 knots. *Mariposa* left Philadelphia on 22 May 1883 on the voyage around Cape Horn to San Francisco, where it arrived on 15 July. A local newspaper reported that there were fifteen large bronze chandeliers in the saloon, of which fourteen had two bulbs lit be electricity while the other one burned sperm whale oil.

The vessel departed San Francisco on its first voyage to Hawaii on 25 July, arriving in Honolulu six days later. The second of the new ships was named *Alameda* when launched on 3 May 1883, departing Philadelphia on 22 September 1883 for the 46 day voyage to San Francisco, departing on 15 October on its first trip to Hawaii.

Mariposa and *Alameda* were 3,150 gross ton, having iron-hulls 314 ft long and 41 ft wide, one funnel and two masts, with yards on the foremast to carry sail. They were powered by compound engines driving a single screw for a service speed of 14 knots. Accommodation was provided for 240 first class and 84 second class passengers, with variable space for third class. The two ships proved extremely popular on the Honolulu route, and soon the company was looking to expand their operations.

When the Pacific Mail decided not to tender for a continuance of their service from San Francisco, the Oceanic Steam Ship Co made a bid for the route, but under the terms of the intended contract, there had to be a British firm involved as well. As a result the American bid was made jointly with the Union Steam Ship Company of New Zealand.

The Union Steam Ship Company of New Zealand was founded by James Mills, and incorporated on 12 July 1875. Initially the company had concentrated on New Zealand coastal services, but expanded very rapidly. In June 1876 the New Zealand Steam Navigation Co Ltd, of Wellington, was bought along with the four small vessels it owned, while the following month the Albion Shipping Co, which owned only one vessel, was also purchased. In 1876 services were expanded across the Tasman Sea to Australia, and the company built new ships at a steady rate over the next few years, and by 1881 they were operating a network of services to the South Pacific islands as well.

When tenders were called for the contract to operate a subsidised service across the Pacific, which had to involve a British company, the Union Line submitted a bid in conjunction with the Oceanic Steam Ship Co that was accepted by the governments of New Zealand and New South

Wales. The five-year contract was finalised on 15 October 1885, and then a further mail contract was obtained by Oceanic from the United States Government to include a call at Pago Pago in American Samoa.

The two contracts required the companies to jointly provide a four-weekly service from Sydney and Auckland to Honolulu and San Francisco and return, which required three vessels, two from the Oceanic company and one from the Union Line. The two vessels that would open the service for the Oceanic company were *Mariposa* and *Alameda*, while the Union Line selected their newest and largest vessel, the 2,598 gross ton *Mararoa*.

Built by Wm Denny and Bros at Dumbarton in Scotland, *Mararoa* was launched on 29 June 1885, and completed on 2 September that year. It was fitted with triple expansion machinery driving a single propeller to provide a service speed of 14 knots. *Mararoa* departed Greenock on 2 October on its delivery voyage, stopping at St Vincent for bunkers, then proceeding to Cape Town, where six days were spent. Leaving there on 8 November, *Mararoa* voyaged non-stop to Hobart, arriving there on 23 November.

When *Mararoa* was ordered it was planned that the vessel would be placed on the burgeoning trade across the Tasman Sea between New Zealand and Australia, but with the award of the trans-Pacific contract while the vessel was on its delivery voyage, these plans were quickly changed, as *Mararoa* was the only vessel owned by the Union Line with the capacity to operate the longer route. So, instead of going from Hobart to Dunedin as originally intended, *Mararoa* headed for Sydney, arriving on 27 November. Next day the *Sydney Morning Herald* reported:

The Union Company's new steamship Mararoa arrived here yesterday from Glasgow, via the Cape and Hobart, with a number of passengers, but no cargo. The Union Company have almost a world-wide reputation for the splendidly built and equipped vessels of their numerous fleet, and they are evidently determined to maintain their prestige, as the Mararoa is an improvement even on the best of the boats previously owned by them; in fact the vessel is one of the finest of her class that has yet been seen here. She is equipped with every modern appliance for the efficient and economical working of the ship; her accommodation is of the first class; her lines are very fine, and there is a general appearance of finish about her which adds to greatly to her attractiveness. The saloon and the drawing rooms are models of artistic taste. Particularly is the drawing room deserving of praise, as it is an exquisite apartment, and should find ready appreciation from all passengers. The electric light is in every part of the ship, and during the voyage out it has not given the slightest trouble.

Messrs Denny Brothers, of Dumbarton, were the builders of the Mararoa, and even to them the vessel is a splendid advertisement. They also supplied the engines, which are on the triple expansion principle, and have worked admirably. At the trials they developed a speed of 16 knots, but on the voyage out only half boiler power was used, and no special effort was made to push ahead.

On the 19th October, at 11am, a slight mishap occurred to the engines, the high pressure piston breaking, which caused the engine to stop until 9pm. On entering Table

Mararoa (WSS VIC)

Bay, on the 39th ultimo, Archibold Johnston, a second class passenger, died from consumption, and was buried at Cape Town. The Mararoa stayed six days at Cape Town, where she was engaged in repairing breakages and coaling ship.

The Mararoa left Glasgow at 3pm on 1st October, anchored at Greenock for the night, and embarked passengers at 1pm on 2nd; got under weigh at 3pm, and at 5pm anchored in Rothesay Bay, the weather being thick and blowing hard. Left again at 1pm on 3rd, and landed pilot off Waterford at 1am on 4th October. Passed Madeira 8am on 8th, and arrived at St Vincent at 5pm on 11th. Finished coaling there, and proceeded on at 11am on the 13th, arriving at Cape Town at 4.30am on the 30th October. Left Cape Town at 3.30am on the 5th instant, and passed the barque Sussex, of London, from Cardiff to Hongkong, 66 days out, all well, on the 8th instant. Sighted the Tasmanian coast at 4am on the 23rd and reached Hobart at 3pm same date. Left again at 5.30am on the 25th, and entered the Heads at 11am on the 27th, arriving at Fitzroy Dock at 12.30pm. At Hobart the passengers for southern ports of New Zealand were transferred to the steamship Tarawera, and the passengers for Auckland were sent on by the steamship Manapouri. The Mararoa will be taken into Fitzroy Dock today for an overhaul.

Despite the decision to award the new mail contract to Oceanic and the Union Line, and the end of the charter arrangement to Pacific Mail, *Australia* and *Zealandia* continued to operate across the Pacific, though it was doubtful they could survive without a Government subsidy. Initially, however, until the two companies could begin their contract service, *Australia* and *Zealandia* were able to remain operating on a temporary subsidy arrangement. Even when the new service did begin, *Zealandia* and *Australia* continued to be advertised as offered a monthly departure from Sydney on a shorter route to San Francisco, going direct from Sydney to Honolulu. In an attempt to eclipse the start of the new service, *Australia* was scheduled to depart Sydney two days before *Mararoa*, and as it would follow a shorter route, would arrive in San Francisco quicker, thus attracting the majority of passengers wishing to travel at that time.

Mararoa was fitted with accommodation for 150 first class and 120 second class passengers, but there were only 49 passengers on board when the vessel, under the command of Captain J Edie, departed Sydney on 4 December for Auckland, Honolulu and San Francisco. Although a broken piston caused a two-day delay on the passage, *Mararoa* arrived in San Francisco on 29 December, only one day late.

Mararoa was the first steamship with triple expansion engines to arrive in San Francisco, and also the best appointed vessel to visit the port up to that time, creating a great deal of interest. A local newspaper reporter was very taken by the bathing facilities provided for the ship, writing that "Bathrooms are very large, and there are enough of them to secure the luxury of a bath for every passenger, an important item while sailing through the tropics".

The first westbound departure under the new contract was taken by *Alameda*, which departed San Francisco on 23 November 1885, while *Mariposa* followed from San Francisco on 20 December. In the hope of denting the pride of these American ships on their entry into the trade, *Zealandia* was programmed to depart San Francisco on the same day as *Alameda*, and great interest was created in the unofficial race between these two ships. *Alameda* called at Honolulu on 30 November, arriving in Auckland on 13 December and Sydney on 17 December.

A report that appeared in the *Sydney Morning Herald* on 18 December was headlined "Ocean Race from San Francisco to Sydney":

Considerable excitement was felt in shipping circles at San Francisco by the sailing on the same date for Sydney, via Honolulu and Auckland, of the Oceanic SS Co's Alameda and the PMSS Co's Zealandia – the friends of each steamer willingly backing their fancy in regard to the steaming qualities of the two vessels. Nearly £2000 has changed hands over the event. The sailing date was set for November 21, but, owing to the detention of the mails, the Alameda had to wait until the 23rd. The Zealandia waited for her rival.

The Zealandia sailed from San Francisco at 2pm on November 23rd, the Alameda following at 4pm, and meeting with very stormy headwind and sea. On the 24th at 4pm the Alameda passed the Zealandia, and arrived at Honolulu on November 30 at 6am, the Zealandia following at 10pm, the Alameda thus winning the first event by 18 hours.

The Zealandia sailed from Honolulu on 1st December at 1am and the Alameda at 9.30am same date. The Alameda arrived at Auckland on December 13, at 1am, and the Zealandia on December 14 at 3.30am; the Alameda thus won the second event by 26½ hours from Honolulu. The Alameda sailed from Auckland at 3.30am on December 14, and arrived in Sydney at 9pm, when there was no sign of the Zealandia. Alameda thus also won the third event.

Also on 18 December the *Sydney Morning Herald* provided an extensive description of *Alameda*:

The steamship Alameda, belonging to the Oceanic Steam Navigation Company of San Francisco, arrived in port last night with the English and American mails, after the fastest passage on record between the two ports, by way of Honolulu and Auckland. The Alameda is a remarkably attractive spar-deck steamer of 3,200 tons gross register, being not unlike in general design and interior arrangement to the Union Steamship Company's new steamer Mararoa, with which she will in future run the mail service to and from San Francisco.

Alameda (Alexander Turnbull Library)

Her lines are so fine and her finish so good that she does not seem so large a vessel as she really is. The Alameda is wholly an American production, and as such speaks well for the future of American iron shipbuilding, as she will certainly compare most favourably with any vessel of her class that has yet visited these waters. The hull is divided into six watertight compartments, and there is provision for water ballast to the extent of 17,000 gallons. The stem is straight, and the stern elliptical, and the vessel is lightly rigged as a topsail schooner.

There is accommodation for 145 cabin and 85 steerage passengers. The saloon, like that of the Mararoa, is situated amidships, and is approached from the upper deck by staircases leading from both sides of the ship with elaborately carved hand rails and posts. The apartment extends the full width of the ship, is roomy, exceedingly well ventilated, and particularly noticeable for the quiet tone of the ornamentation and decoration. It is upholstered in maroon velvet, as are the other parts of the ship. The state rooms run along the sides of the ship, and down the centre, both forward and aft of the saloon, and are exceptionally large. Spring mattresses and the latest type of lavatory are to be found in each, and the ventilation and light are ample. A ladies room forward is quite a feature in the ship, and should be greatly appreciated by those for whom it is designed, as it is convenient and exceedingly comfortable.

The electric light, on the Edison principle, extends throughout the ship, and is unanimously voted to be a great improvement upon the old style of lighting with oil, as it is not only much cooler (a great attraction in warmer latitudes), but gives a brighter, yet softer, light.

On the upper deck commander and officers have rooms fitted and furnished in a very taking style, and in addition to these there are 15 upper deck state rooms, four of which are for families, and number of them are fitted with Pullman berths similar to those of the Mararoa. The drawing room is on the upper deck above the saloon, and is furnished with a library, piano etc. The smoking room, in a house aft of the funnel, is fitted with movable tables and cushioned seats etc, and should make an agreeable resort.

The Alameda is driven by compound surface-condensing engines of the three-cylinder type, which were made by the builders of the vessel. Steam is generated in four steel boilers, which carry a working pressure of 90lb to the square inch. With ordinary weather the Alameda can steam 16 knots, but this can be exceeded though the average running maintained is between 15 and 16 knots. At a speed of 14½ knots the consumption of coal is 50 tons per day, but to get a speed of 16 knots 65 tons are required to be consumed in the 24 hours.

In every cabin are steam heaters, so that if necessary the rooms can be warmed. The Alameda is steered by steam, and has all the latest appliances in the shape of winches, hoists etc for the rapid hauling of cargo, besides steam capstan and steam fire pumps. The latter are unusually powerful, being capable of throwing a jet of water through a 2½ inch hose and an inch nozzle with a force of 60lb to the sq inch, so that fire on board would have little chance of making headway.

The decks of the vessel are very fine, forming most agreeable promenades, and during the voyage just completed they have been constantly used. In every detail it is evident that the Alameda has been well and carefully built for a large passenger traffic, and there is but little doubt that the reputation she has already achieved for herself while running between San Francisco and Honolulu will not be lessened in her new sphere of labour. There were 45 passengers from San Francisco and Honolulu and 37 from Auckland on board, and all speak in highest terms of the ship, of the food supplied, of the way in which it was served, and of the courtesy, kindness and attention of Captain Morse, her commander, and his officers.

The Alameda sailed from San Francisco at 4.20pm on November 23, and arrived at Honolulu on November 30 at 5.30am, the passage having been made in 6 days 12 hours. Departure was taken from Honolulu at 9.27am on the 1st instant after a detention of 27 hours 38 minutes, and the steamer arrived off Tutiula at midnight on the 8th, starting again an hour afterwards. At 1.50pm on the 13th she stopped for a pilot at Auckland, having accomplished the run from San Francisco in 17 days 18 hours 35 minutes actual steaming time. After landing mails, passengers and cargo, the Alameda started again for Sydney on the 14th, and entered the Heads at 5.15pm, having made the run across in 3 days 15 hours 15 minutes. The actual steaming time between San Francisco and Sydney was thus 21 days 9 hours 49 minutes, considerably under the fastest passage hitherto recorded. The Alameda anchored in the lower part of Neutral Bay, but will be berthed at the Union Company's Wharf this morning.

A list was provided of the cargo brought to Sydney from San Francisco and Auckland aboard *Alameda*, which included "75 bales broom corn, 400 boxes apples, 25 packages dried fruits, 3 packages hams, 200 half-barrels salmon, 900 cases canned fruits, 14 horses, Woodyear's circus outfit, and sundries; also 100 bales broom corn, 45 boxes medicine, and sundries for Melbourne".

Zealandia eventually arrived in Sydney on 18 December, almost a day behind *Alameda*. Although the "race" proved the superiority of the American ship, in the *Sydney Morning Herald* on 19 December it was advertised that *Zealandia* and *Australia* would continue to depart Sydney every four weeks, providing a direct service to San Francisco via Honolulu only, with an overland route through America and on to Britain by steamer. The advertisement stated;

The magnificent steamers AUSTRALIA and ZEALANDIA will depart Sydney for SAN FRANCISCO DIRECT, via Honolulu, as under, without transshipment. Passengers are booked to San Francisco or through to European destinations with special advantages, and have at San Francisco choice of the unrivalled Atlantic Steamship Lines of the Cunard, Inman, White Star, or other companies. All first class passengers are allowed 350lb of luggage to San Francisco, and 250lb 'overland' free of charge.

The published schedule showed *Zealandia* leaving Sydney on 28 December, followed by *Australia* on 26 January 1886, then *Zealandia* on 24 February, *Australia* on 24 March and *Zealandia* on 22 April.

Immediately below was an advertisement for the new San Francisco Royal Mail Service, connecting to an overland route to England via San Francisco and New York. The schedule showed *Alameda* was due to depart Sydney on 31 December, followed by *Mariposa* on 28 January, *Mararoa* on 25 February, *Alameda* again on 25 March and *Mariposa* on 22 April. The advertisement also stated:

Passengers adopting this route avoid the heat and discomfort of the Red Sea, and have the privilege of remaining at any or all ports en route, thus adding to the pleasure and value of the trip. It is also to be particularly noted that these steamers are specially designed for tropical trades, being fitted with electric light throughout, and with a refrigerating chamber for ship's provisions, thus ensuring every comfort and convenience when passing through the tropics.

However, without a contract to support them, the Pearce ships were soon forced to withdraw from the Pacific trade. *Australia* arrived in San Francisco on 3 March 1886, followed by *Zealandia* on 20 March 1886, by which time both vessels had been sold to the Oceanic Steamship Company, the sale being finalised on 24 February 1886.

In a strange series of deals, both ships were on-sold almost immediately to William G Irwin, a partner in the Oceanic operation, *Zealandia* on 25 March and *Australia* on 5 April, with both vessels being re-registered in Hawaii. On 9 April *Zealandia* was sold by Irwin to John S Walker, another of the partners, who also purchased *Australia* on 29 May. Just why these transactions happened is not clear, but they did not affect the two ships joining the Oceanic operation.

Surprisingly, *Zealandia* and *Australia* were not renamed, even though they were placed on the short service between San Francisco and Honolulu as replacements for *Alameda* and *Mariposa*. *Zealandia* departed San Francisco on 27 March on its first voyage on the new service, but *Australia* did not make its first departure from San Francisco until 19 May, and thereafter a departure was scheduled every two weeks.

Within a short time it was obvious that *Mararoa* was not suited to the long trans-Pacific trade. Having been designed for the shorter trans-Tasman routes, there was insufficient bunker space for the longer sectors, and valuable cargo space had to utilised for coal. Also, *Mararoa* was a very difficult vessel to handle, being fitted with a tiller rather than a conventional wheel, and the rudder was moved by hydraulic power, which meant a full head of steam had to be maintained at all times.

On 12 August 1886 *Mararoa* departed Sydney on its fourth, and last voyage across the Pacific to San Francisco and on the return trip went only as far as Auckland, then was taken off the route. *Mararoa* joined the trans-Tasman trade for which it had been built, and proved very successful in this role. However, the Union Line did not have another vessel available to replace *Mararoa*, so the Oceanic company had to supply the Union Line with the third vessel required under the contract.

For the first voyage under the new arrangement, *Australia* departed San Francisco on 1 October, going to Honolulu then directly to Sydney, where it arrived on 27 October, a bit later than planned. Next day the *Sydney Morning Herald* reported:

> The steamship Australia, from San Francisco, via Honolulu, with mails, passengers and cargo, entered the Heads at 11 o'clock yesterday forenoon. The cause of the delay in the arrival of the Australia is attributed to the fact that the bottom is foul, the vessel having been running between Honolulu and San Francisco for some time past without having been docked. Otherwise she presents a most creditable appearance inside and out.
>
> Since she was here in January last, extensive alterations and repairs have been made to her by her new owners, Mr J D Spreckels and Bros. The interior of the hull has been cleaned and painted, the saloon and staterooms redecorated and upholstered, spring beds put in the cabins, and electric bells fitted throughout the ship. The steerage has also received attention, having been entirely remodelled; the engines and boilers have been put in thorough order, and the ship has been reclassed A1 at Lloyds. Prior to sailing in October, new fore and main masts were put in, together with a complete set of new yards, booms, sails and rigging. The masts are single spars, specially ordered from Puget Sound, and are 130 feet long.
>
> It is not yet decided whether the Australia will be kept on the present line, but it is the intention of Messrs Spreckels to dispatch the RMS Zealandia from San Francisco with the December mails. The Zealandia has been laid up for some time, undergoing extensive repairs to her engines. Her steam capacity is being increased, and patent corrugated furnaces (imported from Leeds, England) fitted. Her rudder has been renewed, and the entire ship put in splendid order; and it is confidently expected that she will keep up a high rate of speed.
>
> Of the voyage, Captain Webber reports as follows: The Australia left San Francisco at 2pm on October 1, arrived at Honolulu at 6am on October 9, discharged 600 tons of cargo, and took on board 400 tons of coal, and sailed for Sydney direct at 2pm October 10; crossed the Equator on October 16, passed Mitchell's Island (Ellice Group) at 1pm on October 19, Rotumah Island at 10am on October 20, rounded Walpole Island at midnight on October 22, and made the Australian coast at 5pm on October 26, off Smoky Cape. The Australia experienced most exceptionally fine weather from the time of leaving San Francisco to arrival at Sydney, with smooth sea throughout, except 20 hours heavy swell on the 26th instant.

Australia departed Sydney on 4 November, calling at Auckland and Honolulu, and arriving in San Francisco on 29 November. As mentioned in the newspaper story, *Zealandia* departed San Francisco on 18 December 1886, going via Honolulu and Auckland to Sydney. No doubt due to the extensive work performed so recently on *Zealandia*, it was retained on the service to partner *Alameda* and *Mariposa*. The three ships were able to provide a departure from San Francisco and Sydney every four weeks, and this situation continued for the next three years.

In April 1889, *Mariposa* came close to disaster when a fire broke out in a cargo of flax that had been loaded in Auckland, as reported in the *Hawkes Bay Herald* on Wednesday, 25 April 1889:

> The RMS Mariposa, which left for San Francisco on Monday last, returned to port at half-past 3 o'clock this morning. The cause of her return was an outbreak of fire among a quantity of flax that had been stored in the lower forehold. The fire was discovered when the Mariposa was 220 miles distant from Auckland. An attempt was immediately made to extinguish the flames by removing the flax, but it failed, the men being nearly suffocated. The vessel's speed was reduced by half, and she put back for Auckland. The hatches were battened down, and the fire was smothered with steam by midnight yesterday after working for six hours. All hands behaved splendidly, the utmost good order was observed throughout the occurrence, and the passengers exhibited no alarm. A large quantity of flax has been damaged, but the exact amount of the injury is not yet ascertained. The mails were uninjured, and the New Zealand mail is as dry as when shipped. Two bags in the Sydney mail were soaked. The Mariposa resumed her voyage at 4pm today.
>
> The fire was discovered at 6.30 yesterday morning, when the Mariposa was about 220 miles out from the New Zealand coast, but it must have commenced within a very few hours of the steamer leaving the wharf. The first indication of the fire were dense volumes of smoke, which were seen issuing from the mail room and forehold of the ship, and when the hatches of the forehold were lifted thick smoke burst out. It was then seen that the seat of the fire was in the large cargo of flax, which was stored in the lower hold. The engines were slowed down and streams of water were directed down the hatch. About 30 bales of flax were got out.

Mariposa (John Mathieson collection)

The smoke and heat experienced became so severe that one man was carried on deck insensible, and it took two hours nursing to bring him round. Three other men were also almost suffocated, whilst many of the officers suffered from the effects of the smoke. As the fire could not be extinguished by the means adopted, the hatches were again battened down and steamed turned into holes which were cut in the deck. By 3 o'clock the fire was under control and by midnight yesterday all danger had ceased. Between 7 and 8 o'clock yesterday morning the vessel's head was turned to New Zealand, Captain Hayward having decided to return to Auckland. Had the fire gained much more headway before it was discovered the great majority of the people on board must have perished. The women and children alone would have filled the boats, and there would have been little chance of their reaching land against the southerly wind that was blowing and the heavy sea that was running.

The flax on board the steamer comprised 580 bales. When the Mariposa was berthed at the Queen Street wharf the mails were landed and spread out on the wharf. It was found that the New Zealand mail was quite uninjured, and as dry as when shipped. The mail from Sydney included two bags saturated with water, but which were fortunately empty. Experts were set to work at once to find out the condition of the vessel and cargo. Captains Worsp and Clayton examined the vessel and found there was no injury beyond a slight charring of the deck where the holes had been cut. The hold where the fire broke out is of iron. They found that the outside of some of the bales of flax had been charred, whilst the inside was uninjured; this going to show that the fire had not originated from spontaneous combustion. Some of the flax was stowed in the after hold where it was not touched by either fire or water, and it was remarked by many persons that some of the bales were not as dry as they should have been before being shipped. It is possible that a match dropped into a bale when the flax was being put on board. The flax had been stored in the sheds on the Auckland wharf for over three weeks. The whole of the flax having been discharged the Mariposa left again tonight for San Francisco. As the vessel moved off the band played several airs, and the captain and crew were loudly cheered.

The Wellington *Evening Press* published this eye-witness account of the incident, written by the editor of that paper, Mr Wakefield, who was a passenger on the *Mariposa*:

At 6 o'clock on Tuesday morning the Mariposa slackened speed, and almost immediately slowed down till she was making scarcely any way. In answer to inquiries as to the cause of this by the passengers, who were early on deck, the officers were very reticent, merely saying with an air of indifference that the speed had been slackened for a bit for some purpose, but she would soon go ahead again. It was at once noticed that something very unusual had occurred or was going on. The deck before the pilothouse, which usually forms a part of the cabin promenade, was fenced off with cable. None of the crew were to be seen anywhere about the ship, except around the fore-hatch, where a number of them were crowded under the command of Captain Hayward, apparently working with all their might and main at some operations in the forehold, while hosepipes lay all along the deck. Smoke and steam were issuing from the fore-hatch, and though no passengers were allowed to go forward, it soon became known that the cargo was on fire. At this time most of the passengers were in bed or in the bathroom, and the few who were on deck and learnt the state of the case were easily made to understand the necessity for self-control, and for making as light of the matter as possible, so as to avoid a panic, especially among the women and children, who numbered between fifty and sixty. One or two ladies sleeping in the deck cabins were aroused, and came out on deck in a state of alarm, but were quieted by the assurance that there was no danger, and all without exception behaved admirably. Not the slightest panic or disorder of any kind occurred, but everything went on throughout the crowded ship just as if she were steaming safely on her course, and the social hall was well filled with ladies and children by half-past-seven. By 9 o'clock four men had dropped down in a state of suffocation, and had been taken aft unconscious, and several officers were very much exhausted, and suffering severely from the smoke which now pervaded the ship. Still the most complete confidence was felt in Captain Hayward, who never left the forehatch, and whose coolness and firm good sense almost did away with all idea of danger. The boats were got ready without attracting more notice than was necessary, and so well was the impression of safety maintained that breakfast was served just as usual, and very fairly patronised, even by the ladies and children. By ten o'clock the work of getting out the flax was in full progress, the men going down in shifts to fix the tackle on the bales in the great heat and stifling atmosphere of the hold, and others rolling them along the deck. This went on all morning until about fifty bales had been brought up and piled on the deck, filling up nearly all the space forward. The flooding of the hold where the flax was stowed went on simultaneously, the watertight compartments being closed. The flax, water, and smoke together made it impossible for the passengers to remain on deck, and a good deal of discomfort was felt, but everybody seemed determined to make the best of the situation.

The *Te Aroha News* carried the following report sent from Auckland on 27 April:

We learn that prior to the departure of the mail steamer from port a careful examination was made of the hull, when it was found that the whole extent of the damage done could be covered by the expenditure of a few pounds. The deck was scorched between the 2nd, 3rd and 4th beams abaft the fore hatchway of the lower hold. In addition to this four holes were cut in the deck between these beams to admit of the water being poured upon the fire below. The two tie-plates were also warped with the heat. The small amount of damage is due to the coolness of Captain Hayward, and the promptitude with which he grasped the situation and turned on the steam as well as the water immediately the locality of the fire was discovered. As steam penetrates where water cannot reach, this shows the necessity for steam pipes being fitted in all vessels so as to lend additional security in case of fire. The action of Captain Hayward in carrying out these arrangements for subduing the fire undoubtedly saved the vessel from very serious consequences. As it is, the damage is very slight.

The amount of damage to the cargo has not yet been ascertained. With regard to the flax it is known that 46 bales were more or less damaged. Some were very much burned, whilst others were saturated with steam and water so that they also will be reduced in value. In addition to this 90 hides are more or less damaged.

Early in 1889 the Union Line had finally placed an order with the Denny shipyard at Dumbarton for the construction of a new liner specifically designed for the trans-Pacific service, which was christened *Monowai* when launched on 11 December 1889. The vessel was completed on 4 April 1890, and soon after departed on its delivery voyage to Australia. *Monowai* was the largest ship yet built for the Union Line, and would remain so for the next seven years. Accommodation was provided for 133 first class and 100 second class passengers, and there was also a large cargo capacity, as well as enormous bunkers.

On 16 June 1890 the *Sydney Morning Herald* carried this extensive description of the vessel:

The Monowai, which is the largest of the Union Company's magnificent fleet, was launched from the yards of Messrs W Denny Bros, Dumbarton, on December 11, 1889. The vessel is built entirely of mild steel on the cellular bottom principle, with five watertight compartments, with provision for 348 tons of water ballast in five separate tanks. She has a straight stem and elliptical stern, and is rigged as a two-masted schooner, her gross tonnage being 3,400 tons.

There are four decks in all – spar deck, main deck, 'tween deck, and shade deck, which runs right aft to the flying bridge, forward of the funnel, only broken at the necessary places to allow of cargo being worked, under which passengers are completely independent of the weather. She is finely appointed in every apartment, and has accommodation aft and amidships for 133 first-class passengers, and forward for 100 second-class passengers – the latter being quartered in the fore part of the main deck. The saloon, which is on the main deck, is approached by a very handsome double staircase from the music saloon, and is very tastefully decorated throughout; dining tables are placed along the centre and sides; the couches and revolving chairs are upholstered in amber-coloured plush; one feature in the chairs being that the seats are reversible, so that cane bottoms can be used in hot climates. At the fore end of the saloon is a magnificent sideboard, which was exhibited by Messrs Denny Bros at the Glasgow Exhibition. On each side of the stairs is a very handsome bookcase. At the fore end of the saloon, but not entered directly from it, is the bar, and a large pantry fitted with hot plates and every requisite, also a room in which is a splendid service of plate.

Passing through the doors at either end of the saloon access is given to the staterooms, which are arranged in the centre and sides of the vessel – the side rooms being of larger dimensions than those in the centre – and all fitted up in the same manner with crimson velvet cushions, and in each of the staterooms is a mahogany racks in which are placed lifebelts; while there is electric communication from each room to the bar. There are five bathrooms, four of which are solid marble tepid baths and one a shower bath, the room being tiled all over. The washbasins are also set in solid marble slabs, in fact, nothing has been left undone which would conduce to the comfort of her passengers.

The ladies cabins adjoins the main saloon, and is a

very handsome apartment finished in terra cotta, and communicating with it are dressing rooms and two baths of solid marble, the washstands being also of marble, with hot and cold water. Every provision has been made in the event of fire, there being a hose and patent fire extinguisher placed in various parts of the main deck.

The music saloon, which is on the spar deck, is the finest got up apartment we have ever had the pleasure of seeing on any vessel afloat. It is some 11ft in height. About 8ft of the height of the walls are finished in magnificent satinwood panels, above which is coloured glass, which has a very pleasing effect. At the fore end of this apartment stands the alcove containing one of Brinsmead's pianos, while at the after end is a very large handsome mirror, on each side of which is a special stateroom, containing two berths each. There are six other similar staterooms in the after deckhouse, where there is also the smoking room, most tastefully finished in sycamore, satinwood, walnut and marqueterie, the walls being of polished woods of various colours, and the floor is laid with encaustic tiling, sofas covered with buffalo hide, and divisioned off into single seats, with five marble-top tables, glass racks, and electric bells.

The second saloon, which is also on the main deck, and approached from the spar deck, is a very roomy apartment, the upholstery being of buffalo hide. There are separate enclosed staterooms, baths, lavatories etc.

Surprisingly, instead of joining the trans-Pacific trade *Monowai* was placed on the Trans-Tasman "horseshoe" service, departing Sydney on 19 June for Auckland, then visiting several ports in both North and South Islands before crossing the Tasman again to Hobart, with the voyage terminating in Melbourne, from where the return voyage commenced on 16 July.

In the meantime, *Zealandia* remained on the Pacific route, departing Sydney on 9 July, and again on 1 October, followed *Alameda* on 29 October and *Mariposa* on 26 November. *Zealandia* was then scheduled to depart Sydney on 20 December, but the Union Line decided to place *Monowai* on the Pacific trade, with a departure on 24 December.

There was a bit of consternation when the Union Line insisted that the mails that had been destined to be carried by *Zealandia* instead be taken by *Monowai*. The Oceanic Company protested about this, but under the terms of the contract the Union Line was legally justified in this demand, and eventually the two vessels departed Sydney together. As *Monowai* was carrying enough coal for the entire round trip to San Francisco, it was not able to keep up with *Zealandia*, which arrived in San Francisco almost a day earlier than *Monowai*, which berthed on 17 January 1891.

Zealandia then resumed service between San Francisco and Honolulu alongside *Australia*, but the trade was in a state of decline, and could not support two ships. On 22 August 1891 *Zealandia* left San Francisco on a regular round trip to Hawaii, but on returning to the mainland the vessel was taken out of service and laid up, leaving *Australia* to operate the route on its own.

One of the passengers on board *Monowai* was the chairman of the Union Line, Mr George McLean, who was on his way to meet with John Spreckels regarding the future of the joint service. Spreckels had threatened he would withdraw the Oceanic

Monowai (Fred Roderick collection)

Alameda

ships from the South Pacific trade in March 1891 if the United States Government did not come up with a better subsidy arrangement for his ships, but McLean was able to assure Spreckels that the New Zealand Government would provide a suitable subsidy, and the service continued.

When *Monowai* departed San Francisco on 8 February 1891, there were only 40 first class and 48 second class passengers on board, and not a large volume of cargo. Despite all the planning that had gone into *Monowai*, the vessel proved to be too slow to maintain the contract schedule, and the Union Line received a complaint from the New Zealand Government to this effect.

Over the next few years the Pacific service was maintained by *Alameda*, *Mariposa* and *Monowai*, and on one occasion in 1894 *Monowai* managed to land mail in Auckland only 31 days after it had left London, being carried by ship to New York, then train to San Francisco. However, there was still a general dissatisfaction with the performance of *Monowai*, though the following report in the *Sydney Morning Herald* on 2 August 1894 did not indicate this, stating:

> The Monowai, one of the most popular steamers running in the trade between Sydney and San Francisco, had a stormy time of it on her last run across the Pacific northward. The Honolulu report says: The steamer Monowai was sighted about 4 o'clock and reached the wharf about 6 o'clock. Her delay was caused by rough weather and head winds. On the 14th instant the seas were running over the vessel, and one of the seamen named M'Alister was swept about the deck, and, when he was picked up it was found that his right leg was fractured in two places. He was taken to the Queen's Hospital. Her sailing dates were: Left Sydney 11th June at 5pm; left Auckland on the 16th at 2pm; left Apia on the 21st at 6pm. The Monowai reached Honolulu on the 30th and San Francisco 7th July.

On 22 August the following report on the return voyage was published:

> The Monowai, in command of Captain M Carey, reached the Union Company's wharf at 11am yesterday. She left San Francisco wharf at 10pm on the 26th ultimo, discharged pilot at 11.20pm, and arrived at Honolulu on the 2nd instant at 3.30pm, made a stay of six hours, and left for Apia; reached Apia at 11.40pm on the 9th, and left again at 9 o'clock next morning, reaching Auckland at 10.25am on the 16th; left again same day at 6.15pm; entered Sydney Heads at 6.30am on the 21st, and berthed alongside Margaret Street Wharf at 10.45am. Fine weather was met until leaving Auckland, when a WSW gale was encountered, which lasted until the morning of the 20th instant; from thence light E wind and fine weather to arrival. Was detained four hours in the bay on account of dense fog.

The Oceanic vessels were very popular on the trans-Pacific trade, as evidenced by the following item that appeared in the *Sydney Morning Herald* on 16 October 1894:

> The Oceanic Steamship Company of San Francisco has reason to be proud of the work which its steamers Mariposa and Alameda have performed on the Australian line. Both ships have maintained a wonderful regularity in their voyages across the Pacific, and have almost without

exception exceeded the speed required under the mail contract. The Mariposa on arrival yesterday was a good 24 hours ahead. Captain M Haywood is in command, and is ably seconded by an efficient staff. Mr Thomas Smith is not surpassed as a purser, always being up to date in matters of business with the Mariposa, and pressmen in particular are under obligations to him.

The mail steamer sailed from San Francisco at 5pm 20th September, reached Honolulu at 7am, 27th September, left at 8pm same day, and at 7am on 5th October was in Apia Harbour; left there at noon of the 5th instant, arrived at Auckland at 10am on the 11th, and left at 7pm, arriving at Sydney Heads at 3pm yesterday, and berthed at the Margaret Street wharf of the USS Company.

One reason for the reluctance of the Union Line to consider building a new vessel to replace Monowai may well have been a response to the establishment in 1893 of a second service across the Pacific, this one being from Sydney to Vancouver, which provided travellers with a good alternative to the San Francisco route.

Mariposa

Chapter Six

The All Red Route

Although a regular steamship service was now operating between Australia, New Zealand and the United States, there were many people attracted to the idea of an "All Red Route", or an all British route connecting Britain to New Zealand and Australia via Canada. This would entail the use of the Canadian Pacific steamer services across the Atlantic from Britain to ports in eastern Canada, transportation overland to the west coast port of Vancouver, and another steamer across the Pacific to New Zealand and Australia.

The major problem facing the establishment of this route was the difficulty of the trip from coast to coast across Canada, but this was overcome by the construction of a railroad, which was completed in 1887. In 1885 the Canadian Pacific Railway Co had proposed the development of an "Imperial" service once the train service was operating, but this was not followed up, as they paid more attention to establishing a service from Vancouver to Japan and Hong Kong.

In 1890 the Imperial Steam Navigation Company was formed in London to operate a through service via Vancouver, which planned to make the trip from London to Australia in 35 days. For this purpose a subsidy of £80,000 per year was sought from the Governments of Australia and New Zealand, but when no agreement was reached the planned service did not proceed.

Moves to establish a service across the Pacific between Australia and Vancouver were revived in 1893 by James Huddart, the nephew of Captain Peter Huddart, who in 1852 had arrived in Port Phillip Bay from Britain as master of the sailing ship *Aberfoyle*, settling in Geelong and established himself as a merchant and shipbroker. His major interest was transporting coal to Melbourne from Newcastle, and the business soon flourished. In the early 1860s, Captain Huddart brought his nephew, James Huddart, out from Britain. The Huddart family came from Whitehaven in Cumberland, where James' father was a shipbuilder, and James was born in February 1847, so he was still in his teens when he came to Australia. A few years later Captain Huddart returned to his British home in Cumberland, leaving James Huddart in sole control of the Australian business.

By 1875, James Huddart was operating two sailing ships of his own, *Medea* of 453 gross tons and *Queen Emma*, 314 gross tons, on the coal trade between Newcastle and Melbourne. On 1 August 1876, the coal importing business interests of James Huddart and Thomas J Parker were merged to form Huddart, Parker and Company, with John Traill and Captain Tom Webb as equal partners in the new venture. By 1890 the company had developed a network of coastal services using a fleet of steamships, and was a highly successful operation, with James Huddart as company chairman.

Despite this, by 1890 James Huddart found his attention diverted by the proposal to develop an

James Huddart

"All Red Route" for travel between Britain and Australia via the Pacific. Huddart placed orders with the C S Swan & Hunter shipyard at Newcastle, in England, for the construction of two sister ships, to be completed in 1892. These ships would be owned outright by James Huddart, but managed for him by Huddart Parker.

Unfortunately, when the two ships were completed, arrangements for the trans-Pacific service had not been finalised, so James Huddart was forced to find alternative employment for his vessels, or lay them up. As they were too large to join the Australian coastal trade, Huddart opted to enter the trans-Tasman trade, giving his company the impressive title of the New Zealand & Australasian Steamship Company, to operate in direct competition with the Union Steam Ship Company. At the same time Huddart relinquished his position as chairman of Huddart Parker, though retaining a financial interest in the company, which was appointed to be managing agents of the two new ships when they entered service.

The first of the new ships was named *Warrimoo* when launched on 28 May 1892, attaining 17 knots on trials before being handed over to James Huddart on 23 July. Departing Newcastle on 31 August 1892, *Warrimoo* ran into a full gale while passing through the English Channel, but reportedly coped well with the heavy seas. *Warrimoo* arrived in Plymouth at 5.15pm on 2 September to embark passengers, leaving there at 4pm on 3 September.

The voyage to Sydney was made without any further stops, *Warrimoo* passing the Cape of Good Hope on 22 September, and Cape Leeuwin on 6 October. Rounding Wilson's Promontory at 4am on 11 October, and Gabo Island at 8.30 that evening, *Warrimoo* steamed up the New South Wales coast to pass through Sydney Heads at 10.15pm on 12 October. The distance steamed from Plymouth to Sydney was 12,456 miles, and the voyage had been completed in a steaming time of 37 days 18 hours.

Two days after *Warrimoo* arrived in Sydney, an extensive description of the vessel appeared in the *Sydney Morning Herald*, including the following excerpts:

> What the public feel the most interest in is that which conduces best towards making first a safe voyage, and next a comfortable one. The matter of speed also accounts for a good deal, no doubt.
>
> With regard to safety, the vessel is divided into numerous watertight compartments. In order to bring her within the scope of Admiralty requirements for a troopship and scout, she has to be as nearly unsinkable as it is possible to build a ship.
>
> Built of steel, the Warrimoo is constructed on the three deck grade, with long poop extending over engines and boilers, long topgallant forecastle, and a complete water ballast arrangement on the double-bottom system. The decks are of specially selected teak wood of unusual thickness, and the strength of the vessel generally is considered in excess of Lloyd's and Board of Trade rules, the exceptional weight of the framing admitting of hold beams being dispensed with. Her fine lines, double bottom, numerous watertight compartments, and high rate of speed combine to render the vessel eminently fitted to fly the white ensign should the emergency ever arise.
>
> Also with regard to safety from a passenger point of view is the provision made for saving life. In this respect she has eight lifeboats, two of which are constructed of steel, and under the pillow of every passenger on board a lifebelt is placed day and night.
>
> She is fitted with rolling chocks, of steel plates of exceptional width, which will add very much to the comfort of the passengers by diminishing rolling and pitching motions, and the question of ventilation has not been overlooked. In these semi-tropical latitudes pure air and plenty of it are no less vital at sea than an abundance of shower-bath accommodation and unlimited supply of fresh water. "There is not a stuffy place on board," was the declaration of one of the officers yesterday, and marble baths are provided, with fittings of electro-plated silver to match the mountings in the saloon and staterooms. Every berth and compartment, including the vessel's holds, are ventilated on the latest and most approved methods known to naval architects.
>
> The whole of the passenger accommodation is on the main deck, with alleyways running after from the break of the three-quarter poop, thus affording a fine current of air right through on both sides of the ship.
>
> The dining saloon is a magnificent apartment, immediately under the poop. It is 50 feet in length and its width extends over the whole breadth of the ship. The panelling is of chaste design, the polished framing and panels in walnut, maple and carved oak presenting a very fine effect. Upwards of 100 revolving chairs, upholstered in blue Utrecht velvet, are arranged round the tables, and along the port and starboard sides of the saloon there are sofas upholstered to match. The antique sideboards and rich surroundings impart an air of grandeur to the saloon, the effect being heightened by the subdued light from the tinted glass in a large cupola skylight, which, in addition to the large sidelights admits air and light to the apartment.
>
> There are about 50 staterooms, all richly furnished, and fitted with patent spring mattresses, iron folding beds, and patent folding lavatory. The upholstery, selected by Mrs Huddart, wife of the managing owner, is the same as in the dining saloon. There is a complete electric light installation, with reserve engine to meet emergencies, and electric bells are connected with all the berths, fore and aft.
>
> The smoking hall, which is on the forward deck, is a handsome apartment, the panelling of which is carried out in slabs of polished vein marble, ornamented with chaste gilded designs between pilasters of Parmarga marble, the whole being surmounted with a crimson

ermine freise, with gilded lines. The seats are fitted with arms, the tables are of tinted bronze with marble tops, and the floor is laid with encaustic tiles of bright colours and rich design.

A richly furnished boudoir is reserved for the ladies, and there is a spacious music hall directly over the dining saloon, to which entrance is obtained by a descending corridor of exceptional width, the balustrades being richly carved.

There are an exceptional number of fresh water tanks, and machinery capable of condensing upwards of 10,000 gallons is fitted on board. The engines and boilers have been built by the Wallsend Slipway and Engineering Company, Limited. The diameter of shifting and strength of the engines generally are much in excess of Lloyd's rules. The guaranteed speed is 16 knots per hour, but as a matter of fact, the vessel made 16½ knots against the tide, and with her propeller only partly immersed, so that even better results may be anticipated when the ship is loaded.

All the latest improvements have been introduced in connection with the deck appliances, including patent silent winches, three steam whips, Muir and Caldwell's steering gear, stockless anchors, and patent cold air refrigerating machinery for the preservation of dead meat and fruit is also provided.

With passengers having boarded the previous evening, at 6.30 am on Saturday, 15 October, *Warrimoo* departed on the first voyage by the new company to New Zealand, going to Auckland, Wellington, Lyttelton, Dunedin and Bluff before crossing the Tasman Sea to Melbourne, then back to Sydney. Once two ships were in service, the route would be operated in both directions, and also include a call at Hobart.

Meanwhile, on 25 July the second vessel had been launched and named *Miowera*, being completed less than three months later. On its delivery voyage, *Miowera* had first loaded cargo and embarked passengers in London, leaving there on 26 October, voyaging non-stop to Cape Town, and then to Melbourne. The vessel arrived in Sydney on 12 December, and next day the *Sydney Morning Herald* reported:

The Miowera arrived yesterday – 38 hours from Port Phillip to Sydney Heads. This is equal to a mean speed of 13½ knots per hour. Perhaps this is not the speed Miowera is equal to under best conditions; but it is worth noticing as the performance of a vessel on her first voyage, and following a straight out run of 13,000 miles as the Miowera has to Melbourne. The weather conditions were also very unfavourable, and a mean steaming speed of 13.7 knots against heavy heads seas, strong head current, and fresh contrary winds is not often logged by an intercolonial steamer over a distance of 522 miles.

Though she is built on the same lines as the Warrimoo, there are minor improvements made in the passenger spaces of the ship, the saloon fittings, lavatory accommodation, and the staterooms, all tending to render shipboard life more comfortable to the traveller. The thorough ventilation of the vessel from end to end, and in and through each cabin and compartment, is compassed by a special system, and in warm weather or in tropical latitudes, this abundance of fresh air will be appreciated.

Warrimoo

The saloons and state cabins are fitted up and furnished in luxurious style. The dining saloon and staterooms are on the main deck. The general effect is tasteful and elegant. Polished woods have been freely made use of in the fittings, and the rich hangings and expensive cut Utrecht velvet employed in the upholstery work add to the general sumptuousness of the apartment. The saloon is lit by a large stained-glass cupola or skylight of beautiful design, and the social hall or lounge over the saloon is luxuriously appointed.

There are marble baths and lavatories, and the appointments of the various cabins are those of a first class hotel. The electric light is installed throughout, and each cabin has its electric bell. The saloon can dine 120 passengers comfortably. For the ladies there is a handsome boudoir, and for the gentlemen there is a smoking room, the latter being very cosy and comfortable in its arrangements.

The vessel is rigged with three light spars stepped without yards, in accordance with the most modern practice, but capable of carrying sufficient canvas in the shape of three trysails to steady her in a heavy beam sea. On each side of the funnel is a large metal cross bearing a representation of the five stars which form the Southern Cross, the whole design giving a picturesque finish to the appearance of the steamer as seen from the land.

In the matter of safety, it may be mentioned that the Miowera belongs to the description of vessels termed unsinkable, from the numerous watertight compartments into which she is partitioned. There is quite an array of lifeboats at the davits, and two of these are of steel. A lifebelt is also provided for each passenger.

Warrimoo and *Miowera* were identical in size, being 3,529 gross tons, 357 feet/108.7 m long, with a breadth of 42 feet 3 inches/13 m, and moulded depth of 28 feet/8.5 m. They were powered by triple expansion machinery driving a single propeller, giving a service speed of 15 knots. Accommodation was provided on each ship for a maximum of 233 first class and 127 second class passengers. They had very distinctive funnel markings, white with a black top and on the white a blue cross with the Southern Cross star pattern in gold.

Miowera departed Sydney on its first voyage to New Zealand on 17 December, carrying 400 passengers. The New Zealand & Australasian Steamship Company was now able to offer regular departures on the Tasman trade, and immediately proved to be major competition to the Union Line. The Australian company undercut the fares being charged by the New Zealand firm, who immediately responded by reducing their fares to match. This started a rate war, as each company began to undercut the other. In addition, the Union Line began organising direct competition to the Australian company by having one of their fastest ships depart Sydney on the same day as a vessel of the New Zealand & Australasian Steamship Company, and follow the same schedule around the New Zealand coast and on to Melbourne.

As passenger fares and freight charges continued to tumble, it soon became evident that one company was going to be forced out of the Tasman passenger shipping business. By the middle of 1892 Australia was in the grip of a financial depression, with 23 banks going out of business in the first half of that year, and many companies were forced to close down. Going into 1893 the financial situation began to slowly improve, and by the middle of the year some banks were able to reopen, and the future looked a bit brighter.

During this period James Huddart had been finalising plans to establish his intended service from Australia to Canada. Huddart was successful in obtaining the mail contract between Sydney and Vancouver, and annual subsidies of £10,000 from the New South Wales Government and £25,000 from the Canadian Government.

The new service to Canada was ready to commence in May 1893, by which time *Miowera* and *Warrimoo* had been taken off the New Zealand trade. James Huddart named his new service the Canadian-Australian Royal Mail Line.

On 18 May 1893, *Miowera* departed Sydney for Brisbane, Honolulu and Victoria, where the vessel arrived on 8 June, and Vancouver the next day. The first departure from Vancouver was on 14 June, and Victoria the next day. *Warrimoo* followed from Sydney on 18 June, with future departures from Sydney monthly.

At first the venture seemed to be heading for great success, and when *Warrimoo* returned to Sydney from its second voyage the following report appeared in the Shipping column of the *Sydney Morning Herald* on 10 October:

After a fast and very pleasant voyage, the RMS Warrimoo made this port before dark last night and berthed at the AUSN Company's wharf. Captain C R Bird, RNR, reports having left Vancouver at 4am the 17th September, Victoria at 4.30pm same date, arrived at Honolulu at 4pm the 24th, sailed again at 2am the 25th, arrived at Suva at 7am the 4th instant, left the latter port at 4.30pm same date, and entered the Heads 6.15pm: after passing the Health Officer arrived alongside the Grafton Wharf at 7.45pm. Experienced fair weather on leaving Victoria till rounding Cape Flattery, thence very fine weather to Honolulu, which continued till making the Fiji Group, where thick rainy weather was met with to arrival at Suva, thence strong ESE, NE and SW wind with variable weather to arrival.

Mr Boswell, at the close of the voyage, and on behalf of saloon passengers, in a happy speech, presented Mr R E Arundel and Mr J D S Phillips, first and third officers, each with a purse of sovereigns on the occasion of their approaching marriages.

Miowera arriving at Vancouver (Vancouver Maritime Museum)

The Brisbane call had been included in the hope it would encourage the Queensland Government to provide a subsidy as well. When this was not forthcoming Brisbane was omitted from the itinerary after only four northbound and three southbound voyages, as *Warrimoo* came directly from Honolulu to Sydney on its second round trip.

When *Miowera* departed Sydney on 18 September on the fifth northbound voyage, it did not call at Brisbane either, instead heading directly to Honolulu, but went aground at the entrance to Pearl Harbour on the night of 2 October. Reports of the incident took several weeks to reach Australia, and on 20 October the *Sydney Morning Herald* published two reports from their London correspondent:

> The Miowera struck at 8 o'clock on the night of the 2nd October at Honolulu. She is resting on the rocks amidships. All attempts to get her off have up to the present proved futile. A tug failed to move her. The steamer is making but little water. The rudder post is gone. It is expected that the Miowera will break up if bad weather comes on. The cargo was saved in good condition.
>
> The Miowera went on the rocks at the entrance to the harbour of Honolulu. An American man-of-war made an attempt to tow her off, but failed to move her. Mr James Huddart, the managing owner of the Canadian-Australian line, expects to be able to maintain the timetable unbroken from Australia. The Miowera lies in 11 feet of water.

In the same issue of the newspaper there was a description of Honolulu Harbour, which said in part:

> It is sheltered from the NE trades, but is an awkward place to make owing to the coral reefs and banks that stretch east and west of the entrance. This entrance is not more than 500 feet in width, and a narrow channel then takes the vessels a distance of about two miles up to the wharfs at the Hawaiian capital. The entrance itself is the narrowest part of the channel. It is a dangerous and difficult place to make, and the mail steamers of the San Francisco lines make a point of not making Honolulu at night. Only a few months ago one of the largest of the Pacific Mail steamers, the China, in command of a very old shipmaster, grounded on one of these coral beds, but, by lightening forward, got off. Many vessels have met disaster at Honolulu, nor is it to be wondered at, if one may judge from the Admiralty charts of the port, and the character of the place given by many shipmasters. The position of a vessel on the reef at the mouth of the channel would be exposed one to any bad weather from almost all points between east and west by south, and a heavy southerly blow would quickly break up the strongest ship ever built.

From the news to hand it is not clear whether the

Miowera was bound inward or outward at the time. The cargo, consisting of fruit, preserved meats and sundry merchandise, is reported to have been saved in good condition. Insurance risks are, therefore, easy in this respect; but the underwriters of the ship are likely to sustain with the owners a very serious loss. The docking facilities at Honolulu are not very complete. There is a slip that would take up a ship of 1,000 tons, but too small for the Miowera. If she can be floated off by the help of pontoons and temporarily repaired by building a caisson around her, it would not be difficult to get her across to San Francisco.

From the above it was clear that the *Miowera* was in a very precarious position, and it was quite possible that the vessel would become a total loss. It later transpired that the vessel was trying to enter the harbour at the time of the grounding, but as Diamond Head was obscured that evening, the vessel's captain had mistaken high land to the north of the crater as being Diamond Head and brought his ship too close to the shore. At this time there was no lighthouse on Diamond Head, but after another major grounding one was built and began operating in 1899.

When initial refloating attempts failed, passengers, cargo and the mail were removed from the ship, and taken aboard *Australia*, which took them to San Francisco on its regular run from Honolulu. Another item to appear in the *Sydney Morning Herald* on 20 October, sourced from Brisbane, stated:

Immediately on hearing of the accident to the Miowera, the local representatives of the AUSN Company, communicated with Huddart, Parker and Co, placing their steamship Wodonga at their service. It is probable that this vessel will be dispatched from Sydney for Vancouver on the Miowera's sailing date.

The *Wodonga* was quite a new vessel, built at Glasgow in 1890, and having accommodation for about 150 passengers. It was designed for the east coast trade from Melbourne and Sydney to ports in northern Queensland, but at 2,341 gross tons was considerably smaller than *Miowera*, and also had a service speed of only 13 knots. Whether the offer from the AUSN was given serious consideration is not known, but on 26 October the *Sydney Morning Herald* reported:

Mr James Huddart, managing owner of the Canadian-Australian line, has chartered the Shaw, Savill, and Albion Company's steamer Arawa to replace the Miowera, which lies stranded at the entrance to the harbour of Honolulu. The Arawa will leave Sydney for Vancouver on 18th November.

The placing of the Arawa in the Vancouver service is regarded as a favourable chance for testing the practicability of opening up a frozen meat trade with Canada.

The Arawa is one of the best known, as indeed she is one of the finest, vessels specially built for the mail service between London and New Zealand. She has made voyages from Plymouth to Hobart in 35 days 7½ hours via the Cape of Good Hope, speed 14 knots per hour right through. Her best from Plymouth to Otago was 38

Arawa (WSS Vic)

days 30 minutes steaming, and on that performance she claims to have beaten everything over the same route.

The Arawa and Tainui are sister ships. They are fitted with the new triple-expansion form cylindered engines introduced by Messrs Denny and Co, and they use their steam at a pressure of 160lb per square inch. The saving, however, is very large, through the steam being used over and over again, so long, in fact, as it has any force remaining. Consequently, the Arawa, a ship of 5,250 tons, maintained an average speed of 14 knots per hour on a coal consumption of 52 tons per diem. Probably no finer looking vessels of their size have ever been turned out by a builder than the Arawa and the Tainui. Their great length, 460 feet over all, is made to appear even greater by there being four masts instead of the usual three, and two funnels instead of one. The Arawa, fitted with refrigerating machinery and insulated compartments for the conveyance of frozen mutton, has an advantage over the two other ships. She is due at Sydney from New Zealand, where she is at present, on 10th November, and will be dispatched by Messrs Burns, Philp, and Co to Vancouver on 18th November.

The first vessel to be built for Shaw, Savill & Albion Line, *Arawa* came from the Denny shipyard at Dumbarton in 1884, and had operated for almost ten years on the trade from London to New Zealand via Cape Town, its final departure from London being on 31 August 1893. *Arawa* was considerably larger than the two Huddart vessels, at 5,026 gross tons, and provided accommodation for 95 first, 52 second and 260 third class passengers. *Arawa* arrived in Sydney on 10 November, and was prepared for the Canadian trade.

When the Fijian Government offered to provide a subsidy, a call at Suva was instituted. *Arawa* took *Miowera*'s next scheduled departure on 18 November, making the first call at Suva on 24 November, and arriving in Vancouver on 12 December. A call at Suva was included for the first time on a southbound voyage on 3 December 1893 by *Warrimoo*.

It was not until 10 November that a first-hand report on the grounding of the *Miowera* appeared in the *Sydney Morning Herald*. It is indicative of the state of international communications at that time that this report came from a newspaper picked up in Honolulu by the *Mariposa* on a regular voyage from San Francisco. When *Mariposa* arrived in Auckland, the local correspondent for the *Herald* cabled the following story to Sydney:

The following particulars are to hand from Honolulu concerning the grounding of the Miowera. On the evening of Monday, the 2nd October, about 7 o'clock, the lookout on Diamond Head signal station reported by telephone the Miowera 15 miles off. One of the regulations of the Board of Health here is that no pilot shall board the vessel until the port physician has made his examination. In pursuance of this order it has been customary for all the officials to go out in the same boat, but it has generally only taken them half an hour to get started. On this particular occasion they were 55 minutes in reaching the entrance to the channel – some say much more – and when they got there, the electric lights of the steamer showed her to be hard and fast on the outer reef. When they boarded her she had been fast for some minutes.

At 8.20pm the vessel struck the reef at quarter speed, bow on, and ploughed her way through the sand, and plumped right down on the coral in the centre, where she came to a stop. There was little or no shock, the sand having stopped her headway, and no alarm was felt by anyone on board. The engines were immediately reversed at full speed, but no effort could budge her. At midnight, when the press representatives reached the Miowera, there was not a particle of excitement on board, only two or three of the male passengers were on deck. All others, ladies included, were sound asleep in their cabins, having been assured that there was no immediate danger, and that the vessel would get off in the morning, if not before.

Captain Stott made the following statement to the press representatives: "I wish to say that the first land I saw was the hill directly at the back of the town, which I took for Diamond Head, as that was entirely covered by clouds and there was no light upon it. I naturally took the land further to westward for Diamond Head. We took our bearings by the sun at noon and later on also, and reckoning our speed from the last sights I thought we were several miles further off than we were, and would have been of the speed had been correctly registered. There were no lights on the buoys, and there was absolutely nothing to warn me of any danger. I came along at slow speed until I picked up the red light, and a little later the green. At that time I was a long way to windward of the line of lights, and of course knew that when I had that in line I would have a leading light. Consequently, I came very slowly to leeward, and while yet to windward of the leading light the green light suddenly went out. I stopped the engines, and just then a man in the bows sang out that there was a buoy on the starboard bow and close aboard. I took soundings and found six fathoms of water, and while I apprehended no danger I believed that there was little enough water, and rang to back slowly. It was then I first learned that we were aground, as the screw would not move her. We had drifted aground, bow on, and the rollers had swung her around until she rested where she does now broadside on to the rocks. There was no pilot aboard, and I saw no pilot boat till after we were aground, and then he was lighting the lamps on the buoys to show us where we were when it was too late. In any other country the pilot would have been outside, and not in the mouth of the channel lighting lamps to show a stranded vessel her position."

Messrs Davies and Co, agents for Canadian Australian line called on Admiral Skerrett and asked for assistance. He did all that he possibly could under the circumstances; the Adams weighed anchor, and joined the fleet of small steamers in the final efforts to tow the unfortunate steamer towards the channel. Several blue-jackets from the Philadelphia were on hand to help, but the tremendous power brought to bear on the wreck scarcely effected a change in her position, and after consultation with the agents it was agreed to abandon all efforts to tow her off until the owners could be communicated with.

The vessel is stranded on a reef, which is proved disastrous to more than one ship in the past. Her 30 cabin and 20 steerage passengers were all cared for by the agents, and were taken to the best hotel in Honolulu, where the citizens exerted themselves to make them comfortable during their sojourn. On the 7th October the steamer Australia arrived from San Francisco, and negotiations were entered into by the agents of the companies interested to have the vessel leave on her return trip four days before her regular advertised sailing time. It was agreed to pay the Oceanic Company 3000 dollars for accommodation, one-half of which amount was generously contributed by the Provisional Government of the Hawaiian Islands.

On Monday afternoon a thorough examination of the hold of the Miowera was held, and it was found that she was not making any water, and had not done so. Her engineers say that the engines are unhurt, and not even strained. When the Mariposa left Honolulu, the Miowera was on an even keel, and it was confidently believed that she would, unless bad weather came on, be floated off in a day or two.

The last statement was extremely optimistic, as in fact it would take six weeks to refloat the *Miowera*. When *Mariposa* arrived in Sydney, the full text of the decision of the Court of Inquiry into the grounding of the *Miowera*, which was also brought by the *Mariposa*, was reported in the *Sydney Morning Herald* on 15 November, and said in part:

That Captain Stott having got the green light well open to the east of the red, was using a small starboard helm to bring them nearly together, as by sailing directions, when the sudden disappearance of the green light deprived him of his leading mark, and while so deprived of the green light he must have crossed the line of bearing and got too far to the west and stranded on the west side of the harbour entrance about 45 feet from the outside buoy on the west side, while endeavouring with a port helm to turn the ship's head to sea eastward. With regard to the disappearance of the green light, the evidence of Captains Smyth, Davies, Sorendon and Campbell, all men of great experience as masters of steamers running in and out of Honolulu at all hours of the night as well as by day, proved indisputedly that the green light is frequently obscured by masts and spars or even the funnel of a vessel or vessels lying at the Kinau or Likelike wharfs. On the 2nd October last the British barque County of Merioneth was in such a position that the green light, being situated inshore on the wharf, struck on her masts or yards, the latter being squared at the time in such a manner as to prevent it from being seen from a ship having her marks nearly on in the entrance of the passage.

On 24 November the *Sydney Morning Herald* carried a report sent from London by cable the previous day that *Miowera* had been refloated, but it did not state the date this had happened. However, *Warrimoo* had departed Vancouver on 16 November, and it was known that *Miowera* had been refloated before its sister passed through Honolulu. When *Warrimoo* arrived in Sydney on 9 December it was carrying 25 crew members from *Miowera*, and the next day the *Sydney Morning Herald* reported that the first company engaged to refloat the vessel had failed, but the second company had succeeded.

Miowera was fitted with a temporary stern post and rudder at Honolulu, and left on 24 December on its way to San Francisco, where it was drydocked. It was found that the damage sustained in the grounding would be very expensive to have repaired in the United States, and it would be cheaper for the vessel to steam to Britain to have the necessary repairs completed, which was done at the Swan & Hunter shipyard on the Tyne.

While *Miowera* was under repair in England the opportunity was taken to install refrigeration plant in some of the cargo spaces, for the carrying of fruit and mutton. Also, the accommodation was revamped to cater for 112 first class and 60 second class passengers, while the hull was repainted white, and soon after, the accommodation in *Warrimoo* was similarly altered during a refit in Sydney, and its hull painted white.

When the work was completed *Miowera* did not immediately return to Australia, but was scheduled to operate three cruises from London to Norway. On the second of these trips, *Miowera* departed Shields on 9 July, reported to be heading for Odde, but a few days later had the misfortune to run aground again, as reported in the *Brisbane Courier* on 2 August 1894, from cables sent from London:

THE MIOWERA.
AGROUND ON THE COAST OF NORWAY.
A DISASTROUS PLEASURE TRIP.
[BY. CABLE MESSAGE]
LONDON, July 31.
Information has been received that Messrs. Huddart, Parker, and Co's steamship Miowera has gone aground at Askervola, in Norway, and her passengers have been landed on an uninhabited island.

Since her narrow escape from being totally wrecked at Honolulu last year the Miowera has been repaired and refitted in a superior style, and also fitted with freezing machinery, but previous to again taking up the running on the Pacific line she was making several excursion trips to Norway with summer tourists.

Further information concerning the grounding of the

steamer Miowera states that she struck on an unknown rock on the coast of Norway. A pilot was in charge of the vessel at the time of the accident. According to latest reports there is 7ft. of water in the hold.

LONDON, August 1.
In consequence of the stranding of the Miowera, the steamship Arawa will be retained on the line between Canada and Vancouver. The Miowera was to have made only one more trip to Norway after the one that has ended so disastrously, leaving London on the 10th August. She was then to sail for Sydney, en route to Vancouver, to resume her running on the Pacific line.

It was also on 2 August that the *Sydney Morning Herald* carried another report concerning James Huddart, and his ambitious plans to develop an "All Red Route" between Britain and Australia via Canada:

> The particulars of Mr James Huddart's scheme for the establishment of a full-powered Atlantic steam service between Canada and Great Britain will be embodied in a prospectus to be issued shortly.
> The capital will be fixed at £2,000,000.

Initial reports sent from Norway indicated that *Miowera* had been wrecked, and the passengers removed to an uninhabited island, from where they were picked up by another ship, taken to Bergen, and taken back to Newcastle on the regular passenger service. However, on 9 August the *Sydney Morning Herald* carried a brief report from London that *Miowera* had been refloated, and towed to Bergen. An interesting account of the *Miowera* after this incident was recorded by an unnamed passenger on another vessel, the *Venus*, which had left Newcastle on 7 August 1894 on a cruise to the Norwegian fjords. Although the date is not noted, it was recorded that:

> When we went on deck after breakfast, the morning following our rest-breaking call at Bergen, the Venus was steaming up the coast, within the chain of islands, in smooth water. The mainland, as seen from the ship, consisted of hills of no very remarkable height, and chiefly barren. Rocks and islands innumerable studded the seaward side, and on some of them were small clusters of cottages, others were pictures of craggy desolation.
> The Captain told us that we should probably meet the SS Miowera, which had had the misfortune to run on a rock about seventy-five miles north of Bergen a few weeks previously. We remembered reading in the papers that she struck the rock at night, when all the passengers were in their berths, and we can well imagine their consternation and dismay as they rushed on deck in all sorts of dishabille. The Captain had heard at Bergen that the Miowera had been floated off the rock and might be expected to enter that port during the day. She came in sight soon after, attended by two tugs, one in front and the other astern. She was a fine boat, painted slate colour, and we gazed at her with much curiosity. Above the water she did not seem much the worse for the accident, but we were given to understand that below the water-line there was a great rent in her bow, which had been temporarily covered over. We gave her a cheer as she steamed slowly by, and the officer on deck acknowledged the salutation by raising his hat. Of course there were no passengers on board, they having been taken back to England by one of the Norwegian mail steamers, a few days after the tragic termination of their cruise.

Once again *Miowera* had to go to the Swan & Hunter shipyard on the Tyne for repairs, and the third cruise to Norway was cancelled. It was not until 1 September 1894 that *Miowera* left the Tyne, voyaging by way of Cape Town to Sydney, arriving there on 13 October. On Monday 15 October a voyage report appeared in the *Sydney Morning Herald*:

> The Canadian-Australian Steamship liner Miowera left the Tyne at 7.30am on Saturday, 1st September, and arrived at Plymouth at 5.30pm on Sunday, 2nd September. Embarked passengers for Cape Town and Sydney, and left Plymouth same night at 10.15pm. The passage began with thick weather till the 5th instant, then followed with moderate NE winds and fine weather until reaching lat 2°2. Teneriffe Island was passed at 7am on 7th September, and the equator was crossed on 18 September in long 9°15W. Got the SE trades in lat 1°S. Carried west SE wind all the way to Cape Town, arriving there at 11.45am on Saturday, 22nd September, 10 days 12 hours from Plymouth. Left Cape Town the same day at 7pm, and experienced moderate to fresh SE wind and hazy weather for the first 1,500 miles from the Cape of Good Hope, followed by the usual westerly winds for the remainder of the passage. The easting was run down on the parallel 44°30S. Cape Otway was passed on Thursday, 11th October at 8am. Light airs and fine clear weather on the coast, arriving at Sydney Heads at 8am on Saturday, 13th October, or 20 days 15 hours 15 minutes from the Cape, 30 days 20 hours 20 minutes steaming from Plymouth. The machinery worked smoothly throughout voyage, and without stoppage, as no coaling was done on the voyage. The consumption of coal being restricted to 50 tons per day, speed had to be moderated accordingly.

Miowera returned to the Vancouver trade with a departure from Sydney on 20 October. Meanwhile, *Arawa* had left Sydney on its final round trip to Canada on 18 September, departing Vancouver for the last time on 16 October, arriving in Sydney on 12 November. The charter of *Arawa* was terminated shortly afterwards.

Warrimoo had arrived back in Sydney from Canada on 9 October, but as the next voyage was taken by *Miowera*, the opportunity was taken to

Warrimoo with a white hull (WSS Vic)

withdraw *Warrimoo* from service for an overhaul and refurbishment. On 17 November the *Sydney Morning Herald* reported:

> The Canadian-Australian liner Warrimoo yesterday completed a very successful trial trip. The Warrimoo left Sydney and proceeded north as far as Barranjoey, and on the return voyage she was put to her top speed and averaged between Barranjoey and Sydney 17½ knots per hour. She was previously docked, and amongst her alterations is a new second saloon, beautifully fitted, and capable of holding about 50 people. She is also fitted with a Lindo British refrigerating machine in her afterhold, with chambers fitted for fruit and dairy produce, etc, also a chamber for frozen meat. The Warrimoo is fitted with a See patent ash ejector, worked by water, and capable of discharging one ton of ash per minute. There is also a Weir evaporator and a Kirkaldy evaporator, so that fresh water can be used for the boilers, a most important matter, protecting the tubes against the corrosion which is so destructive to them when salt water is used. Leaving the engine-room, a visit was made to the culinary department of the ship, where it was found that the whole of the cooking in both galleys is carried on by a steam process, having also in reserve the usual fire arrangements. The cooking arrangements are very extensive, and are fitted up in the very latest style, and the strong feature about the place is the exquisite cleanliness of the galleys. Of the passenger accommodation, the main saloon has been refitted and painted and decorated, and is the full width of the ship. The ports are contrived so as to allow the breeze to penetrate all through. The new second cabin before mentioned is beautifully fitted up to accommodate about 50 passengers. There are large ports in the cabins, affording splendid ventilation. The cabins are two-berth, while others are suitable for families. All are well fitted up with conveniences for the voyagers. On deck, in connection with the passenger equipment, is a commodious smoking room; the panels are of marble, and the floor tessellated.
>
> It was just 1 o'clock yesterday afternoon when the Warrimoo cleared the Heads and shaped her course north. There was a strong nor-easter blowing at the time. She had a very pleasant trip as far as Barranjoey, and on her return voyage the full-speed trial was made; wind and current in favour, the high rate of speed mentioned above was realised. The Warrimoo has booked a fair number of passengers for Fiji, Honolulu, and Vancouver, and will sail on Monday at 4pm.

Warrimoo returned to service with a departure from Sydney on 19 November, followed by *Miowera* on 18 December, so once again the service was maintained by *Miowera* and *Warrimoo* on a monthly basis. Going into 1895 a regular schedule of departures was being maintained, leaving Sydney on or just after the 18th of each month, with the return voyage from Vancouver leaving on the 16th of the month in most instances, though this was upset by a couple of accidents in quick succession that affected both ships.

In early May 1895, when *Miowera* was northbound from Honolulu, engine trouble caused the speed to be reduced to just 5 knots, and the vessel arrived in Vancouver two days late, on 13 May. Repairs caused the departure from Vancouver to be delayed to 21 May, and the vessel did not arrive in Sydney until 15 June, so the next departure from Sydney was put back to 20 June.

On 9 August, *Warrimoo*, on a northbound voyage,

ran aground on a rocky reef off Bonilla Point in the Juan de Fuca Strait, but was refloated quite quickly, arriving in Victoria the next day and reaching Vancouver on 11 August. The vessel had to go into drydock at Esquimalt for repairs, and did not leave Vancouver until 23 August.

On this voyage south *Warrimoo* did not call at Honolulu, as there had been an outbreak of cholera there. When *Miowera* departed Sydney on 20 August it carried no mail or passengers for Honolulu, and while the vessel did stop briefly off Honolulu on 4 September, it did not enter the harbour, and continued its voyage to Canada.

With *Warrimoo* running late, not arriving back in Sydney until 15 September, there was no departure from Sydney in September 1895, with *Warrimoo* leaving again on 21 October, while *Miowera* also spent a month in Sydney before leaving on 18 November. Departing Vancouver on 16 December, the vessel was scheduled to reach Sydney on 8 January, but did not arrive until twelve days later.

The reason for this was that, when between Victoria and Honolulu, *Miowera* had come upon the disabled steamer *Strathnevis*, operating on charter to the Northern Pacific Steamship Co, and attempted to tow the stricken vessel to safety, but off Cape Flattery, at the entrance to the Strait of Juan de Fuca, the towline had snapped in very heavy weather, and *Miowera* was unable to find the other vessel again, so resumed its voyage to Australia, causing some anxiety for the safety of the vessel.

The *New York Times* carried the following report on 27 December, sent from Seattle the previous day:

The disabled Northern Pacific steamer Strathnevis, in tow of the collier Mineola, arrived in Port Townsend at midnight. Telegraphic communication with that point is interrupted, and only meager particulars of the rescue are at hand.

The Strathnevis was picked up a week ago Monday morning by the Australian steamship Miowera, bound for Australia. The Miowera took the disabled ship in tow for five days. They journeyed along together until within fifty miles of Cape Flattery, when a strong westerly gale was encountered, during which the hawsers parted. The Miowera was unable to pick her up again. The Strathnevis then drifted to Destruction Island, where she anchored last Monday morning, and where she lay until Tuesday, when she was picked up by the Mineola, a Southern Pacific collier, on her way from Tacoma to San Francisco.

The Mineola and her tow passed in by Cape Flattery yesterday morning as far as Race Rocks, where the hawser was parted. It took four hours to pick her up again, during which the tug Tye, Capt Bailey, stood by to give assistance if needed.

The Strathnevis has gone through a succession of severe storms during the past week, but has weathered them all without mishap. The breaking of her wheel [*sic*], the accident that caused her to drift about the ocean for so long, is her only injury. The people on board, although all well, have, according to Capt Bailey, had a very hard time, and will be delighted when they can set foot on firm ground once more.

The Strathnevis left Tacoma Oct 12, for Yokohama, and is commanded by Capt James Beattie. She carried 2,000 tons of general freight, and had on board, besides the crew, 125 Chinese passengers.

Just how severe the storm was can be gathered from reports that appeared in the *San Francisco Call* on 28 December regarding the *Strathnevis*. The newspaper item contained the following report sent from Tacoma, in Washington State, on 27 December:

The steamship Miowera, which had the Strathnevis in tow five days and brought her to within twelve miles of the Tatoosh light, where the hawsers snapped and the steamers parted company, has not yet been heard from. The prospects for her safe return to port are gloomy, and those interested in the steamer are greatly alarmed.

Anxiety continues to grow for the safety of the steamer Danube, which left Victoria about two weeks ago to search for the Strathnevis and has not returned. Whilst she has been at sea the severest gales ever known on the Pacific have swept along the west coast, and it is feared she may have foundered in the same storm in which the Miowera disappeared.

The amount of compensation to be awarded the steamer Mineola for towing the Strathnevis to port has not yet been settled, and no authentic information can be secured at present on the question. Maritime men believe the salvage award will be between $50,000 and $100,000, to be divided about equally between the Miowera and Mineola.

Once its search for the *Strathnevis* was abandoned, *Miowera* had resumed its voyage, but was slowed by the very heavy weather, not reaching Honolulu until 31 December, having been at sea for fifteen days, instead of the usual seven day voyage. The sector from Honolulu to Brisbane was two days longer than usual due to engine problems, and two more days were lost undergoing repairs before the vessel continued its voyage to Sydney, arriving on 20 January. The episode was reported in the *Sydney Morning Herald* on 21 January as follows:

Mr Andrew Holland, one of the official reporters of the Canadian Senate at Ottawa, who arrived in Sydney yesterday by the Miowera, last night made a statement of the finding of the Strathnevis by that vessel. "We left Victoria on the 16th December, and when we were 450 or 500 miles out we sighted a steamer in distress. She proved to be the long-missing Strathnevis, that had sailed from Victoria on the 13th October with a small cargo of flour and tinned salmon and with 165 Chinese passengers and 39 of a crew, bound for Yokohama, Japan.

We subsequently learned that when 1,700 miles out from port the Strathnevis encountered a heavy gale, in which she broke her shaft and lost her propeller, and had then drifted away for 60 days utterly helpless on the great Japan current. The provisions ran out, and those on board were living on the flour and tinned salmon. When we approached the vessel they asked us to take her in tow and help them to the nearest port, otherwise at the rate they were drifting they would be on the rocks on the American coast inside of 10 days.

Captain Stott, of the Miowera, as soon as he heard the story of the disaster that had befallen the Strathnevis, consulted his passengers. He placed the whole situation before them, and asked them for an expression of their opinion as to what action should be taken with regard to the distressed ship. The passengers immediately carried a unanimous resolution that there was only one course open to them, and that was to approve of the Strathnevis being towed to the nearest port. The two vessels were connected by a 6in steel hawser, and the Strathnevis was taken in tow. The good intentions of the captain, however, were frustrated, for early in the night the hawser parted in a heavy sea. The Miowera stood up to her till morning, and the sea continuing heavy it was 42 hours before another cable could be passed between the two vessels.

There was one remarkable feature about the finding of the ship that I might mention. It was the stolid manner in which the Chinese passengers regarded our going to their relief. They did not utter a word; they seemed to take it as a matter of course. If they had been English, French or American sailors on board, the heavens would have rung with their cheers. The chief mate of the Strathnevis, however, took the matter differently. When he came on board our vessel to make his report he was unable to speak for some time. He was greatly affected.

That night we stood by the vessel. Every attempt made at grappling the line that was thrown over by the Strathnevis failed, and the work became almost hopeless. Then the Miowera put over one of her boats with a volunteer crew in her of six men, headed by Chief Mate Hay. All of the crew of the boat had lifebelts strapped about them. After a heavy pull they succeeded in catching the line thrown from the Strathnevis. By this time another 6in wire hawser was secured to the vessel. The sea was running mountains high at the time. At last, before night had come, they succeeded in getting a 12in Manilla hawser fixed between the two ships, and the work of towing was recommenced. It would seem that our renewed efforts were to be frustrated also. The wind increased to a gale, and finally blew with hurricane force. The hawsers were unable to stand the strain, and some time after midnight on the 23rd both of them parted.

The waves were so terrific that they broke in by the skylights of the Miowera, and it seemed that we were in danger of having the engine-room flooded. The wind had carried us so near the lee shore that prior to the cables parting the Miowera tried to stand out to sea with her tow, and the strain on her was so heavy that her stern was brought under water at times, so much so that the man who was on duty watching the cables was frequently up to his knees in water.

When the cables parted we lost sight of the Strathnevis. At daylight we started to cruise after her, and searched for eight hours. Finally the search had to be abandoned owing to the uncertainty of the Miowera's position, no observation having been taken for about 24 hours. The crew of the Miowera state that the storm was the worst they ever encountered on the Pacific.

It was only when we arrived in Sydney that we heard that the Strathnevis had been towed into port by some other vessel. The exact position where the Strathnevis broke loose from us the second time was somewhere near Cape Flattery. Had the gale held off for seven hours more we would have had her safe in port, and the owners of the Miowera would have been £25,000 better off in salvage money.

In order to keep to the advertised schedule, *Miowera* was prepared for its next departure in just five days. *Miowera* departed Sydney on 25 January 1896, but had to return to port two days later due to major engine problems, which no doubt developed when towing the *Strathnevis*. On 28 January the *Sydney Morning Herald* reported:

In the early hours of yesterday a brightly lighted steamer hove in sight to the north-east of the Heads, and as she drew near to the South Head lookout station her white hull and yellow funnel gave rise to the opinion that she must be a warship. As she shaped a course in to the Heads curiosity increased, and her identity was discovered and the signals made, "The mail steamer Miowera returned to port."

The steamer left Sydney on Saturday evening last bound to Vancouver in command of Captain Stott, having a number of passengers and a general cargo. The report of her return to Sydney had created no little surprise. She had just completed an eventful voyage from Vancouver, had picked up the broken down steamer Strathnevis and stood nobly by her until the Strathnevis broke away, and in consequence of this the Miowera had herself met with a longer passage than was anticipated. The firm to which she belongs had handled her very smartly in turning her round within a few days of her arrival here, and when she left on Saturday it was amid congratulations and best wishes. She had not, however, got very far from the coast when something went wrong below, said to be the circulating fans which are used in the forced draught system aboard. A piston was shattered, and her troubles were of such a character that the passengers were asked whether it would not be better, rather then proceed at a reduced speed, to head the ship to Sydney and get the repairs done that could not be done at sea. On that the ship's course was reversed, and Sydney made at six knots to seven knots speed.

The officers on board are very chary of saying anything as to the extent of the injury, but from other sources it is learnt that the steamer had a very trying time, and the passengers a corresponding period of anxiety. The chief engineer of the steamer, Mr Scott, said that he had not more than a couple of hours rest since the accident happened. On being asked whether it was true that the members of the engine staff were working up to their knees in water, he replied, "Oh, no, not as bad as that; the place" (meaning the engine-room) "was in a mess, but the reports referred to as to water were exaggerated. Her machinery broke down in such a way that nothing could be done without a return to port, and that is the long and short of it."

The engineer did not say so, but there is a strong opinion abroad that the service is under-shipped, and that a third vessel is imperatively needed to fulfil the requirements the requirements of an efficient service. The owners of the Miowera have sent the following notifications respecting the accident: "Whilst the Miowera was proceeding on her voyage, and some hundred miles from the Heads, a slight derangement occurred in connection with a fan engine. It was deemed advisable to return to port to effect repairs in preference to proceeding at reduced speed. The vessel is lying in Neutral Bay, and repairs are being carried out by Mort's Dock Company. She is expected to get away again on her voyage this (Monday) evening or early tomorrow (Tuesday) morning."

It appears from a statement made last night by a passenger that when the Miowera was about 100 miles off the Australian coast and making her course at a satisfactory rate an accident befell her machinery. The engines operating the oscillating fans which give draught to the furnaces suddenly broke down, the piston of one of them being completely shattered. Other injuries resultant upon this smash followed before steam could be turned off, and although the engineers did all that was possible to repair the damages, it was soon found that it would be impossible to continue the voyage unless at a very much reduced speed. The accident happened at about 11 o'clock on Saturday evening, and when at 8 o'clock on Sunday morning it was found that the repairs that could be made were only of the character that has been stated, it was decided to return to Sydney. It is stated that the passengers were consulted in the matter, and that 13 of those who had taken saloon berths strongly protested against the continuance of the voyage, and also that the firemen made similar objections. The Miowera is now at anchor in Athol Bight. She has a slight list to starboard, but for all that a number of her passengers are still "by the ship."

Captain Stott later refuted the claim that he had asked the passengers their opinion on whether the ship should return to Sydney. He said he discussed the matter only with the chief engineer, who recommended the ship return to port, and on that advice he turned around and came back to Sydney. Repairs took several days longer than originally anticipated, *Miowera* not leaving Sydney again until Saturday, 1 February. The voyage subsequently went without further problems, *Miowera* arriving in Vancouver on 26 February, and after another quick turnaround, departed on 1 March on the return voyage, only four days later than the original schedule.

For the rest of 1896 *Miowera* and *Warrimoo* maintained a regular schedule, making eleven round trips between them during the year, and this pattern continued into the first half of 1897.

Chapter Seven

Changes

On 28 October 1894 the Union Steam Ship Company of New Zealand suffered the loss of one of their trans-Tasman ships, *Wairarapa*, which was wrecked on Great Barrier Island, north of Auckland, on a voyage from Sydney, with a heavy loss of life. The Union Line decided to temporarily transfer *Monowai* from the San Francisco service to the trans-Tasman trade as a replacement for the lost ship, had to find an alternative ship to cover the next departure of *Monowai* from Sydney, scheduled for 26 November.

Fortunately, *Arawa* was on its way back from Vancouver on the last voyage of its charter to Canadian-Australian Royal Mail Line, being due to arrive in Sydney on 12 November. On that same day the *Sydney Morning Herald* reported:

> The SS Arawa has been chartered by the Union Steam Ship Company of New Zealand for the mail service between Sydney and San Francisco. This change has been made in order to release the fine steamer Monowai for service in the New Zealand and intercolonial trade. The Arawa is therefore advertised to leave Sydney for San Francisco on the 26th November, and it is anticipated she will be well patronised by the traveling public. Passengers during the coming season to New Zealand will no doubt appreciate the re-entry of the Monowai into the New Zealand trade, and the Union Company is to be commended for arranging to place her in the same service as the Mararoa, thus placing their largest and finest vessels at the service of passengers between here and New Zealand.

Monowai had departed San Francisco on 18 October, and arrived in Sydney on 13 November. Four days later *Monowai* departed on a voyage to Wellington and Lyttelton. *Arawa* left Sydney on 26 November, passing through Auckland on 1 December, and arriving in San Francisco on 20 December, departing on 10 January 1895 for the voyage back to Sydney. The second voyage by *Arawa* left Sydney on 18 February, reaching San Francisco on 14 March, and leaving on 4 April.

When the vessel returned to Sydney the charter arrangement was terminated, and *Monowai* had to be brought back to partner *Alameda* and *Mariposa*, which were providing very reliable service. Through the rest of 1895 and all of 1896, these three ships maintained the route between Sydney and San Francisco on a regular basis.

At the end of 1896 *Mariposa* had to be taken out of service for a major overhaul, which was done at the Risdon Iron Works in San Francisco. Instead of missing one voyage, the Oceanic company sent *Zealandia* on its final trip across the Pacific. This meant reactivating this vessel, as in September 1891 *Zealandia* had been taken off the route between San Francisco and Honolulu, and laid up, leaving *Australia* to operate the Hawaii service on its own.

Zealandia departed San Francisco on 7 January 1897, arriving in Sydney on 6 February, leaving on 15 February, and by the time it returned to California, *Mariposa* was ready to resume its place in the schedule.

However, the Union Line was awaiting delivery of their latest liner, which had been specially designed for the San Francisco trade. Also built by the Wm Denny & Bros yard at Dumbarton, the vessel was named *Moana* when launched on 24 December 1896. Departing Glasgow on 12 April 1897 and not carrying any passengers or cargo, *Moana* steamed non-stop to Sydney, where it arrived on 22 May. At 3,915 gross tons, and 350 feet long, *Moana* was the largest vessel in the Union Line fleet, and provided accommodation for 198 first class and 100 second class passengers, as well as having a large cargo capacity.

Newspaper advertisements for the new vessel declared *Moana* was "Specially built for tropical running, and ventilated throughout by means of electric motors, with numerous sleeping state rooms on deck, and every modern convenience tending to add to the comfort of travelers. This steamer attained a speed of 17 knots on recent trial trip."

On 24 May the *Sydney Morning Herald* ran a report on the new vessel, which said in part:

A palatial ship is the Moana. The name is from a beautiful lake in New Zealand, and by adoption serves to identify one of the most superb passenger ships crossing the Pacific, a vessel which in fact can be compared with the best of any of the liners without suffering disparagement, and can give points to many of greater tonnage and in the enjoyment of heavy subsidies.

Create the facilities of a luxurious home while at sea and the patronage will surely follow, and the better the facilities, the more attractive they are, the more liberal will be the public favour. It was with this purpose that the sumptuously furnished Moana was built, not that the Monowai was what could in any sense of the term be described as behind the times, for she is almost a new ship herself, but something larger and grander, possessing all the very latest inventions known to passenger ship building was to be aimed at, and in the Moana will be found the embodiment of the director's conception of a floating palace.

It was with such thoughts in mind that the guests aboard the new ship on Saturday were impressed as they roamed through Moana's wide passages, bounded on either hand with richly-furnished staterooms, or, stepping into the open spaces, found themselves in the richly-upholstered saloons, boudoirs, social halls, libraries, music-rooms, and, specially for the smoker, a patent ventilated deck smoking room, in which are noiselessly working at how many thousand revolutions per minutes one forgets, the automatic fans. These, indeed, abound in all parts of the ship.

There are some charmingly-situated cabins fitted up in quite a novel style with bureaus, chests of drawers, wardrobes, and escritoires, at the latter of which the traveller may in the perfect privacy of his own cabin sit and write to his hearts content. There are baths, hot and cold, spray and plunge, fresh and salt; electric bells at your elbow in every part of the steamer, and signal bells hanging over the tables in the saloons by which the attendance of the stewards is ensured.

A very striking advance has been made in the second saloon space, so much so that, except for the upholstering being a trifle plainer, the visitor will not realise that he has merged into the second class from the first. There are the couches and the lavatories, and there is the second saloon upon a lavish scale, with revolving chairs of a recent patent design, exactly the same as in the first saloon, and with the difference of being a shade plainer.

It is no mere 'steerage', as is generally understood by that term, though there are but the two classes. This part of the ship will at once strike the visitor as being specially noteworthy. Many people nowadays take the second class on board the liners when three classes are carried – first, second and steerage – because there are not the obligations to dress for dinners and so forth enjoyed in the more expensive saloon, and for several years it has been the aim of shipowners to improve the second saloons and make them more attractive every way until today it is found at the large shipping offices that the second-class is filled in every berth when the first saloon space is not more than half taken up. The Moana stands well in the front line in respect to this feature of the passenger space.

The general description of the accommodation is

Moana (John Mathieson collection)

as follows. The principle saloon is on the main deck aft, and is a magnificent apartment of 50ft by 40, with accommodation for dining 110 at once. At the after end a large recess has been arranged, specially adapted for use as a stage for amateur theatricals. The framing of the apartment is polished sycamore, slightly tinted, having narrow architraves, round side lights flanked by pilasters, and surmounted by decorated pediments. The room is panelled, the beams boxed, and the whole decorated in an elegant manner. The sofas are in blue moquette, and the floor is laid in handsome Brussels.

The passengers rooms are arranged forward the saloon, with accommodation for 180 first and 116 second. When the doors are opened in the broad alleyways it is possible to see from one end of the vessel to the other in an unbroken line. Here are in the upper deck houses a very large number of deck cabins, light and airy, specially suited for tropical weather; and on the upper deck, adjoining the music room and deck cabins, is the smoking room, already referred to.

The second-class saloon is large, comfortable and airy, the sides framed in pine painted, and the seats upholstered with railway cloth, the general effect being one of thorough comfort, while avoiding anything to cause stuffiness in a tropical service. The dining-room seats 74 passengers. As stated the cabins are plainer than the first, but with sofas and spring mattresses. Over every berth are lifebelts and electric light and bells as elsewhere.

The Moana's trial trip gave a mean speed of 17 knots over two runs. She is 360 ft in length between perpendiculars, 44 ft beam, 34 ft deep, with a tonnage of 3,915 tons gross, and has been built to the highest class of the British Corporation. The hull is divided by seven watertight bulkheads, and has a double bottom for carrying water ballast. All the cargo gear is hydraulic, the derrick being of the latest Edinburgh design, working rapidly and without noise.

The machinery, supplied by Denny & Co, of Dumbarton, is triple expansion, cylinders 35 in, 53 1/2 in, 85 in, diameter, with a stroke of 4 ft 6 in. Steam is supplied by two double-ended boilers of 15 ft diameter and having 12 furnaces. Forced draught is employed, and the steam pressure is 170lb.

The Moana is flush-decked, with an awning or promenade deck aft. The space for passengers' promenades is commodious. She is rigged on two pole masts, and when down to her marks sits gracefully on the water. It is intended to dock her on Wednesday for cleaning, and the 7th of June will see her take her departure upon her maiden voyage to San Francisco.

On 7 June 1897 *Moana* departed Sydney on its first voyage to San Francisco, calling at Auckland on 11 June, then visiting Honolulu before reaching San Francisco on 29 June, two days earlier than scheduled. The return trip began on 22 July, and *Moana* made a record passage to reach Auckland in 17 days 15 hours actual steaming time.

Meanwhile, the Sydney to Vancouver service continued being operated by Canadian-Australian Royal Mail Line, and in 1895 James Huddart moved back to England, where he tried to establish a twenty-knot Atlantic service, the other sea leg of the 'All-Red Route'. It required much larger steamers than the Pacific service, and an annual subsidy of £225,000 of which Canada was expected to pay two-thirds and England one-third.

Huddart's plan initially won full support from the Canadian government and the postmaster-general in London, but was opposed by vested interests and critics within the British government. After a change of minister in London Huddart's plans were shelved and later rejected. The implied lack of confidence in his ability resulted in a new government in Canada rejecting the Atlantic scheme. However, in recognition of his efforts to establish the England-Canada-Australia route, James Huddart was elected a fellow of the Royal Geographical Society on 25 November 1895.

Huddart continued to promote the Canadian-Australasian service in hope of gaining financial support from New Zealand. His contract with the Canadian and New South Wales governments demanded a fourteen-knot, four-weekly mail service and after four years a third steamer was needed, but his private fortune was exhausted and he had to seek finance elsewhere. A new Canadian-Australian Royal Mail Steamship Company was floated with shares held equally by Huddart and the New Zealand Shipping Company, and *Aorangi* was purchased from the NZSC.

Built in 1883 by John Elder & Co in Glasgow, *Aorangi* had been the second of three sisters, the others being *Tongariro* and *Ruapehu*. *Aorangi* had accommodation for 60 first class, 40 second class and 200 third class passengers, with extra temporary quarters for migrants in the holds when possible. The vessel departed London on 29 November 1883 on its maiden voyage to New Zealand via Cape Town, returning to Britain around Cape Horn.

For ten years *Aorangi* operated regular voyages between London and New Zealand, but on 26 July 1894 Aorangi departed London on its final round trip to New Zealand, then was withdrawn and laid up in Britain at the end of 1894. In 1896, James Huddart initially arranged to charter the ship, but then decided to purchase it outright. *Aorangi* was sent to the Swan & Hunter shipyard at Newcastle-on-Tyne for an extensive refit.

The original compound engine was replaced by triple expansion machinery, with four new boilers, while the funnel was heightened by ten feet to increase the draught to the boilers. The hull was repainted white, which gave the vessel the appearance of a large private yacht. The interior was also rebuilt to carry 100 first class and 50 second class passengers. This work cost £40,000, a huge amount at that time.

On 17 March 1897, the Canadian Australian Royal Mail Steamship Company Limited was incorporated in London for the purpose of taking over the Canadian Australian Royal Mail Line and its three ships, *Warrimoo*, *Miowera* and *Aorangi*. The issued capital was £120,000, with James Huddart & Co and the New Zealand Shipping Company each taking up £60,000. James Huddart & Co was appointed the managers of the new company, and these changes did not affect the operation of the service in any major way.

Aorangi went first to London to load cargo, leaving there on 18 March 1897, calling at Plymouth the next day to board a full complement of passengers. Coaling was done at Teneriffe on 24 March, and the vessel reached Cape Town on 9 April. After a non-stop voyage across the Southern Ocean, *Aorangi* arrived in Melbourne on 29 April and Sydney on 1 May. The same day the *Sydney Morning Herald* reported:

> The Aorangi is intended to be the consort of the Miowera and the Warrimoo...but it is said to be the purpose of the owners to include a New Zealand port in the route shortly after the Aorangi gets running.
>
> The Aorangi was built a few years ago by Messrs John Elder & Co, of Fairfield, and she has now been examined and renovated from stem to stern and from keel to truck. The builders' contract included the fitting up of a new dining saloon for first-class passengers, and new first-class accommodation throughout, with a new music saloon and social hall on the bridge deck, with numerous other additions and alterations, and the effect is to improve the Aorangi and give her all the appearance of a Royal Mail express passenger steamer. What was formerly the first saloon is now the second, so that the accommodation throughout both first and second saloons is comfortable, and all that could be desired for travelers across the Pacific or round the world. The ship is excellently ventilated throughout, is fitted with the electric light, and has every improvement that could be suggested for the comfort of travellers.
>
> Ample accommodation is provided for cold storage both for the ship's use and for cargo. In the engine-room department everything is new, and the engines are supplied by four large boilers.

Newspaper advertisements for the Canadian-Australian service from Sydney to Canada and on to Britain stated that, "Passengers for Europe will find the voyage via Canada very enjoyable compared to the discomforting heat of the Red Sea and Suez Canal. The scenery on the Canadian Pacific Railway is unequalled in grandeur. Stop-over privileges allowed at the various points of interest, such as Banff (Canadian National Park), Niagara Falls etc."

Aorangi entered service for the Canadian-Australian Royal Mail Steamship Company with a departure from Sydney on 10 May 1897, going to Suva and Honolulu on the way to Vancouver, where it arrived on 8 June, departing on 16 June for the return trip. It was also in 1897 that James Huddart severed all his ties with Huddart Parker Limited.

Meanwhile, in mid-1897 the New Zealand Government offered to pay a £20,000 annual subsidy if the vessels of the Canadian-Australasian Royal Mail Steamship Company would include a call at Wellington on their voyages between Sydney

Aorangi in Canadian-Australian colours (WSS Vic)

and Vancouver, and this was agreed to, even though it increased the voyage time between the two terminal ports by five days.

The first northbound departure on the new route was taken by *Aorangi* from Sydney on 7 August, leaving Wellington on 15 August for Suva and Honolulu and on to Vancouver, arriving there on 8 September. The second departure on the northbound route was taken by *Warrimoo* on 16 August, passing through Wellington on 22 August, but it arrived in Vancouver only three days after *Aorangi*, on 11 September. *Warrimoo* left Vancouver on 16 September on its trip back to Sydney, but did not include a call at Wellington, instead going directly from Suva to Sydney. *Aorangi* left Vancouver on 20 September, passing through Wellington on 14 October on the first southbound voyage to include the port. Subsequently all voyages in both directions included a call at Wellington, *Miowera* making its first call there on 18 September.

Unfortunately, the expense incurred by James Huddart in refitting *Aorangi* caused him to go bankrupt in January 1898. When Huddart defaulted on payments for *Aorangi*, the company he had founded went into liquidation. In February 1898 the New Zealand Shipping Company, which was the chief creditor, was appointed receiver, and took over the Canadian-Australasian Royal Steamship Company and its three ships, and the service continued without interruption.

Huddart's health had been deteriorating since 1893 and the mental strain and subsequent failure of his company broke his health completely. He died at Eastbourne, England, on 27 February 1901, five days after his 54th birthday.

During 1898 the discovery of gold in Alaska resulted in another rush of hopeful miners seeking the chance to make their fortune. To cash in on this expected exodus of men from the gold fields in Australia, both companies operating to North America began a new advertising campaign. The Canadian-Australasian Line promoted the fact that they operated the "nearest route to Goldfields", and "Passengers booked to Dawson City or any of the intermediate points." The joint service by the Union Line and Oceanic Steamship Company to San Francisco promoted "Klondyke and Yukon via San Francisco, Victoria or Vancouver. San Francisco is the main port of entry of the Pacific Coast, and controls the bulk of the trade to these famous Gold Regions."

When the New Zealand Government did not renew their subsidy with the Canadian-Australasian company for 1898/99, the Wellington call was dropped from the schedule. The last vessel to call at Wellington northbound was *Aorangi*, on 30 March 1899, while *Miowera* made the final southbound visit on 1 April.

However, the Queensland Government then offered a subsidy, so a call at Brisbane was reinstated to replace Wellington. *Miowera* took the first sailing on the revised route from Sydney on 25 April, leaving Brisbane three days later and calling at Suva, Honolulu and Victoria before arriving in Vancouver on 19 May. Meanwhile *Warrimoo*, which had left Vancouver on 7 April, made the first southbound call at Brisbane, on 29 April, arriving in Sydney two days later.

This new route would only be followed for six months, as in August 1899 the Fijian Government terminated its subsidy arrangement, and the vessels ceased calling at Suva, the last ship to call there being *Warrimoo* when northbound on 23 August, *Aorangi* having made the last southbound call on 13 August.

With the departure of *Aorangi* from Sydney on 12 September, the ships now only called at Brisbane, Honolulu and Victoria on their way to Vancouver, the passage taking about 23 days. *Miowera* took the first southbound voyage on the new route, departing Vancouver on 25 August. There were no calls at Honolulu in December 1899 and January, February and March of 1900 due to an outbreak of Bubonic plague, though on 18 January *Miowera* did stop outside Honolulu and take on board mail that had been fumigated. During 1900 the three ships between them completed fourteen voyages from Sydney to Vancouver and return.

Chapter Eight

The *Sierra* Trio

The service from Sydney and Auckland to Honolulu and San Francisco continued unchanged for three years following the arrival in June 1897 of *Moana*, which was partnered by *Mariposa* and *Alameda*, but then the situation changed dramatically.

On 21 April 1898 the Spanish-American War started, with American troops being sent to the Philippines to take control of that country from Spain. However, there were also concerns in the United States regarding the position of Hawaii, and proceedings were started to have the islands annexed. The annexation order was signed by President McKinley on 7 July 1898, to take effect on 14 June 1900, when Hawaii would become a Territory of the United States.

This change in the status of Hawaii would have a major effect on the operation of the service from San Francisco and Honolulu to Auckland and Sydney. As Hawaii would be considered a part of the United States, the "Jones Act" would come into effect, which precluded non-American ships from carrying passengers and cargo between two American ports.

While this would not affect the Oceanic ships at all, the British registered *Moana* would no longer be able to carry passengers or cargo solely between San Francisco and Hawaii, which had always been quite a lucrative part of the entire service. As a result, the Union Steam Ship Company decided that they would withdraw completely from the San Francisco trade, and transfer *Moana* to other trades.

Initially *Moana* was being advertised to operate its last departure from Sydney on 21 November 1900, but from 23 October this was deleted from the sailing schedule. *Moana* arrived in Sydney on 28 October 1900 at the end of its final voyage from San Francisco. The vessel was placed in the trans-Tasman trade, with a departure from Sydney for Wellington on 3 November. At the same time the New Zealand and New South Wales governments terminated their subsidy arrangements for the San Francisco service.

This left the Oceanic company in a difficult position, as they would not be able to maintain the service without a subsidy, so John Spreckels went to Washington for talks with the United States Government, which resulted in an agreement that the Government would pay a subsidy to Oceanic to maintain the service, while for their part Oceanic would order three new ships that would be ready to enter service in 1900, and provide a three weekly subsidised service between San Francisco, Auckland and Sydney, calling en route at Honolulu and Pago Pago. They were built by William Cramp & Sons of Philadelphia, and named *Sierra*, *Sonoma* and *Ventura*, these being Californian names of Spanish origin.

Work on the first two ships began almost together, the keel of *Sierra* being laid down on 19 June 1899, followed by *Sonoma* three days later, while the keel of *Ventura* was not laid down until 4 November 1899. *Sierra* was launched on 29 May 1900, but completion was slowed, and the vessel was not ready to leave the Cramp shipyard until October. By then both the other ships had been launched, *Sonoma* on 7 August and *Ventura* on 28 September. Fitting out work on these two vessels proceeded much quicker, with *Sonoma* being completed in November and *Ventura* in December. Each vessel had to make the long journey from Philadelphia around South America to San Francisco before they could enter service.

Though each ship was 400 ft/121.9m in length and 50.2 ft/15.3m wide, they were not exact sister ships, as the gross tonnage of *Sierra* at 5,989 was a little less than the 6,253 of each of the other two. There was accommodation for 231 first class, 48 second class and 20 third class passengers. To provide the service speed of 17 knots the twin screws were driven by two triple expansion steam engines, with steam at 175psi being supplied by eight single ended boilers operating under forced draught. Both engines together developed a total of 7,500 indicated horse power. The vessels had a bunker capacity of 3,500 tons of coal.

They were nicely proportioned vessels, with two masts and two short black funnels, and initially they had white hulls. Built to Lloyds highest class, their construction was also in accordance with the US naval requirements regarding their being converted for service auxiliary cruisers.

With the introduction of the three new vessels, *Alameda* and *Mariposa* would be withdrawn from the South Pacific trade. *Mariposa* left Sydney for the last time on 24 October, leaving Auckland five days later, arriving in San Francisco on 10 November. *Alameda* made its final departure from Sydney on 4 December, reaching San Francisco on 24 December. Originally *Mariposa* had been scheduled to make one further round trip to the South Pacific, but was replaced by the first of the new ships, *Sierra*.

Sierra made its maiden departure from San Francisco for Australia on 13 December 1900, under the command of Captain H C Houndlette. The vessel arrived in Sydney on 9 January 1901, berthing at the Margaret Street wharf. The local agent for the ship was the Union Steam Ship Company. The *Sydney Morning Herald* reported on 10 January:

> The largest American-built steamer that has visited Australia came into Port Jackson yesterday – the Sierra of the Oceanic Line. The vessel has excellent lines. She sits handsomely in the water, has fine weatherly bows, an easy sheer the length of 425ft, terminating in a clear run from the quarter. As she came up to the Union Company's wharf these well-proportioned features in her were seen to advantage, and a hearty cheer came spontaneously from the spectators. Many were present who called up a recollection of the old paddle-boats that carried Australia's tourists to the land of the Stars and Stripes, and B Holliday's Line, the Hall line, and the other early efforts which nearly a generation ago were made to bring within touch the Land of the Golden Fleece and the Golden Gate of the Pacific.
>
> The Sierra was boarded by several hundreds of visitors who praised her roomy staterooms and promenaded along her saloon deck. There are in reality four decks available for passengers. The highest is the promenade deck, on which are the social hall and two "bridal cabins". The deck beneath is occupied by drawing room, smoking room, main saloon, and the greatest feature of the Sierra – a large number of "upper deck" cabins or staterooms. These latter are very fine, light, airy, and wide for two. Then on the main deck are more staterooms, also the second-cabin accommodation, which is quite up to date. The visitor will be disappointed who looks for gorgeousness in the furnishings. Everything is good, plain, and substantial. Oak, walnut and maple predominate, with white and gold bulkheads. Baths abound throughout the ship, which, by the way, is a twin-screw, and has a guaranteed speed of 17 knots.
>
> That she has not done the voyage as quickly as expected was due to an accident, but coming from the finest shipbuilding works in the United States – Cramps, of Philadelphia – there is little doubt that she will, when properly going, shorten the time between Australia and San Francisco. As a weatherly ship the testimony of those who voyaged by her was that they never travelled on a steadier vessel, a report fully borne out by her fine beam and shapely hull.

The *Sydney Morning Herald* also published the following voyage report, revealing how bad the weather had been on the trip from San Francisco:

> The Oceanic Company's new steamer Sierra which yesterday arrived from San Francisco, reports having sailed from San Francisco on December 13 at 3.30pm, and passed bar light at 5.10pm. Weather dull and cloudy, with fresh SW wind and a heavy NW swell. At 1am wind freshened and rain squalls at 6am, blowing a strong gale with very high sea, causing ship to labour and take on large quantities of water. 9am had to slow down. At 2pm December 14, still blowing a strong gale, with wind from WNW. Shipped a heavy sea over forward, unshipping one of the derrick booms, and smashing in the woodwork on front of bridge. High wind and sea all day December 15, strong gale from SSW, heavy seas and again had to slow down. December 16, gale still blowing, moderated about midnight. 6pm wind shifted to WNW. Shipped a big sea, washing away awning, ridge poles, and iron stanchions, also iron door off from windlass. High wind and sea all day. Barometer 29.25. December 17, still blowing hard with high sea, and continued so until 2am. Increased our speed from slow to half speed. At 6am wind moderated. At noon weather better, with fair to strong SW winds. December 18 weather fine with fresh SW winds and high westerly swell. Continued about the same to Honolulu. Sailed from Honolulu December 21, 11pm. Had fine weather, with moderate to fresh SE to SSW winds. December 24 port engine broke down by the splitting of low pressure piston. Removed broken piston and reduced the revolutions of both engines. Arrived Pago Pago December 29 at 8.30pm. Had fine weather with moderate to fresh SE and S winds to Auckland, arriving January 4, 1901, at 6.35am. Left Auckland 9.20am January 5. Had fine weather to North Cape. Since then had head winds and sea. Arrived at Sydney yesterday morning.

While in Sydney *Sierra* went into Mort's Dock for cleaning and painting before departing West Circular Quay on 17 January for Auckland, Pago Pago, Honolulu and San Francisco.

Sonoma departed San Francisco for the first time on 23 January 1901, under the command of Captain K Van Oterendorf, reaching Sydney on 16 February, and berthing at Circular Quay West. Sonoma also went into dry dock at Mort's Dock, and after being refloated lay for several days in Neutral Bay before going to East Circular Quay, and departing for San Francisco on 26 February.

Ventura entered service with a departure from San Francisco on 14 February 1901, being commanded by Captain H M Hayward. *Ventura* arrived in Sydney on 9 March, berthing at Circular Quay

Sonoma as built with white hull (Matson collection)

West, having made a fast trip from San Francisco in a steaming time of 20 days 2 hours, the best day's run being 403 nautical miles. This vessel also went into dry dock in Sydney, this time at the Sutherland Dock on Cockatoo Island, and departed for San Francisco on 19 March.

After only one voyage, each ship had its hull repainted black, as it had been found that keeping the white hull clean was a major problem.

When *Sierra* arrived in Sydney on its second voyage on 30 March 1901 and berthed at East Circular Quay, the Sydney agency had been transferred to Burns, Philp & Co Ltd, who continued as local agent for the next five years.

Quite early it became apparent that there were some serious defects with the new vessels. The two short funnels were not providing sufficient draft for the boilers to work effectively, while the blower engines were also ineffective, and the engine foundations themselves were too weak. It became necessary to withdraw each vessel in turn for some major repairs and alterations, which would include a considerable increase in the height of the funnels. The work was done at the Risdon Iron Works in San Francisco, and took about four weeks.

The first of the ships to be withdrawn for this work was *Sonoma*, whose scheduled departure from San Francisco had to be taken by *Mariposa* on 30 May 1901. On arrival in Sydney *Mariposa* anchored in Neutral Bay and the passengers were taken off by tender. *Mariposa* finally berthed at East Circular Quay the day before sailing.

Over the next few months both *Ventura* and *Sierra* were given a similar refit. The result was a drastic alteration in their appearance, as the funnels were now twice their original height, but the increased draft to the boilers enabled them to work much more efficiently. On one of its early voyages *Sierra* created a new record for the Pacific crossing by travelling from San Francisco to Sydney in 19 days 17 hours actual steaming time.

A major selling point for the new service was the offer of a thirty-three day passage between London and Sydney, which was faster than that operated by

Sonoma with black hull (Alexander Turnbull collection)

ships using the Suez Canal route.

The introduction of the three new ships had such a marked effect that in 1901 they carried twice as many passengers than had the three smaller ships used in the previous year. Over the next five years the three Oceanic ships maintained a regular service across the Pacific, with very few interruptions.

However, considerable disruption was caused by the massive earthquake and subsequent fire that devastated San Francisco on 18 April 1906, the Oceanic facilities being so adversely affected that scheduled sailings could not be maintained. *Ventura* had departed Sydney on 9 April, and arrived in San Francisco on 30 April, to find a scene of total devastation. *Sierra* arrived in Sydney on 20 April, and left as scheduled on 30 April for San Francisco.

On 2 May, the *Sydney Morning Herald* carried two stories regarding the San Francisco service, the first appearing in the shipping news, the second in the general news section:

> A cable message received from Messrs J D Spreckels & Bros Co yesterday by Messrs Burns, Philp & Co Ltd, the managing agents of the Oceanic Co in Australia, stated that the mail service between San Francisco and Sydney has been indefinitely suspended. It is however probable that freight steamers, with limited accommodation for passengers, will be dispatched from Sydney at intervals. Messrs Burns, Philp & Co Ltd, have received some further cables from the Oceanic Co, which state that business in San Francisco is utterly demoralized for the present, and that consequently there is much uncertainty as to the future sailings of the company's steamers. It would appear that, owing to the destruction of wharfage property, berths and cargo for outward steamers are not presently available, while coaling and victualling facilities are also temporarily suspended, and crews are unobtainable, so much other employment offering. Under these conditions the general agents of the line, Messrs J D Spreckels & Bros Co, are meantime unable to definitely advise further sailings from Sydney. However, should sufficient cargo offer, steamers may be placed upon the berth, and the Sydney agents, Messrs Burns, Philp & Co Ltd, will endeavour to fill the places of the regular vessels when they learn what cargo is available. With these cargo steamers it would be possible to take a limited number of passengers, while the speed could not be expected to be anything like that of the regular mail steamers of the line.

However, on Saturday, 5 May, the following item was published:

> Messrs Burns, Philp & Co Ltd, managing agents for the Oceanic Company's A and A line, have received further cable advice from Messrs Spreckels, the general agents of the line in San Francisco, stating that the RMS Sonoma will leave San Francisco on May 31. This announcement indicates that two sailings have been dropped, and that the Sonoma will take the running of the Sierra, time tabled to leave on the date mentioned.
>
> The Sonoma will leave Sydney on the return voyage on July 2, and will be followed by the Ventura and Sierra at intervals of three weeks, in accordance with the timetable previously arranged. Many people have no doubt been inconvenienced during the unfortunate suspension of the service, and will now be glad to learn that the running has been resumed with so little delay.
>
> It is expected there will be a considerable rush of people to the Pacific Coast now that the service has been resumed. A large number have transferred from earlier steamers, owing to their stay here during the enforced suspension of the service.

In the midst of all this confusion regarding the San Francisco service, there was apparently a controversy going on regarding which ships were the fastest across the Pacific, those of Canadian-

Sierra after rebuilding

Australasian Line or the Oceanic Company trio. The following item appeared in the shipping news of the *Sydney Morning Herald* on 12 May 1906:

> A controversy seems to be going on about the record steaming across the Pacific, and Messrs Burns, Philp & Co Ltd, managing agents for the Oceanic Co's A and A line, write to point out that the route via New Zealand and Samoa to Honolulu is 341 miles longer than via Brisbane and Suva. Notwithstanding this greater steaming distance, they maintain that the Sierra, which left Sydney on August 8, 1904, and arrived in Honolulu early on the morning of Monday, August 22, holds the record from Sydney. Continuing this voyage on to San Francisco the next day the Sierra arrived there at 4am on Monday, August 29, thus also making a record across the Pacific from Sydney to a terminal port on the Pacific Coast. It may be mentioned, however, that the route from Sydney to San Francisco is but 11 miles greater than the route to Vancouver.

Burns, Philp & Co retained the Sydney agency for the Oceanic ships until the *Sierra* departed Sydney on 7 January 1907, but when *Sonoma* arrived on 24 January the agency had been transferred to Thos S Jones, who had been appointed general manager in Australia for the Oceanic Steamship Co.

However, by then the service was in serious trouble caused by a number of factors. First, the New Zealand Government withdrew its share of the subsidy, and this was followed by an economic downturn in the United States, which by 1907 had become a financial panic. Despite the subsidy still being paid by the United States Government, losses on the service had been increasing each year, and when the Government declined to increase its financial assistance to the Oceanic company, the future looked particularly bleak.

Just to compound matters, boiler troubles delayed the arrival in Sydney of *Ventura* in February 1907. When the ship did arrive on 19 February it was found that very extensive retubing was necessary. After a general machinery overhaul at Mort's Dock and delays in coaling due to wet weather, *Ventura* finally got away on 19 March.

By the end of March 1907 Oceanic had decided to abandon their South Pacific service altogether, *Sonoma* being their last vessel to leave Sydney, on 12 April 1907. Unfortunately, this voyage did not go to schedule, as on 3 May 1907 the *Sydney Morning Herald* carried the following story under the headline "The Sonoma Again Breaks Down":

> It transpires from advices just to hand that the RMS Sonoma was again in trouble after reaching Auckland on her last trip from Sydney bound to San Francisco. She was detained until 10.20 on the night of 18th ult, when she left for San Francisco with a large number of passengers. The delay was caused by the necessity for repairs to the main engines, including several new castings.

The three vessels were laid up in San Francisco, leaving Australia and New Zealand with no direct passenger ship connection to the United States.

Sierra (Alexander Turnbull Library)

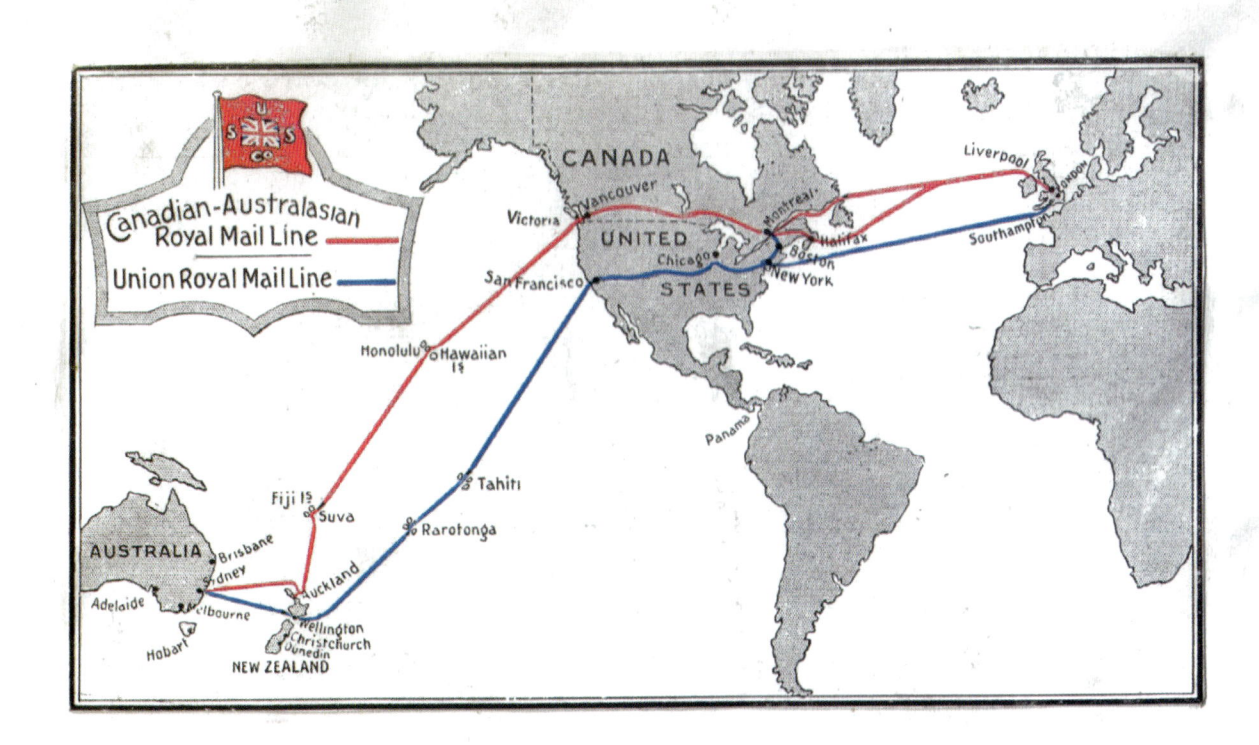

(Above) Map of routes from Sydney and New Zealand to San Francisco and Vancouver and on to Great Britain (Ken Hall collection)

(Below) J E Hobbs painting of *Mararoa* (Museum of Wellington City and Sea)

(Above) J E Hobbs painting of the first *Monowai* (Museum of Wellington City and Sea)

(Below) J E Hobbs painting of *Warrimoo* in Union Line colours (Museum of Wellington City and Sea)

(Above) W W Stewart painting of the first *Aorangi* in early Canadian-Australasian Line colours (Dallas Hogan collection)

(Below) J E Hobbs painting of *Makura*, the first ship built for the Vancouver service (Museum of Wellington City and Sea)

(Above) J E Hobbs painting of *Tahiti* (Museum of Wellington City and Sea)

(Below) J E Hobbs painting of *Maunganui* (Museum of Wellington City and Sea)

Chapter Nine

The Vancouver Route 1901–1914

When the Union Steam Ship Company of New Zealand had been forced to withdraw from the San Francisco service in 1900, *Moana* arrived in Sydney on 28 October 1900 on its last voyage from California. *Moana* was then transferred to the famous "horseshoe" service across the Tasman. On this route the vessel went from Sydney to Wellington, several ports in South Island, then back across the Tasman to Hobart, with the voyage terminating at Melbourne, and following the reverse route back to Sydney.

However, in March 1901 the New Zealand Shipping Company, which had become the owners of the Canadian-Australian Royal Mail Line when James Huddart went bankrupt, sold a half-share in the Canadian trade to the Union Steam Ship Company, who also took over management of the ships, whose hulls were repainted in the standard Union Line dark green.

Warrimoo departed Vancouver for the last time on 8 March 1901, and on its arrival in Sydney on 1 April the vessel was transferred to the Union Line trans-Tasman trades. Its place on the Canadian trade was taken by *Moana*, which departed Sydney on 22 April, arriving in Vancouver for the first time on 15 May.

Surprisingly, considering the fact that the Canadian-Australian Royal Mail Line was now owned by the two major New Zealand shipping companies, the route did not include a call at any New Zealand port, instead going from Sydney to Brisbane, Honolulu, Victoria and Vancouver. In March 1902 a call at Suva in Fiji was reinstated, *Aorangi* being the first to arrive northbound, on 4 March, while *Miowera* stopped on 28 March southbound.

The operation was now on a much firmer footing than at any previous time, and provided regular monthly departures from both Sydney and Vancouver. In 1903 the mail contract held by the Canadian-Australian Royal Mail Line was renewed, the original subsidy of £35,000 being increased by £16,000.

On 25 November 1903, when nearing Victoria

Miowera in Union Line colours (WSS Vic)

Moana joined the Canadian service in 1901 (Vancouver Maritime Museum)

from Sydney, *Moana* had the misfortune to run aground off the William Head quarantine station, close to Victoria on Vancouver Island, damaging the rudder stock and propeller. After being refloated *Moana* was able to steam to Victoria, but had to go to a drydock at Esquimalt for repairs. The Vancouver passengers, cargo and mail were taken from Victoria on 26 November by a local vessel, the *Charmer*. The scheduled December voyage by *Moana* had to be cancelled, and the vessel was not refloated from the drydock on 29 January 1904.

Moana left Victoria on 2 February 1904, and steamed non-stop to Sydney, where it was expected to arrive on 24 February, but in fact did not berth there until 27 February. *Moana* had been scheduled to leave again on 29 February, but this was put back to 3 March.

Aorangi took the 21 March 1904 departure, followed by *Miowera* on 18 April, but when *Moana* returned from Vancouver to Sydney on 26 April the vessel was withdrawn from the Canadian service, and placed on the horseshoe service. The next departure for Canada from Sydney was taken by the latest addition to the Union Line fleet, *Manuka*.

The first passenger ship to be built for the Union Line in the twentieth century was *Moeraki*, which was the first vessel in the fleet to be fitted with twin propellers. Completed in September 1902, *Moeraki* was placed on the Tasman trade. The next year the Union Line took delivery of a sister ship to *Moeraki*, which came from the same shipyard, Wm Denny & Bros at Dumbarton, and was named *Manuka* when launched on 8 September 1903.

Manuka provided accommodation for 232 first class and 135 second class passengers, and at 4,534 gross tons was the largest passenger vessel in the Union Line fleet, though the recently delivered cargo ship *Aparima* was bigger. Departing Glasgow on 25 November, *Manuka* called at Cape Town on 16 December, and arrived in Melbourne on 2 January 1904.

Manuka joined the horseshoe service, departing Melbourne on 6 January 1904, calling at Bluff on 11 January and Wellington five days later, arriving in Sydney on 20 January. For three months *Manuka* remained on the horseshoe service, but was then transferred to the Canadian service.

Manuka left Sydney on 16 May on its first voyage to Vancouver, where it arrived on 7 June, departing on 24 June and returning to Sydney on 16 July. *Aorangi* had followed *Manuka* from Sydney on 13 June, then *Miowera* on 11 July, with *Manuka* taking the 8 August departure on its second trip to Vancouver. *Manuka* departed Vancouver on 16 September, arriving back in Sydney on 9 October, and was transferred back to the horseshoe service, with *Moana* resuming its place on the Canadian route with a departure from Sydney on 31 October.

On this voyage north, *Moana* left Suva on 8 November, and made a brief stop on 12 November at Fanning Island, a remote coral atoll lying 3.54 degrees north of the Equator, just off the Suva-Honolulu trade route. The total area of the island was just 15 square miles, the average height being only 17 feet above sea level. Most of the 250 to 270 natives were employed on the coconut plantations which cover the island.

There was also an important cable station located there, and cable station and plantation administration officials made up a European community of about thirty, but there was no regular steamer service to Fanning Island, so the inhabitants relied on the occasional diversion of passing ships for their supplies.

For the next three years the vessels on the Vancouver service would call at Fanning Island on every second northbound voyage, the final call being made by *Aorangi* in January 1908.

Manuka (John Mathieson collection)

During 1905 the subsidy provided by various Governments for the Canadian service was increased again, to £66,000, of which Canada contributed £37,090, Australia £26,628 and Fiji £2,282. Also during 1905, *Moana* was taken off the Canadian trade from March to October and placed on the Tasman services again, being replaced for two round trips by *Manuka*, which departed Sydney on 17 April and 10 July. *Moana* resumed its place on the route with a departure from Sydney on 2 October.

Moana left Sydney on 19 March 1906 on a regular voyage to Vancouver. At this time there were many visitors to America from Australia and New Zealand whose travel arrangements from San Francisco had been affected by the earthquake on 18 April. The Governments of both countries issued statements that they would be prepared to "take any reasonable responsibility" for the repatriation of their nationals, under certain circumstances. No doubt there were many people from both countries who wanted to get away from San Francisco, but with no ships departing the city, alternative arrangements had to be made.

Moana was due to depart Vancouver on 28 April on a regular Canadian-Australasian Line voyage to Sydney via Honolulu, Suva and Brisbane. It was arranged that persons booked to travel from San Francisco would be taken to Vancouver overland, and join the *Moana* for the voyage south. Instead of the ship calling at Brisbane, *Moana* went from Suva to Auckland, where the New Zealand passengers from San Francisco disembarked on 17 May, then the vessel continued to Sydney, arriving on 21 May, the shipping news next day mentioning it was carrying "a large number of passengers from San Francisco".

In December 1905, the Union Line had begun advertising that their newest liner, the 5,282 gross ton *Maheno*, would be transferred temporarily to the Vancouver route in April 1906, to enable the veteran *Aorangi* to have a major refit.

Built by Wm Denny & Bros at Dumbarton, and launched on 19 June 1905, *Maheno* is generally considered to be the most beautiful of all the ships built at that shipyard for the Union Company. *Maheno* was the first of their liners to be given two funnels, which gave a most imposing appearance. The first Union Line ship to exceed 5,000 gross tons, *Maheno* was 400 ft/212.9m long with a beam of 50 ft/15.2m.

The new ship was powered by direct drive turbines connected to three propellers to provide a service speed of 16 knots, but during first trials in September 1905, *Maheno* achieved a top speed of 17.5 knots.

Maheno departed Glasgow on 29 September on its delivery voyage, carrying over two hundred passengers bound for Australia and New Zealand, and a further 170 passengers joined the ship at Durban on 15 October.

Designed for the Tasman horseshoe service, *Maheno* had superb accommodation for 234 passengers in first class, 116 in second class and 60 in third class. *Maheno* entered service with a departure from Sydney on 18 November.

After arriving in Sydney on 3 April 1906, *Maheno* had been prepared for its first Pacific crossing, which departed Sydney on 16 April. *Maheno* called at Brisbane three days later, then continued to Suva, arriving on 23 April, reaching Vancouver on 7 May, completing the fastest voyage yet made across the Pacific to the Canadian port. On 9 May the *Sydney Morning Herald* reported:

> The turbine steamer Maheno has proved her speed in crossing the Pacific as well as in Australian waters. She reached Victoria, BC, on Sunday afternoon, and after

remaining there for some time proceeded to Vancouver, where she arrived at 4pm on Monday last. As she left Brisbane on Thursday, April 19, and got to Victoria on Sunday last, the passage between Australia and America was the smartest trip that has ever been accomplished by any steamer across the Pacific. The Maheno leaves Vancouver on the return trip on May 25, and sails from Sydney on July 9. The excellence of her accommodation ensured a full list of passengers on her maiden voyage.

Maheno left the Canadian port as scheduled on 25 May and called at the same ports en route back to Sydney, arriving there on 16 June. *Maheno* made one more voyage to Canada, departing Sydney on 9 July, sailing from Vancouver on 17 August and arriving back in Sydney on 8 September. *Maheno* then returned to the Tasman trades, and these were destined to be the only voyages this magnificent vessel would make across the Pacific.

For the rest of 1906 and into 1907 the Vancouver service continued to be operated by *Moana*, *Miowera* and *Aorangi*, with a call at Fanning Island every second departure from Sydney. However, *Manuka* returned to the Canadian route with a departure from Sydney on 15 April 1907, replacing *Miowera* for two round trips. The second voyage by *Manuka* left Sydney on 8 July, arriving in Vancouver on 31 July, leaving there on 16 August and returning to Sydney on 8 September. *Manuka* then went back on the Tasman trades, and *Miowera* took the 30 September departure from Sydney.

On 23 December 1907, *Miowera* left Sydney on its final trip to Canada, but after leaving Suva on 1 January 1908 diverted to make a call at Navua the next day, then continued to Honolulu, and on to Vancouver, arriving there on 20 January. Departing Vancouver on 31 January, *Miowera* made its last visit to Honolulu on 8 February, and Suva ten days later, and after calling at Brisbane on 23 February arrived back in Sydney on 25 February.

Miowera was withdrawn from the Canadian service, then bought outright by the Union Steam Ship Company. After a refit, the vessel was renamed *Maitai* and placed on the Union Line Tasman trades.

The 20 January 1908 departure from Sydney of *Aorangi* was the last northbound voyage that would include a call at Fanning Island, as this was subsequently included on every second voyage in the southbound schedule instead. The first vessel to stop at Fanning Island southbound was *Moana* on 7 April, after a call at Honolulu.

In 1907 the Union Steam Ship Company had taken delivery of another new liner, the 6,437 gross ton *Marama*, which briefly became the largest ship yet to be owned by the company, a title it would hold for less than a year. Built by Caird & Co at Glasgow, *Marama* was launched on 22 June 1907, and completed in September that year. Although larger than *Maheno*, *Marama* lacked the grace of that vessel, being given only one funnel, and had triple expansion machinery driving twin propellers, chosen for reliability rather than speed. Accommodation was provided for 229 first class, 79 second class and 153 third class passengers, with the accent being on comfort rather than luxury.

Departing Glasgow on 28 September, *Marama* called at Cape Town on 12 October, and proceeded directly to Melbourne, arriving on 30 October. *Marama* then crossed the Tasman Sea to Port Chalmers, where it arrived on 4 November, and

Maheno

was prepared for entry into service by the Union Company workshops there.

Leaving Port Chalmers on 20 November, *Marama* went to Wellington to board passengers, departing on 26 November for its first trip to Sydney, where it arrived on 30 November.

Marama was placed on the horseshoe service between Sydney and Melbourne, but after three months on this route *Marama* was transferred to the Vancouver trade to replace *Miowera*. *Marama* departed Sydney on 16 March 1908 on its first voyage to Brisbane, Suva and Vancouver, arriving there on 8 April. Departing Vancouver on 24 April, *Marama* arrived back in Sydney on 20 May.

After *Moana* arrived in Sydney on 20 April 1908 it was again taken off the Vancouver service and placed on the Tasman trades, being replaced once more for two round trips by *Manuka*, which departed Sydney on 11 May and 3 August. On 11 September, *Manuka* departed Vancouver on its way back to Sydney, but between Honolulu and Suva was diverted to Christmas Island to pick up 54 survivors of the steamship *Aeon*, which had been wrecked there.

Built in 1905 for Australian shipowner, Howard Smith Limited, the 4,221 gross ton *Aeon* was a cargo ship that could carry a few passengers, and operated a regular service from Australia, New Zealand and several Pacific islands to San Francisco. The fate of the *Aeon* is indicative of the dangers that faced ships crossing the Pacific Ocean before modern navigational aids were available, and the *Aeon* also did not have a radio.

Aeon had left San Francisco on 6 July 1905 with over two million feet of timber, 1,000 tons of general cargo, and nine passengers, including four ladies and two children, all of whom were due to disembark at Pago Pago, their ultimate destination being Apia. Captain Downie and his eight officers were all European, assisted by 35 Chinese seamen. The vessel was due at Auckland on 25 July, and when it failed to arrive ships crossing the Pacific were ordered to keep an eye out for it.

Captain Welch, of the *Aorangi*, ordered that a lookout be kept for the *Aeon* during the voyage from Sydney to Honolulu, while an American squadron of six cruisers, bound from San Francisco to Samoa, also became involved in the search, but no trace of the missing ship was found.

Captain Downie stated in his report that the weather was fine up to 16 July when the wind veered to the south-east. The night of the 18th was dark and cloudy, and, after setting a course he calculated would keep them twenty miles from Christmas Island, the captain left the bridge, leaving the third mate on watch, but he was not aware that a strong current was pushing the ship off course.

At 9.30 on the night of 18 July the *Aeon* had run smoothly on to a coral reef off Christmas Island, which was uninhabited. The engines were run at full speed astern for an hour and a half, but the wind swung the vessel broadside on to the reef. All hands remained aboard till dawn, when a safe landing was completed. Plenty of provisions were in the cargo, and a good supply of water was found on the island, where huts were erected containing beds removed from the ship. A high platform with a flagstaff was set up in the hopes that their plight would be seen from a passing vessel as they were close to the main shipping route to Samoa.

Over the next four weeks one of the lifeboats was fitted with an oil engine found in a consignment of cargo being sent to Auckland. In this improvised motor launch the captain, second mate, first and

Marama berthed in Vancouver (Vancouver Maritime Museum)

third engineer, set off on 17 August for Fanning Island, 196 miles away, where there was a radio relay station. After going only 18 miles the rudder was disabled, and the motor stopped, but the party was able to drift back to Christmas Island. A month was spent in making more complete preparations, and on 15 September the same party again set out, reaching Fanning Island on 18 September. A radio message was sent to Australia advising the fate of the *Aeon*, and the fact that everyone had survived.

Manuka, which had left Honolulu on 18 September, received a radio message instructing the vessel to divert to Fanning Island, pick up the four men who had arrived from Christmas Island, then go to the rescue of the other survivors. Captain Downing later stated, "the *Manuka* picked us up on September 22 with a boat. We sighted Christmas Island, opposite the *Aeon*, at 2 pm on September 23, and saw the ship. At 4 o'clock we sent a rocket, and received no reply, but at the third attempt got a response." As it was getting late, and a strong current was running, no rescue attempt was made that day, and *Manuka* remained off the island throughout the night, then came in as close as possible early the next morning.

One of the ladies on the *Aeon*, Mrs Patrick, had been heavily pregnant when the ship left San Francisco, and on 21 September she gave birth to a daughter. At that time the survivors on Christmas Island had no idea whether the captain had managed to reach Fanning Island or not, so the sudden arrival of *Manuka* was a heartwarming sight for them all.

A report sent to newspapers in Australia stated,:

The skilful manner in which the *Manuka* was handled by Captain Morrisby and officers as she lay all night off a dangerous shore, with a strong current running, and took aboard the 500 bags of mails without the slightest mishap, excited great admiration among the passengers, and led to their meeting and passing a resolution of commendation. After 7 am the castaways safely embarked despite a jumping sea, which made the bringing aboard of Mrs Patrick especially a difficult feat. The whole party were brought away.

Once all the survivors were safely aboard *Manuka*, the vessel resumed its voyage, reaching Suva on 1 October. Here the passengers that had been on *Aeon* disembarked, and joined another vessel to take them to Apia. After calling at Brisbane, *Manuka* arrived in Sydney on 8 October. *Manuka* then returned to the Tasman trades, and *Moana* resumed its place on the Vancouver service with a 26 October departure from Sydney.

In September 1908 the Union Steam Ship Company took delivery of another new vessel, *Makura*, which was the first liner specially designed to operate on the service to Canada. *Makura* was built at the Alexander Stephen shipyard in Glasgow, being launched on 14 July 1908.

Handed over to the Union Company on 17 September, *Makura* departed Glasgow on 26 September on its delivery voyage, calling at Durban on 18 October, then making a record passage directly to Melbourne in fifteen and a half days, reaching there on 2 November, and arriving in Sydney on 4 November.

With a length of 470 feet, and a 65 foot beam,

Manuka

Makura was the largest vessel to be owned by the Union Company until 1913. It was fitted with triple expansion machinery driving twin propellers for a service speed of 16.5 knots.

Makura received much favourable comment for the excellence of the accommodation provided for 220 first class, 170 second class and 120 third class passengers. On 4 November 1908 the *Sydney Morning Herald* reported:

The Union SS Company's new steamer Makura – specially designed and built for the Canadian-Australian mail service – is due at Sydney this afternoon on her maiden voyage.

The Makura, which is the largest vessel of the company's extensive fleet, is of 8,530 tons gross – larger than the P&O Company's RMS China, and the Orient Company's RMS Ortona, now in these waters. She has accommodation for 220 passengers in the first saloon, 170 in the second saloon, and 120 in the third class – a total of 510 – and when she reached Melbourne on Monday had 416 passengers on board. The name selected for the ship signifies "all red" in the Maori language, and is very appropriate in view of the fact she will be chiefly employed on the "All Red" mail service.

It is claimed that the internal arrangements of the Makura are superior to those of any vessel that has previously left the Clyde, and all the first saloon berths are fitted on the most modern style, each having an electric fan. Those on the main deck are on the "Bibby" plan, whereby each is lighted from the side, and has a porthole of its own. The dining saloon, extending the whole width of the ship, is panelled in oak, and decorated elaborately, the upholstering being in rich, though subdued, green moquette, which hamonises splendidly with the surroundings.

On the occasion of her official trials before leaving Glasgow the Makura maintained a speed of 17½ knots over the measured mile, and during a 24 hours run steamed at a service speed of 16½ knots. Captain Livingstone, an old employee of the company, is in command. So delighted were the passengers with the vessel that all on board – first, second, and third class – united in a presentation to Captain Livingstone and his officers of an address. The Makura is timed to leave Sydney on her first voyage to Vancouver on the 23rd inst.

The next day the following report appeared:

The Union Company's new twin-screwsteamer Makura, which is to be employed on the Canadian-Australian mail service, arrived at Sydney yesterday afternoon on her maiden voyage, and was berthed at the Orient Company's wharf at the Circular Quay. The graceful lines and huge proportions of the great liner – she exceeds a tonnage of 8,000 – called forth much favourable comment along the waterside.

This magnificent vessel made an exceptionally smart run from Melbourne. She cleared Queenscliffe at 9.25am on Tuesday morning, signalled Wilson's Promontory at 3.15pm the same day, and entered Sydney Heads shortly after 3pm yesterday. The run from Heads to Heads was, therefore, accomplished within 30 hours.

She sailed from Glasgow on September 26, and from Durban on October 18. Her actual steaming time from Durban to Melbourne was 13 days 20 hours. The distance traversed between these ports was 5,579 miles, the average speed the Makura maintained being 16.8 knots per hour. Her best 24-hours steaming was 416 knots, a most creditable performance, having regard to the fact that no attempt was being made to lower any existing records. She was going under practically easy steam, only seven out of her eight boilers being used.

On 23 November 1908, *Makura* departed Sydney

Makura departing Vancouver (Vancouver Maritime Museum)

on its first voyage to Canada, calling at Brisbane on 26 November and Suva on 30 November, then Honolulu and Victoria, arriving in Vancouver on 16 December. Departing there on 1 January 1909, *Makura* included a stop at Fanning Island on its way back to Sydney, where it arrived on 25 January.

With the arrival of *Makura*, *Marama* was temporarily taken off the Vancouver trade after arriving back in Sydney in November 1908, and placed on the trans-Tasman trades. On 21 December, *Aorangi* departed Sydney on a regular voyage north, but after leaving Suva on 29 December went to Navua, leaving there the next day to continue its voyage north.

When *Moana* returned to Sydney on 23 March it was again transferred to the Tasman trades, and *Marama* came back to the Vancouver trade with a departure from Sydney on 12 April. *Makura*, *Marama* and *Aorangi* maintained the Canadian-Australian service until the end of 1909, but on 22 November, *Aorangi* departed Sydney on its final voyage to Canada.

After calling at Victoria early on 16 December, *Aorangi* continued to Vancouver, but due to a heavy fog was not able to berth there, instead anchoring out in English Bay. As the fog persisted the next day the passengers and mail were taken ashore in tenders, but *Aorangi* was not able to go alongside the wharf until 18 December.

On 1 January 1910, *Aorangi* departed Vancouver for the last time, calling at Victoria the same afternoon, leaving Honolulu on 9 January and Suva on 17 January, with a call at Brisbane on 23 January before arriving back in Sydney on 25 January. In all, *Aorangi* completed 55 round trips between Sydney and Vancouver. Initially the vessel was laid up in Sydney, but later in 1910 was purchased outright by the Union Line, given an extensive refit, and began operating from New Zealand to San Francisco.

To temporarily fill the gap in the schedule created by the withdrawal of *Aorangi*, the former *Miowera*, now renamed *Maitai*, was brought back for one round trip, departing Sydney on 14 February. Departing Vancouver on 25 March, *Maitai* included a call at Fanning Island on its way back to Sydney, where it arrived on 20 April. This was the only voyage this vessel would make to Vancouver under its new name.

The March voyage from Sydney was taken by *Marama*, followed by *Makura* in April, while *Manuka* was brought in to take the departure from Sydney on 9 May. On its way from Suva to Honolulu, *Makura* made a visit to Fanning Island, and the vessel arrived in Vancouver on 1 June. Departing Vancouver on 17 June, *Manuka* arrived back in Sydney on 11 July. This was the last voyage *Manuka* would make on the Canadian trade.

Early in 1910 the Union Steam Ship Company bought out the New Zealand Shipping Company interest in the Canadian-Australian Line, which enabled the Union Line to initiate improvements in the service.

Aorangi departing Vancouver (Vancouver Maritime Museum)

Rather than build another liner for the Canadian-Australian Line, the Union Company was able to arrange the charter of a vessel nearing completion in Britain for Huddart Parker Limited. Built by John Brown & Co in Glasgow, the vessel was named *Zealandia* when launched on 20 November 1909, being completed in May 1910. It had been ordered by the Australian company for their services across the Tasman Sea to New Zealand.

In May 1910 James Mills, chairman and managing director of the Union Line, made a special trip to Melbourne for talks with the chairman of Huddart Parker Limited, Mr W T Appleton. Mills made an offer to Appleton that if Huddart Parker would refit *Zealandia* to suit it for the Canadian trade, and take a one-third stake in Canadian-Australian Line, the Union Line would take a one-quarter interest in a reconstructed Huddart Parker, and also extend for a further five years the current agreement between the two companies involving the joint services they were operating on the Tasman trades. Appleton agreed to the last two terms, but refused to take an interest in Canadian-Australian Line, instead offering to charter *Zealandia* to the Union Company at a favourable rate. This was agreed to by both parties, and *Zealandia* was fitted with space for 500 tons of refrigerated cargo in the holds prior to completion.

Departing the Clyde on 14 May 1910, *Zealandia* steamed non-stop to Durban, berthing there on 8 June to take on bunkers, then proceeded directly to Melbourne, arriving on 25 June, and Sydney on 2 July. The next day the *Sydney Morning Herald* carried a report on the new vessel, including the fact that, instead of going into the Tasman trade as planned, it would instead be operating between Australia and Canada:

The first vessel built for Australian owners which is fitted with a wireless telegraphy installation, the Zealandia (owned by Huddart, Parker Proprietary Limited) arrived in Sydney yesterday from Glasgow and Durban, via Melbourne. She maintained communication with England for some days. When 1,100 miles off Durban a message was sent to the Postmaster-General of the South African Federation, and was duly acknowledged.

The vessel maintained an average speed of 13½ knots using only five boilers out of seven, and burned only 63 tons of coal per day. This was before reaching Melbourne. From Melbourne to Sydney she made 14.1 knots, using three boilers. Captain Free says the vessel is equal to a speed of 16½ knots loaded, and to 17 knots half loaded. The steamer is intended for the Canadian-Australian, in substitution for the Manuka, which is to go into the interstate and New Zealand trade. "The size, capacity, and equipment of the Zealandia," says a London shipping expert, "will undoubtedly give her a foremost place among the vessels of 1910 constructed for colonial owners."

Accommodation is provided for about 200 first-class passengers, 120 second-class, and 120 third-class. The officers and crew number about 130. The first-class accommodation, consisting of two and three-berth staterooms and public rooms, is arranged amidships on the upper shelter and promenade decks. The second-

Zealandia (John Mathieson collection)

class accommodation is arranged at the aft end on the upper and shelter decks, and comprises staterooms, dining saloon, music room, and smoking rooms. The dining saloon, placed on the upper deck, occupies the full width of the vessel, and seats 90 persons. The third-class accommodation is arranged forward on the main, upper and shelter decks. The cabins are arranged for from two to six passengers.

On 1 August 1910 *Zealandia* departed Sydney on its first voyage to Canada, calling at Brisbane and Suva on the way to Vancouver, where it arrived on 24 August. The new vessel was a more than adequate consort for *Makura* and *Marama*, and the three ships together were able to provide a very well balanced service, providing a departure from each terminal port every four weeks.

Zealandia was notable in being the first Australian-owned ship to be fitted with wireless telegraphy. Although this was primarily a safety device, it also found other uses when the ship was at sea. Soon after *Zealandia* began operating across the Pacific, it was reported in the newspapers that the wireless operator on the ship had engaged in a long-range chess match with the wireless operator on board the *Makura* as the two liners were crossing the Pacific in opposite directions.

Marama was withdrawn from service for a major overhaul late in 1910, and *Moana* was brought back on the route for two round trips, the first departing Sydney on 21 November, and the second on 13 February 1911. This would be the last time *Moana* operated on the Canadian service, the vessel arriving in Vancouver on 10 March and leaving on 24 March, arriving back in Sydney on 24 March 1911. In future years *Moana* was only used on the trans-Tasman trades or the service from Sydney to Fiji. *Marama* returned to the Canadian service with a departure from Sydney on 8 May.

Up to 24 April 1911 the advertisements for the Vancouver service appearing in local newspapers showed the route followed being from Sydney to Brisbane, Suva and Honolulu to Vancouver, but from 25 April it was shown that from the August departure Brisbane was being dropped in favour of a call at Auckland. With this change, the subsidy being paid by Australia was withdrawn, but New Zealand began paying a subsidy.

The last departure from Sydney to include a call at Brisbane was taken by *Zealandia* on 3 July, calling at Brisbane two days later, and arriving in Vancouver on 26 July. On its return voyage, which included a stop at Fanning Island, *Zealandia* called at Brisbane for the last time on 2 September, arriving back in Sydney two days later.

The first voyage to go by way of Auckland was taken by *Marama*, which left Sydney on 31 July, calling at Auckland on 4 August, then going to Suva and Honolulu as usual on the way to Vancouver.

Marama returned to Sydney on 30 September, and on 2 October the *Sydney Morning Herald* reported:

The RMS Marama, which left Vancouver on September 6, at 11 am, arrived at the E&A wharf on Saturday, she being the first boat to come via Auckland. On the evening before reaching Honolulu a successful ball was held. From Honolulu to Suva, in beautiful weather, sports and competitions of all kinds were carried out. A gymkhana, which lasted two days, was a source of great amusement to all, the several events being keenly competed. On the last night out from Suva a very successful fancy-dress ball was held, and went off with great zest. The weather still held good, and was carried right till arrival in Auckland. The evening before arrival at Auckland a concert was held, during which the prizes for the various competitions were given out. The committee were to be congratulated on the quality of the prizes, and in the general arrangements throughout the voyage. The Marama has on board 69 first class, 51 second class, 61 third class passengers. She lands 950 tons general cargo, which includes 730 tons Sydney, 2 tons Hobart, 7 tons Perth, 2 tons Maryborough, 1 ton Thursday Island, 3 tons Devonport, 160 tons Brisbane, 28 tons Melbourne, 17 tons Adelaide. 350 tons cargo, seventy passengers were landed at Auckland.

Makura made a departure from Sydney on 28 August, followed by *Zealandia* on 25 September. On its southbound voyage that departed Vancouver on 4 October, *Makura* made the last call at Fanning Island by ships on the Canadian service, as all subsequent sailings went directly from Honolulu to Suva.

The introduction of a New Zealand call increased the economic viability of the service, as the ships were also allowed to transport passengers between Sydney and Auckland. In addition to the business and holiday passengers carried on these ships, there was also a steady flow of new settlers. These were mostly British people who had originally migrated to Canada, but found the country not to their liking. On 27 November 1911 the *Sydney Morning Herald* reported on the arrival in Sydney the previous day of *Zealandia* as follows:

The RMS Zealandia, which arrived yesterday morning, and berthed at the Huddart Parker wharf, landed 130 passengers at Auckland and brought 247 to Australia. Her cargo for New Zealand comprised 587 tons and for Australia 1,234 tons. Generally fine weather was experienced throughout the passage. Heavy rains were met in the Fiji Islands, and after rounding North Cape (NZ) strong head winds and seas were encountered. The Sydney cargo comprised the following: General, 117 packages; machinery, 415; sewing machines, 78; shoes, 13; drugs, 623; corsets, 14; rubbers, 1; autos and parts, 15; typewriters, 16; dry goods, 6; scales, 85; soap powder, 225; salmon, 2,605; apples, 11,731; timber, 3472.

Mr Frank Coffee, who returned to Sydney by the Zealandia yesterday, brings disquieting information as to the factors operating against immigration to Australia.

"There are many Canadian settlers," remarked Mr Coffee, "who are turning their eyes to Australia, but find difficulty in arranging transport. The Zealandia carried 360 passengers in all classes, of whom 160 were third class. A large percentage were Englishmen, and a large proportion of these were Lancashire men. I asked them why they were leaving Canada, and they replied that work was scarce in the winter months, and it cost a lot to buy warm clothing to protect them from the rigours of a Canadian winter."

"About 40 third class passengers left the Zealandia at Auckland. Some of these had through tickets to Sydney and Melbourne. Some New Zealanders in the steerage ran down Australia and boosted New Zealand, and persuaded them to leave the steamer at Auckland."

In 1910 the Union Line had ordered another new liner to be built for them by the Fairfield shipyard in Glasgow, to enter service at the end of 1911. Meanwhile, in 1911 the Union Line placed an order for yet another new liner which would be much larger than any previous vessel owned by the company, and placed on the service to Vancouver. With these two ships under construction, there was some speculation as to where the first vessel would initially be operated. The following item appeared in the *Sydney Morning Herald* on 9 August 1911:

The new steamer Maunganui, now under construction in Scotland, will probably be used by the Union Company for the Pacific Royal Mail Line pending the completion of the 10,000 tons steamer which has been specially ordered for the Sydney, Auckland and Vancouver service. The latest order provides for a speed of from 16 to 17 knots. The vessel will be used in conjunction with the *Makura* and *Marama*, the Zealandia reverting to the New Zealand service, for which she was specially constructed.

Maunganui was launched on 24 August 1911, and was nearing completion when the following description appeared in the *Sydney Morning Herald* on 4 November:

A twin screw steamer, built by the Fairfield Shipbuilding and Engineering Company, she is 430ft in length, 55ft 6in in breadth, 42ft 6in in depth to promenade deck, and of about 7,000 tons gross. She is divided into nine watertight compartments, and there are five decks – boat, promenade, upper, main and lower. Accommodation is provided for 244 first class, 175 second class and 86 third class passengers, and for a crew of 135 men. According to advices received, there is a spacious entrance hall, which contains the main stairway leading to the upper deck, and the lounge and music room and smoking lounge are on the promenade deck. Forward of the main stairway there is a dining saloon over 50ft in length, and extending the full width of the vessel. The tables are arranged on the café principle, and are capable of sitting 144 persons. The second class dining saloon has sitting accommodation for 110 persons. The first class staterooms are on the Bibby system, with berths for one, two, or three persons. Forward of the main saloon is the third class saloon, with seating accommodation for 58 persons, and staterooms adjacent. The propelling machinery will consist of two sets of quadruple-expansion balanced engines. Steam at a pressure of 220lb will be supplied by two double-ended and two single-ended cylindrical boilers adapted for forced draught. The Maunganui is intended for the Australian-New Zealand-Vancouver trade.

After embarking 300 passengers at Plymouth, *Maunganui* left on 29 December on its delivery voyage, arriving in Sydney on 5 February. At 7,527 gross tons *Maunganui* was the largest vessel yet built for the Union Steam Ship Company. Instead of joining the Vancouver service, *Maunganui* was placed on the trans-Tasman horseshoe service from Sydney to Wellington, Lyttelton, Port Chalmers, Bluff, Hobart and Melbourne and Union Line continued the charter of *Zealandia* on the Canadian service.

However, the Union Line realised the Vancouver service needed upgrading, and on 7 October 1911 the *Sydney Morning Herald* carried the following item:

Sir James Mills, of Dunedin, has undertaken his present visit to London with a view to placing orders for two new steamers of 10,000 tons each, to be used in the new mail service between Vancouver and Auckland. The time of transit from London to New Zealand will be about 23 days, as compared with the 37 taken by the vessels on the Suez Canal route. The new steamers will have a speed of 17 knots, and will, according to an estimate prepared by Sir James Mills, have to earn £10,000 a month each to clear their heavy expenses.

In the event, no orders were placed for the two liners. The Canadian service throughout 1912 was operated exclusively by *Makura*, *Marama* and *Zealandia*, with a departure every four weeks from both Sydney and Vancouver, providing thirteen trips in each direction during the year.

Construction of one new liner that had been ordered to replace *Zealandia* had begun at the John Brown shipyard in Glasgow during 1911. When the time came to choose a name for the new liner, the Union Line initially wanted to have it begin with 'M' and have a Canadian connection, but nothing suitable could be found.

Various other names were submitted and rejected, though at one time *Calgary* was seriously considered, before it was announced that the new liner would be named *Sicamous*, and an early artists' impression of the ship showed it with this name on

The launch of *Niagara* (Alexander Turnbull Library)

the bow. However, the numerous uncomplimentary nicknames that could be derived from this name caused the directors of the Union Line to have a rethink.

After the alternative of *Kootenay* had been seriously considered, it was finally decided that the new liner would be named *Niagara* when it was launched on 17 August 1912.

The following item about the *Niagara* appeared in the *Sydney Morning Herald* on 24 September 1912, and it is interesting to note, in view of the *Titanic* disaster only five months previously, the emphasis placed on the fact that lifeboats would be able to carry all passengers and crew.

> Mails to hand yesterday contain an account of the successful launching on August 17 of the triple-screw Royal mail steamer Niagara, which has been built to the order of the Union Steamship Company of New Zealand Ltd, for the Canadian-Australasian Royal Mail Line, by Messrs John Brown and Co Ltd, Clydebank, to the highest class at Lloyd's. The Niagara will be the largest and finest vessel of the fleet, and will take up the company's service between Australia and Vancouver about April next year.
>
> Though principally designed for passengers, the Niagara will carry a considerable amount of cargo, and a large part of the hold space has been insulated for the carriage of frozen meat, butter, chilled fruit, etc.
>
> Accommodation for 281 first-class passengers is provided amidships on main, upper, shelter, and promenade decks, the staterooms being arranged for one, two, three, or four passengers, while several groups of cabins have been provided for family parties. Two cabins de luxe are situated on the shelter deck. The first-class dining saloon, with dining accommodation for 100 passengers, is decorated in Louis XVI style. It is situated on the upper deck amidships, convenient to the main entrance, and has a large well overhead. A feature of the saloon is that the tables are all arranged for small parties. Besides the well-equipped library, writing, music and smoke rooms, an electric elevator is arranged at the main stairway, between the main and promenade decks, for the convenience of passengers. The second-

Niagara (Vancouver Maritime Museum)

class accommodation provides for 210 passengers, and is arranged aft, with the dining saloon on the upper deck. Accommodation is also provided for 176 third-class passengers.

The lifeboat accommodation is more than ample to provide for all passengers and every member of the crew. The boats are fitted with Welin's patent quick-acting davits, Mills' disengaging gear, and Welin's patent chocks. A steam launch is also provided for service when the ship is lying off some of the intended ports of call. A leading feature of the steamer is the large amount of promenade space allotted to the various classes of passengers. There is also a complete system of wireless telegraphy. Telephonic communication is arranged between the various public rooms and different parts of the ship

The propelling machinery, a combination of reciprocating engines, with a Parson's low-pressure turbine, is one of the latest examples of progress in marine engineering, and has been constructed by the builders. A new feature is that this will be the first vessel burning oil fuel to have a British Board of Trade certificate for carrying passengers.

The hydraulic engine installed in the engine-room is capable of working the whole of 10 hoists through a complete cycle within the space of one minute.

Work on fitting out the interior of the ship took twelve months, followed by sea trials, after which the ship was handed over to the Union Line. *Niagara* was the largest vessel to have been owned by the Union Line up to that time, but it was registered in London rather than in New Zealand.

Niagara was notable in being the first large

First class smoking lounge (Ken Hall collection)

passenger liner to use oil fuel under a British Board of Trade certificate, with four of her eight boilers being capable of burning either oil or coal.

The vessel was fitted with three propellers, the outer propellers being driven by triple expansion reciprocating engines, from which the exhaust was passed to a low pressure turbine to drive the centre propeller, providing a service speed of 17 knots at about 130 tons of oil consumed per day, the bunker capacity being 3,660 tons of oil.

On 8 March 1913, *Niagara* left Glasgow on its delivery voyage, going first to Plymouth to embark passengers, departing on 14 March. The liner went directly to Durban, then crossed the Indian Ocean to reach Melbourne on 21 April, arriving in Sydney on 28 April. Due to the lack of adequate facilities en route to refuel with oil, the voyage was made using coal, and to enable the liner to carry enough fuel for the entire trip, coal was loaded into holds two, three and five.

At 13,415 gross tons, for a few months *Niagara* held the title of the biggest vessel operating to Australia, being slightly larger than the newest P&O and Orient Line ships. However, when *Ceramic* entered service in July 1913 on the trade from Britain to Australia it took the title from *Niagara*.

The arrival of *Niagara* meant the end of the Union Line charter of *Zealandia* from Huddart Parker. *Zealandia* left Sydney on 10 February 1913 on its final voyage to Vancouver, arriving on 4 March, leaving there for the last time on 19 March, leaving

First class dining saloon (Ken Hall collection)

First class music saloon (Ken Hall collection)

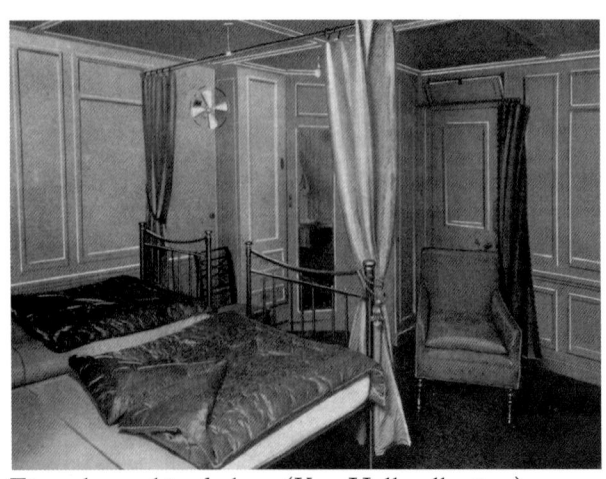

First class cabin de luxe (Ken Hall collection)

First class bedstead cabin (Ken Hall collection)

Third class accommodation (Ken Hall collection)

Second class dining room (Ken Hall collection)

Second class cabin (Ken Hall collection)

Honolulu on 26 February, Suva on 4 April and Auckland on 8 April, arriving back in Sydney on 12 April. *Zealandia* was returned to Huddart Parker, who placed the vessel on the coastal trade between Sydney and Fremantle.

Marama took the 10 March departure from Sydney, with *Makura* scheduled to depart on 7 April. On that day a fire broke out in the mail room on *Makura*, which damaged 20 bags of mail destined for New Zealand.

On 5 May 1913, *Niagara* departed Sydney on its first trans-Pacific voyage, calling at Auckland on 9 May, and the next day the *Auckland Star* reported:

> Not only is the mail steamer Niagara, which arrived here yesterday from Sydney, and continues her voyage to Vancouver today, the largest vessel of the mercantile marine to enter this port, but she also holds that proud distinction in Australia. Another claim that can be made for her is that she is the first British liner to be constructed for the development of horsepower by oil fuel. But the points that will more directly interest the public are that in place of the combined social and music room, the Niagara is provided with a lounge on the promenade deck and a music room adjoining, as well as a large library and writing room on the shelter deck. Also, there is a lift, that modern convenience that seems more than any one thing to impress on the passengers the size of a vessel.

The newspaper also noted that there were two "cinematograph photographers" on board to make a film promoting the All Red Route. *Niagara* called at Suva on 14 May and Honolulu on 20 May before arriving in Vancouver on 28 May. However, on this northbound voyage the *Niagara* used coal, and the oil tanks were only filled when the vessel reached Vancouver. The first southbound voyage by *Niagara* left Vancouver on 11 June, arriving back in Sydney on 5 July, this being the first trip done on oil firing.

The Union Line was now able to operate the Canadian-Australasian Line service with three of their own ships, *Niagara* being partnered by the smaller *Makura* and *Marama*, and these three vessels provided a departure every four weeks from both Sydney and Vancouver through the rest of 1913 and into 1914.

Niagara

Chapter Ten

Reviving the San Francisco Service

The Union Steam Ship Company had been forced out of the service from Sydney to Honolulu and San Francisco in 1900, and it had been maintained by the American flag ships of the Oceanic Steamship Company until April 1907, when they had withdrawn from the route. This meant that there was no steamship service from the South Pacific to the United States of America.

However, the Oceanic Company had continued operating their original service from San Francisco to Honolulu, using *Mariposa* and *Alameda*, but in 1909 they placed *Mariposa* on a new service from San Francisco to Honolulu and Papeete in Tahiti. The Union Steam Ship Company was operating a service from Auckland and Rarotonga to Papeete at that time using vessels like *Navua*, which was primarily a cargo vessel with basic accommodation for a few passengers.

On 30 November 1908, advertisements first appeared advising that a new five-weekly service was to be commenced early in 1909 from Wellington to Papeete, to connect with the *Mariposa* for onward passage to San Francisco. The vessel selected by the Union Company to inaugurate the service to Tahiti was *Manapouri*, which departed Wellington on 3 January 1909 on the first sailing on the new route to Rarotonga and Tahiti, meeting up with *Mariposa* at Tahiti.

Built by Wm Denny & Bros at Dumbarton, being launched on 20 December 1881, and arriving in New Zealand in May 1882, *Manapouri* was notable in being the first merchant vessel to have incandescent lighting installed. *Manapouri* and its sister vessel, *Wairarapa*, also completed in 1882, were the largest vessels in the Union Company fleet when new, being 1,780 gross tons, and could carry about 200 passengers in rather cramped conditions as well as a large amount of cargo.

Placed on the trans-Tasman trades, *Manapouri* and *Wairarapa* were claimed to be the fastest ships owned by any company in Australia and New Zealand, though they were soon surpassed by newer and larger vessels. On 29 October 1894 *Wairarapa* ran aground on Great Barrier

Manapouri opened the Tahiti service

Island when approaching Auckland on a voyage from Sydney, and sank. A total of 121 persons lost their lives, 107 of whom were passengers, in one of the worst disasters to befall the Union Company.

In 1895 *Manapouri* was transferred to a new service from Sydney to Fijian ports, and in 1899 the vessel was extensively rebuilt. An extra deck was built on the top of the existing midships superstructure, to improve passenger facilities, and the wheelhouse was moved forward to allow for an extra hold between it and the funnel. After these alterations, *Manapouri* was measured at 2,060 gross tons. *Manapouri* then served for the next ten years on the Fijian service.

Manapouri made its final departure on the Tahiti service from Wellington on 17 September, then returned to the Fijian trade. In the meantime, the service from Auckland to Rarotonga and Papeete had continued, but it did not connect with *Mariposa*. In July 1909 this was being operated by *Hauroto*, which was replaced by *Talune* for the departure from Auckland on 31 August 1909.

Manapouri was initially scheduled to be replaced on the service from Wellington by *Tarawera*, a 2,003 gross ton vessel dating from 1882, but this was changed to *Hauroto*, which departed Wellington on 23 October. Built by Wm Denny & Bros in 1882, *Hauroto* was 1,988 gross tons, and primarily a cargo ship with limited passenger accommodation. *Hauroto* made four round trips on the service from Wellington to Tahiti, its final departure being on 18 February.

The Union Line must have decided on a major upgrade to the service they were providing, as the next departure was scheduled for *Mokoia*, which at 3,502 gross tons was much larger than *Hauroto*, and had been built by Wm Denny & Bros at Dumbarton in 1898. With a sister ship, *Waikare*, *Mokoia* was placed on the various trans-Tasman trades, and served there until being transferred to the Tahiti trade, becoming the largest vessel yet to be seen in Rarotonga and Papeete. *Mokoia* provided accommodation for about 150 first class and 100 second class passengers, and also had a sizeable cargo capacity.

Mokoia departed Wellington for Tahiti on 16 March 1910, but the initial voyage was not a great success. A Press Association report published in New Zealand papers on 6 April stated:

When the Mokoia was at Papeete the inhabitants manifested great interest in the steamer as the largest passenger vessel that ever visited the group.

The results attending the placing of the Mokoia on the Wellington-Tahiti run are somewhat disappointing, as only ten passengers travelled from Tahiti and Rarotonga to Wellington, where the vessel arrived this morning. The number carried outwards, however, was satisfactory.

To publicise the connecting service to San Francisco, and also promote the delights of Tahiti, the following advertisement began appearing in Australian newspapers:

Mokoia

TAHITI, THE GOLDEN
A NEW ROUTE
TO
SAN FRANCISCO AND LONDON

New Zealand, Tahiti, San Francisco

THROUGH TO LONDON IN 35 DAYS
NEW ZEALAND'S MAIL ROUTE

Captain Cook, Robert Louis Stevenson, and Doctor Nicholas Senn have all panegyrised the scenery, the climate, and the natives of Tahiti. It is the Paradise of the Pacific, and a pearl in the "Easy Stage Route" from Australasia to Europe. Sydney to Wellington in 3½ days sail, Wellington to Tahiti 9 days, and Tahiti to San Francisco 12 days. San Francisco of today is the most modern city in the world, and from it radiates a great choice of Transcontinental railway lines, with Europe only 11 days eastward.

NO OTHER ROUTE TO LONDON IS SO
DIRECT
SAILINGS FROM SYDNEY
APRIL 16TH AND MAY 21ST
ROUND-WORLD TICKETS ISSUED

Not mentioned in the advertisement was the fact that passengers from Australia would have to travel on three separate vessels between Sydney and San Francisco, then take a train trip across the United States to New York, from where another steamship would complete the journey to Britain or Europe.

The 16 April departure from Sydney was taken by *Moeraki*, and *Mokoia* departed Wellington on 21 April, connecting with *Mariposa* at Papeete. *Mokoia* made four more departures from Wellington over the next five months, the final voyage from Wellington to Tahiti by *Mokoia* leaving on 16 September.

By then the Union Steam Ship Company had been granted a new subsidy from the New Zealand Government to extend their Tahiti service to San Francisco, giving them a monopoly on the Trans-Pacific passenger trade to North America. As the service would still start from Wellington, passengers from Australia would have to continue catching a connecting steamer to and from Sydney.

To operate this new service, the Union Line purchased *Aorangi* outright from the New Zealand Shipping Company. The old vessel was given an extensive overhaul, and fitted with accommodation for 94 first class, 52 second class and 42 third class passengers. To partner *Aorangi*, the Union Line selected *Maitai*, which was formerly *Miowera* on the Vancouver trade.

On 3 October 1910, the *San Francisco Chronicle* carried an advertisement for the "new through passenger and freight service, San Francisco to Wellington without change via Tahiti and Rarotonga". It advised that *Aorangi* would depart San Francisco on 16 November, followed by *Maitai* on 14 December, with a departure every 28 days after that. The Oceanic Steamship Company would act as agents for the Union Line in San Francisco.

On 19 October 1910, *Aorangi* departed Wellington on the first voyage by a Union Line ship to San Francisco since 1900, calling first at Auckland, leaving there on 22 October and stopping at Rarotonga and Papeete before arriving at San Francisco on 11 November. While in port there wireless was installed on *Aorangi*, which left as scheduled on 16 November, carrying 54 cabin passengers and cargo that included 4,000 boxes of California apples.

Maitai departed Wellington on 16 November and Auckland on 19 November on its first voyage via Tahiti to San Francisco, arriving there on 9 December and departing as scheduled on 14 December.

Aorangi and *Maitai* provided a departure from Wellington every four weeks, though when *Aorangi* arrived back in Wellington in early April 1911 it was withdrawn for maintenance, and the next departure from Wellington, on 5 April, was taken by *Manuka*, while *Maitai* took the 3 May departure.

When *Aorangi* completed its overhaul, the vessel made a voyage from Wellington to Sydney, arriving there on 23 May. *Aorangi* departed Sydney on 27 May, providing Australian passengers with the comfort of a through voyage to San Francisco, calling at Wellington, Rarotonga and Papeete.

However, subsequent voyages reverted to the initial schedule from Wellington, requiring a connecting service to and from Sydney.

Aorangi and *Maitai* were a far cry from the vessels that the Union Line had previously used on the San Francisco trade, and the company soon became aware that something better was needed, and in August 1911 they were able to purchase a suitable second-hand vessel, *Port Kingston*, from the Imperial Direct West India Mail Company.

In 1901, Elder Dempster & Co, a British company based in Liverpool, had been awarded a mail contract by the British and Jamaican Governments, and formed a subsidiary company, Imperial Direct West India Mail Company, to operate the new service, which started the same year using four ships. In 1903 an order was placed for a larger vessel, which was launched on 19 April 1904 as *Port Kingston*. Running trials on 12 July the vessel averaged 18.53 knots, and on 7 September departed on its maiden voyage from Avonmouth, in the Bristol Channel, on a service to Bermuda and Jamaica.

Accommodation was provided for 160 first class and 60 second class passengers, and set new

Aorangi reopened the Union Line service to San Francisco (Alexander Turnbull Library)

Maitai in Wellington Harbour (Alexander Turnbull Library)

Port Kingston

standards for the West Indies trade. There was also 124,684 cubic feet of insulated cargo spaces, in which 40,000 stems of bananas could be carried to Britain from Jamaica. Painted all white with a tall yellow funnel and masts, the vessel looked particularly attractive. Initially the service prospered, but problems developed and plans to build several sister ships to *Port Kingston* never came to fruition.

On 16 January 1905, when *Port Kingston* was outbound from Avonmouth to Kingston the vessel ran into a severe storm, and one of the crew members was killed. On 14 January 1907, *Port Kingston* was at anchor off Kingston, Jamaica, when an earthquake devastated the island. *Port Kingston* was driven ashore by huge waves, but was refloated undamaged shortly after, and the ship served as a hospital for casualties for several days. Another year a hurricane decimated the banana crop in Jamaica, and later the number of tourists being carried on the ship began to decrease.

When the mail contract came up for renewal in 1910 the Jamaican Government would not meet the amount requested by the Imperial Direct West India Mail Company, and without this subsidy the service was no longer economically viable. *Port Kingston* arrived in Avonmouth in February 1911 at the end of its final voyage from Jamaica, then was laid up at Bristol, and offered for sale.

In August 1911 the Union Steam Ship Company of New Zealand purchased *Port Kingston* for £100,000. Renamed *Tahiti*, the vessel was given an extensive refit in Glasgow, during which the accommodation was altered to cater for 277 first class, 97 second class and 141 third class passengers. The ship was repainted in standard Union Line colours, dark green hull with yellow band, and red funnel with black top and two narrow black bands.

It was not until 6 November that advertisements for the Union Line service to San Francisco began including the *Tahiti*. Up to that time the company had been advertising that *Maitai* would be departing Wellington on 15 December, but subsequent schedules indicated that *Tahiti* would be departing Sydney on 11 December, with a call at Wellington on 15 December, continuing on to Tahiti and San Francisco.

The extension of the San Francisco was very welcome in Sydney, and on 6 November the *Sydney Morning Herald* stated:

The enterprise of the Union SS Company in establishing a new mail service between Sydney and San Francisco is likely to be of immense benefit to the port of Sydney. It means that the three vessels will make this their headquarters, getting locally all that is necessary in the way of provisions, coal, repairs etc. In addition Sydney will become the principal home of 350 wage-earning men – with wives and families in many cases – whose money will go into general circulation in the city.

There has been an outcry for direct communication with America ever since the old service was discontinued after the great earthquake in San Francisco. The Union Company has risen to the occasion, and promises to provide a better service than there has ever been. In addition to affording good passenger accommodation, ample freight will be provided for perishable products, such as fruit, meat, and other marketable products. In the season, advantage, doubtless, will be largely taken of the opportunities for shipping fruit.

It is possible that in future the service will call at Melbourne if the Victorian Government offers any inducement. As there will be three steamers running, there will be no difficulty about this. The great object of the company is to make the new service permanent. It is an Australian venture. Application has been made to the Commonwealth Government for a subsidy, and if this is granted permanency is assured. Much depends upon the future. If the trade warrants it, larger vessels of a higher speed will be added to the fleet.

No sooner had the Union Line announced the establishment of their service from Sydney to San Francisco than reports appeared that the Oceanic Steamship Company would be returning to the same trade in 1912. On 7 November 1911, the *Sydney Morning Herald* reported:

According to a cable message received yesterday by Mr

Tahiti (WSS Vic)

V A Sproul, of this city, from J D Spreckels and Bros Company, managing agents of the Oceanic Steamship Company, it has been definitely decided to resume the service between San Francisco and Sydney in May next.

The ports of call will be Honolulu and Pago Pago in Samoa, and the voyage will occupy 21 days. Before the service was suspended a few years ago the steamers of this line called regularly at Auckland, but as far as can be ascertained, it is not intended in future to visit any New Zealand port.

The Sonoma and Ventura, which are now being reconstructed at the works of the Union Iron Company, San Francisco, will conduct the resumed service for a time, but at a later period larger and faster vessels will be employed. Oil fuel will be used, and it is anticipated that both the Sonoma and Ventura will be capable of maintaining an average speed of 17 knots at sea. Sufficient oil will be shipped at San Francisco each voyage to enable the vessels to complete the journey to Sydney, and to steam on the return journey as far as Honolulu, where supplies will be replenished.

The service will be a four-weekly one, and the steamers will remain in port at Sydney for five days, and at San Francisco from nine to 10 days each trip. Advices containing complete details of the resumed service are now on their way to Sydney, but it would appear from information received by Mr Sproul, who was formerly manager of the Oceanic Company in New Zealand, that an arrangement has been made with the United States Government for a fast time-table service between the Californian port and Sydney.

The Sonoma will probably be selected to reopen the line, and she will sail from San Francisco on May 12, and will arrive at Sydney on June 2.

Within a few months, therefore, there will be two distinct lines of steamers trading between Sydney and San Francisco, in addition to the Canadian mail liners, which will continue to run between Sydney and Vancouver. As already stated, the ports of call of the steamers of the Union Steamship Company of New Zealand will be Sydney, Wellington, Rarotonga (Cook Islands), and Papeete (Tahiti).

Immediately below this story, the following item appeared concerning the attempts being made by the Union Steam Ship Company to obtain subsidies from various Australian Governments, which would affect the route to be operated:

The Union Company is endeavouring to get a subsidy from the Commonwealth Government for the service for mail purposes, and is said to be in negotiation with the Queensland and Victorian Governments also, with a view to including Brisbane and Melbourne as ports of call in addition to Sydney.

"There is no doubt," said Mr Val Johnson, the Melbourne manager of the company, to an interviewer, "that this new service will be of considerable importance to Australia, and it is a bold step on our part to initiate it without first securing subsidies from the Governments concerned. If we are subsided the service will come direct from Wellington to Melbourne, thus making that city the first port of call, and Sydney the last."

Tahiti had departed Glasgow on 30 September, and arrived in Sydney on 24 November. It was reported the vessel brought 208 saloon passengers and 294 in third class from Britain. For the delivery voyage *Tahiti* was under the command of Captain Hammond, but he handed over to Captain F P

Evans, who had formerly been in charge of *Aorangi*. To replace him, the chief officer of *Aorangi*, Captain Ferguson was promoted to command that vessel.

After discharging passengers and cargo, *Tahiti* moved to an anchorage in Rose Bay to be prepared for its first trans-Pacific voyage, moving to the Messageries Maritime wharf at Circular Quay East on 8 December. On 11 December 1911, *Tahiti* departed Sydney, arriving in Wellington four days later, and calling at Papeete before arriving in San Francisco for the first time on 4 January 1912. *Tahiti* was much larger than its running mates, *Aorangi* and *Maitai*, making it a rather lopsided service.

On 8 February 1912 the Oceanic Steamship Company won a mail contract from the United States Government for the resumption of their service from San Francisco to Honolulu, Pago Pago and Sydney. The Oceanic Company's service between San Francisco and Honolulu had been maintained by several steamers including the old *Alameda*, which was sold in 1910. As a replacement, *Sierra*, which had been idle since being withdrawn from the service to Sydney, was given an extensive modernisation. The boilers were converted to oil burning and the funnels somewhat shortened, and *Sierra* then entered the Honolulu service.

With the company about to resume their place on the trans-Pacific service, *Sonoma* and *Ventura* were brought out of lay-up and sent to the Union Iron Works shipyard for major refitting. The passenger accommodation on both ships was extensively upgraded and expanded, while the engines were overhauled, new boilers fitted that burned oil instead of coal, and the forward funnel removed, while the remaining stack was enlarged.

At the same time the United States Government awarded the new Sydney mail contract to Oceanic in 1912, they terminated the previous contract to carry mail to Tahiti. As a result the veteran *Mariposa* was taken off this service, as without the mail subsidy the route was economically unviable. *Mariposa* arrived in San Francisco from Tahiti for the last time on 25 January 1912, and only six days later the vessel was sold to the Alaska Steamship Company. Not renamed, the vessel was lost in Alaskan waters in 1917.

The work on the *Sonoma* was finished first, and prior to returning to the South Pacific it was sent on a special voyage to Panama, in connection with the Panama-Pacific Exposition, departing San Francisco on 25 April 1912. Under the command of Captain J A Trask, *Sonoma* then left San Francisco on 2 July 1912 on its first voyage across the Pacific, arriving in Sydney on 22 July. On the previous day the *Tahiti* had also arrived in Sydney from San Francisco and on 23 July the *Sydney Morning Herald* reported:

> Yesterday Sydney received San Francisco mails by the Union Steamship Company's RMS Tahiti, which left the Pacific coast on June 26. Today we shall have additional mails by Messrs Spreckels and Co's Oceanic oil-burning steamer Sonoma, which left San Francisco on July 2, and came by way of Honolulu and Pago Pago. Captain Trask brought the vessel to the Heads at an early hour

Sonoma with a single funnel (WSS Vic)

last night, but too late for the doctor. She was therefore anchored in Watsons Bay for the night.

The approach up the harbour of this oil-burning mail steamer is being looked forward to with peculiar interest. She has brought about 50 passengers for this port, and has 1,000 tons of cargo to discharge. She also has a large mail of 581 bags on board, and for the first time in the history of this port London newspapers will be delivered here 30 days after their sale in the English metropolis.

The vessel has accomplished a splendid run across, covering the 6,727 miles in 19 days, inclusive of the stops. To do the distance between San Francisco and Sydney in the Sonoma's time, without including lost time at way ports, a steamer would require to maintain 15 knots on an average.

Captain Hayward, who used to be connected with this Oceanic service years ago, and who was looking forward to bringing the first steamer back, will be missed by many old friends. He died recently at San Francisco.

On 24 July the *Sydney Morning Herald* reported:

Much interest was taken in the reappearance of the Oceanic Company's steamer Sonoma. The run from San Francisco to Honolulu was accomplished in 5 days 17 hours 18 minutes. The ship received a good send-off from there, and in 6 days 12 hours 55 minutes was at anchor in the harbour of Pago Pago – the American Samoa. 3,000 islanders assembled to greet the vessel.

Also in the 24 July issue of the *Sydney Morning Herald* was the following item:

Mr F S Samuels, managing director of the Oceanic Steamship Company, was a passenger by the Sonoma, which arrived on Monday night, inaugurating the new service between San Francisco and Sydney.

Mr Samuels stated they had entered into a contract with the United States Government for a service between San Francisco and Sydney, the running time to be twenty days. This contract did not cover the return trip from Australia to San Francisco, but their schedule time for that would be 19 days. This should result in putting the Australian mail in London in 29 or 30 days.

"We have had a very large experience in operating oil-burning steamers, covering a period of many years," he continued, "and probably not more than once in that time has a steamer of our lines failed to arrive at the hour designated at either of the terminal ports. This proves that oil-burning steamers ensure regularity. As our steamers are capable of steaming up to 17 knots and our schedule does not exceed 15 knots, we have a large reserve in case of bad weather. On our initial trip to Sydney we would have arrived, as planned, at 3.30 on Monday, had we not been detained at Pago Pago, in Samoa, by having to discharge a large amount of cargo, while the natives, instead of helping us to do it with the dispatch we desired, indulged in celebrations on account of the renewal of the service. It was a red-letter day there. We also encountered a heavy swell, which put us back considerably."

Mr Samuels claimed that theirs was the speediest mail service to London. "Our highest day's run was 395 miles," he said. We brought newspapers from London, dated June 23, the mail coming over from London to San Francisco in nine days, which was nothing exceptional. We will deliver the mails in from 29 to 30 days."

"We converted our steamers into oil-burners because coal in California costs six dollars seventy-five cents per ton, while crude oil costs only four and a half dollars. There is a large saving in the engine department through the use of oil as against coal. We employ 42 less in the Sonoma's stokehole since the introduction of oil fuel than we did when we burnt coal. Thus it makes an enormous difference in wages, and we have that number of men less to accommodate and to feed. Another advantage we have found is that we can keep a steadier steam pressure with oil than with coal. We have brought with us sufficient fuel for the round trip. If oil of the sort we want can be bought here at a reasonable price, we would consider the matter of obtaining some of our supplies in Sydney."

Mr Samuels mentioned that the company was receiving a subsidy from the United States Government of two dollars per statute mile, which amounted to 15,600 dollars (£3,200) per trip.

Touching the development of trade between the United States and Australia, Mr Samuels said that their steamers, commencing with the last sailing in August, were booked full as far as freight for Australia was concerned for the following four months at least, fruit constituting the largest portion. If trade developed as they hoped it would, it was quite possible that they might have to put on larger steamers, but he thought that those at present employed would be found large enough for a year or two at least.

Sonoma berthed at McIlwraith's wharf, No.4 Darling Harbour, which became the permanent berth for the Company's vessels for the next five years, and left Sydney on 27 July on the return voyage. *Ventura* left San Francisco on 30 July 1912 under Captain John Cowell and arrived in Sydney on 19 August. The managing agent for the company in Sydney was now Mr V A Sproul.

The two vessels subsequently provided a four-weekly service across the Pacific to Sydney, calling at Honolulu and Pago Pago, the round trip taking 45 days, and there was an 11-day stop-over in San Francisco between voyages. The service became known as the "Sydney Short Line", as the ships reached Sydney quicker than the Union Line vessels, which followed a longer route.

However, the vessels operated by the Union Line remained coal burners, as coal was plentiful in both Australia and New Zealand, while oil was in very limited supply, and quite expensive, as it had to be imported. The Union Line ships would carry enough coal in their bunkers for the round trip to San Francisco, so did not have to purchase any bunkers in California.

Moana returned to the San Francisco trade in 1912 (Alexander Turnbull Library)

Faced with this serious competition, the Union Line realised they needed better ships to partner *Tahiti* than *Aorangi* and *Maitai*. As a result *Maitai* was transferred to the Tasman trades, being replaced by *Moana*, which had made the last Union Line voyage to San Francisco via Honolulu in October 1900. *Moana* departed Sydney on 16 October 1912 on its first voyage to San Francisco via Tahiti.

In 1913, the misfortune of another company gave the Union Line the opportunity to obtain a brand new ship quite quickly. In 1910 the Adelaide Steamship Company had ordered two large liners from the Beardmore shipyard on the Clyde, to be placed on the coastal trade between Sydney and Fremantle. However, following the loss of their coastal liner *Yongala* in March 1911, the order had been increased to three ships. The first of these vessels entered service as *Warilda* in September 1912, being joined by *Wandilla* in January 1913.

The third ship of the class was named *Willochra* when launched on 14 August 1912, and completed on 7 February 1913, with accommodation for 250 first class, 120 second class and 60 third class passengers. *Willochra* departed the Clyde on 15 February, going first to Plymouth to embark passengers for the voyage to Australia, and arrived in Fremantle on 25 March. The vessel went on to Adelaide, from where it proceeded directly to Sydney, arriving on 4 April.

Unfortunately, this fine liner arrived in Australia at a time when the coastal trade was in a slump, and also overtonnaged, with five other large new liners being completed for the trade in 1912 and 1913. So *Willochra* was laid up in Sydney Harbour, and offered for charter or sale.

The vessel was inspected by representatives of the Union Steam Ship Company, and a two-year bareboat charter agreement was quickly reached, with an option to purchase. At the time it was stated that the vessel would replace the veteran *Warrimoo* on the "horseshoe" service, but it could also be used if necessary on the San Francisco trade.

On 29 April, *Willochra* departed Sydney for Port Chalmers, where it arrived on 4 May, and Union Line staff refitted the vessel to suit their requirements. Having completed its refit, *Willochra* departed Port Chalmers for Melbourne, where it arrived on 5 July, departing there on 9 July on a 'horseshoe route' voyage to Sydney via New Zealand ports. Also on 9 July, sister ship *Warilda* departed Melbourne on a regular coastal passage to Adelaide and Fremantle for the Adelaide Steamship Company. However, by that date advertisements began appearing for *Willochra* to make a voyage to San Francisco departing Sydney on 6 September.

Willochra called at Hobart on 11 July and Bluff on 14 July, remaining in Port Chalmers overnight 15-16 July, Lyttelton on 17 July and Wellington on 18 July. The liner then crossed the Tasman Sea to

Sydney, arriving there on Tuesday, 22 July. Next day the *Sydney Morning Herald* noted:

> Throughout the voyage from Wellington the Union Company's steamer Willochra experienced fine weather generally. The Willochra arrived yesterday morning. A large cargo of sundries was landed at this port.

In the same shipping column the following items also appeared regarding ships involved in the Union Line services to San Francisco and Vancouver:

> The RMS Aorangi leaves San Francisco at 11am today, for Sydney, via the usual ports of call.
>
> The Union Company's RMS Tahiti leaves Rarotonga at 3pm today, in continuation of her voyage from Sydney to San Francisco. She is due at her destination on August 7.
>
> A wireless message from the RMS Moana states that she will arrive from San Francisco, via Wellington, at daylight today.
>
> The RMS Marama leaves Suva next Friday evening for Sydney, via Auckland, and should arrive here next Saturday week.
>
> Makura, RMS (Canadian Australian Line), arrived at Vancouver yesterday, at 3pm, from Australasian ports.

Willochra had been scheduled to depart Sydney on 26 July to follow the reverse route to Melbourne, arriving there on 9 August, and also make the voyage back from Melbourne to Sydney at the end of August, then enter the San Francisco trade. However, in July 1913 there was a smallpox outbreak in Australia, which was gradually spreading to New Zealand, and this was having an effect on the Tasman trade, as New Zealand was insisting that all passengers arriving from Australia must have a valid vaccination certificate. As a result, the voyage planned for *Willochra* was cancelled, as stated in the following item from the *Sydney Morning Herald* on Friday, 25 July:

> There will be no steamer leaving Sydney for New Zealand tomorrow. This, of course, is due to the Union Company's decision to withdraw the steamer Willochra until she takes up her San Francisco running in September, a step which has been found necessary owing to the quarantine restrictions in connection with the outbreak of smallpox. The absence of a boat for New Zealand tomorrow should not cause any great inconvenience, as the RMS Niagara is leaving on Monday next.

In the meantime, *Aorangi* had departed Sydney for San Francisco on 14 June, followed by *Tahiti* on 12 July and *Moana* on 9 August. *Willochra* remained laid up in Sydney until it joined the trade with a departure from Sydney on 6 September. *Willochra* replaced the veteran *Aorangi*, which had departed San Francisco on 23 July, and on its arrival back in Sydney was laid up.

Willochra departed San Francisco at 11am on 15 October on its voyage back to New Zealand and Australia, and after calling at Papeete continued

Willochra in Wellington Harbour (Alexander Turnbull Library)

to Rarotonga, where it arrived on 30 October, and was due to reach Wellington a week later. Instead of being scheduled to make another voyage to San Francisco, advertisements in Sydney newspapers showed that *Aorangi* was being reactivated to take the 29 November departure for San Francisco, while *Willochra* was to make a departure from Melbourne on 26 November on the horseshoe service.

However, in October 1913 a maritime strike had started in Wellington, which was soon affecting the operation of Union Line vessels. The trouble began when shipwrights employed by the Union Steam Ship Company in their facility at Evans Bay in Wellington went on strike on 18 October. Two days later, wharf labourers held a stop work meeting and decided to refer the dispute to the Federation of Labour and returned to work, only to find that scabs had been hired in their place.

In defiance of their president another meeting was held and 1,500 workers decided "That no work shall be accepted until such time as the victimised men are re-instated". On 24 October wharf labourers invaded several ships and stopped them being worked. The same day the shipowners offered to reinstate a 1912 agreement if work was resumed, but the union rejected this proposal.

The situation remained relatively peaceful until the morning of 30 October, when strikers in Wellington attacked a squad of mounted special constables at Waterloo Quay. That evening the special constables charged into a crowd that had gathered in Post Office Square, but the strikers were able to drive them off, and some constables were besieged in a local store, and had to be defended by shop staff with drawn revolvers.

On 3 and 4 November there were riots around the Mount Cook Garrison Hall in Buckle Street, where the special constables were quartered, and the Royal Tiger Hotel. Dozens of people were injured, including a man and a boy who suffered bullet wounds. The following day, 5 November, saw the "Battle of Featherston Street", when the strikers tried in vain to prevent the shipment of racehorses to the New Zealand Cup meeting at Christchurch.

By the time *Willochra* arrived in Wellington on 6 November, waterside workers were refusing to handle Union Line ships, and working the cargo had to be done by office staff. As a result *Willochra* remained in Wellington for a week. The strike also affected the voyage to San Francisco by *Moana*, which departed Sydney on 1 November. Due to leave Wellington on 7 November, *Moana* did not get away until 13 November.

Meanwhile, the strike had gradually spread to other New Zealand ports, though without the violence that had occurred in Wellington or the major disruptions to shipping. In addition, a number of non-maritime unions went on strike in sympathy with the waterside workers. The strike in New Zealand also spread to Australia, with waterside workers in Sydney refusing to handle any ships bringing cargo from Wellington.

Willochra did not reach Sydney until 18 November, a week later than scheduled, and after disembarking passengers, left Sydney on 19 November for Newcastle, to take on coal, returning to Sydney two days later. However, with office staff called in to discharge the cargo brought from Wellington, the work took much longer than usual, and the plan for the ship to make a positioning voyage to Melbourne to take the scheduled 26 November departure had to be abandoned.

When crew began leaving their ships in support of the strikers, the Tasman services operated by the Union Line were seriously disrupted. On the Vancouver service *Makura*, which had been scheduled to depart Sydney on 26 November, was also affected by the strike. In addition, two ships owned by Huddart Parker Limited that operated across the Tasman, *Ulimaroa* and *Riverina*, became involved as well, thus bringing the trade between Australia and New Zealand to a virtual halt. On Monday, 24 November the *Sydney Morning Herald* reported:

> The Manuka, of the Union Line, was still hung up in Sydney on Sunday. It was intended she should sail at noon on Saturday, but the crew left her, after having given 24 hours notice. It was then decided to postpone her departure till 2 o'clock, and when that hour arrived 6 o'clock was fixed upon. But evening came and the Manuka was still fast at the wharf, the efforts to obtain a crew having evidently proved unsuccessful. The passengers were told she would probably not get away before Monday. The men, it is apparent, have decided they will not man the boat.
>
> The Willochra will remain till Wednesday. Her crew has been paid off, but on the day mentioned it is believed an attempt will be made to get her away. It appears that trouble has arisen with the stewards, who have been attending to the meals for the office staff. It is known the stewards are restive by reason of a wire from Wellington a week or two ago, and it is now stated that they have refused to serve the office staff, who have been unloading the boats.
>
> Mr Kavanagh, MLC, secretary of the NSW Labour Council, in the course of remarks made on Saturday, said he hoped the stewards, who were unionists, would not be asked to wait on the staff engaged in unloading the vessels. He had no wish to see the trouble extend to this State. Such an extension would not help the New Zealanders, and it is a thing to be avoided. He expressed regret that the company had not refrained from bringing cargo from Wellington, and the responsibility of causing any trouble here must rest on the company's shoulders.

As days passed, the sympathy strikes in other parts of New Zealand than Wellington were beginning to collapse, as support by non-maritime unions was withdrawn, and their members went back to work. On 26 November the *Sydney Morning Herald* carried the following report from Auckland:

> The collapse of the strike is further emphasised by the decision of the bricklayers to return to work. The trams will resume this morning. Conditions are rapidly approaching normal. Special foot police will remain camped at the wharfs until the whole trouble is settled. Trade prospects are improving.

The same day the newspaper reported on the situation in Sydney:

> The New Zealand strike is still affecting shipping in Australia.
>
> The Makura, which was to have left at midnight, is still at the Union Company's wharf, and appears likely to remain there, unless the seamen change their minds. As was stated yesterday, they had given notice at 1 o'clock on Monday. If this is so, it would seem that the 24 hours did not elapse before they left the ship. It is said that the men had two months' pay due to them, which may be in danger of being forfeited.
>
> The company hope to get the Maheno, at present anchored at Cremorne Point, away today. Should they do so she will carry with her the mails which were to have been taken by the Manuka. These mails were taken back to the GPO when it was found that the Manuka could not get a crew, and today they will be taken down stream to the Maheno.
>
> The work of unloading the Willochra is proceeding quietly with the aid of the office staff, the greater portion of her cargo being stacked in the shed.
>
> The stewards on the Makura and Willochra have decided not to carry any more meals to the company's staff who are engaged in unloading.
>
> There were crowds of men, women and children at the Union Company's office, making inquiries as to when the Maheno and Manuka would be leaving. They all received the one reply, "Come back in the morning."
>
> To sum up the position, the Willochra, Makura and Manuka are lying idle at the wharfs, and the Maheno is in midstream, with a possibility of getting away today.

On 26 November another Union Line vessel, *Tofua*, arrived in Sydney from Suva, carrying a large cargo of hay as well as 28,000 bunches and 2,500 cases of bananas. Wharf labourers started unloading the hay, but after only a short time they stopped working, and refused to move any more cargo. Local merchants, concerned the bananas would rot, decided to go to the wharf and unload them themselves, while postal authorities also went on the ship to collect the mails.

Meanwhile, office staff continued to work cargo on both *Makura* and *Willochra*, but their union then stepped in and demanded that this work be stopped too, leaving all the Union Line ships idle. The departure of *Aorangi* for San Francisco on 29 November was delayed several hours, but the vessel managed to get away about midnight, though not with a complete crew.

On 20 December the unions decided to abandon their strike, having gained nothing from the two month disruption other than a loss of wages for their members, and within days operations across the Tasman were back to normal.

Willochra began operating on the horseshoe service, while *Tahiti* left Sydney on 27 December for San Francisco, followed by *Moana* on 24 January. *Aorangi* took the departure on 21 February, but this was destined to be the final voyage this vessel would make across the Pacific.

Aorangi departed San Francisco on 1 April 1914, and on completion of that voyage the vessel was chartered to the Royal Australian Navy, and fitted out as a supply ship at the Garden Island naval base in Sydney Harbour. The work was completed in August 1914, but the vessel was not commissioned into the Navy, instead retaining civilian status and crew. During the first few months of the war, *Aorangi* was attached to the naval fleet operating in the waters around New Guinea, capturing German settlements, but once this had been accomplished *Aorangi* was handed back to the Union Line on 3 May 1915.

Sold to the British Admiralty on 15 July 1915, *Aorangi* voyaged to Britain, but instead of being used as a store ship as planned, the vessel was sent to Scapa Flow and sunk as a blockship, following a successful submarine raid on the Royal Navy fleet based there. Refloated on 8 September 1920, *Aorangi* was refitted as a storage hulk, and towed to Malta, where it served for five years before being scrapped in 1925.

Willochra was brought back to replace *Aorangi* on the San Francisco trade. On 15 April, *Willochra* left Melbourne on its final voyage on the horseshoe service, arriving in Sydney on 28 April. On 2 May the liner left on a voyage to Wellington only, returning to Sydney on 12 May, and on 16 May *Willochra* departed Sydney on its second voyage to San Francisco, leaving Wellington on 16 May.

The future schedule advertised in local newspapers showed *Tahiti* would depart Sydney on 13 June for San Francisco, and *Moana* on 11 July, to be followed by *Willochra* on 8 August.

For the Vancouver service *Niagara* was scheduled to depart Sydney on 29 June, followed by *Marama* on 27 July, and *Makura* on 25 August. The three Oceanic vessels operating from San Francisco were also scheduled to maintain their four-weekly departures through the middle of the year, but events happening half a world away would soon bring major changes to these plans.

Chapter Eleven

The First World War

On 4 August 1914 Great Britain declared war on Germany when troops of that country invaded Belgium, in breach of an agreement Germany had made with Britain and France in 1839 to respect the neutrality of Belgium. In Australia and New Zealand it was initially thought that the war in Europe would not have any major effect on the liner services then being operated across the Pacific by the Union Steam Ship Company. This would soon be proved wrong, but as the United States was not immediately involved in the war, it was inevitable that the Oceanic Line service would not be adversely affected.

In August 1914, the Union Steam Ship Company was operating two services across the Pacific from Sydney and New Zealand, the San Francisco trade being maintained by the *Tahiti*, *Willochra* and *Moana*, while the Vancouver service was operated by *Niagara*, *Makura* and *Marama*. The Oceanic Steamship Company was operating two ships, *Sonoma* and *Ventura*, from San Francisco to Auckland and Sydney. Despite the outbreak of war in Europe, shipping companies continued to advertise schedules in local newspapers, and details of arrivals and departures were reported in full.

On the Vancouver service *Niagara* had departed Sydney on 29 June, followed by *Marama* on 27 July, with *Makura* scheduled to leave on 25 August. When the war started it was known that a German cruiser, *Leipzig*, was somewhere off the coast of North America, and it was considered unsafe for British merchant vessels to operate in the North Pacific until its exact location was known. On 15 August the *Sydney Morning Herald* reported that both *Niagara* and *Marama* were held up in Honolulu "due to the proximity of the German cruiser *Leipzig* to the British Columbia coast".

On the day war was declared, *Marama* had departed Suva, and in an unusual diversion made a stop at Fanning Island on its way to Honolulu, but on arrival there on 12 August the vessel remained in port. Meanwhile, *Niagara* departed Vancouver one day later than originally scheduled, on 6 August, and Victoria the next day, arriving in Honolulu on 15 August, and also remained there.

On 18 August it was reported that the *Leipzig* was coaling in San Francisco, which it was allowed to do as the United States was still neutral. *Marama* and *Niagara* both left Honolulu on 18 August to continue their voyages, *Marama* arriving in Vancouver on 26 August. *Niagara* did not stop at Suva but went directly to Auckland, arriving on 30 August, reaching Sydney on 5 September.

Due to the concern about the whereabouts of the *Leipzig*, the departure of *Makura* from Sydney was delayed to 4 September, but after calling at Auckland and Suva, *Makura* went directly to Victoria, arriving on 25 September, and Vancouver the next day.

Meanwhile, another German cruiser, the *Nurnberg*, had been sent by Admiral von Spee to Fanning Island to cut the cable of the relay station located there. On 7 September a German landing party destroyed the cable station operating room and the power generating plant, then pulled up the underwater cable and cut it, thus putting the cable station out of action at a vital time.

Meanwhile, as soon as war was declared the New Zealand Government had offered to send an Expeditionary Force comprising almost eight and a half thousand troops from New Zealand to Britain, to assist the "mother land" as it was known to most New Zealanders. This would require a convoy of ten ships being assembled, and the New Zealand Government began requisitioning them.

Tahiti had departed Sydney on 13 June for San Francisco, while *Moana* left on 11 July, and was to be followed by *Willochra* on 8 August. The departure of *Willochra* was put back a day due to clearance delays, with the vessel passing through Sydney Heads at 3.20pm on Sunday, 9 August. Although it was not known at the time, this was destined to be the final time *Willochra* would leave an Australian port with passengers on board.

At the same time, *Tahiti* was on its way back from San Francisco, and was scheduled to depart Sydney again on 5 September. Both *Willochra* and *Tahiti* arrived in Wellington on the morning of 13 August 1914, and *Tahiti* was immediately requisitioned for military service instead of continuing as planned to Sydney. On 14 August the *Sydney Morning Herald* reported:

> The Union Company's steamer Tahiti arrived at Wellington from San Francisco at 7am yesterday. The steamer is not coming on to Sydney this trip, and her Sydney mails and passengers are being transferred to the steamer Manuka. The Manuka will leave Wellington for Sydney today.
>
> The same company's steamer Willochra, which left Sydney on August 9 for San Francisco, arrived at Wellington at 6am yesterday. It is uncertain whether she will continue on her voyage to San Francisco. If she does not do so arrangements will be made to despatch another steamer in her place.

Tahiti went to Port Chalmers to be converted into a troopship by the Union Line's own staff. Apart from the installation of facilities for troops, the ship was repainted warship grey. Designated His Majesty's New Zealand Troopship No 4, *Tahiti* later went to Lyttelton to complete preparations for a voyage to Britain, and embark troops.

Willochra remained in Wellington almost a week before a decision was made that the vessel would not be going any further, so passengers and cargo were transferred to *Maitai*, which was taken off the Tasman trade and departed Wellington on 21 August for San Francisco. *Willochra* remained in Wellington until 21 August, when it left to return to Sydney, arriving on 25 August, and it was reported that *Willochra* would be "laid up indefinitely."

The withdrawal of *Tahiti* and *Willochra* threw the San Francisco service into disarray. It was arranged that passengers and cargo that had been booked to leave on 5 September on *Tahiti* would instead be carried from Sydney to Wellington aboard *Manuka* on its regular Tasman service, departing Sydney on 11 September. Meanwhile, *Moana*, which was on its way back to from San Francisco and due to take the October departure from Sydney, would terminate its voyage in Wellington, and all passengers and cargo would be transferred to another vessel for the trip across the Tasman. *Moana* would then embark the passengers and load the cargo from *Manuka*, and leave Wellington on 17 September for San Francisco.

Another Union Line passenger vessel to be requisitioned was *Maunganui*, which had been operating on the Tasman trade, and was taken over on arrival in Wellington on 23 August, also being converted to carry troops in the first convoy organised to carry New Zealand troops to Britain

On the Canadian service, *Marama* had departed Vancouver on 3 September, and arrived at Auckland on the morning of Friday, 25 September, but the same evening the *Auckland Star* reported:

> The RMS Marama, which was to have resumed her passage to Sydney at five o'clock will not sail at that hour. The time of departure has in the meanwhile been formally postponed to seven o'clock, but enquiry at the Union Company's office elicited the information that it is not known when the Marama will leave Auckland.

It could have been fear of possible German warships in the area that caused this delay, as the next day the *New Zealand Herald* reported:

> Though no other vessels of any description were sighted from the Marama during her voyage from Vancouver to Auckland , wireless signals – in code – were intercepted by the vessel's apparatus in the vicinity of Fanning Island. From the character of the signals, the Marama's operator considered that they originated from Telefunken apparatus, and since they were in a naval code it was presumed that the signals were being made by a German warship.
>
> The wireless signals were first heard on September 15, when the Marama was eastward of Christmas Island and about 200 miles from Fanning Island. News of the cable cutting at Fanning Island on September 8 had been received at Honolulu, and as the loudness of the signals suggested that the enemy's ship was not far distant, they added to the anxiety of the passengers. Signals were also heard during the following evening, but they apparently came from a greater distance. When the voyage was commenced most of the passengers believed that they were taking a considerable risk; in fact, many of those who intended to make the trip decided, at the last moment, to remain behind.
>
> The Marama sailed from Vancouver on September 3, and throughout the voyage steamed at night with all deck lights out, and with specially constructed shutters over the portholes and other openings whence gleams of light might escape. The arrival of the Nurnburg at Honolulu to coal shortly before the Marama left the Canadian port naturally caused much excitement among the passengers.
>
> For some distance, both before and after leaving Honolulu on September 11, the Marama followed a course a long way out of the ordinary track taken on the trip to New Zealand. Upon arriving at Suva on Monday last the passengers learned that the people were somewhat alarmed by rumours that two German warships had been hovering around Samoa a day or two previously, but of this statement no confirmation was obtained.
>
> Notwithstanding the general opinion that the trip was not without danger the passengers were perfectly calm throughout the voyage, a fact which was largely brought about by the confidence inspired by Captain Crawford and his officers. On Thursday night an address of appreciation, signed by all the passengers, was handed to Captain Crawford.

Marama finally departed Auckland at 4pm on 26 September, but this was destined to be the final voyage this vessel would make on the Canadian trade, as on 28 September the *New Zealand Herald* noted, "The Marama has made her last trip in the Vancouver mail service for the present". At the same time the latest Union Line schedules indicated that *Marama* was being transferred to the San Francisco trade, with its first voyage departing Wellington on 15 October. As the Union Line had no spare ships available, the Canadian service was reduced to just two ships, *Niagara* and *Makura*.

Niagara had been scheduled to leave Sydney on 21 September, but this departure was delayed to 2 October, and on this voyage *Niagara* also bypassed Honolulu. *Makura* had departed Vancouver on 1 October and Victoria the next day, but bypassed both Honolulu and Suva, going directly to Auckland, where it arrived on 19 October, and Sydney five days later.

Both *Niagara* and *Makura* bypassed Suva and Honolulu on their next northbound and southbound voyages, but when *Makura* departed Sydney on 24 December, and on the same day *Niagara* left Vancouver, both ships reverted to their normal route, with calls at Suva and Honolulu, and this continued into 1915. *Marama* departed Sydney on 10 October on its first voyage to Wellington, Rarotonga, Tahiti and San Francisco.

Shortly after 6am on 16 October, *Tahiti*, with Captain F P Evans in command, and *Maunganui*, under Captain L C H Worrall, left Wellington in company with eight other ships, carrying between them 8,454 men, this being the largest number of New Zealand troops ever to be sent overseas at one time, as well as 3,550 horses.

Escorted by a British battleship, a Japanese battle-cruiser, and two smaller "P" class Royal Navy cruisers, the convoy steamed westward towards Hobart, where it arrived on 20 October. Most of the ships were able to go alongside a wharf, *Tahiti* being at Princes Wharf with one of the small cruisers berthed ahead. On 22 October the convoy departed Hobart to continue its voyage to Albany, where the ships arrived on the morning of 28 October, and anchored out in King George Sound, joining 26 vessels carrying Australian troops and horses.

On the morning of 1 November the entire armada of 36 vessels and three escorting cruisers, HMS *Minotaur*, HMAS *Melbourne* and HMAS *Sydney*, departed King George Sound in a pre-arranged order, the Australian transports forming up in three lines, while the New Zealand ships brought up the rear in two lines. The convoy was increased by two more ships carrying Australian troops as it passed Fremantle, as well as the Japanese battle-cruiser *Ibuki*.

The reason the convoy was given such a strong escort was the danger posed to the troopships by the German cruiser *Emden*, which was known to be somewhere in the Indian Ocean, having already sunk over a dozen ships. It was feared that if the *Emden* was aware of the presence of the convoy it

Tahiti berthed in Hobart

could cause havoc to the ships.

On the morning of 9 November a message was received from the signal station on Cocos Island that an unknown warship was approaching. At that time the convoy was just fifty miles northeast of the islands, and HMAS *Sydney* was sent to investigate. *Sydney* came upon *Emden*, which had sent a raiding party ashore to wreck the signal station. In a short, desperate battle, *Sydney* managed to overwhelm *Emden*, which was run ashore to prevent it sinking.

With the threat to the convoy removed, the ships continued on their way to Colombo, and then to Aden, but as the ships were proceeding through the Red Sea their destination was changed to Egypt, with the troops being disembarked in Alexandria.

Over the remaining years of the war, *Tahiti* and *Maunganui* would each make a further ten voyages carrying troops. On nine of these trips, six from New Zealand to Egypt and three that went all the way to Britain, *Tahiti* and *Maunganui* sailed in company. When the United States came into the war in 1917, both *Tahiti* and *Maunganui* made several trips across the Atlantic carrying American troops to Europe, this continuing right up to the Armistices.

After the withdrawal of both *Tahiti* and *Willochra* from the San Francisco service, *Moana* continued to operate on the route, being partnered by *Marama*, which made four return trips. In September 1915 *Marama* was requisitioned for a second time, being sent to Port Chalmers for conversion into a hospital ship.

The work was completed in just twenty-three days, with numerous internal walls and fittings being removed to allow for the installation of 600 beds, plus all other necessary medical facilities. The engines were also given an extensive overhaul, while externally the hull was painted white with a green band broken by three large red crosses on each side, while the funnel was painted yellow.

On 4 December 1915, *Marama* departed Wellington on a voyage to Britain, and over the next four years the vessel made a further eight return trips to Britain bringing home wounded New Zealand soldiers.

The requisitioning of *Marama* once again left the San Francisco service with just one ship, *Moana*, so the veteran *Maitai* was again taken off the Tasman trades and went back on the Pacific run.

However, the Vancouver service was considered to be of such national importance that neither *Niagara* nor *Makura* was taken over for military duty, and both remained on the Canadian service throughout the war.

Back in Sydney *Willochra* remained idle until 4 November, when it was requisitioned for service as a troop transport by the New Zealand Government. *Willochra* left Sydney for Port Chalmers, where it was converted by Union Line staff. *Willochra* was assigned to the second convoy to be sent overseas from Australia and New Zealand.

This convoy was considerably smaller than the first convoy, consisting of only seventeen ships, three of which were carrying New Zealand troops. These ships also assembled in King George Sound, departing on 1 December 1914. With the threat of German raiders gone, no escort was provided, and the ships disembarked their troops at Alexandria on 1 February 1915.

Over the next three years, *Willochra* made a further

Marama as a hospital ship

Niagara was painted grey during the war

eight trips from New Zealand with troops, four to Egypt and four to Britain. On 17 April 1918, *Willochra* was taken over by the British Government, though at the time the vessel was actually in New Zealand. *Willochra* left Wellington for Suez, and after disembarking troops there steamed to Cape Town for a short refit before continuing to Britain, arriving at Southampton on 5 October. *Willochra* then began transporting American troops across the Atlantic to Europe until the Armistices, after which the vessel was used to transport troops home.

At the time the war started, the Union Line had a new ship being constructed for them at the Fairfield shipyard in Glasgow, which was due to be launched in August 1914, completed in 1915 and placed on the service to Vancouver to partner *Niagara*. When the new ship entered service it would be possible to operate the Canadian route with just two ships instead of three.

The new liner was to be larger than *Niagara*, and would be fitted with geared turbines driving two propellers for a service speed of 18 knots, with

Willochra in dazzle colours when carrying American troops

HMS *Avenger*

accommodation for over 600 passengers divided between three classes. Having broken with their tradition by giving *Niagara* a non-Maori name, the Union Line reverted to their regular practice by announcing that the new ship would be named *Aotearoa*, the Maori name for New Zealand, which actually translates as 'land of the long white cloud.'

Aotearoa was almost to the launching stage when war broke out, and all work ceased immediately when the British Government ordered all shipyards to concentrate on building warships. *Aotearoa* sat on the stocks for almost a year, but in June 1915 the British Government ordered that work be recommenced on all merchant ships sitting on slipways, so they could be launched to clear the slipway for more urgent warship construction.

On 30 June 1915 *Aotearoa* was launched, without any fanfare or ceremony. At that time the hull had been completed and the machinery installed, but there was no superstructure. The incomplete vessel was towed to a nearby berth, and it was thought it would remain there until the war ended.

However, a few months later the British Government requisitioned *Aotearoa* for conversion into an armed merchant cruiser. The two planned superstructure decks were dispensed with, and the vessel was armed with guns and quickly made ready for sea. In July 1916 the vessel was commissioned into the Royal Navy, being renamed HMS *Avenger*.

Assigned to the 9th Cruiser Squadron, *Avenger* was sent into the Atlantic to search for the German commerce raider Mowe in the St Vincent-Cape Verde area. After two months of fruitless searching, *Avenger* was transferred to the 10th Cruiser Squadron, which was based at Scapa Flow, and began blockade duty in the stormy waters between the Orkney Islands and Iceland.

On 25 December 1916 *Avenger* intercepted the German sailing ship *Seeaddler*, which was attempting to break out into the Atlantic, but a clever bluff on the part of the Germans enabled them to convince the British ship that they were neutrals, and they were allowed to pass through.

Over the next six months, *Avenger* made several patrols on blockade duty, being under the command of Captain A L Ashby, RN. In June 1917 the vessel completed another patrol, and began its voyage back to Scapa Flow to refuel. At 2am on 14 June, *Avenger* was hit on the port side by a torpedo fired by the German submarine, U69, the explosion killing one member of the crew. *Avenger* came to a halt, and began to settle in the water, but it was hoped the vessel could be saved. About an hour after the torpedo hit, two destroyers, HMS *Nessus* and HMS *Noble*, which had been detailed to escort *Avenger*, but were about 30 miles away when the torpedo hit, arrived on the scene and took off most of the crew, leaving just Captain Ashby, four officers and two ratings on board.

During the morning of 14 June *Avenger* settled lower in the water, and eventually it became clear that the vessel could not be saved. The men still on board the stricken vessel were taken off, and early in the afternoon *Avenger* sank.

With the United States maintaining a neutral status after the war started, the operations of the Oceanic Steamship Company were not subject to the same disruptions as the services operated by the Union Steam Ship Company of New Zealand. In fact, with many potential passengers being fearful of travelling aboard a British ship, the American company experienced a considerable increase in patronage on their service, which was advertised in local newspapers as follows:

Sierra returned to the Pacific trade in 1915 (John Mathieson collection)

UNDER NEUTRAL FLAG
TO
AMERICA AND LONDON

19 DAYS TO SAN FRANCISCO
29 DAYS TO LONDON

SPECIAL NOTICE
STEAMERS OF THE OCEANIC STEAMSHIP COMPANY ARE OWNED IN AMERICA AND UNDER CONTRACT TO THE WASHINGTON GOVERNMENT. They will SAIL UNDER THE AMERICAN FLAG, AND TRANSFER ENGLISH PASSENGERS TO AMERICAN-OWNED STEAMERS AT NEW YORK, THUS ASSURING SAFETY ALL THE WAY TO AMERICA AND ENGLAND.

The Oceanic service was being operated on a four-weekly schedule by *Sonoma* and *Ventura*, with calls at Honolulu and American Samoa in each direction. The third sister, *Sierra*, was being used on the short service from San Francisco to Honolulu, but their opposition on this route, Matson Line, had improved their service by the introduction of two new ships, *Matsonia* and *Manoa*, in 1914. Faced with this serious competition, Oceanic decided to withdraw completely from the Hawaiian trade, and concentrate on the South Pacific service. *Sierra* left San Francisco on 3 February 1915 on its final round trip to Honolulu, returning on 15 February.

Sierra was then sent to the Union Iron Works in San Francisco for a major refit. All the accommodation was rebuilt and modernised, while in the engine room new boilers were installed as well as new bed plates under the engines. One funnel was removed and the remaining one shortened, to conform to the appearance of *Sonoma* and *Ventura* after their refits. The only difference between *Sierra* and the other pair was the fitting of a new wheelhouse one deck higher.

On 7 December 1915, *Sierra* departed San Francisco for New Zealand and Australia once again, and with three ships on the route Oceanic was once again able to offer a departure from each end every three weeks.

Meanwhile, *Maitai*, under the command of Captain Charles McLean, had continued to operate on the San Francisco service, and on 7 December 1916 departed the California port on a regular southbound voyage. Apart from a small number of passengers the vessel was carrying cargo, including a consignment of Ford Model T cars.

On 25 December 1916 *Maitai* dropped anchor in the roadstead off Avarua, the main township in Rarotonga, a location the vessel had used many times before. On this occasion there was a strong current running, and during the day a wind came up, which became so strong during the afternoon that *Maitai* began to drag its anchor across the lagoon. Before any action could be taken to correct this, the anchor chain suddenly snapped, the bow of *Maitai* quickly swung to starboard, and the ship began to move sideways towards the Avarua Reef.

Captain McLean tried his best to extricate his ship from its precarious position, but a lack of steam in the boilers and the adverse sea conditions combined to push *Maitai* onto the reef, where it came to rest with a list to port, while the starboard side was held firmly by the reef. Salvage attempts proved fruitless, and the ship became a total loss.

A subsequent court of inquiry into the accident was unable to find a reason for the anchor chain breaking, and commended Captain McLean for his actions in trying to save his ship. The anchor was subsequently raised from the seabed and is now a feature in the Peace Gardens at Avarua, while the wreck has become a popular dive site, though only the rusted boiler is still identifiable.

News of the loss of *Maitai* did not reach San Francisco until the survivors arrived there on 31 December, at which time *Moana* was in the port. *Moana* departed as scheduled on 5 January 1917, but there was no suitable replacement available for *Maitai*. This meant that one complete round voyage was missed, but *Moana* maintained its schedule, arriving in San Francisco in late February 1917, departing on 28 February on the return trip.

Up to this time the American newspapers had continued to report the arrivals and departures of overseas shipping, and on 2 March 1917 the *San Francisco Chronicle* carried the rather unusual statement that "with utmost secrecy the Union liner *Moana* left port late Wednesday for Wellington." However, on 26 March the same newspaper reported that they would "respond to the wishes of the Navy Department and not note the departure of vessels, wireless reports, or movements of mail. Arrivals will be reported without port of departure."

From May 1917 American newspaper carried no reports on overseas shipping arrivals and departures at all. One reason for this increase in security was the danger posed to shipping by German surface raiders that were becoming active in the Pacific, though how many, and where they were, was not accurately known.

As a temporary replacement for *Maitai*, the Union Line placed *Paloona* on the San Francisco trade for one round trip, arriving in San Francisco at the end of March, while the next voyage was taken by *Moana* as previously scheduled.

For the next voyage to San Francisco the Union Line could only come up with a cargo ship, *Wairuna*. This 3,947 gross ton vessel had been built by Armstrong Whitworth at Newcastle in England, and named *Lady Strathcona* when launched on 5 November 1903, entering service in May 1904 for Bucknall Steamship Lines Ltd, of London, but the following year it changed hands, being bought by the Union Steam Ship Company and renamed.

Maitai aground at Rarotonga

Wairuna loaded a cargo of animal hides, flax, kauri gum, coal and some live sheep in Auckland, and left on a direct route to San Francisco which took it on a course that passed through the Kermadec Islands. As *Wairuna* approached Sunday Island (now called Raoul Island) from the south on 2 June, the officers on the bridge saw the mast of a ship anchored to the northeast of the island. Second Officer Rees suggested it might be a German raider, but Captain Saunders thought it was probably loading copra.

Suddenly a two-seater biplane swooped so low over the ship it just missed the top of *Wairuna*'s masts, and black crosses could be seen on the lower wings of the aircraft, while the observer held a bomb over the side ready to drop. A seaman ran up to Captain Saunders with a message attached to a sandbag which the plane's observer had dropped onto the fore deck. It read, "Do not use your wireless. Stop your engines. Take orders from the cruiser or you will be bombed." The seaplane had then dropped the bomb just ahead of the ship to emphasise the order. When the officers on *Wairuna* looked they could see the other ship had several guns trained on their ship, and an armed boarding party was approaching in life boats. Captain Saunders told the wireless operator not to touch his transmitter, and ordered the engines be stopped.

The other ship turned out to be the German raider *Wolf*, which was formerly the Hansa Line cargo ship *Wachtfels*. Armed with six 150mm and one 105mm guns, four torpedo tubes and 465 mines, *Wolf* also carried a Friedrichshafen F33e seaplane for scouting. Leaving Germany in November 1916, *Wolf* avoided the Royal Navy blockade to escape into the Atlantic, and laid mines off the Cape of Good Hope, Bombay and Colombo. Having sunk the sailing barque *Dee* south of Cape Leeuwin, Western Australia, the raider then sailed to the south of Australia and New Zealand and arrived in the Kermadecs on 27 May.

The vessel was undertaking self maintenance on 2 June when a plume of smoke was sighted on the horizon. With a boiler dismantled for repair, *Wolf* was only able to make six knots, so the aircraft was sent aloft to investigate. After the boarding party from *Wolf* took possession of *Wairuna* it was tied up alongside *Wolf*, and stripped of its cargo of cheese, meat and milk plus 1,200 tons of coal. The capture of *Wairuna* is the first recorded combat use of naval aircraft in the Pacific.

On 17 June *Wairuna* was taken out of the anchorage into deeper water to be sunk. When time bombs failed to sink the vessel, *Wolf*'s 150mm guns put holes into the waterline. After a couple of hours *Wairuna* finally rolled over to port and sank.

On the night of 25/26 June, *Wolf* laid 25 mines between the Three Kings Islands and Cape Maria van Diemen and a further 35 mines were laid off Farewell Spit the next night. *Wolf* then sailed across the Tasman to lay 17 mines near Gabo Island south west of Cape Howe, Australia. During five months in the Pacific, *Wolf* sank five vessels and its mines sank another three.

The captured crew of *Wairuna*, and those of other ships sunk by *Wolf*, remained on board the raider until it returned to Germany on 19 February 1918 after 452 days at sea and an estimated 64,000 miles. The loss of *Wairuna* was not reported in newspapers until the war was over.

Throughout the rest of 1917 and through 1918 the Union Line only operated *Moana* on their service to San Francisco, with a departure every second month. However, with the three Oceanic ships, *Sonoma*, *Ventura* and *Sierra*, providing regular departures every three weeks, initially there was an adequate service being provided between the United States and the South Pacific. This continued after the United States entered the war on 6 April 1917, but came to an end in November that year when the United States Government requisitioned all American flag vessels over 2,500 gross tons.

Sonoma, *Ventura* and *Sierra* were all taken over by the Government, but as the South Pacific service was declared an essential trade route, *Sonoma* and *Ventura* were retained on the service, though operating under the control of the United States War Shipping Board. *Sierra* was not included in this arrangement, and on 28 December it was handed over to the Army Transport Service, and delegated to transport troops across the Atlantic. On 24 May 1918, *Sierra* was transferred to the control of the United States Navy, which continued into 1919.

To cope with the freight side of the trade in the absence of *Sierra*, the Oceanic Company chartered several cargo vessels including *Selandia*, owned by the East Asiatic Company, which arrived in Sydney for the first time on 10 June 1918. This 4,950 gross ton vessel holds a special place in maritime history, as when it was built in 1912 it was the first ocean-going motor ship in the world, being fitted with Burmeister & Wain diesel machinery, and not having a conventional funnel, which was replaced by a thin exhaust pipe. *Selandia* made several voyages across the Pacific, at times returning to San Francisco via the Philippines.

Chapter Twelve

The Post-War Years

At the end of the war in November 1918, the Vancouver service was being operated by *Makura* and *Niagara* of the Union Line, neither of which had been taken over for military duty during the conflict, though the third vessel that had been on the route, *Marama*, was requisitioned in October 1914. For the rest of the conflict *Niagara* and *Makura* were able to maintain regular departures, which continued after the Armistices.

The San Francisco route had also undergone minor alterations during the war years. The Oceanic Steamship Company had maintained a regular service to Australia and New Zealand with three ships, *Sierra*, *Sonoma* and *Ventura*, until late in 1917. The United States had entered the conflict in April 1917, but it was not until November 1917 that the United States Shipping Board took control of all American flag shipping. At that time *Sierra* was taken over for military duty, and this continued until the end of the conflict, but *Sonoma* and *Ventura* remained on the South Pacific trade as before.

Since the Oceanic service had been resumed in 1912 the vessels had been berthing in Sydney at 4 Darling Harbour, but in 1918 this changed. When *Sonoma* arrived on 7 May 1918 the local agency was styled "Oceanic Steamship Company". *Sonoma* berthed at 4 Darling Harbour to disembark passengers, but took on cargo and passengers at Pyrmont, leaving on 15 May.

The next arrival was *Ventura*, on 18 June 1918 under Captain J Dawson, which berthed at Woolloomooloo for a few days, then loaded at Pyrmont before sailing on 26 June. With the arrival of *Sonoma* on 9 July, passengers disembarked at No1 Dawes Point and cargo was loaded at Pyrmont, but when *Ventura* arrived on 20 August 1918, it berthed at No. 4 Circular Quay West, and this became the permanent wharf for the Company's vessels until 1929.

Usually the ships operated without any problems, but, after leaving Sydney on 23 January 1919, *Sonoma* returned two days later on one engine. It was found that the starboard propeller had been "fouled by a piece of wire", and after divers cleared the obstruction the vessel sailed again for San Francisco on 29 January.

When *Sierra* was returned to Oceanic on 1 October 1919, the company decided that the San Francisco route would only require two ships in the post-war years, so *Sierra* was offered for sale, and purchased by the Green Star Steamship Company, of New York, on 27 December 1919. This left *Sonoma* and *Ventura* to maintain a schedule of four-weekly departures going into the 1920s.

Of the three liners that had been maintaining the San Francisco trade for the Union Line in 1914, *Tahiti* had been requisitioned within days of war breaking out, and spent the rest of the war carrying troops. This left *Moana* and *Maitai* to maintain the route on a revised schedule, but following the loss of *Maitai* in December 1916, *Moana* maintained the San Francisco alone for the next two years until another ship was added to the route, this being *Paloona*.

Paloona had been built by Gourlay Bros at Dundee as the first *Zealandia* for Huddart Parker Limited, being completed in May 1899. The vessel measured 2,771 gross tons, and provided accommodation for 180 saloon class passengers in cabins, while a further 200 persons could be carried in dormitories in steerage class.

On arrival in Australia, *Zealandia* had been placed on the Tasman trade from Sydney to Auckland, Wellington, Lyttelton and Dunedin, with calls at several intermediate ports in New Zealand. The vessel had remained on the Tasman trade until early in 1908, when it was replaced by the new *Ulimaroa*.

In April 1908, *Zealandia* had been chartered to the Union Steam Ship Company and placed on their service between Sydney and Hobart. In September 1908 *Zealandia* was purchased outright by the Union Line, and given an extensive refit during which the funnel was heightened. The vessel was then renamed *Paloona*, and returned to the Hobart trade, but was also used from time to time on services across the Tasman. In October 1914 *Paloona* was placed permanently on the Tasman trade, replacing larger vessels that had been taken

Paloona

over for military duty until the end of 1918.

On 7 December 1918, *Paloona* departed Wellington on its first trans-Pacific voyage to Rarotonga, Papeete and San Francisco. Despite its small size and limited cabin accommodation, *Paloona* made a second voyage from Wellington, departing on 25 February 1919, while a third and final voyage left Wellington on 3 May.

After returning to Wellington on 30 June, *Paloona* was placed on the trade to the Pacific islands for a short time, visiting Fiji, Samoa and Tonga, then in 1920 the vessel returned to the Tasman trade until 1922, when it was laid up at Port Chalmers. *Paloona* remained idle for the next six years before work began on dismantling the vessel, until only the bare hull remained. This was then towed to Otago Heads and sunk alongside the mole on 20 September 1928.

With the withdrawal of *Paloona* from the San Francisco service, *Moana* was joined in July 1919 by the Union Line vessel *Tofua*, which had been built by Denny Bros in 1908 for the passenger and cargo trade to the Pacific Islands. *Tofua* loaded a full cargo at Liverpool, departing on 12 April 1908 on its delivery voyage, reaching Sydney on 4 June.

Tofua left Sydney on 23 June on its first voyage to Fiji, Tonga and Samoa, and visited several ports in New Zealand before returning to Sydney. *Tofua* was fitted with refrigerated holds for transporting fruit and vegetables, and had some passenger accommodation in the superstructure.

When war broke out, *Tofua* initially continued to operate on its regular trade, but in 1916 the vessel was requisitioned by the New Zealand Government. The holds were fitted out with basic accommodation for up to a thousand troops, and the entire exterior was repainted in striped dazzle colours. Over the next three years *Tofua* made nine return trips between New Zealand and Britain, leaving London for the last time on 20 April 1919, and being handed back to the Union Line at Port Chalmers on 28 May.

Tofua was given a quick refit by the Union Line's own staff at Port Chalmers, and on 7 July 1919 the vessel departed Wellington on its first voyage to San Francisco. *Tofua* and *Moana* maintained monthly departures from Wellington, with passengers from Australia being carried across the Tasman Sea on vessels employed on the weekly service between Wellington and Sydney.

Moana made its final departure from Wellington for San Francisco on 22 April 1920, being replaced by *Marama*, which had been returned to the Union Line in late 1919, and sent to Vancouver for a major refit, during which it was converted from coal to oil firing. On completion of the refit, *Marama* did not return to the Vancouver route, but instead was placed on the San Francisco trade. *Marama* departed Wellington on 15 June for its first voyage to San Francisco, being partnered by *Tofua*, while *Moana* was transferred to the trans-Tasman trades.

Moana remained on the Tasman trades until 13 March 1921, when the vessel was laid up at Port Chalmers. After six years of idleness, work began in 1927 on dismantling *Moana*, and the bare hull was then sold to the Otago Harbour Board to be sunk on 31 October 1927 alongside the breakwater sheltering Port Chalmers, being reported a few days later as follows:

Tofua

When a ship has been out of commission for a while the question arises whether it would pay to recondition her. Several issues are involved. The Moana did not emerge among those regarded as economically worth reconditioning. She was dismantled at Dunedin, her fittings and machinery sold, and the hull disposed of to the Harbour Board. For several weeks a favourable opportunity to sink her had been awaited, for success depended on fine weather, ebb tide, and smooth water. While awaiting such disposal she had sunk at her berth, and after being refloated had been ballasted with sand to prevent her from turning turtle. The Moana was on an even keel when towed to the scene of her final resting place.

The ebb tide carried the Moana broadside on to the rocky portion of the Mole. Everything being in readiness for sinking the covers were removed from a series of holes previously cut in the side of the hull. A charge of explosive was fired, and the old vessel quickly began to droop by the head. Presently the water was rushing in through all the holes in the sides, and in 15 minutes the Moana was on the bottom, with a sharp list outwards from the stonework of the Mole. At high water a portion of the deck was awash.

On 3 May 1919, *Tahiti* left London carrying New Zealand troops home, arriving in Auckland on 4 July. *Tahiti* was then handed back to the Union Line, but was in need of an extensive refit before it could return to their service. With all the Union Line workshops in New Zealand working flat out on other ships being prepared for a return to service, it was decided to send *Tahiti* to Vancouver.

The vessel departed Auckland on 11 August for the Canadian port, and during the refit the boilers were converted to oil firing.

Meanwhile, the Vancouver service was still being operated by *Niagara* and *Makura*, but they had received virtually no maintenance during the war years, and were in need of refits. Until this could be organised the two liners continued to operate departures across the Pacific every four weeks. However, there were also various maritime disputes occurring in Australia, one of which involved the Marine Stewards and Pantrymens Union, who refused to work on certain ships, one of which was *Niagara*.

Niagara was scheduled to take the February 1920 departure from Sydney, but this was delayed by the strike. For a week the Union Line advertisement in local newspapers simply stated "early departure" for the ship, but as the strike dragged on, it was decided to abandon the voyage altogether, and on 24 February *Niagara* entered Woolwich Dock for major maintenance.

By the time *Makura* arrived back in Sydney from its voyage to Vancouver the strike was over, so *Makura* departed as scheduled on 26 March, while *Niagara* resumed its place in the trade with a departure from Sydney on 29 April.

Makura was in desperate need of a docking, so when the refit of *Tahiti* in Vancouver was completed in June 1920, that vessel was temporarily placed on the Vancouver trade, enabling *Makura* to be withdrawn, and sent to San Francisco for its refit. *Makura* had left Sydney on 3 June on a regular

Niagara (John Mathieson collection)

voyage to Vancouver, where it arrived on 29 June. After off-loading passengers and cargo, *Makura* went down the coast to San Francisco to undergo an extensive refit, which included conversion to oil-firing. The crew of *Makura* was taken aboard *Marama*, which left San Francisco on 13 July on its way back to Wellington.

Tahiti departed Vancouver on 16 June, calling at Honolulu and Suva en route to Auckland, where wet weather caused a delay in unloading cargo. As a result *Tahiti* did not reach Sydney Harbour until late on 16 July, having to anchor in Watson's Bay overnight and going to a berth the next day. *Tahiti* had been scheduled to depart for Vancouver on 15 July, which had been put back to 17 July, but it was not until 22 July that the vessel left. *Niagara* took the next departure from Sydney on 19 August, followed by *Tahiti* again on 16 September.

Tahiti made its third departure from Sydney for Vancouver on 11 November, arriving at the Canadian port on 19 December. By that time, *Makura* had completed its refit, and left Vancouver on 17 December on a regular voyage, arriving in Auckland on 6 January, and Sydney on 11 January. *Makura* had originally been scheduled to depart for Vancouver on 6 January, but due to its late arrival this was put back a week. However, by that time the operation of the Vancouver service had been thrown into complete disarray.

In early December 1920 a strike involving members of the Australian Marine Stewards and Pantrymens Union working on coastal steamers had started in Sydney. This quickly brought the coastal trade to a stop as members of the union walked off ships when they arrived in Sydney. Within a few days the strike had spread to other ports, and then began involving Australian-crewed ships operating on other trades. *Niagara* had been scheduled to depart Sydney on 9 December on a voyage to Vancouver, but the union members of the crew refused to man the ship, and the sailing was cancelled. This brought some changes involving both the Vancouver and San Francisco trades.

Tahiti had been scheduled to make a departure from Vancouver on 20 December to return to Sydney, following which the vessel would be transferred to the San Francisco trade, while *Niagara* had been scheduled to depart Vancouver on 12 January on its return trip to Sydney on the voyage that was cancelled.

To fill this gap, and also reorganise their fleet, the Union Line announced that *Marama* would be taking the voyage from Vancouver originally scheduled for *Niagara*, while *Tahiti* would be going to San Francisco to take the voyage to Wellington originally scheduled for *Marama*.

Tahiti left Vancouver on 20 December and made the voyage down the coast to San Francisco. *Marama*, which had departed Wellington on 2 December, arrived in San Francisco on 30 December, then went to Vancouver. However, after this one voyage, *Marama* would return to the San Francisco trade, partnering *Tahiti*, while *Niagara* and *Makura* would maintain the Vancouver service.

Tahiti would be replacing *Tofua*, which arrived in San Francisco for the last time on 11 December 1920, departing on 16 December for the voyage back to Wellington, arriving there on 11 January 1921. On 4 January 1921, *Tahiti* departed San Francisco, carrying 86 passengers and 300 tons of cargo, resuming its place on the trade it operated before the war, calling at Papeete and Raratonga before arriving in Wellington on 28 January, where the voyage terminated. Passengers and cargo for Sydney were transferred to the regular weekly steamer from Wellington. *Marama* departed Vancouver on 12 January on its special voyage to Auckland and Sydney.

The continuing strike by stewards in Sydney resulted in *Makura* joining the list of idle ships, and also brought about a change of plan for *Tofua*, as reported in the *Sydney Morning Herald* on 13 January:

> The crew of the Union Coy's RMS Makura refused to sign on yesterday, and the vessel has in consequence been added to the idle fleet now in port.
>
> It has been decided to bring the RMS Tofua, which arrived in Wellington on Tuesday from San Francisco, on to Sydney. This vessel's voyage usually terminates at Wellington, and the reason for her coming on to Sydney is, it is understood, to take passengers from here to either Vancouver or San Francisco.

Tofua, which was manned by New Zealand stewards and therefore not affected by events in Australia, arrived in Sydney on 18 January, but instead of being sent across the Pacific was placed on the Tasman trades with a departure for Auckland on 22 January. This was probably to meet the overwhelming demand for passages on this route, as the Australian vessels operated by Huddart Parker Limited had had to cancel all their sailings. The problems being caused on the Tasman trade were reported as follows in the *Sydney Morning Herald* on 13 January:

> The position of the New Zealanders stranded in Sydney owing to the shipping strike is daily becoming more acute. This afternoon, at 2.15, a public meeting will be held in the Town Hall to discuss the situation, and all those anxious to return to New Zealand by the first available steamer are invited to attend.

Tofua spent several months operating between Sydney and Auckland, and later served the Union Line on various trades for the next twelve years and on 11 April 1932 arrived in Auckland at the end of its final voyage. Late in 1933 the vessel was sold to a Japanese firm, Miyachi Kaisen KK, which took delivery of the ship in Auckland in January 1934. *Tofua* voyaged under its own steam to Kobe, where it was broken up.

The operation of the Oceanic Steamship Company service from San Francisco by *Sonoma* and *Ventura* was not affected by the strike, but it was slightly upset by a smallpox scare when *Ventura* arrived in Sydney on 18 January 1921. It was reported the next day that:

> A case of smallpox was discovered on the Oceanic Company's steamer Ventura on arrival here from San Francisco early yesterday morning.
>
> By the Health Officer's orders the vessel immediately went into quarantine. A second-class passenger was found to be affected; but the smallpox is only of a mild character. The Ventura will remain in quarantine for at least three weeks.
>
> On board are 137 passengers and a crew of 130. The former will probably be landed in quarantine tomorrow. The usual precautions will be taken by the quarantine authorities, but if successfully vaccinated some of the passengers may be released in a few days.

Ventura was forced to anchor just inside the entrance to Sydney Harbour, off the North Head Quarantine Station, but with the suspected case of smallpox being of a minor nature, the liner was released from quarantine on 21 January, and allowed to berth at Circular Quay east, where a few of the passengers who possessed valid vaccination certificates were able to disembark. However the majority of the passengers along with 50 crew members were forced to remain at the North Head Quarantine Station until their quarantine period expired.

Despite this, *Ventura* was able to depart as scheduled on 27 January for the voyage back to San Francisco. On 7 February the *Sydney Morning Herald* reported:

> The Oceanic Steamship Company received a cable message yesterday from Captain Dawson of the AMS Ventura, stating that the vessel left Pago Pago, Samoa, in progress of her voyage to San Francisco on Wednesday. Captain Dawson advised that all on board well. It will be remembered that the Ventura on her last trip from San Francisco landed practically all her passengers and crew into quarantine at Sydney, on account of a suspected case of smallpox, and it is only today that the last of the passengers are leaving quarantine for the city.

On 24 January 1921, at mass meetings held at several major ports, the unionists had given up their fight against the shipowners and agreed to return to work under the same conditions that had applied when the strike began. However, the shipowners refused to allow the union members to return to work until the union leadership had given a written undertaking not to start similar strikes in the future over the same issues. The initial response from the unions was not accepted by the shipowners, and

Marama

they decided to leave their ships idle until the union gave them the requested assurances. As a result the dispute dragged on for a further month, though some ships did start moving before the union finally capitulated totally on 25 February.

To maintain the San Francisco trade, on 27 January Sydney passengers for San Francisco joined the Union Line steamer *Moeraki* for the voyage to Wellington, where they transferred to *Tahiti*, which departed on 1 February. Meanwhile, *Marama* arrived in Sydney from Vancouver on 7 February, and was scheduled to depart Wellington on 1 March for San Francisco. *Marama* remained in Sydney until 23 February, boarding passengers for the through trip to San Francisco, still leaving Wellington on 1 March.

With the settlement of the strike, shipowners moved as quickly as possible for a full resumption of services. The departure of *Makura* on 3 March marked the resumption of the Vancouver service, but *Niagara*, which had been laid up in Sydney since early December 1920, remained idle in the port. Originally scheduled to depart on 10 February, this was cancelled when the dispute was not resolved, and then a 31 March departure for Vancouver was advertised, but this was put back to 7 April, enabling the liner to take up the original schedule arranged before the strike began, with *Makura* leaving Sydney again on 5 May.

Since the end of the war, the San Francisco service had been operated from Wellington, with Australian passengers being transported to and from New Zealand by Union Line steamers engaged on the weekly service between Wellington and Sydney.

This pattern continued for the departure of *Tahiti* from Wellington on 30 March, followed by *Marama* on 26 April, but subsequent voyages commenced in Sydney. *Tahiti* took the first sailing from Sydney on 28 May 1921, with *Marama* departing on its next voyage on 23 June.

After two years on the San Francisco trade, in July 1922 *Marama* was replaced by *Maunganui*, which had been released from military duty in late 1919 after a hectic war career. *Maunganui* underwent an extensive refit in Wellington, the work being done by Union Line staff. The accommodation was restored to its original configuration, while the boilers were converted from coal to oil firing. Unfortunately the work was subjected to numerous delays through industrial disputes and other problems, and it was not until the middle of 1922 that *Maunganui* was ready to resume commercial service.

Instead of returning to the Tasman trades, *Maunganui* was placed on the San Francisco route, making its first departure from Sydney on 6 July 1922. The vessel departed Wellington five days later, calling at Rarotonga on 16 July and Papeete on 19 July before arriving in San Francisco on 2 August.

Marama was transferred to the trans-Tasman trades, for which the vessel had originally been built, but this did not mark the end of *Marama*'s involvement in the San Francisco service. During the next eight years, whenever one of the regular steamers on the San Francisco trade was withdrawn for overhaul, *Marama* would be brought in as a replacement for one or two round trips.

However, the various maritime unions in both Australia and New Zealand continued to cause

Maunganui (Alexander Turnbull Library)

major problems for shipowners from time to time with strikes and other disruptive activities. In November 1922 waterside workers in New Zealand refused to handle any ships operated by the Union Steam Ship Company, and soon were joined by seamen, which virtually brought their fleet to a halt.

When *Makura*, which was crewed by Australian seamen, arrived in Auckland on 10 November on a voyage from Vancouver, it filled its empty cabins with passengers wishing to travel to Sydney. Meanwhile, *Maunganui*, which had a New Zealand crew, left Sydney on 9 November on a voyage to San Francisco, and it was feared the vessel might be held up in Wellington on 13 November, but it left only a few hours late to continue its voyage.

On 16 November 1922 a meeting of the Federated Seamen's Union in Australia decided to support their New Zealand mates, and began a series of actions aimed specifically at the Union Steam Ship Company which caused some disruption to the trans-Pacific services. *Makura* had been scheduled to depart Sydney for Vancouver on 23 November, but when a call for crew was made the previous day no seamen applied, and the departure was delayed, though passengers were allowed to board the ship the following day. A week later the Union Line decided to call for a volunteer crew, which was successful, as reported on Thursday, 30 November 1922, in the *Sydney Morning Herald*:

> As a result of a call for seamen to man the Canadian-Australian mail liner, RMS Makura, made yesterday morning by the Union Steamship Company, a large number of men have been engaged, and it is regarded as certain that the vessel will sail for Vancouver tomorrow afternoon.
>
> The members of the Sydney branch of the Marine Stewards Union at a mass meeting yesterday afternoon decided that they would not man any vessel belonging to the Union Steamship Company where volunteer labour was involved.
>
> Following on the decision at Tuesday's meeting of the Federated Seamen's Union to continue its boycott of the Union Steamship Company's vessels, instructions were received in Sydney yesterday morning from the company's head office in New Zealand to call for a volunteer crew to man the RMS Makura and enable that liner to make her voyage to Vancouver. The men to be selected were to be competent to take the vessel to sea.
>
> There was a surprising response to the call by the company, and a large number of men offered immediately. Many of them were members of the English Seamen's organisation, who had been thrown idle in Sydney owing to the stand taken during the past few months by the Seamen's Union in Australia. The men bore excellent characters and had good experience. Over twenty men were engaged, and some were sent down into the ship. It is expected that this morning the whole complement will be engaged.
>
> The question of securing cooks, stewards, and bakers is presenting no difficulty to the company. If ordinary stewards are not forthcoming, the company has plenty of offers to fill their places on the vessel.
>
> The deck and fire hands and firemen necessary to man the vessel for sea comprise 19 able-bodied seamen, three ordinary seamen, one donkeyman, six greasers, six oil burners, two wipers, and one fireman's steward.
>
> The company announced yesterday afternoon that all

Makura departing Sydney

men employed on the Makura will be paid full rates of pay and will work under conditions laid down by the awards. The rates of pay are as follows: AB seaman £15/14/3 per month; ordinary seamen £9/14/3 to £16/14/3 according to experience; greasers £17/14/3; oil burners £17/14/3; donkeyman £19/14/3; wipers £15/14/3 per month. These rates include board, beds, and bedding being found by the ship.

The rates of pay under the same conditions for stewards and cooks are £15/16/- per month for first-grade stewards; £15/6/- for second grades, with £13 to £22/10/- per month for cooks and bakers.

The Makura has a full list of passengers booked for her voyage, the total number being 367. In addition to this, she will leave with a heavy mail, representing the ordinary mail and the accumulation of the past week.

In order to prevent any trouble, the Makura was removed to a harbour anchorage yesterday afternoon off Double Bay, and it is from there that she will sail on Friday afternoon. Arrangements have been made for passengers to be embarked from No 5 Wharf, Darling Harbour, at 3 o'clock tomorrow afternoon, and the vessel will sail as soon as they are on board.

Although the Makura will leave Sydney eight days behind time, she will be able to catch up some of the lost time during the voyage, and her next sailing from Sydney will possibly be at the scheduled date.

As soon as it was learned that the company was asking for a volunteer crew, a large number of pickets were posted outside Union House yesterday. They remained there all day but business inside was carried out without interruption. As far as is known, none of the applicants for positions was stopped.

Despite more and more Union Line ships being able to return to service with volunteer crews, the hard core of the union refused to back down, and the strike dragged on, though having less and less effect on the waterfront. With *Makura* having managed to depart with a full crew, when *Niagara* was due to depart on 29 December a call was made for crew the previous day, and soon all position had been filled. In order to avoid any possible disruption to the departure of the ship by union members, on the evening of 27 November *Niagara* was moved from its berth to Neutral Bay, and it was planned that boarding passengers would be transported by tenders from the shore to the ship on the afternoon of 29 December.

However, that night a fire broke out on board *Niagara* which could have had disastrous consequences. As the *Sydney Morning Herald* reported on 29 December:

At an early hour yesterday morning the Union Company's liner Niagara caught fire owing to the fusing of an electric wire in the engineer's storeroom. No serious damage was done.

Mr Vigers, the fifth engineer, who was on duty early yesterday morning, noticed smoke coming through a ventilator on the top deck. Immediately the alarm was given, and the seat of the fire was found to be in the engineer's storeroom.

The firefloat Pluvius, under the command of Captain Carter, of the Harbour Trust, went out to the vessel, where she was anchored off Neutral Bay. Inspector Beatty and Sergeant Shakespeare, with a posse of water police, also steamed out to the liner. Their assistance was, however, not required, the crew having, with the aid of the ship's hose, and with buckets of water, already subdued the flames.

Within a few feet of the seat of the fire on one side, were 10 cases of turpentine, while the other side was stacked high with bags of coal. The fact that fire was burning for an hour without spreading to either is regarded as an extraordinary circumstance.

At the time of the outbreak the Niagara, under the command of Captain Crawford, was lying in the stream off Neutral Bay, having the previous night been moved from No 5 wharf, Darling Harbour. No passengers were on board at the time.

The Niagara is due to sail today, manned by a volunteer crew, and it is stated that the fire will not interfere with the scheduled time of sailing.

In the light of the recent shipping trouble Inspector Fowler dispatched Detectives Garlick and Jones to investigate. No suspicious circumstances, however, were reported.

Niagara did manage to get away on the scheduled time, and the service continued without any further problems as the seamen's strike gradually fizzled out over the next few weeks.

Meanwhile, the Oceanic Steamship Company service from San Francisco had continued to operate a regular schedule with two ships, *Sonoma* and *Ventura*, into the 1920s. The ten-year mail contract the company held with the United States Government expired on 30 June 1922, and was replaced by a new two-year contract at a higher rate, which was renewed at two-yearly intervals.

By 1923 the trade from San Francisco to the South Pacific was increasing steadily, and the Oceanic Company could not meet the demand for passages with just two ships, so they went looking for a suitable vessel to purchase.

In a surprise move, they were able to buy back the ship they had sold in 1919, *Sierra*. After a year of service for the Green Star Steamship Company without change of name, the vessel had been sold in 1920 to the newly formed Polish American Navigation Company. Renamed *Gdansk*, it was used on a regular service from Danzig to New York, but the anticipated surge of passengers wishing to travel to America did not materialise, and in 1921 the service folded.

Gdansk remained idle until being bought by Oceanic, who gave the vessel its original name, but first sent it for an extensive refit. On 8 July 1924, *Sierra* departed San Francisco on a voyage to the South Pacific once again, arriving in Sydney on 29 July, and this enabled the company to resume a schedule offering a departure every third week.

In an attempt to lure more passengers, and possibly gain a mail contract from the Fijian Government, on 3 June 1925 when *Ventura* departed Sydney it included a call at Suva on the way back to San Francisco, and this became a regular stop for all three vessels.

During 1923, *Tahiti* made a record passage of 16.5 days from Wellington to San Francisco. An insight into the experience of travelling on the *Tahiti* at this time is given in a series of letters written to his parents by Harry Gordon Gracie, then aged 24 and working as a bank teller. In 1924 Harry was asked by the Treloar family of Tamworth to accompany their son, Bill, who was being sent to America for treatment at the Mayo Clinic in Rochester, Minnesota. Bill apparently suffered from an ailment which the Australian specialists felt could not be adequately dealt with in Australia.

The two men embarked on *Tahiti* in Sydney for the departure on 14 August 1924, and the first letter sent home by Harry was posted at Wellington on 18 August, having been written the previous day:

At sea on Sunday 17/8/24
(This is written on my knees in the cabin so hope you can read it)
My dear Mother,
The writing room is full up so I know that under the circumstances you will forgive a letter in pencil since we are to reach Wellington only tomorrow morning and that means being able to post this.

We are both well and have not been too bad. It was very rough after leaving Sydney and this is really the only decent day we have yet had. Friday was a rotten day rain and wind all through and very rough. We stayed in bed all day and had three good meals. Yesterday was bleak and cold and the smell of ship permeated everything. We did not attend the saloon that day either but had them in our cabin. So we did not lose them. I have only lost one and Bill still has all his. Mine went west at 9.52pm on the night we sailed.

The best thing about this ship is our bedroom steward. He is a corker. Nothing is a trouble to him and he is always bright and happy and a man that knows his job.

The crowd on board are all wolis but thank goodness most of them leave us in NZ and we are hoping for a big improvement from then on as we will get a lot more flash ones then.

Life on board ship is a very lazy one and not much to my liking. One thing does appeal to me however and that is the hot salt baths in the morning. They are great especially when you are called after morning tea and fruit with "the bath is now ready for you sir".

The meals are not bad but the cooking could be better

Tahiti anchored off Rarotonga (Dallas Hogan collection)

in some lines but there is plenty to choose from.

Well no more to say this time but will write decently from Tahiti after our first port of call.

Hope you are all well at home

The next letter was written to his father while the ship was en route from Wellington to Rarotonga. Unfortunately the bad weather had continued, in addition to which Harry had not been very impressed by Wellington.

Still at Sea
22nd Aug 1924.
Dear Father,
Again I am forced to write in pencil as the writing room (four tables) is full up as this morning it was announced a mail would close at 5 this afternoon so we are all busy.

I doubt very much if I could write in ink as it is a very rough day and the old ship is both rolling and pitching so you can picture me on the couch in the cabin with the paper on my knees rolling first one way and then the other. I am quite a good sailor after all and have felt no ill effects since the first night and even then I was not too bad.

So far it has been a rotten trip no one on board worth bothering about as they are all either very old or very young and the weather has been far from the best, nearly all dull days and lots of misty rain and consequently we spend lots of time in bed as there is nothing to do when we do get up.

Bill is goodo and now concentrates well enough to read books and magazines and he also butts in now and again in different conversations. He is going to see the Mayo Bros however as soon as we get to the Eastern side of the States which I think will be about the end of September.

We had about 30 hours at Wellington and it was about 28 too long for me. It rained and blew the whole time and was bitterly cold.

It is a very quaint place with streets similar to Sydney in so much as they twist and turn all over the place. The buildings are all small and nothing higher than four storeys. Bricks are seldom used and there are very few reinforced concrete buildings. The finest public office is the Post Office and the poorest the Railway Station. The latter is woefully small and falling to pieces. It is not as good as Warialda or anywhere near it. It puts me in mind of the old Point Station in appearances only and only has one platform.

We spent the morning looking around the town and in the afternoon took the tourists bus around the outlying surroundings and drove for 2 hours for 5/- which was reasonable. There are no homes of any great beauty that I saw but they certainly have some fine scenery as the town or City rather is built on the edge of the harbour and is surrounded by high towering mountains on all sides and I certainly would not like to have to reach some of their homes if I had a few aboard.

Their trams are owned by a Corp's and are very nice and clean but I think much dearer than ours. Safety first is their motto alright and they close the blind side of the tram up so there is no getting on or off the wrong side and nobody moves from their seat until the tram has stopped. Their harbour is a very fine one indeed and they try to class it with ours but I still remain firm for Aussie. Ours is much prettier I think and certainly is made more use of.

We saw lots of snow on a mountain quite close to Wellington.

At night we went to Fullers Vauds show and saw Jim Gerald. He was awful but quite good with the crowd there and was recalled time and again for singing "Mr Gallagher and Mr Shean" and other songs about the same calibre and maturity. It was a pleasure to get to bed at the Grand Hotel where we stayed as there was plenty of nap on the bed and after being there about 2 hours for the first time I was warm. The next day was cold bleak windy and rainy so after a few purchases we came back to the boat and have been here ever since.

We have Stewart Dawson aboard of Ambassador fame and Davies and family of Davies and Davies the Ford car kings of NSW and Stefansson the Arctic explorer and Miss Steinberg late Sec for Melba.

I am excelling myself today but the seat is comfortable and so I roam on. I hope you can read it at all as the boat is as rough as bags and one wants a good saddle and a pair of spurs to stick on with.

Tomorrow we lob in at Rarotonga and if fine and calm enough we can go ashore in a boat from the ship for about 3 hours but if it is at all rough or likely to be we will not be allowed off as there is no wharf and if it blows up at all they are forced to put to sea at once. So that is that.

36 hours after that we land at Papeete for a day and then the long 10 day stretch to the completion of our long first stage of the journey. This will be the last time you will hear from me before San Fran as there is no other mail I can catch.

There was a gap of ten days before the next letter was written, by which time the *Tahiti* had visited both Rarotonga and Papeete, and was nearing San Francisco. Harry wrote:

At Sea Still
3rd Sept 1924
My dear Mother,
We will be in San Francisco in two days now (Friday 10am) so that is good news as we are both a bit tired of the boat and looking forward to a day or two at least on dry land. It is now nine days since we saw the last palm tree of the wonderful South Seas Islands.
Rarotonga - Cook Islands
To retrace our steps a little. I think the last time I wrote was a day out from Rarotonga and it was posted there to catch the boat back in about 2 days so I will carry on from there and tell you a few of the things that have happened since.

We first sighted Cook Islands about midday and anchored off the reef at about 2pm as there is no harbour there and all copra and fruit comes off the island in surf boats and these land passengers on the return trip. It is a thrilling ride as the surf is always fair and a big swell runs. We had a safe trip and then had our first taste of island life.

Rarotonga is only small but very pretty and abounds with nigs who all play Ukulele or guitars all day long even returning from work on the plantations. They are a very happy crowd and there seems to be no discontent among them. The population of the island is distributed amongst 4 villages none of any size so we took a car and toured the island going right around the island in under 1 hr and a half 20 miles so you can imagine it is not very large.

On our return we looked around the villages and it was then time to return to the ship as we sailed again at 6.30pm that night on another 3 day stretch to Papeete on the island of Tahiti and this place I am sure must be wonder island of the Pacific.

We picked up the island about midday and sailed through the Straits with Tahiti through the shadow of its mountains on one side of us and the lofty needle like pinnacles of the Morea on the other.

The coral reef encircles these islands also but Tahiti has a break in the coral 40 yards wide which forms a natural harbour for the ships and through this we sailed and berthed along side the wharf right in the town. Coming in to Papeete was the prettiest sight I have yet seen.

The water was a rich colour blue, the houses beyond with red tiled roofs and behind the great mountains covered with coconut palms and tropical vegetation of all description and then the great ravines and gorges between the mountains was sufficient alone to turn a perfectly normal suburbanite like myself into a bushman right away to explore this wonderful island.

I will have to wait until my return to tell you about all the things we saw and did there as it was great.

Why the best champagne there is only 5/- per large bottle but one is hit well to leg for other things.

We spent the afternoon firstly in the glass bottomed boat out on the coral reef to see the wonders of the deep and then we explored the town.

At night we went to the pictures and the fight and had a great time as everything was in French except the fight. That was Aussie from start to finish, (in the sixth round) when the nig had had enough and so lay down and took the count then got up and retired smiling to the crowd.

We slept on board and next morning took a car and went to Venus Point where Cook landed to observe the transit of Venus. It was a great drive full of interest as we crossed gorges and mountains in profusion and finally came back to the sea about 14 miles from Papeete at a lighthouse and monument erected to commemorate the voyage of Capt Cook.

We returned in time for lunch and left Tahiti at about 3pm on the long run of 11 days to 'Frisco and we arrive there on Friday morning at 10am we hope and this is Wednesday.

Since leaving our last post, games have been started on board and Bill and his partner beat my partner and me for the final of the mixed doubles in the quoit championship which is not too bad for us.

Last night was the fancy dress ball and it was a great

success as nearly everyone dressed for it. I rigged out in a sheik outfit made up of a pair of highly ornate silk pyjamas, a sheet, a large scarlet silk h'chief and a multicoloured head band all found around the ship and together made rather an attractive outfit.

Well that is that and it brings me I think up to date and if you will keep all my letters till my return I will fill in detail where required on my return as I find it impractical to write a diary so far.

We are both well and I think Bill is improving but we intend going straight to Rochester in Minnesota to see the Mayo's and then enjoy the trip after.

I hope you can read this as the boat is rolling and pitching this afternoon and it makes hard work of writing letters.

The next letter indicated the pair was very glad the trip across the Pacific was over, as it started:

9th Sept 1924
Dear Mother,
We are well and truly on land at last and having a great time. After a rotten trip of bad weather and no lively passengers we finally came ashore at San Fran at about four p.m. on Friday last and came straight to the above address.

Harry and Bill apparently stayed in San Francisco for a couple of weeks, then travelled overland for Bill's treatment in Rochester where they stayed four weeks. Following this they went on to New York via Chicago and Buffalo, and then boarded the White Star liner *Homeric* to cross the Atlantic, staying in London for two months. Leaving Bill in Cornwall to continue his recovery, Harry also visited Paris before returning to Sydney via the Suez Canal on the Orient liner *Ormonde*.

Chapter Thirteen

The Second *Aorangi*

In September 1922 the Union Steam Ship Company placed an order with the Fairfield Shipbuilding & Engineering Company at Glasgow for the construction of a new liner for the Vancouver trade. The Fairfield company had also built the ill-fated *Aotearoa*, but the new ship would be substantially larger than that vessel. When the first designs were drawn up for the new ship it was to be steam driven, but this was changed, and it became the first large passenger liner to be fitted with diesel engines.

The Union Line had been one of the first shipping companies to embrace motor ships, beginning with the freighter *Hauraki*, which was built in 1922 for the cargo service between Sydney and Vancouver. *Hauraki* was one of only six vessels to be fitted with North British Diesels, which unfortunately proved to be less than reliable, but *Hauraki* served the Union Line until it was captured by Japanese naval forces in the Indian Ocean on 12 July 1942.

The Japanese apparently had enormous problems understanding the workings of the ship's engines, but it did operate for them until being sunk by United States air strikes on 17 February 1944.

The keel for the new liner, Fairfield hull number 603, was laid in November 1922, and when launched on 17 June 1924 it was named *Aorangi*, after the Maori name for Mount Cook in New Zealand's South Island, which translates as "cloud piercer". Fitting out the interior took eight months, and the ship was completed in December 1924.

The construction of *Aorangi* created world-wide interest, particularly due to the decision to install diesel engines. It was expected that daily fuel consumption would be half that of ships equipped with geared turbines, and as the diesel engines were smaller there was an extra 18% of space made available for passenger cabins. There would also be a large reduction in the number of stokers and

Aorangi (David Robinson collection)

trimmers that would be required.

The interior fittings were also widely reported. The June 1924 issue of the British magazine *Blue Peter* celebrated the launch of *Aorangi* with a special supplement, which included the following:

> First class consists of mostly single and two-berth cabins, with a few three-berth cabins being provided in case of need, while, in some cases, communicating doors are fitted for the convenience of family parties. Similarly, second-class accommodation is principally in single and two-berth cabins, with the addition of a few family cabins with four berths. In the third class will be found a large number of two-berth cabins, not more than four persons will be berthed in any third class room, open emigrant sleeping accommodation being entirely absent. All cabins are well equipped, well furnished and fitted for natural and forced ventilation by ozonified air. Lavatory and bathroom accommodation is abundant throughout the ship, with tiled rooms, porcelain baths, spray and needle baths, and constant hot and cold water services.
>
> The deck spaces for games, etc., have been planned on the most generous lines.
>
> Adjacent to the main entrance hall is an inquiry office for passengers' information and mails, together with a shop for the sale of newspapers, magazines, etc.
>
> Each of the principal public rooms has accommodation for an orchestra, while highly sensitive microphones will repeat the music to the second and third-class passengers.
>
> A large area of promenade deck near the first-class verandah cafe has been allotted and equipped for open-air dancing, and a comprehensive programme of film displays will be given during voyages in the public rooms.
>
> Barbers' shops, with electrical appliances, will serve not only the first and second class, but also the third-class passengers and crew. A dark room is arranged for passengers' photography. A printing establishment, with electrically driven machinery, is installed for the ship's printing and the production of the ship's magazine.
>
> Two modern electric passenger lifts are provided, communicating with all decks, including the boat deck. There are service staircases for the staff, while pantries on each passenger deck will provide prompt service of refreshments or hot meals in passengers' cabins.
>
> The ship has loud-speaking telephones and telegraphs for navigational purposes, while all departments are connected with the ship's telephone exchange. A wireless station, with continuous wave and spark instruments, will deal with navigational messages, passengers' telegraph traffic, press news and broadcast programmes from shore stations.
>
> Electrically operated clocks, corrected daily by the ship's position, are provided in all the principal passenger spaces of whatever class, and in some of the cabins.
>
> In the kitchens, cooking ranges, fired by a low pressure oil system, electrical appliances, grills, salamanders, potato peelers, mixers, toasters, hot plates, etc., will provide for the passengers' gastronomic welfare.
>
> The pantries exhibit a complete installation of labour-saving devices, including electrically driven dish-washing machines, plate-cleaning machinery, etc. Electrically heated ovens, dough-mixing machines, and whisking machines will serve the ship's bakery; and there are, besides, special facilities for the manufacture of mineral waters, ice cream, etc.
>
> An electrically driven laundry, with water-softening plant, linen and flannel washing equipment, ironing machines, clothes and linen presses, together with receiving, marking, checking and dispatch rooms, give the ship an outfit in this respect of the most modern kind.
>
> There is cabin accommodation for two medical men, with consulting room, waiting room and dispensing room en suite, and four well-equipped hospitals, with bathrooms, for infectious and non-infectious male and female patients respectively.
>
> The ship will carry no less than 1,000 tons of fresh water for drinking purposes. She will have two sets of refrigerating machinery, one for cargo, the other for the chief steward's store-rooms. Electrically driven pressure and exhaust fans will be used, besides natural ventilation, for renewing the air of the public rooms, as well as in the cabins, lavatories, etc.
>
> The vessel is heated by a low pressure steam-heating system, controlled by the individual passenger, while, in various parts of the ship, electric heaters have also been provided.
>
> Besides arrangements for baggage, bullion and mails, the ship has stowage for 225,000 cubic feet of general cargo and 90,000 cubic feet of refrigerated cargo, such as fruit, meat and dairy produce.
>
> Specially designed steam-driven winches, ensuring silent running, will avoid disturbance of passengers. The steering gear, of the electro-hydraulic type, which is in duplicate, is controlled from the navigating bridge by telemotor.
>
> The ship is provided with lifeboats in plenty, each with separate davits and its own launching station, and there is also a motor lifeboat. Aids to navigation of the latest type are also present, including submarine signalling gear, directional wireless equipment, gyro compasses, etc., and the subdivision of the hull into numerous watertight compartments would enable her, in case of accident, to remain afloat with any two compartments open to the sea. Mechanically operated watertight doors are controlled from the navigating bridge.
>
> Fine ship as the Aorangi is designed to be, perhaps her most remarkable feature is her propelling machinery. She will have four screw propellers, each driven by a six-cylinder Fairfield Sulzer-Diesel engine working on the two-stroke single-acting principle. These engines will generate the aggregate equivalent of 20,000 indicated horse-power, and any three of them will, at ordinary pressure, be sufficient to maintain the vessel's normal sea speed. In addition, each engine has a reserve of power which would, should need arise, enable the ship to be driven continuously at a speed much above the normal. This margin of power characterises also the minor machinery on the main engines, scavenging pumps and

First class promenade deck (Ken Hall collection)

First class lounge (Ken Hall collection)

First class smoking room (Ken Hall collection)

air compressors being of a total power substantially in excess of normal requirements, with a reserve unit in each case. The electrical installation for power and lighting also is sufficient to leave one unit normally unemployed and in reserve.

The Union Company maintains two alternating monthly services from Vancouver and San Francisco respectively, thus giving a fortnightly service between the Pacific Coast, New Zealand and Australia. On the former line Niagara has already become world-famous, and is now to be joined by the Aorangi.

In shipbuilding and shipowning circles the performances of the Aorangi will be regarded with keen attention, for upon the measure of her success – and nothing has been left undone to ensure success in the fullest degree – will depend the adoption in general practice of the courageous policy which has inspired the Union Steam Ship Company in their projection of a remarkably attractive passenger steamer. The influence of such ships must tend to create traffic rather than to divert it, and it may be expected that many people will be led by the fame of the Aorangi to become ocean travellers and to journey by the Vancouver route to Honolulu, New Zealand and Australia, perhaps returning via Ceylon and Egypt; and that of those who go out by the Suez Canal route on a visit to the Southern Dominions not a few will avail themselves of the joint facility, offered by the Union Line and its sister companies, of coming back via the South Sea Islands, Hawaii and North America, for, be it noted, a return ticket to Australia nowadays practically franks the traveller right round the world.

Early diesel-engined vessels had been fitted with a very thin exhaust pipe or no funnel at all, which gave them a unique appearance, but *Aorangi* was given two tall raked funnels of equal height along steamship lines, with each funnel serving as the exhaust for one of the two engine rooms, which were separated by the fuel storage tanks.

The four 3,250bhp Sulzer engines fitted into *Aorangi* were the largest diesels that had been built up to that time. Set up side by side in the main engine room across the width of the ship, each engine was connected to one of the four propeller shafts. Four auxiliary diesels were located in a smaller engine room forward, being used to supply electric power around the ship. There were also two oil fired donkey boilers of the single-ended Scotch type, to provide steam for working the fuel transfer pumps, hot water and heating around the ship.

On sea trials run in early December 1924 *Aorangi* achieved a maximum speed of 18.237 knots over the measured mile. The liner was officially completed on 16 December, and on a special demonstration trip carried out that day there were representatives from more than seventy shipping companies on board, mostly superintendent engineers, to gather experience on the operation of a motor ship. Probably the most noticeable thing was the remarkable absence of vibration, even at the stern.

Aorangi was the only Union Steam Ship Company vessel ever to be fitted with four propellers. As with *Niagara* and *Makura*, *Aorangi* was registered in London.

Accommodation was provided for 380 first class passengers, plus 56 interchangeable between first and second class, all situated amidships, 284 second class in the after section of the liner, and 227 third class passengers located forward. Three-quarters of all the cabins were for two persons only, and in first class 50 single berth cabins. There were eight luxury suites, all decorated in a different period style, each having a marble tiled bathroom. Public rooms were particularly attractive and well laid out, with those for first class being noted for their luxury. In his book, *Famous Liners of the Eastern Oceans*, published in 1937, G W P McLachlan described the ship as follows:

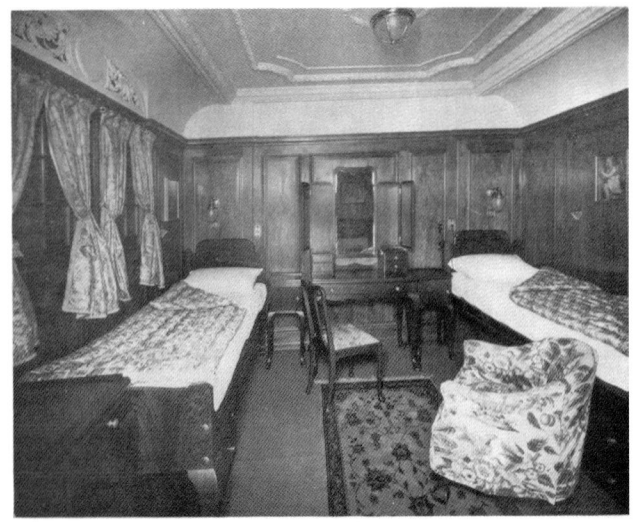

First class cabin de luxe (Ken Hall collection)

She is a handsome two-funnelled vessel, with raked stem and cruiser stern, her two masts being well raked aft, giving her a general appearance not altogether unlike that of the famous old Cunarders *Campania* and *Lucania*.

Her length is 600 ft., beam 72 ft. and depth 42 ft. 6 in., while her gross measurement is 17,491 tons. Accommodation is provided for 440 first-class, 300 second-class and 230 third-class passengers, and it is interesting to note that her name is Maori for Mount Cook, a beautiful oil painting of which eminence adorns the half-landing of the first-class stairway leading from the after end of the lounge to the gallery above.

On the promenade deck, first-class passengers have a music saloon and writing room forward, lounge amidships and smoking room and verandah cafe aft. The design of these rooms provides a happy combination of the stately dignity of historical period decoration with the comfort and hygienic practices of the present day. They form a noble suite of public apartments, all on the one floor and grouped together with through communication. Perhaps the most striking, by reason of its size and appointments, is the lounge hall, which is no less than 64 ft. in length by 43 ft. 6 in. breadth, and of unusual height, with a handsome gallery above. The Georgian scheme of decoration is architecturally and artistically carried out with a large amount of panelling and carefully designed detail, painted in varying shades of warm stone colour.

An open staircase ascends from the after end of the lounge to a gallery, the attractiveness of which is enhanced by recessed settees, wrought iron balustrading and a beautiful skylight. The adjoining smoking room, which is 34 ft. long by 25 ft. wide, is in the Jacobean style, having a stone fireplace and ingle-nook, oak furniture, English tile-pattern floor, grey-toned oak wall panelling and hanging pieces of armour. The music room is of the Louis XVI period, with everything in keeping, even to delicate French prints on the walls, walnut furniture and ormolu ornaments.

The dining saloon, in which 213 people can be seated,

First class bedstead cabin (Ken Hall collection)

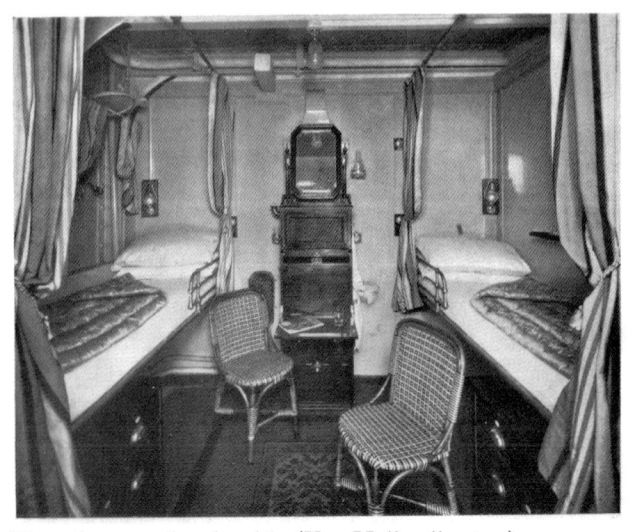

First class two-berth cabin (Ken Hall collection)

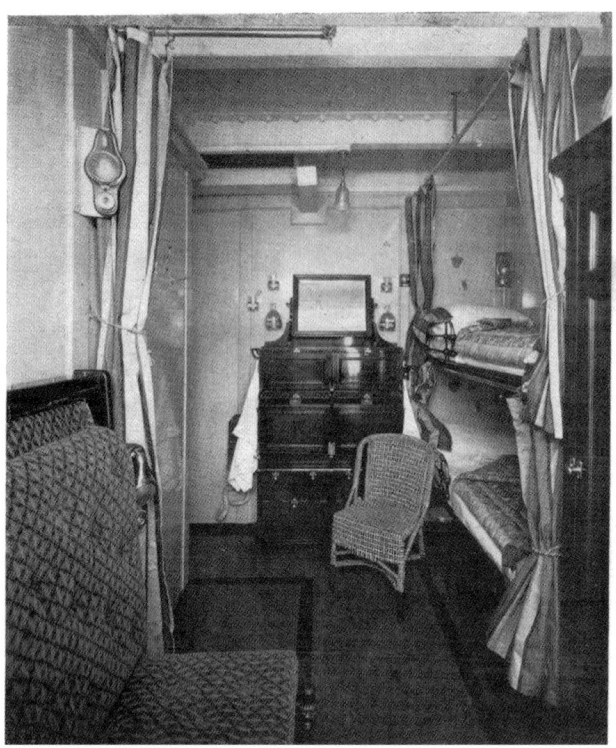

Second class cabin (Ken Hall collection)

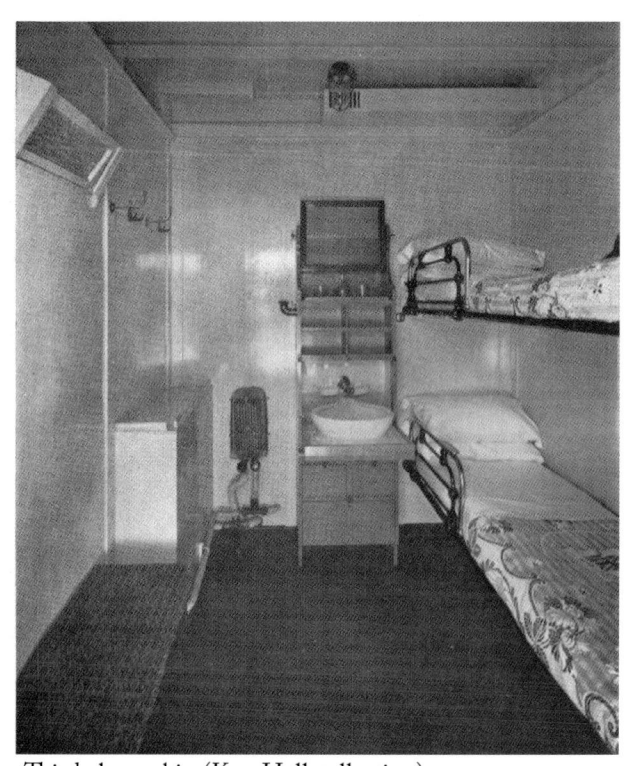

Third class cabin (Ken Hall collection)

is another Louis XVI room, with panelling painted in varying shades of Trianon grey. The cabins are roomy and airy, and no less than 11 per cent have only one berth, while 76 per cent are two-berth rooms. There are also eight special cabins de luxe, each with a marble-lined bathroom attached, on the promenade deck. These suites are all decorated in different period styles, viz., Empire, Adam, Louis XVI, Elizabethan, Queen Anne, Regency, Sheraton and Jacobean.

The propelling machinery of the *Aorangi* comprises four sets of Fairfield-Sulzer Diesel engines, each of which has six cylinders 274 in. in diameter by 39 in. stroke, working on the two-stroke cycle principle. These engines develop a total of 15,500 ihp on four shafts, turning the screws at 127 rpm and giving the vessel a speed of 18 knots.

As 1924 drew to a close, the pending introduction of *Aorangi* on the Canadian service caused a minor dislocation of the services then being operated by the Union Line to San Francisco and Vancouver. At the end of September 1924 the joint advertisement for the two services showed *Makura* scheduled to depart Sydney for Vancouver on 20 November, *Tahiti* leaving for San Francisco on 4 December, then *Niagara* to Vancouver on 18 December, *Maunganui* on 1 January 1925 and *Tahiti* on 29 January, both to San Francisco, then *Niagara* on 12 February to Vancouver. Under this arrangement, there would be no ship leaving Sydney for Vancouver in January 1925.

On 17 October there was a change to this advertisement, showing that on 16 January 1925 *Tahiti* would be leaving Sydney for both Vancouver and San Francisco. However, on 26 December there was another change, with it being indicated that *Tahiti* would be leaving from Auckland on 27 January, but passengers from Sydney for Vancouver and San Francisco would be taken by *Marama* from Sydney on 16 January to Wellington.

While all this was happening, *Tahiti* had arrived in San Francisco on 26 December, leaving on its return trip five days later, which was originally shown as going to Wellington and Sydney. After calling at Rarotonga on 12 January, *Tahiti* arrived on 19 January in Wellington, where the voyage was terminated. Meanwhile, *Marama* had left Sydney on 16 January, and arrived in Wellington on 20 January, at which time the passengers from *Tahiti* going to Sydney and the passengers from Sydney joining *Tahiti* were moved between the ships, and *Marama* left on 22 January for Sydney. On 24 January *Tahiti* left Wellington for Auckland, arriving there on 26 January, departing the next day on the Canadian-Australasian Line route to Vancouver. *Tahiti* then went down the coast to San Francisco, arriving on 18 February, leaving there a few days later for a regular Union Line voyage to Wellington and Sydney.

Aorangi's delivery voyage commenced from Southampton on 2 January 1925, but instead of proceeding to Australia, the liner crossed the Atlantic and passed through the Panama Canal. In the Pacific the liner encountered some very heavy weather, even at one time being hove to until the seas abated. *Aorangi* arrived at San Francisco on 26 January 1925, leaving the next day and arriving at Vancouver on 30 January 1925. The journey of 9,047 nautical miles was made at an average speed of seventeen knots.

Aorangi at Vancouver on its maiden voyage (John Mathieson collection)

Aorangi commenced its maiden Pacific voyage from Vancouver on 6 February, stopping for a day at Honolulu, and arriving in Auckland on Tuesday, 24 February, becoming the largest vessel to have entered the port up to that time. The *Auckland Star* carried an extensive report on the arrival of the new ship, which included the following:

The Aorangi, which made port today on her maiden voyage from England is a ship which has created worldwide interest by the fact that she is the largest motor-driven vessel afloat.

To see her gliding over the placid waters of the harbour steady as the pier to which she was due to tie, one could hardly imagine her as storm-tossed and badly buffeted by giant waves in the Pacific. Yet such was the christening the Pacific gave her when she passed out of the Panama Canal into its waters, after having made the passage across the stormy Atlantic from Southampton without shipping a sea. However, she emerged from the ordeal without any serious damage, and has made a smooth trip from Vancouver.

The huge sides of the Aorangi made a fine broadside for the mountainous seas encountered earlier on the Pacific, and they flung themselves against this new intruder with the full fury of the greatest storm her captain had ever witnessed in those waters. Some towering seas broke aboard and actually invaded the cabins, but the damage done was infinitesimal and the Aorangi emerged triumphant, though she had to be hove to.

As a rule the port health officer and the Customs officials, who look after the passports and such things, board incoming vessels when they drop anchor in the harbour, but the arrival of the big motor liner led to more expeditious arrangements. These officials went out in the Harbour Board's pilot launch Waitemata with the pilot, and met the mail steamer well outside the Rangitoto Beacon. The stranger's two funnels appeared over the horizon shortly after noon, about five miles to the east of Tiritiri, and in a comparatively few minutes she loomed up close at hand. She has a bow like an exaggerated Niagara, and from the deck of a little launch she towered up tremendously above the water.

The companion ladder, which was let down for the boarding, looked a mere pair of house-steps against the long green side of the big visitor, and the side-hatchway when one entered the ship seemed a long way from the top rail, while the commander and other officers on the high bridge suggested mountaineering. Such was the idea of the long-expected motor liner from the view-point of the Press launch.

One of the first things that struck one on stepping over the side was the distance across to the other side seemed as long as some boats one knew. Then, as you turned to the right, you came bang on what might have been a Queen Street shop for the sale of fancy goods and nick-nacks, presided over by a young lady who looked like a nurse.

Then, as one went through the spacious public rooms, one was reminded of hotels more than ships. The public rooms seemed to have received special attention from designers and decorators. Certainly they impressed one as being quite exceptional, even for a Vancouver liner. Then there are 'bureaux', all sorts of offices, and lifts and things that do not seem at all nautical. The Aorangi, in short, is like nothing so much as a small town itself.

Like the tube railways in London, everything is plainly labelled aboard the Aorangi – and there is some necessity for it. For instance, as you descend a wide oaken staircase, and look down at the mat you read in white letters on a green ground "Deck C" or whatever deck you have landed at. Every alleyway is branded, every turning is legibly marked. She is such a vast congress of shops, lounges, restaurants and unexpected places that if she were less freely labelled the Aorangi would be a very maze.

Even the spaces the deck chairs are supposed to occupy are numbered, so that the holder of deck chair No 54 can have no excuse for lolling over into the territory of No 55, no matter how obese No 54 may be, or how much room he may desire.

One would imagine that this numbering and signposting of the ship was essential if anyone making a trip of less than several months duration were to be sure of finding his way about. You might easily lose your way on board the Aorangi if she were not so well identified by labels and tags and brass plates and other things.

Studied with a nautical eye as she came up the harbour, the Aorangi did not strike one as a thing of beauty, stately as she seemed in her way, in the fashion of a "ship-shape ship." Her cruiser stern detracted from the evenness of her lines and her funnels, too, seemed small in proportion to her size. On all sides it was admitted that she was not by any means as beautiful a model as her smaller sister, the Niagara.

Looked at from her wake, however, the cruiser stern appeared to conform to the general design of the hull, which regarded as a whole is not unpicturesque, and of a model to which we are now becoming accustomed. Despite her three passenger decks, with two bridge decks rising above, the Aorangi did not appear to have anything of a top-heavy appearance. Indeed, she has all the looks of a sound, steady sea-boat, in which the traveller might find comfort during the worst weather. There seems little doubt that she will become a most popular ship with passengers.

A most peculiar circumstance marked the first coming to the port of Auckland of the new steamer. Just clearing Rangitoto in a rather stiff breeze, the bunting gaily streaming from the after mast carried away. Rounding North Head, the forward signal lines went, too, and immediately the fore-and-aft line carrying the flags, which stretched between the two masts, snapped. The Aorangi entered the harbour steaming at the rate of sixteen or seventeen knots, thus presenting a majestic picture as she swept into view of the city.

Public interest in the new arrival was amply demonstrated. On every vantage point there was a crowd of people, and hundreds stood on the ends of the King's, Central and Queen's wharves as the vessel reduced speed to dead slow and made in towards her berthing place. When she approached Queen's wharf all the ships in the harbour, large and small, joined in a deafening cock-a-doodle doo, which was continued for several minutes.

Attracted by this unaccustomed din in their lunch hour, thousands of people came rushing along from Queen Street, and speedily crowded the wharf, the only vacant portion of which was where the Aorangi was about to berth. Ships lying on the western side of the Central Wharf and on the eastern side of Queen's Wharf were invaded by eager crowds, the people overrunning them and climbing to every accessible high position in order to get a good view of the Aorangi. It must be confessed that there was a good deal of disappointment expressed, for most people expected to see something much bigger in the way of ships. Appearances are often deceptive in ships, however, and therefore it was not surprising to hear many exclamations of, "Why, she is no bigger than the Niagara!" She is, though, five thousand tons bigger, and that tonnage added to a vessel like the Niagara makes a pretty considerable ship.

This afternoon there is a great crowd exploring the Aorangi, the interior of which resembles a huge modern hotel. This evening the ship will be open to the public on payment of one shilling, the money realised to be devoted to the public charities of Auckland.

Although the number of cases of infantile paralysis are diminishing, the Union Steamship Company have decided to strictly enforce the regulations with regard to children under sixteen years of age visiting the RMS Aorangi. It is therefore understood that children will not be permitted to visit the vessel.

Apparently not everyone was thrilled to be on board the *Aorangi* for its maiden voyage, as on 25 February the following story appeared in the *Auckland Star*:

It would appear that more went on aboard the good ship Aorangi during her voyage from England than one would dream of. An amazing story was told in the Police Court this morning about two stewards who wiled away the time by flinging quantities of ship's cutlery, crockery, and general gear out of the portholes with such reckless abandon that, had the journey lasted a few months, little would have been left.

George Scott was charged with the theft of a dustpan and broom, a settee cushion, a glass tumbler, and a quantity of cutlery, while Joseph Olivier was charged that, on the high seas, he did damage a wooden drawer and steal a cushion. All the goods were the property of the Union Steamship Company. Both accused pleaded not guilty.

Jane Kennedy, a third-class passenger, stated that she had seen Scott take a glass and throw it out a porthole in the third class dining room. She had also seen him throw plates into the sea in the same manner. She remarked about it to the accused, who told witness that it was all right, because "they got a new crate of dishes in every port."

One women stated that she saw Scott fling a broom and a dustpan out the porthole, while on other occasions she had seen plates consigned to the deep. Scott told this witness that the place was a pig-hole, and received the reply that if he swept it out properly, it wouldn't be.

A third-class waiter testified to observing the accused get rid of ship's gear per medium of the porthole, while another swore to seeing him put silverware in his pocket.

D N Miller, steward of the Aorangi, said that on the voyage he began to miss cutlery and silver. He had trouble with Scott, who was later disrated. Since Scott and Olivier had been removed to the third-class, there had been practically no losses.

Regarding the charges against Olivier, Alexander Munroe, second-class steward, said that accused asked him for keys for his drawer. Witness told him that he did not have any. Later he heard a noise, and next morning found the drawer referred to smashed. Robert Ashby, Master-at-Arms, stated that accused had been interviewed regarding the drawer, and had admitted taking a spade to lever it open. In the operations, the drawer came apart. Detective McHugh gave evidence to arresting both accused. Scott denied the charges, but Olivier admitted forcing the drawer with a shovel.

"These fellows are guilty of sabotage," said the magistrate. "They take a delight in damaging other people's property, and they think it funny. They are really fanatics. Their mischief really comes back on the heads of the workers. It's a very bad case. Olivier is sentenced to one month's imprisonment and ordered to pay costs. Scott will receive three months' on the first two charges, the sentences to be cumulative. On the other charge he is convicted and discharged."

From Auckland *Aorangi* went down the east coast of North Island to arrive in Wellington at noon on 27 February, the only time the liner would visit that port. Departing Wellington on 28 February, *Aorangi* arrived in Sydney on 3 March 1925. The liner was flying flags from the foremast as it passed down the harbour, berthing at Circular Quay East, though its regular berth would be in Walsh Bay. The next day the *Sydney Morning Herald* reported:

Fifteen minutes after noon yesterday the Canadian-Australasian Royal Mail Line's new motor ship Aorangi entered Sydney Heads, having completed one of the most novel maiden voyages undertaken by any vessel in modern times. At noon the vessel was two or three miles off, and had completed a little more than 432 miles in the 24 hours, indicating a speed of about 17 knots.

The fact that the arrival of the vessel in the Quay was eagerly awaited by a very large gathering was evidence of the interest which the coming of the vessel has aroused. Gaily beflagged, the new liner made a fine picture in her berth.

The Aorangi, besides her significance as a mark of progress in ship-building and marine engineering, marks another epoch in the history of her owners, the Union Steam Ship Co of New Zealand Ltd, which next year will celebrate its jubilee. During its career the company has been noted for a number of pioneering feats in shipping. The steamer Rotomahana, which has passed into idleness after a useful career, was the first steel vessel to be built in the world. The company was the first to have Lloyd's and the Board of Trade certificates for oil firing under boilers for large passenger liners, and was the first to adopt direct driven and geared turbines for such vessels. A striking comparison is afforded between the present Aorangi and the former vessel of the same name under the Union flag, in the Pacific service. The old Aorangi, built in 1883, was of 4,268 tons gross register and 389 feet in length. The new vessel is 600 feet in length and her gross tonnage is 17,491 tons.

Many features have been included in the design of the vessel's accommodation. Eight cabins de luxe for instance, represent eight distinct periods in their furnishings. Each suite has a marble-lined bathroom, and the periods which the suites typify respectively are Sheraton, Queen Anne, Regency, Jacobean, Elizabethan, Louis XIV, Adam and Empire. The shelter deck is given over mainly to first and second class cabins, and a large proportion of the cabins throughout the ship are one and two berths. In the first class, 11 percent are single berth, 76 percent in two berth, and the remainder three berth rooms.

The vessel, in addition to her passenger accommodation, has capacity for 225,000 cubic feet of cargo, in addition to about 60,000 cubic feet available for refrigerated cargo. In her fore peak and double bottom tanks, the vessel can also carry 1,000 tons of fresh water.

A large number of well known Australians were among the passengers.

A good description of the vessel appeared in the April issue of the magazine, *The Harbour*:

The arrival of the Union Steam Ship Company's new motorship Aorangi in Sydney on March 3 was one of the most epoch making events in the history of Australian shipping, as the Aorangi is the largest motorship in the world.

The dining saloon is a spacious apartment designed after the style of the Louis XVI period, with artistic panelling painted in varying shades of Trianon grey. The well opening above is surrounded by a fine gilded wrought-iron balustrading with a large decorated tapestry panel after the manner of Boucher. The remainder of the extensive range of first-class public rooms are grouped together with through communication on the promenade deck. The first-class lounge hall is 64 feet in length by 43 feet 6 inches in breadth, and is of unusually dignified height, with a handsome gallery above. The smoke room is in the Jacobean style, with a central well skylight. There are two verandah cafes, a music room in the Louis XVI style, an auxiliary dining room for small parties, writing room, ladies room, and gymnasium. The second and third-class accommodation is also of the most approved description.

Every modern convenience for the comfort and safety of passengers has been fitted. The number of saloons and cabins with historical period decoration are particularly attractive, and in particular might be mentioned the eight

First class dining room (Ken Hall collection)

Second class dining room (Ken Hall collection)

Third class dining room (Ken Hall collection)

special cabins deluxe, every one of which represents a certain period in its furnishings.

Apart from the dining room, most of the public rooms, first and second class, are located on the promenade decks, and the promenade space to port and starboard for the first-class passengers is some 275 feet long, special provision having been made for dancing. A very handsome open staircase leads from the after end of the lounge to the gallery above, where are arranged recessed settees, the balustrading being of wrought iron.

The second-class public rooms on the promenade deck are at the after end, and comprise a lounge forward, with a ladies sitting room and a smoking room aft, separated by the main entrance. The second-class promenade space is about 100 feet in length, whilst right at the forward end of this same deck is the third-class promenade space and public rooms, and right aft, a crew's airing space.

On the boat deck above, adjoining the entrance, is a gymnasium, and forward are the captain's and deck officer's quarters, with cabins for the engineers amidships.

The shelter deck is given over mainly to first and second-class passenger cabins, with a third-class promenade forward and accommodation for part of the crew. A large proportion of the cabins throughout the ship, both first and second-class, are of the single and two-berth type, 11 per cent of the first-class passengers being in single berth, and 76 per cent in two-berth cabins, whilst the remainder are accommodated in three-berth cabins.

The dining saloons are all on the upper deck, the first-class being amidships, the second-class aft, and the third-class forward. On this deck is the main first class entrance, which has a very commodious appearance, the office being on the port side, and a large day nursery on the starboard side. Adjoining the latter is a separate room, which may be used as a private dining saloon, or as a dining room for children in the daytime. The first-class dining room seats 213, the second-class 180 and the third-class 144, small tables being a prominent feature of the two former.

A broadcasting system has been provided, so that music, speeches etc, can be transmitted from the central position to all the first, second and third-class public rooms, as well as the first-class lounge. A telephone exchange has been fitted in the bureau with communications between all the principal officers of the ship, while there are a number of loud-speaking telephones for navigation purposes, an enclosed telephone box being arranged in the engine room.

On the boat deck, each boat is controlled by a separate set of davits which are of the new Maclachlan automatic design, and are able to place all the boats in the water in a few minutes. There are sixteen of these gravity davits, 14 of which operate large single lifeboats with a capacity of 86 persons. One handles a motor boat carrying 50 people, and the remaining one is a 28 foot emergency lifeboat, capable of carrying 56 people. The advantage claimed with this installation is that the total complement of passengers is accommodated in single lifeboats directly attached to davits.

The four sets of diesel engines which comprise the main propelling machinery are of the Fairfield-Sulzer type, each having six cylinders, 27½ inch diameter by 39 inch stroke, working on the two-stroke principle, and in order to meet the special requirements of a fast passenger liner, the usual standard Sulzer type of engine has in some respects been modified. Considerations of propeller efficiency necessitated a relatively high speed of revolution, and on the surface the shafts will be turning about 127rpm when developing a total of 19,000 ihp.

Her auxiliaries include a Clayton fire extinguishing apparatus, the Stone system of hydraulically-controlled water-tight doors, Stone spring-balanced windows, and six propellers of Stone's manganese bronze. A Sperry gyro-compass of the latest type, also steering and bearing repeaters, and a Sperry continuous course recorder are fitted, while she is also equipped with the Sperry gyro-pilot for steering the vessel automatically.

In advertisements for the Canadian-Australian Royal Mail Line service from Sydney to Vancouver, it was stated that:

> The magnificent and luxuriously appointed new quadruple screw motor ship AORANGI, 18,000 tons register, 23,000 tons displacement, will leave SYDNEY on 12th March, 1925, and AUCKLAND on 17th March, on her maiden voyage in the Vancouver service. Spacious decks, beautifully designed public rooms, special staterooms, verandah café, electric passenger lifts, and every modern convenience. All cabins fitted with natural and forced ventilation by ozonified air.

While *Aorangi* was the first of a new breed of fast large liners powered by diesel engines, it was run on a schedule more suited to the older, slower vessels. As a result *Aorangi* consistently gained on the timetables, often arriving hours ahead of schedule. On the 'short' legs, such as the 2,400 miles between Honolulu and Vancouver, which was scheduled to take six and a half days, *Aorangi* would easily gain twelve hours on the schedule.

At the end of each voyage *Aorangi* would spend five days in Vancouver and five days in Sydney, of which thirty six hours at each port would be spent on disinfecting the ship. During the first year's operation the average speed of *Aorangi* was 16.54 knots with a daily fuel consumption of 53-56 tons which included fuel for the diesel engines, refrigerating plant, heating and laundry operations.

As marine diesels were still in their infancy when *Aorangi* was built, the propulsion system had not yet been perfected, and it was found that a considerable amount of work was constantly required to keep the ship going. Having four engines, it did not create a major problem when problems arose in one, as the ship could maintain its service speed on three engines. When a piston was damaged in one engine

First class nursery (Ken Hall collection)

First class verandah café (Ken Hall collection)

Second class lounge (Ken Hall collection)

Maunganui made one trip to Vancouver (WSS Vic)

installed within five hours, and the stopped engine brought back into service.

With the arrival of *Aorangi*, *Makura* was no longer required on the Canadian service, and left Sydney on 12 February on its final voyage on the route, departing Vancouver for the last time on 11 March, arriving in Sydney on 4 April.

Makura was then transferred to the San Francisco route to partner *Tahiti*, and *Maunganui* reverted to the trans-Tasman trade once again. However, when *Niagara* arrived in Sydney on 27 May 1927 it was withdrawn from service for an overhaul, being replaced by *Maunganui* for one round trip to Vancouver, the only voyage this vessel would make to the Canadian port.

Maunganui departed Sydney on 2 June, returning on 23 July. The Union Line had no other employment for the liner, so on 26 July *Maunganui* left Sydney for Wellington, where it arrived four days later and was laid up. Three months later *Maunganui* was reactivated and returned to the Tasman trade.

Towards the end of 1927 *Aorangi*'s engines were overhauled for the first time since entering service. To this point the ship had voyaged just over 200,000 nautical miles at an average speed of 16.44 knots. A total of 12,224 engine hours had been run up with an average daily fuel consumption of 45.8 tons for propelling purposes only. By December 1927 the overhaul was complete and the *Aorangi* returned to its regular sailings.

The Vancouver service operated with great regularity, and it was very seldom that either *Aorangi* or *Niagara* rated a mention in the newspapers unless something went wrong. One such occasion was at the end of June 1929, when *Aorangi* arrived in Sydney with a passenger suffering from smallpox on board. As the *Sydney Morning Herald* reported on 25 June 1929:

Consternation was caused among health officials in Sydney yesterday when it was discovered that a case of smallpox had developed on board the motorship Aorangi during the voyage from Vancouver to Sydney.

It was established at the Coast Hospital yesterday that Athol Thomas, of Perth, one of the contingent of Young Australia League boys who had arrived by the ship on Saturday, had contracted the disease. He was removed from the hospital to the quarantine station at North Head yesterday afternoon.

Another member of the contingent was also taken to North Head last night and will be kept under observation. The second boy, who comes from Queensland, was taken ill at an early stage of the voyage across the Pacific and had recovered sufficiently to walk ashore. Both patients were examined at Suva and at Auckland by the port medical authorities, who certified that they were suffering from chicken-pox.

After Thomas was removed to the Coast Hospital the disease developed so rapidly that it was possible to diagnose his condition definitely as smallpox. Since the Aorangi has been given a clean bill of health at Sydney, all of the 488 passengers and many of the 341 members of the crew had left the ship. They were all "contacts" as defined by the Federal Health Act, and officials of the Health Department moved promptly to prevent a possible spread of the infection. The co-operation of the Union Steamship Company was sought, and passengers still in Sydney were directed to report to the Federal health offices. There were many hurried telephone calls, and early in the afternoon the first group of passengers presented themselves for vaccination.

By dusk more than 200 people had been vaccinated. Late arrivals were instructed to report this morning, when it is almost certain that the requirements of the Act will be met by the remainder of the Sydney passengers.

The few members of the Aorangi's crew who had not been vaccinated by the ship's medical officer during recent voyages were among those treated, and notices to attend were also served on people whose business had taken them to the ship when it reached port.

On 26 June 1930 *Aorangi* sailed from Sydney for Canada with the Australian team for the 1930 Commonwealth Games aboard, the team reaching their final destination of Hamilton on 23 July.

Aorangi

Chapter Fourteen

From San Francisco to Wellington

When *Aorangi* replaced *Makura* on the Vancouver service, the older vessel was given an extensive refit to suit it for the San Francisco trade, the accommodation being altered to cater for 207 first class, 114 second class and 72 third class passengers. On 23 April 1925, *Makura* departed Sydney for Wellington, Tahiti and San Francisco, where it berthed on 15 May.

At the end of 1925, American writer Zane Grey, famous for his novels set in the American west, embarked on *Makura* for his first trip to New Zealand, to pursue his great passion for fishing, and wrote about the voyage:

There is always something wonderful about a new fishing adventure trip – for a single day, or for a week, or for months. The enchantment never palls. For years on end I have been trying to tell why, but that has been futile. Fishing is like Jason's quest for the Golden Fleece. On December thirtieth, when I stood on the deck of the Royal Mail SS Makura, steaming out through the Golden Gate bound for the Antipodes to seek new waters, the same potent charm pervaded my being. There was a Lorelei calling from the South Seas; there was a siren bell ringing from the abysmal deep.

San Francisco Bay at that hour was a far cry from the turquoise-blue water of the tropics. A steely sun made pale bright light upon the ruffled bay; gray fog shrouded the dome of Mt Tamalpais; from the northwest a cold wind drove down on the bare brown hills to whip the muddy water into a choppy sea. The broken horizon line of the beautiful city of hills shone dark against the sky. A flock of screaming gulls sailed and swooped about the stern of the vessel. A big French freighter kept abreast of the Makura through the Golden Gate, then turned north, while we headed to the southwest.

The Royal Mail ship Makura was no leviathan, but she certainly was a greyhound of the sea. In less than an hour I saw the mountains fade into the fog. That last glimpse of California had to suffice me for a long time. We ran into a heavy-ridged sea, cold and dark, with sullen whitecaps breaking. I walked the decks, watching as always, until the sky became overspread with dark clouds, and a chill wind drove me inside.

That night after dinner I went out again. The sky was dark, the sea black, except for the pale upheavals of billows which gleamed through the obscurity. The ship was rushing on, now with a graceful, slow forward dip and then with a long rise. She was very steady. Great swells crashed against her bows and heaved back into the black gulfs. There was a continuous roar of chafing waters. An old familiar dread of the ocean mounted in me again. What a mighty force! It was a cold, wintry almost invisible sea, not conducive to the thrill and joy of the angler. It was a northern sea, gusty, turbulent, with rough swells. I leaned over the rail in the darkness, trying to understand its meaning, its mood, trying to be true to the love I bore it in tranquil moments.

Next morning when I went out the decks were wet, the sky gray, except low down in the east where rays of sunlight slipped through to brighten the cold gray buffeting sea. I noted several sea birds following in the wake of the ship. They were new to me. Dark in color, marvelously built, with small compact bodies, sharp as a bullet, and with long narrow wings, they appeared to have been created for perfect control of the air. They sailed aloft and swooped down, skimmed the foamy crests, rode abreast of the rough seas, and dipped into the hollows, all apparently without slightest effort of wing. I did not see them flap a wing once. This is a common habit of many sea birds, especially the shearwaters, but I had never before seen it performed so swiftly and wonderfully. These birds had a wing spread of three feet, and must have belonged to the shearwater family. Lonely wanderers of the barren waste of waters!

Morning and afternoon swiftly passed, the hours flying with the speed of the Makura over the waves. Toward sunset, which was only a dim ruddy glow behind the fog banks, the chill wind, the darkening sea, the black somber fading light, all predicted storm. The last daylight hours of the last day of 1925 were melancholy and drear. I was reminded of November back in Lackawaxen, Pennsylvania, where so often I heard the autumn winds wail under the eaves, and the rain pelt the roof -- mournful prelude to winter.

This rough sea was like that of the north, where off the rugged shores of Puget Sound the contending tides are raw and bold. The winter twilight quickly merged into the blanket of night. Then out there in the opaque blackness the sea roared by the ship, tremendous and inscrutable, with nothing to inspire love, with everything to confound the soul of man. What was the old year to the sea, or the new year soon to dawn with its imagined promise, its bright face, its unquenchable hope? Nevertheless, the thought that overbalanced this depression was of the magic isles of the South Seas, set like mosaics in the eternal summer blue, and the haunting Antipodes, seven thousand miles down the lanes of the Pacific.

All morning of the third day out the Makura sped on over a lumpy leaden sea, mirroring the gray of the sky. How tenaciously the drab shadow of winter clung to us! Yet there had come some degree of warmth, and on the afternoon of this day the cold wind departed. When the sunlight strayed through the fog, it gave the sea its first tinge of blue; but the sun shone only fitfully. There was no life on the sea, and apparently none in it. Neither bird nor fish showed to long-practised eyes. I wondered about this. We were hundreds of miles offshore, out of the track of the schools of sardines and anchovies that birds and fish prey upon. Still there should have been some manifestation of life. How vast the ocean! Were its spaces and depths utterly barren? That was hard to believe.

Sunset that night was rose and gold, a gorgeous color thrown upon a thin webbed mass of mackerel cloud that for long held its radiance. It seemed to be a promise of summer weather. Sunrise next morning likewise was a blazing belt of gold. But these rich colorings were ephemeral and deceiving. The sky grew dark and gray. From all points masses of cumulous clouds rose above the horizon, at last to unite in a canopy of leaden tones. A wind arose and the sea with it. The air still had an edge.

All day the Makura raced over a magnificent sea of long swells rising to white breaking crests. The ship had a slow careen, to and fro, from side to side, making it difficult to walk erect and steadily. The turbulent mass of water was almost black. Its loneliness was as manifest as when calm. No sail! No smoke from steamer down beyond the horizon! No sign of fish or bird! I seemed to have been long on board. The immensity of the sea began to be oppressive. That day and the next we drove on over a gray squally expanse of waters.

The time came when I saw my first flying fish of the trip. It was an event. He appeared to be a tiny little fellow, steely in color, scarcely larger than a humming bird. But for me he meant life on the ocean. Thereafter while on deck I kept watch. We had sunshine for a few hours and then the warmth became evident. The sea was a raging buffeting rolling plain of dark blue and seething white. We were a thousand miles and more off the coast, where I felt sure the wind always blew. We were in the track of the trade winds.

On the sixth day the air became humid. We had reached the zone of summer. Every mile now would carry us toward the tropics. I saw some porpoises, small yellow ones, active in flight. They were a proof of fish, for porpoises seldom roam far away from their food supply. I wondered if they preyed upon the tiny flying fish. Swift as the porpoise is, I doubt that he could catch them. As we sped south I noted more and more schools of flying fish, rising in a cloud, like silvery swallows. Presently I espied

Makura

one that appeared larger, with reddish wings. This was a surprise, and I thought I had made a mistake as I had not a really good look at it. Not long afterward, however, I saw another, quite close, and made certain of the red wings. Then soon following I espied three more of the same species. They certainly could sail and glide and dart over the rough water.

We ran into a squall. Rain and spray wet my face as I paced the deck. Out ahead the gray pall was like a bank of fog. The sea became rougher. Our wireless brought news of a hurricane raging over the South Seas, centering around the Samoan Islands, where tidal waves had caused much damage. What had become of the tranquil Pacific? Late that afternoon we ran out of the squalls into a less-disturbed sea.

On the morning of January sixth before daybreak we crossed the equator. I went out on deck before sunrise. Sea and sky were radiant with a pearly effulgence. There were no reds, purples or golds. White and silver, gray and pearl predominated, which colors intensified as the sun came up, giving a beautiful effect. All around the horizon the trade-wind clouds rode like sails. They had the same ship-like shape, the same level bottoms and round windblown feathery margins as the trade-wind clouds above the Gulf Stream between Cuba and the Keys but not the color! Sunrise off the Keys of Florida is a glorious burst of crimson and gold that flames sky and sea.

We were now in the southern hemisphere, and I felt that it would be interesting for me to note the slow march of the sun to the north. On the equator the sun always sets at six o'clock. So far the voyage had been remarkably free of glaring white sunlight. This day when we crossed the equator we had alternately bright sunlight and soft gray-shaded sky.

The night we entered the Tuamotu Archipelago, or Low Islands, I had a striking sight of the planet Venus, so extraordinarily beautiful and incredibly bright in that latitude. The great star was exceedingly brilliant, yet not white; it had color, almost a gold or red, and left a shining track over the waters almost like that of the moon. Sometimes it seemed like a huge lantern hung close to the ship; again it retreated to the very rim of the world. Then how swiftly it went down into the sea! Another phenomenon I had noted lately was the singularly swift sunset, and the extreme brevity of light afterward.

There are two kinds of islands in the South Pacific, the low and the high. The former consist of atolls with their circular ridge of white sand above the coral, fringed with cocoanut palms; and the latter, mountains of volcanic origin, are characterised by high peaks densely overgrown with tropical verdure. The Paumotus are a vast aggregation of low islands, or atolls, sprinkled all over a great range of water. Yachts are forbidden to adventure in this perilous archipelago. The charts cannot be trusted, the currents are treacherous, the winds more contrary than anywhere else on the globe. Yet the course of the SS Makura ran straight through the archipelago. Probably many atolls were passed close at hand, wholly invisible from the deck; and it was only at the latter part of the long run through, that the course came anywhere near the clustered islands that gave the place its name.

My first and long-yearned-for sight of an atoll came about mid-afternoon on January eighth. I saw with naked eyes what most passengers were using marine glasses to distinguish. It was a low fringe of cocoanut-palm trees rising out of the blue sea. What a singular first impression I had! This islet, or atoll, was the first of many of the Tuamotu Archipelago that were soon to rise gradually out of the heaving blue floor of the ocean. They appeared like green growths on a Hindu magician's carpet. Most were small with just a few trees fringing the sky line; but some were long and large, with thick groves of cocoanut palms. It was impossible, of course, to distinguish these atolls from the Keys of the Florida Peninsula or the islets of the Caribbean Sea. The great beauty of an atoll cannot be seen from afar. The ring of coral sand rising just above the sea, the ring of cocoanuts round it, the ring of turquoise-blue water inside, the ever-framed lagoon, blue as the sky, serene and tranquil, with its sands of gold and pearl, its myriads of colored fish, the tremendous thundering of the surf outside -- these wonderful features could not be appreciated from the ship.

I went up on the third deck where I could see the strips of white beach and the bright-green band of palms. These Paumotus surely called with all the mystery and glory of the South Pacific; but our ship passed swiftly on her way and soon night blotted out sight of the fascinating atolls.

Next morning I was up before dawn. The ship was moving very slowly. I could scarcely hear any sound of swirling waters. I went out on deck in the dim opaque gloom of a South Pacific dawn. The air was fresh, cool, balmy, laden with a scent of land. On the starboard side I saw a black mountain, rising sharp with ragged peaks. This island was Moorea, the first of the Society group.

Soon dead ahead appeared the strange irregular form of Tahiti. It made a marvelous spectacle, with the rose of the east kindling low down in a notch between two peaks. Tahiti was high. I watched the day come and the sun rise over this famous island, and it was indescribable. We went through a gateway in the barrier reef, where the swells curled and roared, and on into the harbor to the French port, Papeete.

Seen from the deck of a vessel Papeete was beautiful, green and luxurious, with its colored roofs, its blossoming trees, its schooners and other South Sea craft moored along the shore. The rise of the island, however, its ridged slopes of emerald green and amber red, its patches of palms, its purple canyons streaked with white waterfalls, its ragged, notched, bold peaks crowned with snowy clouds -- these made a spectator forget that Papeete nestled at its base.

I spent a full day in this world-famed South Sea Island port, the French Papeete. It was long enough for me! Despite all I had read I had arrived there free of impressions, with eager receptive mind. I did not wonder that Robert Louis Stevenson went to the South Seas a romancer and became a militant moralist. It was not fair, however, to judge other places through contact with Papeete.

The French have long been noted for the careless and slovenly way in which they govern provinces. Papeete is a good example. There is no restriction against the Chinese, who appeared to predominate in business. Papeete is also the eddying point for all the riffraff of the South Seas. The beach comber, always a romantic if pathetic figure in my memory, through the South Sea stories I have read, became by actual contact somewhat disconcerting to me, and wholly disgusting. Perhaps I did not see any of the noble ruins.

Every store I entered in Papeete was run by a crafty-eyed little Chinaman. I heard that the Chinese merchants had all the money. It was no wonder. I saw very few French people. I met one kindly-looking priest. All the whites who fell under my gaze seemed to me to be sadly out of place there. They were thin, in most cases pale and unhealthy-looking. It was plain to me that the Creator did not intend white men to live on South Sea Islands. If he had he would have made the pigment of their skins capable of resisting the sun.

This was the early summer for Tahiti. It was hot. New York at 99 degrees in the shade, or Needles, California, at 115 degrees, would give some idea of heat at Papeete. It was a moist, sticky, oppressive, enervating heat that soon prostrated. I always could stand hot weather, and I managed to get around under this. But many of the ship passengers suffered, and by five o'clock that evening were absolutely exhausted.

What amazed me was the fact that this heat did not prevent the drinking of liquor. Champagne and other beverages were exceedingly cheap at Papeete. I found out long ago that a great many people who think they travel to see and learn really travel to eat and drink, and the close of this day on shore at Papeete provided a melancholy example of the fact. If I saw one bottle of liquor come aboard the SS Makura I saw a hundred. Besides such openly avowed bottles, there were cases and cases packed up in the companionway for delivery.

I visited the hotel or resort made famous mostly through Mr O'Brien's book, White Shadows of the South Seas. Luxurious growths of green and wonderfully fragrant flowers surrounded this little low house of many verandas; but that was about all I could see attractive there. It appeared different classes of drinkers had different rooms in which to imbibe. Of those I passed, some approached what in America we would call a dive. It is all in the way people look at a thing. The licentiousness of women and the availability of wine rank high in the properties of renown.

The Tahitian women presented an agreeable surprise to me. From all the exotic photographs I had seen I had not been favorably impressed. But photographs do not do justice to Tahitian women. I saw hundreds of them, and except in a few cases, noticeably the dancers, who in fact were faked to impress the tourists, they were modestly dressed and graceful in appearance. They were strong, well built though not voluptuous, rather light-skinned and not at all suggesting negroid blood. They presented a new race to me. They had large melting melancholy eyes. They wore their hair in braids down their backs, like American schoolgirls of long ago when something of America still survived in our girls. These Tahitians had light-brown, sometimes nut-brown and chestnut hair, rich and thick and beautiful. What a delight to see! What pleasure to walk behind one of these barefooted and free-stepping maidens just for the innocent happiness of gazing at her wonderful braid! No scrawny shaved bristled necks, such as the flappers exhibit now, to man's bewildered disgust; no erotic and abnormal signs of wanting to resemble a male! Goodness only knows why so-called civilized white women of modern times want to look like men, but so it seems they do. If they could see the backs of the heads of these Tahitian girls and their long graceful braids of hair, that even a fool of a man could tell made very little trouble, and was so exquisitely feminine and beautiful, they might have a moment of illumined mind.

The scene at the dock as the S.S. Makura swung off was one I shall not soon forget. Much of Papeete was there, except, most significantly, the Chinese. No doubt they were busily counting the enormous number of French francs they had amassed during the day. The watchers in the background were quiet and orderly, and among these were French ladies who were bidding friends farewell, and other white people whose presence made me divine they were there merely to watch a ship depart for far shores. A ship they longed to be aboard. I could read it in their eyes.

In the foreground, however, were many Tahitian women and some half caste, with the loud-mouthed roustabouts who were raving at the drunken louts on board the ship. It was not a pretty sight. Near me on the rail sat an inebriated youth, decorated with flowers, waving a champagne bottle at those below. I did not see any friendliness in the uplifted dark eyes. This was only another ship going on down to the sea; and I thought most of those on board were held in contempt by those on land.

I did not leave Papeete, however, without most agreeable and beautiful impressions. Outside of the town there were the simplicity and beauty of the native habitations and the sweetness of the naked little Tahitians disporting on the beach. There were the magnificence of the verdure, foliage and flowers and the heavy atmosphere languorous with fragrance. There were the splendour of the surf breaking on the reef seen through the stately cocoanut palms, the burn of the sun and the delicious cool of the shade. There were the utter and ever-growing strangeness of the island and the unknown perceptions that were gradually building up an impression of the vastness of the South Sea. There were the splendor of Nature in her most lavish moods and the unsolvable mystery of human life.

I saw many old Tahitian men who I imagined had eaten human flesh, "long pig", as they called it in their day. The record seemed written in their great strange eyes.

Birds and fish were almost negligible at Tahiti. For all the gazing that I put in I saw only a few small needle fish. Not a shark, not a line, not a break or swirl on the surface! There were no gulls, no sea birds of any kind, and I missed them very much. I saw several small birds about the size of robins, rather drab-colored with white on their wings, black heads and yellow beaks. They were tame and had a musical note.

On the next day out from Papeete we saw steamship smoke on the horizon. It grew into the funnel of a ship,

R.M.S. TAHITI	R.M.S. MAKURA	R.M.S. NIAGARA	R.M.M.S. AORANGI
7,898 tons	8,075 tons	13,415 tons	17,491 tons

(Above) This painting of the four Union Line vessels operating to San Francisco and Vancouver appeared in a brochure produced in the 1920s (Ken Hall collection)

(Below) Stan Stefaniak painting of *Aorangi* and *Tahiti* departing Sydney

(Above) J E Hobbs painting of *Niagara* (Museum of Wellington City and Sea)

(Below) J E Hobbs painting of the second *Aorangi* (Museum of Wellington City and Sea)

(Above) Stan Stefaniak painting of *Mariposa* berthed in Circular Quay and *Aorangi* passing under the Sydney Harbour Bridge on the afternoon of 25 February 1932

(Below) W W Stewart painting of the famous race across the Tasman Sea in June 1938 involving *Awatea* and *Mariposa*

(Above) John Bradley painting of *Monterey* passing under the Sydney Harbour Bridge in the early years of World War Two

(Below) J E Hobbs painting of *Awatea* (Museum of Wellington City and Sea)

then the hull, and at last the bulk of the sister ship of the Makura, the Tahiti. She passed us perhaps five miles away, a noble sight, and especially fascinating because she was the only traveling craft on our horizon throughout the voyage.

A little after daybreak on the following morning I was awakened by the steward, who said Rarotonga was in sight. From a distance this island appeared to be a cone-shaped green mass rising to several high sharp-toothed peaks. Near at hand, in the glory of the sunrise, it looked like a beautiful mountain, verdant and colorful, rising out of a violet sea. I noted the extremely sharp serrated ridges rising to the peaks, all thickly covered with tropic verdure. The island appeared to be surrounded by a barrier reef, against which the heaving sea burst into white breakers.

Schools of flying fish, darting like swarms of silver bees, flew from before our bows. That was a promising sight, for usually where there are schools of small fish the great game fish will be found. Here, as at Tahiti, there was a marked absence of birds.

After Papeete, the weather was delightfully cool. The Makura anchored outside the reef, half a mile from shore, and small launches with canoe-shaped lighters carried cargo and passengers through a narrow gate in the reef to the docks.

Rarotonga was under English control, and certainly presented an inspiring contrast to the decadent and vitiated Papeete. At once we were struck with the cleanliness of streets and wharfs, and the happy, care-free demeanor of the natives. They looked prosperous, and we were to learn that they all owned their bit of cocoanut grove and were independent. We drove around the island, a matter of twenty miles more or less. The road was level and shady all the way, with the violet white-wreathed sea showing through the cocoanut trees on one side and the wonderful sharp peaks rising above the forest on the other.

There were places as near paradise as it has been my good fortune to see. Flowers were as abundant as in a conservatory, with red and white blossoms prevailing. Children ran from every quarter to meet us, decorated with wreaths and crowns of flowers, and waving great bunches of the glorious bloom. They were bright-eyed merry children, sincere in their welcome to the visitors. Some of the native houses were set in open glades, where wide-spreading, fern-leaved trees blazing with crimson blossoms were grouped about the green shady lawns. The glamour of the beautiful colors was irresistible. The rich thick amber light of June in some parts of the United States had always seemed to me to be unsurpassable; but compared with the gold-white and rose-pink lights of Rarotonga it grew pale and dull in memory. The air was warm, fragrant, languorous. It seemed to come from eternal summer. Everywhere sounded the wash of the surf of the reef. You could never forget the haunting presence of the ocean.

After our trip round the island we spent a couple of hours on the beach with the natives. This was in the center of the town. A continual stream of natives strolled and rode by. Their colored garments added to the picturesque attraction of the place. On the reef just outside could be seen the bones of a schooner sticking from the surface; and farther out the ironwork of a huge ship that had been wrecked there years ago. They seemed grim reminders of the remorselessness of the azure sea. The atmosphere of the hour was one of sylvan summer, the gentle and pleasant warmth of the South Seas, the idle, happy tranquillity of a place favored by the gods; but only a step out showed the naked white teeth of the coral reef, and beyond that the inscrutable and changeful sea.

We bought from the natives until our limited stock of English money ran out. Then we were at the pains of seeing the very best of the pearls, baskets, bead necklaces and hatbands, fans and feathers, exhibited for our edification. These natives found their tongues after a while and talked in English very well indeed. What a happy contrast from the melancholy shadow-faced Tahitians!

It was interesting to learn that liquor is prohibited at Rarotonga. If any evidence were needed in favor of prohibition, here it was in the beautiful healthy wholesome life on Rarotonga. Indeed, everyone appeared charmed with the beauty, color, simplicity and happiness of this island. "By Jove! Rarotonga is just what I wanted a South Sea Island to be!" was the felicitous way Mr Radmore put it. Absolutely this charm would grow on one. It might not do to spend a long time at Rarotonga. But I decided that some day I would risk coming for a month or two. We learned that at certain seasons fish were plentiful, especially the giant swordfish. Among the other islands of the Cook group was one over a hundred miles from Rarotonga, rarely visited by whites, and said to be exquisitely beautiful and wonderful.

One of the passengers who boarded the Makura at Rarotonga was Dr Lambert, head of the Rockefeller Foundation in the South Seas. He was an exceedingly interesting man to meet. He had been eight years in the islands, and knew the native life as well as anyone living. He called Papeete an uncovered brothel; and indeed had no good word for any of the French islands. It was of no use, he claimed, to try to interest the French in improvements; and therefore he had not been able to let the Tahitians and Marquesans benefit by the splendid work being done by the foundation.

On Tuesday, January thirteenth, we crossed the 180th meridian, and somewhere along there we were to drop a day, lose it entirely out of the week! I imagine that day should have been Tuesday, but the steamship company, no doubt for reasons of its own, made Saturday the day. How queer to go to bed Friday night and wake up Sunday morning! Where would the Saturday have flown? I resolved to put it down to the mysteries of latitude and longitude.

There was another thing quite as strange, yet wholly visible, and that was the retreat of the sun toward the north; imperceptibly at first, but surely. I saw the sun rise north of east and set north of west. As the Makura rushed tirelessly on her way, this northward trend of the sun became more noticeable. It quite changed my world; turned me upside down. How infinitely vast and appalling seem the earth and the sea! Yet they are but dots in the universe. Verily a traveler sees much to make him think.

There were two pearl traders on the Makura who had

boarded the ship at Rarotonga. One of them, Drury Low, had not been off his particular island for fifteen years. He was a strange low-voiced new type of man to me. I think he was Scotch. He lived at Aitutaki Island, one of the Cook group, said to be the loveliest island in the South Seas. His companion's name was McCloud. They gave me information concerning a great game fish around Aitutaki Island. They excited my curiosity to such extent that I got out photographs of yellow-fin tuna, broadbill swordfish, Marlin swordfish, and sailfish. To my amazement these men identified each, and assured me positively that these species were common in the Cook Islands. They also described to me what must be a sawfish, native to these waters. The yellow-fin tuna was called varu in the Cook Islands, walu in the Fijis, and grew to large size. Low saw one caught recently weighing one hundred and six pounds, and knew of others over a hundred. These were caught on hand-lines, trolling outside the reef. Recently a large one was hooked, and bitten in two by a shark. The smaller part that was hauled in weighed over two hundred.

Never shall I forget my first absolutely certain sight of an albatross. It was on the afternoon of January fifteenth about two o'clock. I heard some one speaking of a wonderful bird following the ship, so I at once ran out. Wonderful bird? How futile are words! When I saw this sea bird of Ancient Mariner fame I just gasped, "Oh! Grand!" But then I have an unusual love for birds.

The albatross had a white body and brown wings that spread ten feet from tip to tip. They were a lighter color underneath. The breast, back and head were pure white; the body appeared to be as large as that of a goose; the head had something of an eagle shape, seen at such a distance. From head to tail there was a slight bow, sometimes seen in sea gulls. But it was the wing spread, the vast bow-shaped, marvelous wings that so fascinated me. I had watched condors, eagles, vultures, falcons, hawks, kites, frigate birds, terns, boobies, all the great performers of the air, but I doubted that I had ever seen the equal of the albatross. What sailing! What a swoop! What splendid poise and ease, and then incredible speed! The albatross would drop back a mile from the ship, and then all in a moment, it seemed, he had caught up again. I watched him through my glass. I devoured him. I yearned to see him close. How free, how glorious! I wondered if that bird had a soul such as Coleridge would endow him with. If dogs were almost human in their understanding of men, why could not wild birds have something as unusual? The albatross had always haunted me, inspired me, filled me with awe, reverence.

Late in the afternoon I espied another albatross, or at least one that on nearer view looked different. I climbed to the top deck and went aft to the stern rail, where I had an hour of delight in watching him from an unobstructed vantage point. The markings differed enough to convince me it might be another albatross. The body was flecked with brown, the neck ringed with the same color; the head like that of a frigate bird, only very much larger; the bill yellow, long and hooked. There was a dark marking on the white tail; the backs of the wings were dark brown, almost black, and the under side cream white except for black tips. He surely was a beautiful and majestic bird, lord of the sea. Where he swooped down from a height, he turned on his side so that one wing tip skimmed the waves and the other stood straight up. He sailed perpendicularly. He was ponderous, graceful, swift. A few motions of the wide wings sent him sailing, careening, swooping. He appeared tireless, as if the air was his native element, as no doubt it is, more than the sea. Once he alighted like a feather, keeping his large wings up, as if not to wet them. When he launched himself again it was to run on the water, like a shearwater, until he had acquired momentum enough to keep him up. Then he lifted himself clear.

Sunday morning at ten, January seventeenth, I sighted land. New Zealand! High pale cliffs rising to dark mountain ranges in the background swept along the western horizon as far as I could see. Wellington, our port of debarkation, was a red-roofed city on hills surrounding a splendid bay. It had for me a distinctly foreign look, different from any city I had ever seen before; a clean, cold, tidy look, severe and substantial.

From Wellington to Auckland was a long ride of fifteen hours, twelve of which were daylight. The country we traversed had been cut and burned over, and reminded me of the lumbered districts of Washington and Oregon. One snow-capped mountain, Tongariro, surrounded at the base by thick, green forests, was really superb; and the active cone-shaped volcano, Ngauruhoe, held my gaze as long as I could see it. A thick column of white and yellow steam or smoke rose from the crater and rolled away with the clouds.

Auckland appeared to be a more pretentious city than the capital; and it likewise was built upon hills. It is New Zealand's hub of industry. From Auckland to Russell was another long day's ride, over partly devastated country and part sylvan, which sustains well the sheep and cattle of the stations thereabout. Farms and villages were numerous. The names of the latter were for me unpronounceable and unrememberable. They were all Maori names. At Opua, the terminus of the railroad, we took a boat for Russell. We were soon among picturesque islands above which the green mountains showed against the sky.

Russell turned out to be a beautiful little hamlet, the oldest in the island, and one with which were connected many historical events. The bay resembled that of Avalon, having a crescent-shaped beach and a line of quaint white houses. It is a summer resort, and children and bobbed-haired girls were much in evidence. The advent of the ZG outfit was apparently one of moment, to judge from the youngsters. They were disappointed in me, however, for they frankly confessed they had expected to see me in sombrero, chaps, spurs and guns. Young ladies of the village, too, were disappointed, for they had shared with people all over the world the illusion that the author Zane Grey was a woman. I found there in the stores, as at Wellington and Auckland, the English editions of my books.

Chapter Fifteen

Disaster on Sydney Harbour

The Union Line San Francisco service continued to be operated by *Tahiti* and *Makura*, with monthly departures from Sydney. On the afternoon of Friday, 3 November 1927, *Tahiti*, under the command of Captain Basil Aldwell, left its wharf in Darling Harbour at the start of another voyage across the Pacific, and as it departed there was an incident on the wharf, which was reported in the *Sydney Morning Herald* as followed:

> As the Tahiti was casting off from No 5 wharf, Darling Harbour, at about 4 o'clock yesterday afternoon, a young woman on the wharf, who was bidding farewell to a friend, fell into the water. A man, who was also seeing the Tahiti off, jumped in a rescued the woman, who was little the worse for her immersion. One of the Stannard Brothers launches took both the rescued and the rescuer aboard.

Usually such an incident would rate a minor mention in the newspaper, but it was included in a two page spread of stories on 4 November that was headlined "Appalling Harbour Disaster", and told the tragic tale of what happened less than half an hour after the *Tahiti* had left its berth. As the liner was proceeding down Sydney Harbour in the main shipping channel, one of the local ferries, *Greycliffe*, was making its usual 4.10pm run from Circular Quay to Watson's Bay, with calls at Garden Island, Nielsen Park and Parsley Bay. Suddenly the *Greycliffe* was sighted directly in front of *Tahiti*, and in the subsequent collision the bow of *Tahiti* sliced through the ferry and sent it to the bottom, with the loss of 39 lives, including many school children on their way home. At the time the liner was under the control of Captain Thomas Carson, who had been a harbour pilot since 1909. As the newspaper reported in one story headlined "The Disaster":

> The greatest disaster that has ever occurred on Sydney Harbour took place yesterday afternoon about 4.30 o'clock, when the Union Steamship Company's RMS Tahiti rammed and sank the Sydney Ferry Company's steamer Greycliffe, off Bradley's Head.
>
> The accident was accompanied by appalling loss of life. The latest reports last evening stated that 11 bodies had been recovered, 26 persons were reported missing and over 50 had been treated at Sydney Hospital for injuries received in the collision.
>
> It is feared that further loss of life has resulted. Many of the passengers on the Greycliffe were children returning from school in the city or from the sports meeting of the Public Schools Amateur Athletic Association at the Cricket Ground. Strangely, however, children do not figure largely in the list of dead, although many of them were treated for injuries.
>
> An unusual feature of the disaster is that both vessels were traveling in approximately the same direction at the time the collision occurred. The Tahiti had sailed from No 5 Darling Harbour for New Zealand at 4pm, and the Greycliffe had left Circular Quay at approximately the same time, with about 125 passengers on board, on her usual run to Vaucluse, Parsley Bay and Watson's Bay. The ferryboat for that trip is generally known as the 'school boat', as she carries many children returning from schools in the city.
>
> It is not known definitely how the collision occurred. The Tahiti, which is commanded by Captain Aldwell, had reached a point nearly opposite Bradley's Head when the accident happened.

Sydney Harbour ferry *Greycliffe*

The collision occurred so suddenly that the passengers on board the Tahiti did not realise what had happened. The screams of women and children on the stricken Greycliffe rudely enlightened them.

Apparently the Greycliffe was broadside on to the mail steamer. At the moment of impact, the sharp bow of the Tahiti bit into the wooden superstructure of the ferryboat, at first pushing it forward and turning it over, and then tearing right through the smaller vessel amidships, one half of the Greycliffe going to the south side of the Tahiti and the other to the north.

In a moment all was confusion. Terrible scenes were witnessed as the ferryboat's passengers struggled to free themselves from the wreckage, which finally sank. The engine-room boiler burst when it became submerged, adding further to the terrors of the situation for the unfortunate passengers. In a moment many were struggling in the swirling waters and many pitiful scenes were witnessed. Forgetting their danger some of the survivors immediately went to the assistance of others and placed them in comparative safety until assistance arrived. A fireman on the Tahiti dived overboard, rescued two children, and assisted others.

In a remarkably short space of time vessels of all descriptions had hurried to the scene and searched for survivors among the litter of wreckage that covered the surface of the harbour; many were saved. It is feared that many of the passengers were fatally injured when the collision occurred.

The Tahiti swept on for some distance after cutting through the Greycliffe before she could be pulled up. Eventually she returned, anchored off Point Piper, and lowered boats to go to the rescue of the survivors.

The steel plating of the mail steamer prevented her being damaged, and all that was noticeable were two long scratches on either side of her bows, where the wooden superstructure of the Greycliffe had scraped off the paint in passing. She was able to continue her voyage to New Zealand last evening.

Within minutes of the collision a number of small vessels reached the accident scene and began rescuing survivors. Among the first to arrive was the ferry *Kummulla*, closely followed by the ferries *Burra Bra*, *Kurraba* and *Woollahra*, a naval launch, a police launch, the tug *Bimbi*, and various privately owned boats. Once all the people who had been thrown into the water were picked up, most were taken to either Man o' War Steps, but those survivors picked up by other ferries were taken to the wharves at Circular Quay, as the following reports stated:

The open space in front of the naval offices at Man o' War Steps was turned into a temporary casualty station when passengers from the Greycliffe were landed there. The first of the passengers were landed there at about 5 o'clock, and for nearly an hour ambulance wagons were going to and from the hospitals.

A naval launch brought several people, including a woman who was unconscious, and a boy about 12 years of age, whose face was a deathly pale colour. Immediately afterwards a large private launch brought a number of

THE DISASTER ON SYDNEY HARBOUR.

John Allcot drawing of the collision

other passengers from the sunken ferry steamer, and many of them appeared to be bad cases.

Some heartrending scenes were witnessed as the injured were brought ashore. One young woman, shivering from the cold, was crying piteously and inquiring anxiously about her mother, who was also a passenger on the Greycliffe. Another woman, wrapped in a naval overcoat, was brought to Man o' War Steps lying across the bows of a naval launch and she appeared to be dead.

Some of the survivors were almost covered with blood, and most of them were suffering from exposure. One young woman, who was in great pain, had her clothing torn to shreds, and her stockings had been almost ripped off her legs. She was helped off the naval launch by a bluejacket, but she was unable to walk. The bluejacket, without any hesitation, took her in his arms, and carried her to the waiting ambulance wagon. Suffering as she was the young woman offered profuse thanks to the naval man, who merely answered, "That's alright, Miss".

The men among the survivors showed great fortitude and on landing those who had received only an immersion turned to and helped the more unfortunate passengers. Several of the men, without coast, and their shirtsleeves saturated with blood, were particularly helpful in assisting the women and children to the waiting ambulance wagons.

Distressing scenes were witnessed by hundreds of people when the ferry boat Kummulla put in to the Mosman wharf at Circular Quay shortly before 5 o'clock with a number of survivors, all of whom were unconscious or semi-conscious.

The first of the survivors to be carried from the ferry to the waiting ambulance was a young woman, her face blood-stained and her clothes torn in tatters. She had lost consciousness, and efforts by the crew and others on the Kummulla to revive her had failed. Lying about the main deck of the vessel were the limp forms of a number of school girls, of several women and some men. Most of them had evidently been injured at the time of the collision, as the wounds upon their faces and bodies indicated. Their clothes, reduced to shreds, and the expressions of terror upon their ashen faces, told the story of the terrible trial through which they had passed. Members of the crew, police officers and others were working feverishly to restore animation, and in more than one instance they were successful. Two girls, one of whom was wrapped in a man's pyjamas, were presently carried through the agitated crowd and placed in ambulances, which hastened them off to a hospital.

A few of the survivors from the *Greycliffe* were interviewed when they stepped ashore, and gave accounts of the collision and what happened to them.

A dramatic story of the disaster was related by Mr J Corby, one of the survivors, who was picked up by the Kummulla. Trembling violently, and with bleeding face, the first words Mr Corby uttered when he walked unsteadily off the vessel to the wharf were "Oh my God, my poor wife and child. They have gone." Assured by a "Herald" reporter that many of the passengers had been saved, Mr Corby related what he knew of the tragedy.

"I was taking my wife and daughter, aged six years, to Watson's Bay to spend the afternoon," he said, "and as we were sitting talking on the top deck of the Greycliffe we heard some women scream. On looking round I saw a big steamer almost on top of us. I sprang for some lifebelts, and shouted to my wife to rush down the gangway. I seized a lifebelt, and was just making for the gangway to join my wife and daughter when there was a terrific crash. Our boat seemed to have been completely splintered by the impact. I was immediately thrown into the water, and went down with the anguishing screams of women and children still ringing in my ears. My next recollection was that I felt myself coming towards the surface of the water. I thought I would never reach there, so long was it before my head appeared above the surface. I was surrounded by a mass of floating debris, and, clutching hold of something, looked about for my wife and child. Everywhere around me were struggling women and girls, some with their faces horribly mutilated. What happened after that I do not know, for the next I remember was when I 'came round' on the ferry steamer."

Mr Corby is a fettler, employed in the Railway Department, and his home is at Moree. He arrived in Sydney on Tuesday with his wife and daughter on holidays and was staying at the Hotel Burlington, Haymarket. His wife, he said, could not swim. Mr Corby partially collapsed on the wharf during the interview, and was taken charge of by ambulance officers, and placed in hospital.

Mr J S Bithel, employed at Garden Island, and a resident of Watson's Bay, said that he was not among those who believed the Greycliffe was cut in half. The impact was so severe, he said, that the boat was crushed to pieces. He was sitting on the port side when he saw the Tahiti coming along at a fair speed – six or seven knots he thought. Suddenly the Greycliffe seemed to cut off toward Bradley's Head. It was most unusual, and he came to the conclusion immediately that the steering gear had gone wrong. He heard the Tahiti give two blasts of the whistle, and almost at once the Greycliffe was struck amidships. Just before the crash he ran to the other side of the vessel, and when the ferry heaved over his leg was jammed between the seat and part of the boat.

As soon as he was released he was thrown into the water, and went straight down, almost to the bottom of the harbour it seemed to him. "I turned twenty Catherine wheels, I think. I did not know where I was going or what was happening to me. When I came up I was dazed. All around me there was wreckage. I was near to a buoy, but I did not have the strength to grasp it. I got into a sort of coma, and the next thing I knew was that a lifebelt was thrown to me from a tug. With a supreme effort I grasped this, and I was dragged on to the vessel. The passengers who had been thrown into the water were even then scattered all around, struggling and screaming.

I don't think that any people in the cabins could have had any chance. The boat sank, I am sure, in 20 seconds. It was the most nerve-wracking experience I have ever been through, and I have been shipwrecked two or three times."

Seated at the stern of the boat were four schoolboys, Leslie Brook, Len Horler (son of the Town Clerk of Vaucluse), Ken Berliner and Hubert Fairweather. Horler, when seen last night, said they were singing, shouting and "mucking up" generally just before the collision occurred.

Leslie Brook said that he heard the Tahiti's whistle. The vessel seemed to be so close that the boys decided to move away. No sooner had they moved than the crash occurred and the Greycliffe seemed to tip over.

"I was drawn down by suction," Brook said, "and whirled around in all directions by the current. When I came up to the top I grabbed the biggest piece of wood I could find. I saw Doris Garrett struggling in the water, and I helped her to safety. Other passengers were floundering around looking for something to support them, crying and calling for help. I saw one lifeboat come from the *Tahiti*, but it was a long time after the collision. Launches came from every direction, but there was such confusion that nobody seemed to know what to do. I am a good swimmer, and I am sure it was because of that that my life was saved. I saw another boy, Ken Lankshire, in the water. He could not swim, and I do not know what became of him. I saw Dr Read in the water. There was wreckage everywhere, and it seems as though the boat must have been knocked to splinters, because few pieces of wood were large enough to support anybody. It was terrible to see the scrambling and commotion in the water which was whirled round as though it was boiling. I must have gone a long way down, and I took many mouthfuls and felt very sick when I came up again."

Horler must have been dragged down twenty-five feet. He also was a good swimmer, and as it became darker and darker as he sank he knew that he was down a considerable depth. When he came to the top his leg was caught in a rope and he was dragged down again, and he had considerable difficulty in freeing himself. Horler was in bed last night with his head bandaged, his ankle injured, and with cuts and scratches all over his body.

Doris Garrett paid a tribute to the assistance that was given to her by the schoolboys. She said that they saved her life. Her father was on board, but she did not know what had become of him. When the collision seemed to be inevitable some men told a number of girls to go round to the other side of the ship. As soon as she reached the other side the crash occurred, water came onto the deck, and she was knocked into the harbour by the tilting of a seat. "I am a good swimmer," she said, "but I did not have time to swim. The water whirled me round and round, and when I came up after being drawn down I did not know where I was. While under the water I seemed to think that I was asleep, and when I came to I expected to find myself in bed. Leslie Brooks managed to get me onto a floating drum. Nancy Lewis was with me, and the boys managed to get her onto the same drum. Later we were picked up by the tug Bimbi. I saw one lifeboat launched from the *Tahiti*, but that was when everybody was picked up.

Although the engines of the *Tahiti* had been stopped immediately after the collision, the ship took some time to come to a stop. It turned around, and came back down the harbour, anchoring off Point Piper, and then launching a lifeboat, but by then all the survivors had been plucked from the water. A reporter from the *Sydney Morning Herald* was able to board the vessel and interview some of the passengers, who gave graphic descriptions of the tragedy in another item:

Passengers on board the RMS Tahiti were stunned by the suddenness of the happening. They spoke to one another in awed whispers, speech vainly endeavouring to overtake scattered thought. They stood in silent groups, petrified by the disaster. Only a few passengers knew anything about the happening until it was practically over. They had heard the shrill burst from the Tahiti's siren that preceded the impact, and they felt little more than a slight bump as the giant mail steamer crashed through the frail timbers of the ferry. It was not until the screaming of stricken women and children had mingled in chorus that they realised that something serious indeed had occurred. Then there was a rush for the upper decks.

To use one passengers' words; "It was all over before we knew anything about it. We heard the siren, and when the ship trembled slightly, I remarked to a friend, 'They are putting the brakes on.' That was the last time I laughed. Looking over the side I could see the ferry slowly turn over and then, to my horror, she split in halves. One piece swept by on the side on which I was standing. It was terrible to hear the women and children screaming. I could not look any longer, and in a minute or two we had left the wreckage and its struggling occupants behind."

Another passenger vividly described the scene on the ferry boat immediately after the collision. He was idly watching the waves break over the bow, when he suddenly became aware of the second vessel immediately ahead. He could then see that nothing but a miracle could avert disaster, but he was not prepared for the full horror of what was to follow. The actual impact was slight, and for several moments the ferry was carried through the water, turning slowly over until the keelplates were plainly visible. Then, like a huge knife, the bow of the Tahiti cut through the middle of the Greycliffe, shearing through steelwork and wooden superstructure as though it was so much matchboard. A piercing shriek arose from the sinking ferry boat.

In a moment one side had disappeared from view. The other immediately became alive with scrambling, terrified people. Some, clinging frantically to stanchions, to railings, to anything that would afford support, clambered hopelessly upward on the slowly submerging side of the wreck, terror written on their livid faces, but it was those who occupied the lower compartments who were in truly desperate straits. Realising that unless they could fight free through windows or gangway openings before the vessel became submerged they must inevitably perish, they struggled madly to escape. Some achieved their object even after the ferry had sunk, but it is feared that many were trapped. Mercifully some must have been fatally injured when the crash came.

The section of the Greycliffe that passed on the other side of the Tahiti apparently contained the engine and boiler. Passengers on that side say that they heard a muffled explosion, after that half of the ferry boat sank. They described a similar spectacle of terrified people struggling to escape and how, just after the Tahiti had passed, the water closing over the stricken vessel, boilers had cast up into the air a great cloud of steam, intermingled with flying pieces of timber. In this swirling vortex suddenly appeared the heads of men, women, and children, who fought for life against the suction of the sinking ship.

Despite the disastrous nature of the collision, the *Tahiti* suffered virtually no damage, and after an inspection was allowed to continue its voyage, as the *Sydney Morning Herald* reported:

Sometime after the collision the Tahiti was taken to an anchorage near Shark Island. A radio message was sent to Mr C H Hughes, general manager of the Union S S Co at Sydney, informing him of the collision, and the Marine Superintendent. Captain Walton immediately proceeded to the Tahiti. An examination of the liner showed that she was undamaged, and it was decided to resume the voyage. The Tahiti cleared the Heads at 8.08pm.

By the time the *Tahiti* left, work had already started on salvaging the remains of the *Greycliffe*, as was reported in two separate items:

Captain Carter, Chief Officer of the Harbour Trust Fire Brigade, who proceeded to the scene with a staff of men on the Pluvius, said that the superstructure of the Greycliffe was smashed to pieces.

A rigid search was made for people in the water until after 8 o'clock last night by the aid of searchlight, but no further traces were discovered.

The men on the Pluvius gathered up the wreckage, he said, as it was a menace to navigation in the fairway. There were numerous lifebelts in the water indicating that the passengers had little or no time to put them on. The decks of the Pluvius were piled with broken timbers, seats, lifebelts and other debris, and this would be taken to the Sydney Ferry Company's yard this morning.

Captain Carter said that every effort was made to find bodies by means of the searchlight, and all the wreckage was carefully examined. He was of the opinion that when the Greycliffe sank only the hull, boilers, and engines remained. The depth of water at the scene of the disaster was between 40 and 50 feet.

To a late hour last evening, small vessels of the Harbour Trust were engaged in removing the wreckage, which was drifting in the path of the Athol, Clifton, and Manly ferry services. An examination of this, when it was brought to the beach near Taronga Park, showed that not only had the roof of the vessel been completely torn away, but that most of the upper deck had been ripped off also. Portions up to 18 feet long, which served as rafts for many survivors, were towed in and moored with ropes, while in several cases lifebelts were still in their support, indicating that there was no time after the smash to make use of them. Parts of stanchions, ventilators, supporting posts for decks, doors, seats, one side of the steering cabin, parts of decking with advertisements attached, and innumerable sections of wood, inches long, indicating the force of the collision, were washed and towed ashore. Darkness set in before all of it had been removed.

Over the next two days, divers were sent down to look through the wreckage spread over the bottom of the harbour, and 13 bodies were recovered. Extensive searches continued, the last two bodies

Tahiti

not being located until two weeks after the tragedy. The larger pieces of wreckage, including the engines, were raised and deposited on the beach near Taronga Zoo.

As required by law, the Coroner began an inquiry into the deaths, but the main interest centred on the Court of Marine Inquiry, which commenced on 27 December under Mr Justice Campbell. A string of qualified witnesses called on the first day, including several serving members of the Royal Australian Navy, all gave evidence that in their opinion the *Tahiti* was going at a speed of at least 12 knots at the time of the collision. The captain of the Manly ferry *Burra Bra*, which was following the *Tahiti* down the harbour, stated that his vessel was going about 13 knots and not catching up to the *Tahiti*. All the witnesses stated that they saw the *Greycliffe* and *Tahiti* running on parallel courses, with the ferry ahead of the liner, until the ferry suddenly swung to port, and the collision occurred.

The final witness on the first day, the master of the *Greycliffe*, Captain William T Barnes, said:

> I was standing on the starboard side of the wheelhouse against the telegraph when I heard two blasts. I looked over my shoulder through a window at the back of the wheelhouse. I did not see anything at all. I stepped to the port side and looked out and then I saw the bows of the Tahiti right on my port quarter aft, only a few feet away. Just as I moved across I felt a wave hit my stern and swing me to port. I immediately stepped back to the centre of the wheelhouse and pulled the wheel over to starboard, but it did not take effect. Then crash, bang. The Greycliffe went over on her starboard side with her stern down and I was thrown into the water. I came up and got on to a raft and the Kurraba picked me up.

On the second day of the Inquiry it was the turn of the pilot on the *Tahiti*, Captain Carson, to take the stand. He stated he was aware of the *Greycliffe* being ahead of him and on a parallel course on his starboard side, and also claimed the speed of the *Tahiti* was 8 knots. He went on to say:

> After leaving Garden Island the Tahiti began to overtake the Greycliffe rather rapidly. Passing Garden Island, my ship was working up from about 6 knots to about 7 knots. Then the Tahiti practically ceased to overtake the Greycliffe, which seemed to keep stationed about four points on my bow, about a ship's length from the bridge of the Tahiti. When we were nearly abreast of Shark Island I noticed the Greycliffe alter her course very rapidly towards us, closing in very quickly. I made an exclamation to the captain of the Tahiti, ordered the helm hard to starboard, stopped both engines, then ordered the port engine full astern and sounded two short blasts. I thought the two ships would clear, but the Greycliffe seemed to cross more than ever. When the Greycliffe seemed to swing, I ordered both engines full speed astern, but unfortunately, the ships collided.

Captain Carson's evidence was supported by Captain Aldwell, the master of the *Tahiti*, who also claimed his ship was moving at about 7.5 knots at the time of the collision. However, an expert witness, Captain L E Lucas, stated that, by using evidence presented to the court on the time it took the *Tahiti* to travel a distance of 4,040 feet in 3 minutes and 15 seconds, the ship must have been moving at a speed of 12.25 knots at the moment of impact, well above the 8 knots limit in the area.

On 7 January 1928, Mr Justice Campbell gave his judgement, finding that the *Tahiti* was solely to blame for the collision, as it had been moving at an excessive speed, and the officers on the bridge failed to observe regulations and keep out of the way of the *Greycliffe*, stating:

> I am unable to accept the case put forward on behalf of the Tahiti and those in charge of that vessel that the Greycliffe, when she was about 400 feet away from the Tahiti's bridge and about four points on the starboard bow suddenly swung to port with a sharp angle of turn that would head her almost north and to the west of Bradleys Head. No one was able to suggest any reason for this as a voluntary act and it is not otherwise sought to be explained or accounted for and it is flatly denied by the master of the Greycliffe.

The pilot, Captain Carson was subsequently suspended, it being stated that he had breached Article 24, which required that a vessel overtaking another vessel keep out of the way of the vessel being overtaken, and also Regulation 43 of the Sydney Harbour Trust Regulations, which prescribed a maximum speed of 8 knots between Shark Island and Bradley's Head.

The engines from the *Greycliffe* were later sold to a New Zealand dairy products firm, who used them in their factory until 1964, when they were acquired by the Auckland Museum of Transport, where they are still on display.

Chapter Sixteen

Times of Change

By 1925 the three ships being operated by the Oceanic Steamship Company, *Sierra*, *Sonoma* and *Ventura*, were completing twenty five years of service, and well past their prime. Oceanic realised only too well that to remain a viable force in the San Francisco trade they had to acquire newer and larger vessels, but since their service to New Zealand and Australia had lost about US$3½ million in the forty years it had operated, the company was loath to invest further in the trade without generous government assistance.

When *Sonoma* had arrived in Sydney on 3 March 1925, one of the passengers on board was Mr F S Samuels, assistant to the president of the Oceanic Steamship Company. Next day the *Sydney Morning Herald* reported that Mr Samuels had said, "Provided the American Government gives us a satisfactory contract, full consideration will be given to the construction of two large steamers to be used solely on the Australian service."

When the requested assistance was not forthcoming, the Oceanic Steamship Company faced an uncertain future, and by the end of 1925 the company was for sale. The Matson Line decided to buy Oceanic, the purchase price being US$1½ million. The sale was finalised on 21 April 1926, when a new company was started as a subsidiary of Matson Line, with "The" being added to the original title to form The Oceanic Steamship Company. Included in the sale were the three passenger ships plus one cargo ship, *Carriso*, which was sold in November 1926. The Matson Line also negotiated another two year mail contract with the United States Government for the Oceanic service.

Each of the passenger vessels was upgraded to Matson standards during a refit in San Francisco,

Ventura (WSS Vic)

Sierra in Matson colours arriving in Sydney on 21 August 1930

and their funnels were repainted in Matson colours, buff with a blue top and large blue "M". The first departure from San Francisco by a passenger ship under the new ownership was taken by *Sierra* on 8 June 1926. On the same day, John D Spreckels, the founder of the Oceanic Steamship Company, died. *Sierra* arrived in Sydney for the first time under the new colours on 29 June, *Sonoma* made its first departure from San Francisco under the new ownership on 23 June, and *Ventura* on 7 July.

At this time the vessels would berth in Sydney at No 4 Circular Quay West, or occasionally at No 5, but in 1929 this was changed, and No 2 Circular Quay East became the Matson Line wharf in Sydney. The last vessel to use Circular Quay West was *Sonoma* in December 1928, and the first to berth at Circular Quay East was *Ventura*, on 10 January 1929.

The movements of ships across the Pacific to either San Francisco or Vancouver passed without much mention in the newspapers apart from when something unfortunate happened, or a celebrity travelled.

In 1927, two of the biggest celebrities in Australia were the aviators Charles Kingsford Smith and Charles Ulm, who were regularly creating new records with their flights. Early in 1927 they set a new record for a flight around Australia, 10 days and 6 hours, but their ambition was to become the first to fly across the Pacific.

In pursuit of this, on 14 July 1927 Kingsford Smith and Ulm boarded the *Tahiti* in Sydney to go to San Francisco, purchase a suitable aircraft, and fly it back to Australia, but apart from their names appearing in the list of passengers joining the ship, no other mention was made.

However, also on 14 July, the Oceanic steamer *Sierra* arrived in Sydney from San Francisco, and in addition to the passengers and cargo on board, there were three monkeys, whose arrival was deemed worthy of a story in the *Sydney Morning Herald* on 15 July:

Showing the results of a sea voyage, when they were affected by sea sickness, three monkeys of international fame arrived in Sydney by the Sierra from San Francisco yesterday to fulfil an engagement at the Tivoli.

Max, Moritz, and Akka are known probably the world over as the result of their appearance both in the circus tent and in the films. Their managers, Messrs Charles Judge and Caratang, claim that "there is nothing in reason which they cannot do," and those who are acquainted with the pictures in which they have been the principal actors, will not regard this as a great exaggeration. They were captured in 1920 in the forests of Sierra Leone, West Africa.

So delicate are these animals that not only have they to be kept in a specially constructed cage in order to meet changes of climate, but they must be fed on special diet.

After arriving in Sydney on 10 June 1928, *Tahiti* was taken off the Union Line San Francisco service for a major overhaul. The work was done at the Union Line workshops in Port Chalmers, with

Tahiti departing Sydney on 12 June on a voyage to Wellington, where all passengers and cargo were offloaded before the ship proceeded south.

Maunganui was brought back to replace *Tahiti*, arriving in Sydney from Auckland on 12 June, and departing two days later for San Francisco. *Maunganui* made two more round trips to San Francisco, the first departing Sydney on 9 August. The voyage across the Tasman Sea was particularly rough, making the ship almost a day late arriving in Wellington. The third voyage *Maunganui* made to San Francisco left on 4 October, the vessel returning to Sydney on 28 November.

The refit of *Tahiti* was completed in the middle of November, and the liner went first to Wellington to load passengers and cargo, arriving in Sydney on 27 November. *Tahiti* then entered Woolwich dock for a final cleaning of the hull, being refloated on 28 November and leaving the next day to resume its place on the San Francisco trade.

On 9 June 1929 *Makura* arrived in Sydney from San Francisco, and was then prepared for a voyage to Vancouver, replacing *Aorangi* while that vessel underwent an overhaul. *Makura* was replaced by *Maunganui*, which arrived in Sydney from Wellington on 10 June, and left three days later for San Francisco.

Makura left Sydney on 27 June, arriving in Vancouver on 19 July, leaving on 24 July, this being the last time *Makura* would visit the Canadian city.

It was also in June 1929 that *Tahiti* came close to disaster on its voyage from San Francisco to Sydney, as the following report in the *Sydney Morning Herald* on 9 July indicated:

> Passengers from San Francisco, who reached Sydney by the Tahiti yesterday, had a startling experience when the vessel struck one of the numerous coral reefs, near the entrance to Papeete Harbour, on June 22.
>
> The day was a perfect one, and most of the passengers were leaning over the rails enjoying the warm sunshine, and the fine view of adjacent islands. Suddenly, there was a scraping sound, and then the Tahiti gave a dangerous lurch, righting herself quickly, to the immense relief of all.
>
> "There was dead low water at the time," remarked Captain Aldwell, of the vessel. "My explanation of the mishap is that the ship probably touched bottom, and sheering off, struck a submerged reef. The first impact came amidships on the port side. The vessel was quickly on an even keel again, in deep water."
>
> The damage is not thought to be serious. A plate on the port side was dented, and a rivet started. A temporary rivet was replaced at Wellington. An inspection by a diver at Wellington also disclosed that slight damage had resulted to a propeller. All cargo was taken out of the holds at Wellington, and will be carried to Sydney by another mail steamer.
>
> The Tahiti will be drydocked at Sydney, and permanent repairs effected.

Canadian-Australasian Royal Mail Line

SAILINGS

1929-30 SOUTHBOUND 1929-30

STEAMSHIP	Vancouver B.C. Depart (Noon)	Honolulu T.H. Arrive	Suva Fiji Arrive	Auckland N.Z. Arrive	Sydney Australia Arrive
"NIAGARA"	Mar. 6	Mar. 13	Mar. 22	Mar. 25	Mar. 30
"AORANGI"	April 3	April 10	April 19	April 22	April 27
"NIAGARA"	May 1	May 8	May 17	May 20	May 25
"AORANGI"	May 29	June 5	June 14	June 17	June 22
"NIAGARA"	June 25	July 3	July 12	July 15	July 20
"MAKURA"	July 24	July 31	Aug. 9	Aug. 12	Aug. 17
"AORANGI"	Aug. 21	Aug. 28	Sept. 6	Sept. 9	Sept. 14
"NIAGARA"	Sept. 18	Sept. 25	Oct. 4	Oct. 7	Oct. 12
"AORANGI"	Oct. 16	Oct. 23	Nov. 1	Nov. 4	Nov. 9
"NIAGARA"	Nov. 13	Nov. 20	Nov. 29	Dec. 2	Dec. 7
"AORANGI"	Dec. 11	Dec. 18	Dec. 27	Dec. 30	Jan. 4
"NIAGARA"	Jan. 8	Jan. 15	Jan. 24	Jan. 27	Feb. 1

SAILINGS SUBJECT TO CHANGE WITHOUT NOTICE.
Steamships call at Victoria several hours after leaving Vancouver.
Ships usually remain at Honolulu and Suva from 6 to 8 hours, and at Auckland 12 to 24 hours.

1929-30 NORTHBOUND 1929-30

STEAMSHIP	Sydney Australia Depart	Auckland N.Z. Depart	Suva Fiji Depart	Honolulu T.H. Depart	Vancouver B.C. Arrive
"AORANGI"	Mar. 7	Mar. 12	Mar. 15	Mar. 22	Mar. 29
"NIAGARA"	April 4	April 9	April 12	April 19	April 26
"AORANGI"	May 2	May 7	May 10	May 17	May 24
"NIAGARA"	May 30	June 4	June 7	June 14	June 21
"MAKURA"	June 27	July 2	July 5	July 12	July 19
"AORANGI"	July 25	July 30	Aug. 2	Aug. 9	Aug. 16
"NIAGARA"	Aug. 22	Aug. 27	Aug. 30	Sept. 6	Sept. 13
"AORANGI"	Sept. 19	Sept. 24	Sept. 27	Oct. 4	Oct. 11
"NIAGARA"	Oct. 17	Oct. 22	Oct. 25	Nov. 1	Nov. 8
"AORANGI"	Nov. 14	Nov. 19	Nov. 22	Nov. 29	Dec. 6
"NIAGARA"	Dec. 12	Dec. 17	Dec. 20	Dec. 27	Jan. 3

1929-30 Sailing schedule (Ken Hall collection)

Fortunately repairs to *Tahiti* were completed quickly enough for the vessel to depart as previously scheduled on 11 July for its next trip to San Francisco.

Meanwhile, *Maunganui* made a second voyage to San Francisco, departing Sydney on 8 August, and when *Makura* arrived back in Sydney from Vancouver on 17 August it made several return trips to Wellington, the last arriving back in Sydney on 30 September, before resuming its place on the San Francisco service with a departure on 3 October. *Maunganui* returned to Sydney from San Francisco on 28 September, and went back to the Tasman trades with a departure for Wellington on 4 October. Going into 1930 the San Francisco was again being maintained by *Tahiti* and *Makura*.

Having departed Sydney on 7 August 1930, on 12 August, *Tahiti* left Wellington to continue its voyage to Rarotonga, Papeete and San Francisco. The vessel was under the command of Captain A T Toten, and had 103 passengers on board, a crew of 149, and 500 tons of general cargo, as well as mail and some bullion.

At about 4.30 on the morning of 15 August 1930, the starboard propeller shaft suddenly snapped just inboard of the stern tube, and fell off.

Before the engine could be stopped the inboard end of the broken shaft had torn a hole in the side of the ship. The second engineer, Mr A Thompson, who was in charge of the engine room at the time, went into the shaft tunnel to inspect the damage, and was confronted by a huge torrent of inrushing water, so he returned quickly to the engine-room and ordered the watertight door be closed.

However, the watertight bulkhead that separated the shaft tunnel and No 3 hold had also been damaged, and needed to be shored up, but water began seeping into the engine-room and the after holds. Pumps could not prevent the inflow of water steadily rising, and it was soon apparent that the *Tahiti* was doomed. At the time the *Tahiti* was 460 miles from Rarotonga, and it was not possible for the ship to make that port. However, it was also clear that the *Tahiti* would take some time to sink.

Radio calls for help brought responses from four ships, but none of them were close enough to render immediate assistance. One of the vessels to respond was the Union Line vessel *Tofua*, which was on its way from Suva to Tonga, and would take several days to reach the *Tahiti*. The cargo steamer *Penbryn*, was the closest to the scene of the accident, but would not arrive there until shortly after 10pm on 16 December some forty hours after the shaft had broken, while the French steamer *Antinous* would reach the stricken vessel some hours later.

The fourth vessel to respond was *Ventura* of The Oceanic Steamship Co, which was berthed in Pago Pago on its way from Sydney to San Francisco when the distress call was received. *Ventura*, under the command of Captain William R Meyer, left port immediately and made its way as fast as possible through heavy seas, but would not arrive at the scene until the morning of 17 August.

The sequence of events was reported in the *Sydney Morning Herald* as follows:

After drifting helplessly in mid-Pacific for more than 60 hours, the Union Royal Mail steamer Tahiti foundered at 4.42 o'clock yesterday afternoon (Ventura's time).

All the passengers and the entire crew are safe on board the American mail steamer Ventura which reached the scene about 9.30 o'clock in the morning. The freighter Penbryn, which arrived at 9.30 o'clock (local time) on Sunday night, stood by all night. As the Ventura appeared on the horizon the Tahiti's engine-room bulkhead began to give way, and Captain Toten ordered the passengers into boats. Five boats were in the water when the Ventura arrived.

Tahiti drifting in the Pacific (John Bennett collection)

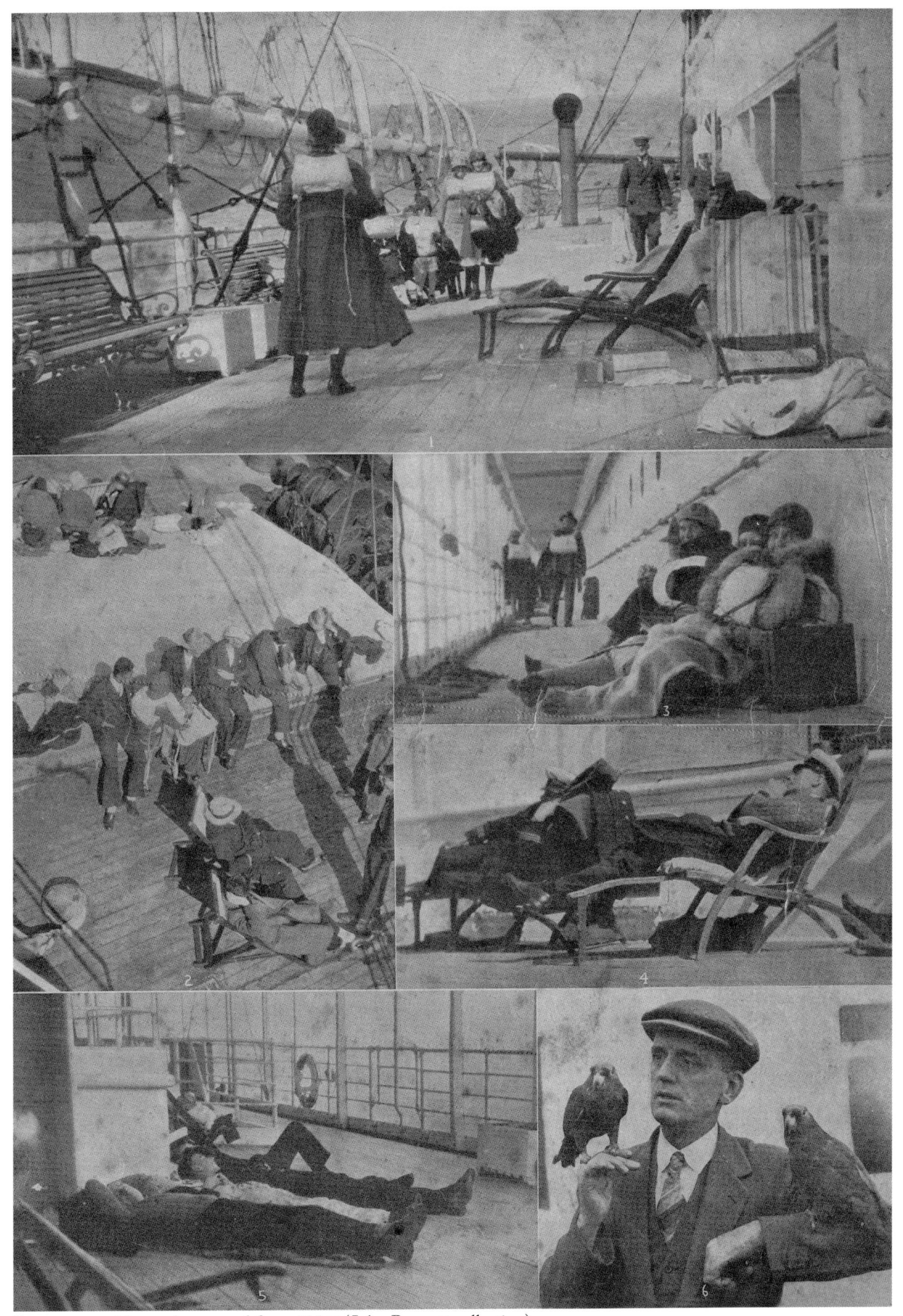

Passengers waiting to be rescued from *Tahiti* (John Bennett collection)

The bulk of the Tahiti's light mail matter and some light personal luggage was safely transferred to the Ventura before the Tahiti sank. The Ventura is now making for Pago Pago, in American Samoa.

When the Penbryn reached the Tahiti on Sunday night, Captain Toten decided that the position was sufficiently reassuring to justify remaining on board the sinking ship until the Ventura arrived. The crew continued to work the pumps all night, but when day broke it was apparently obvious that there was little hope of saving the vessel.

An anxious wait for the Ventura then ensued, although the presence of the Penbryn to render immediate assistance should the Tahiti show any signs of foundering quickly must have been definitely comforting.

Passengers were not fated to remain on board until the Ventura had come up. Signs that the bulkhead, which was holding back the water from the fore part of the vessel, was giving way, were noticed just after the Ventura's smoke was seen. By the time the rescuing liner was within hail five lifeboats had got safely away from the doomed vessel's side.

Several hours later came the welcome news that all souls, and even part of the mails and personal luggage, were safe on board the Ventura. Captain Meyer of the Ventura decided to remain on the scene until the Tahiti disappeared, for it was evident that it was only a matter of hours. Late in the afternoon the liner heeled over and sank.

Wireless messages received in Sydney from shortly after 3 o'clock on Saturday morning until last night told a graphic story.

At 2.56am (Sydney time) a message was picked up by Amalgamated Wireless as follows: "Tahiti sends a CQ (all stations) – any ships about 500 south of Raratonga please give positions."

At 5.20am (Sydney time): "Suva radio broadcasts to CQ. The Tahiti, approximately 460 miles from Raratonga, has broken propeller and tailshaft, which have dropped off. Number four hold and engine room filling; all vessels keep lookout and report if in touch."

At 10.56pm (Sydney time): "Tahiti sends to CQ – abandoning ship; position 26 degrees 27 minutes south, 166 degrees 05 minutes west."

At 12.43am (Sunday, Sydney time), from Suva radio: "Tahiti half an hour ago – still holding on and pumping hard; position as before."

At 2.22am (Sydney time): "Tahiti sends following: Engine-room bulkhead badly bulged and leaking, engine-room under control; No 3 hold water level with 'tween decks; passengers still aboard; pumps working full bore, and Captain Toten will give position as daylight appears in about another hour.

At 3.39am (Sydney time), from Suva radio: "Tahiti fifteen minutes ago – engine-room beyond control now; if no further word will abandon ship; probably several miles northwest of former position; look for my lifeboat set."

At noon (Sydney time), from Suva radio: "Report Tahiti – passengers and crew still aboard. Penbryn arriving on scene early in afternoon today when passengers will be immediately transferred. For safety, crew will be transferred before dark, standing by on Penbryn till morning: water gaining. Latest from Tahiti 22.33 Greenwich Mean Time (8.33am Sydney time), on coil, "All OK."

Also at noon (Sydney time) from Suva: "Position Tahiti 26 degrees 30 minutes south, 165 degrees 56 minutes west: Penbryn 26 degrees 34 minutes south, 166 degrees 48 minutes west: Tahiti reports engine-room bulkhead bulging and leaking: advises Penbryn to be prepared to take passengers from boats."

6.35pm (Sydney time), from Suva: "Penbryn sighted Tahiti's rockets at 6.55pm (local time): due an hour later."

7.13pm (Sydney time), from Wellington: "Advice received 7 o'clock (New Zealand time) states Penbryn will be alongside Tahiti about 7.30pm (local time): all in readiness to transship passengers; weather overcast but fine."

Later messages were:

From Suva radio: "Penbryn arrived at the Tahiti 9.30pm (Suva time), and is standing by all night: Ventura arrives 9am tomorrow (Suva time), and will transfer passengers: Antinous will arrive at 11am; message from Tahiti describes weather as light breeze and heavy swell; Tahiti's main wireless gear has broken down, and she is using an emergency set to keep in touch with Suva: messages are being retransmitted from Suva to Wellington and Sydney."

From Suva radio at 1.30am (Monday, Sydney time) – "Just heard Tahiti still holding on waiting for daylight."

From Suva radio, 3.50am (Suva time): "Tahiti's position lat 25.15 long 166.10. Ventura expects reach Tahiti 10am."

Later from Suva: "As the Ventura hove in sight at 9.30 this morning (local time) the bulkhead commenced to give way. Passengers had to take to the boats. Up to present five boats have got away without trouble.

From Wellington (NZ): "The Tahiti's passengers, crew, and mails have been transferred to the Ventura."

A message from Suva, by cable and wireless, added that the Ventura was standing by until Tahiti sank, and would then proceed to Pago Pago.

Bearing tidings of the fate of the doomed liner, the last message was dispatched from Wellington at 8.15pm. It read: "Tahiti sank 4.42pm, Ventura time. Captain advises all passengers and crew safe aboard Ventura. Latter now proceeding Pago Pago (American Samoa), where Tahiti's island passengers and crew will be disembarked. Ventura thence to San Francisco with Tahiti's American and European passengers. Tofua diverted to pick up island passengers and crew Pago Pago."

At 9.30 on the morning of 17 August, when the after bulkhead appeared ready to collapse, Captain Toten gave the order for passengers to abandon the ship, and they were placed in the lifeboats and rowed over to the *Ventura* when it arrived shortly

Photographs taken from *Ventura* (John Bennett collection)

Tahiti sinking (John Bennett collection)

after. Meanwhile the crew had remained on board trying to prevent the ship sinking too quickly, and during this period the lifeboats were used to save some of the passengers' and crew's baggage, as well as a portion of the mails and a shipment of bullion from the strong room. By 1.30pm this operation had been completed, and Captain Toten ordered the crew into the lifeboats as well. By then the engine room was completely flooded and the stern almost under water.

Ventura returned to Pago Pago, where the *Tahiti* passengers who had been destined to leave the ship at Rarotonga and Papeete, as well as the crew of *Tahiti*, all disembarked. The Union Line vessel *Tofua*, which had responded to the distress call but was too far away to render assistance, was diverted to Pago Pago to pick up the passengers booked to Rarotonga and Papeete, and the crew of the *Tahiti*. The passengers were taken to their destinations, while the crew remained on *Tofua* until it returned to Auckland.

The passengers from *Tahiti* who had been bound for San Francisco remained on board *Ventura*, which continued its voyage to California, arriving in San Francisco on 1 September. The officers and crew were officially commended for their actions in rescuing the survivors from the *Tahiti*, and feted in a special parade up Market Street.

On Tuesday, 18 August, the *Sydney Morning Herald* carried two further stories concerning the loss of the *Tahiti*:

All the Tahiti's newspapers, packages and parcels mail were lost. During the transference of the letter mail to the Ventura six bags were lost in the sea, and 50 bags became wet. All the remainder of the letter mail was saved intact.

The vessel's cargo comprised 200 tons for Papeete, 100 tons for Raratonga, and 200 tons for San Francisco. It is officially announced that the steamer Maunganui will replace the Tahiti in the Sydney – San Francisco service.

The Marama, which is laid up at Wellington, will take the place of the Maunganui in the Sydney – New Zealand service.

The Maunganui will commence her new run from Sydney on October 3, and the Marama will sail from Auckland on September 26.

A subsequent court of inquiry into the disaster came to the conclusion that "the loss of the *Tahiti* was due to a peril of the sea which no reasonable care or foresight could have avoided". The court declared that the *Tahiti* was "a fine ship, well found, capably manned, with a clear course and fine weather", and the "the ship's company on the *Tahiti*, from Commander down, rose magnificently to the occasion."

The sudden loss of the *Tahiti* left the Union Line in a difficult position, as while they were able to quickly transfer *Maunganui* to take over the *Tahiti's* schedule, they did not have a suitable permanent replacement vessel in their fleet, but they would quickly obtain another ship in a rather unusual way.

At the time the *Tahiti* sank, the Union Line's parent company, P&O, had an almost new passenger ship, *Razmak*, laid up in Britain, with no possible use being found for it. The loss of the *Tahiti* solved that problem, as *Razmak* was an ideal size for the San Francisco service, so the transfer of *Razmak* to the Union Line was completed in September 1930.

Razmak had been designed to operate a fast passenger and mail feeder service between Aden and Bombay. In an unusual arrangement, the hull was built by the Greenock shipyard of Harland & Wolff, being launched on 16 October 1924, then towed to Belfast, where the quadruple expansion machinery, boilers and superstructure were added, and the internal fitting out completed.

Razmak was handed over to P&O on 26 February 1925, and at that time measured 10,602 gross tons, and provided accommodation for 142 first class and 142 second class passengers. The vessel was fitted with twin propellers, and had a service speed of 18 knots. On 13 March *Razmak* left London on a one-way positioning voyage to Aden, then entered service in the Indian Ocean.

In 1926 P&O abandoned the Indian Ocean feeder service, and *Razmak* was placed on a new route from Marseilles to Bombay, but this was abandoned in 1929. *Razmak* returned to England and was laid up in London on 18 July, as P&O had no alternative use for the ship. When fate took a hand with the loss of the *Tahiti*, *Razmak* was quickly transferred to the New Zealand company.

Razmak departed London on 3 October on its delivery voyage, calling at Gibraltar and Marseilles before passing through the Suez Canal and going to Bombay, where it arrived on 23 October, on which day the following item appeared in the shipping column of the *Sydney Morning Herald*:

According to advice received in Sydney yesterday by McDonald, Hamilton, and Company, agents for the P&O Line, the steamer Razmak, which, as the Monowai is to replace the lost Tahiti in the Sydney-Wellington-San Francisco service, is due at Bombay today from London. She will sail on Saturday direct to Wellington, where she is scheduled to arrive on November 11. Various changes will then be made to provide accommodation for third-class passengers (she was built for two classes only), and she will be painted in the Union Company's colours. On December 2, she will leave Wellington for San Francisco, carrying Sydney passengers and cargo transferred from the Maunganui.

It is quite likely that *Razmak* carried passengers on the voyage from London to Bombay, which was a popular route for P&O liners. The vessel then proceeded to Colombo, where 500 tons of cargo for

Razmak

Wellington was loaded. Departing Colombo on 27 October, *Razmak* steamed directly to Wellington, where it arrived on 12 November.

On 13 November, the following item, sent from Wellington, appeared in the Melbourne *Argus*:

> The P&O liner Razmak reached here today from Colombo. She will be renamed the Monowai, and take up the lost Tahiti's running from here on December 2. As the vessel was only built for two classes, fittings from the Mararoa and other dismantled Union Line ships will be used to install third-class accommodation.

Refitting to suit the liner for its new service was done by Union Steam Ship Company staff at their Evans Bay facility in Wellington, with the accommodation being changed to cater for 224 saloon, 69 second class and 108 third class passengers. Externally the hull and funnels were repainted in the standard Union Line colours, with a white superstructure, though the ventilators remained in the P&O buff colour rather than white.

Although the name of the ship was changed to *Monowai* during the refit, it remained registered at Greenock in Scotland, this not being changed to Wellington until 14 November 1932.

On 29 November *Monowai* moved into Wellington Harbour to have the compasses adjusted, then final preparations were completed for the first voyage across the Pacific. Instead of *Monowai* crossing to Sydney, the departure for San Francisco from there on 27 November was taken by *Maunganui*, which brought the Australian passengers, cargo and mail to Wellington, where the vessel arrived on 1 December and everything was transferred to *Monowai*.

On 2 December 1930 *Monowai*, under the command of Captain Toten, departed Wellington for Raratonga, Tahiti and San Francisco, arriving there for the first time on 19 December.

With the arrival of *Monowai*, *Maunganui* was

Razmak berthed in Wellington (Alexander Turnbull Library)

Monowai berthed in Wellington prior to its maiden voyage (Alexander Turnbull Library)

taken off the San Francisco service and went back to the Tasman trade again.

On its return voyage, *Monowai* arrived in Sydney for the first time on Saturday, 17 January 1931. The vessel had embarked some unexpected extra passengers in Wellington, a group of stewards from the Canadian-Australasian liner *Niagara*, which had departed Sydney on 8 January 1931 on a regular voyage to Vancouver. As the *Sydney Morning Herald* reported on 19 January 1931:

> Twenty-five stewards from the liner Niagara, who left the vessel at Auckland, reached Sydney on Saturday by the Monowai. They had volunteered to take leave which was due to them when they found that, because of a depleted passenger list, the Niagara was to continue her voyage to Vancouver over-staffed.
>
> Interviewed on their arrival, the men all expressed loyalty to their employers, and said that a company which treated them well in good times deserved some consideration in bad times.
>
> Their attitude was the subject of much comment by the Monowai's passengers, who applauded their spirit.

On *Monowai*'s first departure from Sydney, on Thursday, 22 January 1931, Captain Toten had been instructed to make a fast trip to Wellington, providing weather conditions were favourable, in order to test the Bauer-Wach low-pressure double-reduction exhaust turbines which had been fitted to the original engines before *Monowai* left Britain.

Departing Sydney Heads at 5.04pm, *Monowai* quickly worked up to full speed, though using only five of its six boilers. On the first day at sea the vessel ran into northerly winds, creating a heavy swell and westerly set, while in Cook Strait there was a strong

First class lounge on *Monowai* (Dallas Hogan collection)

Second class lounge on *Monowai* (Dallas Hogan collection)

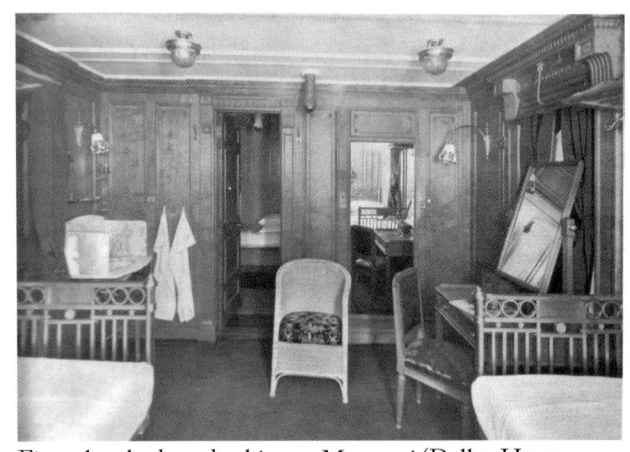

First class bedstead cabin on *Monowai* (Dallas Hogan collection)

First class promenade deck on *Monowai* (Dallas Hogan collection)

ebb tide which delayed the arrival at Wellington Heads by at least half an hour, to 1.47pm, but this was still early enough to break the previous record, set by the Matson liner *Malolo* in November 1930, by one hour and eight minutes, the new time being two days 18 hours 43 minutes.

Unfortunately, the entry of *Monowai* into service coincided with a world trade recession, and the Union Line decided *Monowai* was too large to remain on the San Francisco route all year. On 28 May 1931, *Monowai* departed Sydney on a voyage to Vancouver, while *Aorangi* was undergoing overhaul. *Maunganui* was brought in for two voyages to San Francisco, the first departing Sydney on 14 May and the second on 9 July.

Returning to Sydney on 17 July, *Monowai* was temporarily placed on the shorter trans-Tasman trade until *Maunganui* returned to Sydney from San Francisco on 29 August. *Maunganui* then resumed its place on the trans-Tasman trade with a departure for Auckland. *Monowai* returned to the San Francisco route with a departure from Sydney on 3 September 1931 for Wellington, Papeete and San Francisco.

A description of a voyage from San Francisco to Wellington on board *Monowai*, written by Cecil Gask, was published in the Australian magazine *The Harbour* in June 1932:

> We sailed out of the Golden Gate, and saw its rugged hills become dim on the horizon. 'Frisco had been swept by a cold north wind, and it was good to look south toward the sunshine. Far distant in the Pacific there awaited us our first place of call—the French outpost of Tahiti; beyond was the British isle of Rarotonga, then Wellington itself.
>
> We left the cold weather behind on the third day; on the fourth our awnings were erected—also the swimming tank. On deck the games got under way. There was the variety of circles, pegs, and targets; also the deck-tennis nets, which took early possession of our zest. The ocean was calm, as we had expected it to be. Sometimes it twinkled beneath the sunlight, or was ruffled by a breeze or flecked with tiny breakers; at night there was the moon upon it.
>
> The evenings grew in attraction. The Pacific sky showed us some new effects—tints that were thrown far into the eastern clouds, and blue twilights with a bright star or two. We passed over the Equator in the early hours of the seventh day, and the tropic heat of the Southern Hemisphere took a hold of us. We put on our whitest clothes.
>
> Nine days out—towards evening—land hove in sight. It was the outlying islands of the Taumotu group. They had palm trees, and looked slight and fragile— just a few feet above the ocean. Next day we were due at Tahiti.
>
> We reached Tahiti before dawn, and watched the sun rise behind the peaks. At daybreak the Monowai sailed slowly through the channel in the coral reef, past

the sentinel islet of Motu Uta, and into a glade-like harbour—that of Papeete, capital of the Society Islands. The town lay silent among its trees. Everywhere were the coconut palms. Behind it rose the Green-clad mountains. It had grey, wooden dwellings, and tiny, yellow churches, with red spires ascending through the trees. On the wharf there was a large crowd of people—whites and natives.

Hurriedly we crossed the wharf, and passed into the shadowy, sunlit streets, where we moved among the soft-stepped townfolk with a roving freedom. Curious old carriages, with large wheels and slight capacity, were drawn up against the few inches of pavement here and there—a bicycle or two went by, once or twice there was a motor-car. On either side were open-fronted stores, while at the rear of the town—a short step from the water—was the market-place, already, being French, quit of the day's affairs. Seaward, in the curve of the bay west of the wharf, trim bungalows lined the shore, fringed with hedges—and the red hibiscus.

Feeling good Tahitians, we spoke our French—even to the Chinese storemen. They seemed strange words we used—ten thousand miles from Paris! The children, we found, knew little or nothing of our English. We exchanged a friendly interest with the natives. Some of the dark maidens, fully conscious of their charms, wore remote smiles as they passed us. Some had a lone red flower set in their hair. It spoke of a sweetheart, or the lack of one, according to position. We found a museum—and the leafy prison.

Out of Papeete, we were led into the wild riches the island. Eastward, beyond the outskirts of the town we followed a side-track to Arue Beach. Here, from the many strewn upon the grey sand, we sipped a coconut in its native grove. We found the tomb of Tahiti's former rulers, containing five kings called Pomare, and I climbed the steep hill winding about Radio Bay. Beyond, in a glade by Point Venus, was the first landing-place of Captain Cook. Bread-fruit grew wild, and the large papayas, resembling the Cantaloupe melon; also the pendant branches of bananas.

The road went up and down along the shore. It took us through native villages, with their pale bird-cage huts, and around the peninsula, at one point over thirty miles distant from Papeete. Always the mountains were at our side. Orohena rose to its crest, a mile above the sea. We left the roadway, and dived into pellucid water startling the bright-hued fishes. They were blue and green, like sombre little lanterns—also striped in black and silver.

Toward evening we were upon the wharf. There were some new passengers, their shoulders draped with garlands. Once more the population had descended on the ship. Away to the west lay the rugged island of Moorea. Soon we were sailing past it—and Tahiti grew dim, and disappeared.

For a day and a half we were upon the water. Then Rarotonga hove in sight. Small and circular—seven miles from shore to shore—the island had the green peaks of Polynesia. Upon them was the morning mist. We anchored off Avarua, beyond the reef, in water of an intense blue. Deep below the surface large fish moved lazily. A white launch set out from the land. Behind it came a chain of native boats, laden with fruit. Soon we were gliding shoreward.

Avarua—the trading centre of the Cook Islands—was like a tiny English village, set in the tropics. A road wound landward to the mountains. It was massed with bloom—scarlet flamboyant, white-and-yellow frangipanni, lilac-hued Bougainvillaea, crimson "cat's-tail"—everywhere with the yellow and red hibiscus. On the ground was the fallen blossom of the utu tree—above there hung the fruit, used by the natives as a fish narcotic. Along the seafront were the stores.

The road around the island passed through coconut groves. We saw the natives cutting out the white fruit and spreading it in frames to dry. They were the copra workers. Beyond we came upon an opening in the coral strand—and away in the distance was a native fisherman, wielding his spear. We strolled into a native garden It had a shady house—and there was a friendly maiden. She gave us bananas grown upon the mountain slopes, and cracked passion-fruit for us with her teeth. Later, we swam in the clear water, and watched the native boys diving by the pier. At dusk we sailed away.

In a day or two the Tropic of Capricorn was far behind us. There was a quick moderation of temperature. The sea was calm, and changed from blue to green. After five days we sighted land—the North Island of New Zealand.

At midnight we were among the lights of Wellington.

The Oceanic Steamship Company was also concerned about the declining traffic brought about by the worsening world economic situation. In an attempt to attract more business, from July 1931 *Sierra*, *Sonoma* and *Ventura* began including a call at both Los Angeles and Auckland on their voyages to and from Sydney. From that time the route followed by the three ships was from San Francisco and Los Angeles to Honolulu, Pago Pago, Suva, Auckland and Sydney.

The first departure on the new route was taken by *Sonoma* from San Francisco on 2 July 1931, and Los Angeles on 3 July. The vessel arrived at Auckland for the first time on 24 July, then continued to Sydney. The other two ships began calling at the extra ports on their departures from San Francisco over the next two months, but they were still able to provide a sailing every three weeks from both San Francisco and Sydney.

Meanwhile, changes were also happening on the Vancouver service. On 4 August 1931 there was an announcement that the Union Steam Ship Company of New Zealand had reached an agreement with the Canadian Pacific Railway Company to form a new joint company, Canadian-Australasian Line Limited, in which each company would own a half share in both *Aorangi* and *Niagara*.

The Canadian Pacific Railway Company operated the service across Canada that had always been used as part of the "All Red Route", but the company was also a major force in the shipping industry, with a fleet of 'Empress' liners operating services across the Atlantic from Quebec or Halifax to Liverpool, and also in the Pacific from Vancouver to Japan and Hong Kong.

The Canadian Pacific payment to the Union Line would be in the form of CP Preference Stock, and the new company would be incorporated in Canada, with a head office in Vancouver. Both ships were transferred to the ownership of the new company, but remained registered in London. The Board of Directors would comprise equal representation from both companies, and the Union Line would manage the operation of the two liners. Despite these changes, the two liners retained the Union Line colour scheme, but a new house flag was adopted, which was a variation on that of the original Canadian-Australian Royal Mail Steamship Company formed by James Huddart in 1893.

In an attempt to attract more passengers the Union Line began advertising excursions from Sydney and Auckland to Suva and Honolulu from November to February using the regular voyages to Vancouver being operated by *Aorangi* and *Niagara*. Excursions were also being promoted from Sydney and Wellington to Rarotonga and Papeete on ships employed on the San Francisco service.

Island Excursions at Concession Rates

A unique opportunity to enjoy the glamour and romance of the Islands for less than the cost of a city holiday.

SUVA, FIJI.
Round Trip, 23 days—
   First-class Return £35

HONOLULU, HAWAII.
Via Auckland and Suva—
Seven Weeks' Tour—
   First-class Return £75
   Cabin-class Return £55

RAROTONGA, COOK ISLAND.
Via Wellington, N.Z.—
Twenty-three Days' Tour—
   First-class Return £45
   Cabin-class Return £34

PAPEETE, TAHITI.
Via Wellington and Rarotonga—
Seven Weeks' Tour—
   First-class Return £55
   Cabin-class Return £40

No Exchange Charges. Bookings now open. Early reservations advisable. Full particulars from:—

CA AND UNION LINES

UNION S. S. CO., 247 George Street, Sydney.
Tel.: B7671.
59 William St., Melbourne. Cent. 8392.

Union Line advertisement

Chapter Seventeen

Mariposa and *Monterey*

The entry of *Aorangi* onto the Vancouver service in 1925 to partner *Niagara* greatly increased the public interest in travelling by this route to North America and sometimes on to Britain and Europe, at the expense of the San Francisco route, which was being serviced by older, smaller and slower vessels. This situation continued until 1932, when The Oceanic Steamship Company introduced two new, large and fast liners on the route.

The original Oceanic Steamship Company had been taken over by the Matson Navigation Company in April 1926, but the operating name was retained, and the company continued as a separate entity. Apart from upgrading the existing ships and repainting their funnels in Matson colours, the new owners did not do anything to improve the service until Oceanic was awarded a lucrative new ten-year mail contract in 1928.

Also in 1928, the United States Government approved the Jones-White Bill, which became known as the Merchant Marine Act, by which an amount of US$250 million would be made available to American shipping companies, which would be able to borrow up to three-quarters of the cost of building new vessels in American shipyards, at a very low rate of interest, provided the design would enable the ship to be converted for service as a naval auxiliary in time of war.

Matson Line decided to take advantage of this, and placed orders for two new liners to be operated by The Oceanic Steamship Company on the South Pacific route. Keeping with Oceanic tradition, they were to be named after counties in California, *Mariposa* and *Monterey*. The Matson Line also took out an option to build a third liner of the same type, to be confirmed by the end of 1930.

Prior to taking over the Oceanic operation the Matson Line had only been involved in the Hawaiian trade as far as passenger ships went, though they had maintained a regular cargo service to New Zealand and Australia for many years. However in 1929 their newest and largest passenger liner, *Malolo*, was sent on an extensive cruise around the Pacific. *Malolo*, which means "flying fish" in Hawaiian, was the first vessel to be designed by William Francis Gibbs and it was built in Philadelphia, by Wm Cramp Shipbuilding & Engineering Co, being launched on 26 July 1926.

At 17,266 gross tons, with a length of 582 feet (177.3m) and a beam of 83 feet (25.4m), *Malolo* was the largest liner yet built in the United States, and the first American liner to be given a cruiser stern. It was also much wider than contemporary liners of similar size, while the lifeboats were located below the level of the Promenade Deck. These features were included to meet the requirements of the United States Navy, so the ship could be converted for military duty if required. *Malolo* was also given a double bottom and twelve watertight bulkheads, far more than was usual in liners of that era. Just how important these were would be proved even before the liner entered service.

Malolo left Philadelphia on 24 May 1927, for ten days of sea trials. Next day, the ship ran into fog, and speed had been reduced to 14 knots as it neared the Nantucket lightship, when the bow of the Norwegian cargo ship *Jacob Christensen* sliced into the port side of *Malolo* almost at a right angle, making a huge hole just under the bridge, forward of the bulkhead separating the two boiler rooms, both of which were flooded within five minutes.

Any other liner then afloat would have sunk, but *Malolo* remained afloat, thanks to the extra bulkheads which prevented the incoming water from spreading throughout the ship. Radio calls for help brought tugs from New York, but because of the fog they did not reach *Malolo* until almost 24 hours after the collision. On the afternoon of 28 May, the damaged liner was tied up at Pier 4 in Hoboken.

Originally due to enter service in June 1927, the liner was not completed until 20 October, and carried passengers from New York to San Francisco on its delivery voyage. *Malolo* left San Francisco on 16 November 1927 for Honolulu, arriving there on 21 November. *Malolo* quickly became a very popular ship, providing a departure from San Francisco every second Friday.

Accommodation was provided for 690 first class

passengers only, almost all in outside cabins with private facilities. Eight steam turbines geared to twin propellers gave a service speed of 20 knots, and a maximum speed of over 22 knots. The hull was painted chocolate-brown, the standard Matson line colour, and the funnels were yellow with a blue top, and a large blue "M".

On 21 September 1929, *Malolo* departed San Francisco on a 90-day Pacific cruise, visiting eleven countries. Ports of call included Yokohama, Kobe, Shanghai, Hong Kong, Manila, Saigon, Bangkok, Singapore, Batavia and Surabaya, then down the west coast of Australia, visiting Fremantle on 17 November before heading to Melbourne, arriving on 21 November and staying for two nights. *Malolo* berthed in Sydney on 25 November, remaining until 28 November. A local newspaper reported the liner had 359 passengers, of whom 209 were women. After leaving Sydney, *Malolo* visited Auckland, Suva, Pago Pago and Honolulu, returning to San Francisco on 20 December.

Malolo resumed its Hawaiian schedule until 20 September 1930, then left San Francisco on its second 90-day Pacific cruise. This visited most of the same Asian ports as the previous year, with the addition of Bali. *Malolo* then called at Thursday Island before going directly to Sydney, arriving on 22 November. *Malolo* again berthed at Circular Quay West, remaining alongside for three nights. It was also reported that the vessel was carrying only 170 passengers when it arrived, and fifteen additional passengers joined the ship in Sydney for the trip back to San Francisco.

Departing Sydney Heads at 4.54pm on 25 November, *Malolo* reached Wellington Heads in 2 days 19 hours 51 minutes, beating the previous record of 2 days 23 hours set in 1905 by *Maheno*, of the Union Steam Ship Company of New Zealand. After Wellington, *Malolo* again called at Auckland, Suva, Pago Pago and Honolulu, returning to San Francisco on 19 December.

Malolo then went into drydock for a major overhaul. The hull was repainted white, with a blue sheer line and green boot topping. Upon returning to service, the liner resumed operating to Hawaii, with departures from both San Francisco and Los Angeles. In 1937 *Malolo* was renamed *Matsonia* by the Matson Line.

Meanwhile, on 25 October 1929 the contract for the construction of the first two new liners for Oceanic had been signed with the Bethlehem Shipbuilding Corporation's Fore River facility in Quincy, Massachusetts. William Francis Gibbs was responsible for the design of the new vessels, which was based on that of *Malolo*, though the new ships would be larger and have a more modern external appearance.

Construction of *Mariposa* commenced first, the keel being laid on 11 June 1930, the first rivet used being made from iron taken from the historic American warship USS *Constitution*, known as "Old Ironsides". Three months later work began on the second ship, *Monterey*. In November 1930 Matson Line exercised their option and placed a firm order for a third ship, which would be placed on the Hawaiian trade, and named *Lurline*.

Mariposa was launched at 1.30pm on 18 July 1931, with a bottle containing water from Sydney Harbour being smashed across the bow instead of the traditional champagne. Fitting out the interior of the vessel then commenced, taking five months.

On 18 September 1931, *Malolo* departed San Francisco on its third long Pacific cruise, lasting 88 days. This time *Malolo* called first at Los Angeles before heading towards Japan, then visited most of the same ports as in previous years, plus Port Moresby. From there *Malolo* proceeded directly to Sydney, arriving on 23 November.

As the liner came down Sydney Harbour, it passed under the nearly finished Sydney Harbour Bridge, going west as far as Balls Head before turning around and berthing at No 4 Circular Quay. The arrival of the liner was again mentioned in the *Sydney Morning Herald*, the story containing the following amusing paragraph, written by one of the reporters who boarded the ship from the Customs launch:

> Pressmen were plied with questions by charming widows, hard-bitten manufacturers, brokers, bankers and all sorts of conditions of men and women. One man thought Sydney's foreshores were wasted. He wanted to see them commercialised. Had he been monarch of all he surveyed, he would have factory stacks belching forth smoke and soot. But he was the exception. The others were delighted with the clean skies, clean fresh air, and the beauty

Malolo berthed in Sydney (Vic Scrivens collection)

of the scene. The commercialising visitor found no support for his views in his immediate neighbourhood. He sought solace in a cigar and silence.

Malolo stayed in Sydney for three nights, and left its berth at 6 am on 26 November. After again calling at Auckland and several Pacific islands, *Malolo* returned to San Francisco on 15 December, and resumed its place on the Hawaiian trade. In 1937 *Malolo* was renamed *Matsonia*.

The second new ship was launched on 10 October 1931 and named *Monterey*. For a couple of months the two liners were berthed opposite each other at the builder's yard being fitted out. During the second half of 1931 work on fitting out *Mariposa* had continued, with accommodation for 475 first class and a maximum of 240 cabin class passengers being installed, as well as facilities for a crew of 359. In addition there were three cargo holds, two forward and one at the stern.

Malolo berthed in Auckland, November 1931 (Tony Ralph collection)

Under the conditions of the Merchant Marine Act, the hull had to be subdivided in excess of the requirements of the 1929 International Convention for Safety of Life at Sea, with particular attention being paid to the stability of the ship should it be involved in an accident. The main steering gear had to be located below the waterline, and the decks reinforced for the fitting of gun foundations should the vessel be taken over for military duty. In addition, a fuel capacity of 6,606 tons was required, which was sufficient for the round trip from San Francisco to Australia.

The new liner ran sea trials on 10 and 11 December 1931, achieving a maximum speed of 22.84 knots, well in excess of the 20.5 knot service

Monterey (left) and *Mariposa* fitting out (Vic Scrivens collection)

speed required under the terms of the mail contract. On 14 December *Mariposa* was handed over to the Oceanic Line, but did not leave the builders' yard until 9 January 1932, when it steamed to New York, to be opened for public inspection and load stores.

The advent of the new Matson liners did not sit well with everyone in the United States. The following appeared in an item on the effects of the depression in the Honolulu journal *The New Freedom* early in 1932:—

> Notwithstanding this state of affairs (the depression in the shipping industry and the huge volume of unemployed tonnage), and while there are so many millions unemployed on the mainland, and with so much wheat and cotton on hand which cannot be sold, the United States is going ahead with this crazy proposition of spending from 300,000,000 to 400,000,000 dollars of our money - not the Matson monopoly's money – in building one hundred new steamers which are not needed and which will only serve to stir up the hatred and ill will of many countries against the USA.
>
> The three new boats which the US Government is building with our money for the Matson monopoly to play with are certainly not needed or wanted at this time in the South Seas. The moderate passenger and freight traffic between Australia, New Zealand and Fiji at one end and the United States mainland and Canada on the other has been very well handled for many years by the old and reliable Union Steamship Co of New Zealand. With the exception of a few American drummers, theatrical types and vagrant writers and deadbeats, all the passengers travelling to and fro between Australia, New Zealand and the north are British, and unless we are mistaken they prefer to go on British boats. The freight does not amount to a great deal, and is likely to be less in the near future owing to the US increasing the duty on New Zealand butter and preventing Australian and New Zealand beef and mutton from being used by the army and navy here.
>
> Down South the tendency is to restrict the importation of American automobiles and other manufactured goods. Australia and New Zealand are now realising that Great Britain is their best customer for their primary products, and if they wish to increase their sales of butter, wool, wheat, etc., they will have to buy more from the Old Country. All this is bound to be reflected in diminished cargoes for the Matson vessels.
>
> If that grasping organisation, instead of abetting the Government to squander our money in building unnecessary new vessels would risk, say, a quarter of the outlay of its own funds in reducing its rates for transporting passengers and goods between Honolulu and the mainland, it would be moving in the right direction and at least make a show of modifying its present "public be damned" policy.
>
> Remember, it's OUR money and not the Matson monopoly's that is building these new vessels.

On 16 January *Mariposa* left New York carrying 300 passengers, and after passing through the Panama Canal arrived in Los Angeles on 29 January and San Francisco on 31 January. For this delivery voyage the liner, commanded by Captain Joseph H Trask, had a large blue "M" painted on each funnel, but this was removed before the liner entered Pacific service, and would not be painted

Mariposa (John Mathieson collection)

on again until Matson had repaid the Government loan in the late 1930s.

At a ceremony to welcome the new liner to San Francisco the San Francisco *Chronicle* quoted Mr Albert C Diericx, vice-president of the Matson Line:

> I know that people have wondered how we can afford to invest 25 million dollars as a gamble in futures when the Sydney-San Francisco trade has been unable to make the run of our three old-timers - Sierra, Ventura and Sonoma - very profitable. We are going on the principle that service makes travel, and travel makes trade. We are out to compete with the P&O and the Orient Line, and with speed, comfort and perfect efficiency divert trade to this route.

Mariposa sailed from San Francisco on 2 February on its first trip to Australia, but instead of following the regular route the voyage was dubbed a "Coronation Cruise", and visited Honolulu, Bora Bora, Pago Pago, and Suva before reaching Auckland on Saturday, 20 February, spending two days in port. That evening the *Auckland Star* reported:

> Like a ship out of a story-book she came – the Mariposa, newest unit of the Matson fleet. Even through an unkindly rainstorm she appeared as a thing of dazzling whiteness, her huge hull and towering upper-works glistening with fresh paint. From each of her two low-set funnels trailed the finest wisp of smoke, and from her raking masts fluttered long strings of bunting. Above her cruiser stern flew the Stars and Stripes. Her smoothly running engines made it seem as if the ship was softly talking to herself as she steamed up harbour, her sharp bows, with just the suggestion of a flare about them, giving birth to thousand upon thousand of long ripples that stretched away on either side to lap the distant shores. And then, when abreast of the long Stanley Bay wharf, the Mariposa, hailed by her owners as the Queen of the Pacific, lowered a brand-new anchor to the bed of the Waitemata.
>
> It was in no way an ideal morning for the white giantess first to display her splendour in Auckland. She rode to her anchor on a sullen tide, and glowering rain clouds emptied their contents from above. But even in this dismal setting the Mariposa, dressed from boat deck to waterline in shimmering white, looked a typical cruise ship, a ship of the tropics.
>
> Half an hour after the liner's anchor had taken the strain of its 19,000 ton load, the port health officer's pinnace and a Customs launch ran alongside. When the Ferry Building struck eight, the ship, with the tug Te Awhina pushing manfully on her starboard bow, was moving in to her berth at the Central wharf.
>
> It is the general spaciousness of the Mariposa that first impresses itself upon the visitor. Everywhere one goes there seems room to spare. The A deck of the liner is a thing to wonder at. Stepping from one of the two silent elevators that carry passengers between decks, the visitor turns to the left into a cosy library, furnished with rich blue carpet, blue leather chairs, and tiny reading tables. Numerous prints of old ships of a bygone age decorate the walls. From the library one passes into a magnificent lounge that measures 48 feet by 54 feet. The decorative scheme here is lavish, and the four highly ornamental pillars carry a host of noiselessly whirring electric fans. Green, gold and pink are the colours that the artist has made most play with in this luxurious quarter of the ship. Even the piano standing on the small stage is decorated in green and gold.
>
> The walls of the smoking room are done in grey panels that give an unusual stone effect, which is relieved by an excellent series of old English sporting prints. The men's club room is but one other unusual feature. Decorated as a palm garden, the first-class verandah measures 45 feet by 60 feet, the large dancing oval being surrounded by numerous small tables. Four revolving coloured spotlights hang ready to leap into instant life at the touch of a switch. Tucked away in a corner of this room is a miniature soda fountain. Also on A deck is the first-class writing room, the colour scheme of which is among the most delicate of all.
>
> On the boat deck above is a finely equipped gymnasium. Besides the usual paraphernalia to be found in such places there is a patent weight reducing machine for passengers wanting to reduce their waist line and an electrically driven horse. Nearby are the electric baths.
>
> The first-class dining saloon on E deck is one of the attractions of the ship. Here the atmosphere is delightfully cool, for the air is continually being "washed", dried, and brought to just the required temperature. The golden and silver work has been done First class smoking room (Tony Ralph collection) with leaf in place of ordinary paint, and the effect, which is added to by the presence on the walls of artistically-painted exotic birds, is palatial.
>
> There are nine decks on the Mariposa, and six are devoted solely to the passengers. Solid teak planking, three inches thick, covers the promenade decks, and there are close on 90,000 square feet of rubber tiling in the interior. Electric switches are everywhere and the ship's dynamo capacity is sufficient for a town of 25,000 inhabitants. In the first class there is accommodation for 475 passengers, and in the cabin class for 229, a total of 704. Liquid refreshments are always on hand when the liner is logging her 20 knots – she averaged 21.5 on one day between Pago Pago and Suva – for, in addition to the soda fountain, there are two bars. In each stateroom there is a private telephone and each lounge is fitted with talkie picture equipment. Special news or entertainments are distributed throughout the vessel by a broadcasting system, and, of course, there is also a newspaper plant. When the ship is at sea the mouths of two of the holds are converted into cooling swimming pools.
>
> Mr Robert L Ripley, cartoonist, writer and radio broadcaster, is a passenger on the Mariposa. Mr Ripley is the author of 'Believe It Or Not', which is published

in many countries, and he is traveling for the purpose of gaining impressions and matter for another series.

"I have gone abroad once or twice a year for the last 18 years, and have visited 124 countries in that time, but Australia and New Zealand are quite new to me," said Mr Ripley this morning. "Like most Americans, I know very little about both. I hope to come back to gain more information and see more of both countries. I am just traveling round collecting strange things so that I can put them into black and white."

At night the funnels were floodlit, and on Sunday, 21 February, *Mariposa* was the biggest attraction in Auckland. Thousands flocked down Queen Street to see the new liner, which was opened for public inspection during the afternoon, and over 2,500 people took advantage of the opportunity to wander through the lavish public rooms. It was also reported that the consulting surgeon on the *Mariposa* had to be rushed to the Auckland Hospital to be operated on for appendicitis, but was able to return to the ship before it departed. The report also stated that, in addition to the consulting surgeon, the ship carried a doctor, dentist and nurse.

There was also an amusing incident reported in the *Auckland Star* on 22 February:

Early last evening a band marched along Quay Street, and when opposite the wharf at which the new liner was berthed, struck up the well-known hymn "For Those in Peril on the Sea". The agents are inquiring facetiously whether the Matson Company has a legal action against the band.

Arriving in Auckland on the morning of 21 February was *Aorangi*, which was on its way back to Sydney from Vancouver. The two liners departed Auckland on 22 February, *Mariposa* at 7am and *Aorangi* at 12.10pm, both heading for Sydney, arriving there on Thursday, 25 February, though ten hours apart.

Mariposa entered the harbour at 5.32am, and anchored off Watson's Bay for a medical check. At 6.26am the P&O liner *Strathnaver* also entered the harbour, passing the American ship as it proceeded to its berth at Circular Quay 4 West, while *Mariposa* was docked shortly after at Circular Quay 4 East. *Strathnaver*, which had entered service from Britain to Australia in October 1931, was making its second visit to Sydney, so for several hours two of the newest liners in the world were together in Circular Quay, making a most imposing sight for the commuters on Sydney Harbour ferries, and sightseers who flocked to the area to have a look.

At 11am, *Strathnaver*, having disembarked all its passengers for Sydney, undocked from Circular Quay 4 West, and was moved under the Harbour Bridge to the Jones Bay wharf used by P&O liners when they were staying in port for several days. Once this had been accomplished, *Mariposa* was moved across to the

First class dining room (Tony Ralph collection)

First class dance pavilion (Tony Ralph collection)

Cabin class lounge (Tony Ralph collection)

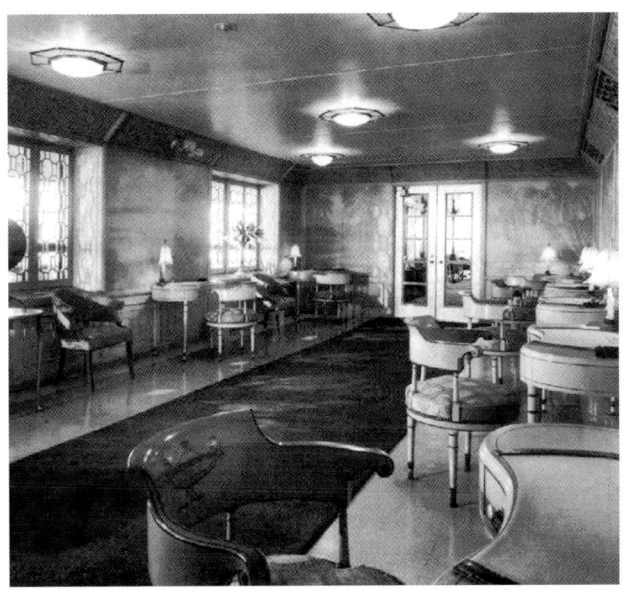

First class writing room (Tony Ralph collection)

vacated berth at Circular Quay 4 West, which was the primary passenger wharf in Sydney, and remained there for the rest of its visit.

At 3.36pm, *Aorangi* passed through Sydney Heads, and having gained medical clearance, moved down the harbour, passing *Mariposa* as it went under the Harbour Bridge to its regular berth in Walsh Bay.

On 26 February the *Sydney Morning Herald* reported:

Few Sydney people had the good fortune to be up early enough yesterday morning to witness the arrival of the new Matson liner Mariposa, which is on her maiden voyage.

While the Mariposa was at anchor off Watson's Bay, during the medical inspection, the new white P&O liner Strathnaver came through the Heads and passed the Mariposa in the stream. The picture was unique for Sydney. The sun by this time lighted the ships with dazzling splendour.

Sydney welcomed the Mariposa with its most beautiful weather, and not less fitting was the welcome given by other craft on the harbour as the new 19,000-ton vessel, the largest to trade to Sydney across the Pacific, came up the harbour. Sirens shrieked, and people on the ferries and foreshores showed keen interest.

The 448 passengers on the Mariposa also showed a keen appreciation of Sydney. They were so absorbed in the views of the harbour and its shores that they left till the last minute the more practical side of their voyage – the changing of dollars into Australian pounds and the checking of baggage.

More than 200 American tourists are making a round cruise by the vessel, which has come from New York and San Francisco by way of Hawaii, Samoa, Fiji and New Zealand, and has yet to pass northward through East to Japan, Hawaii, and San Francisco. As soon as the vessel berthed at Circular Quay the tourists left the ship with great bustle to see as much of Sydney and nearby beauty spots as possible until the Mariposa leaves on Saturday night for Port Moresby.

A party of tourists drove to the Town Hall immediately after disembarking, and were received by the Lord Mayor (Alderman Walder), and the Lady Mayoress, and Mr Roy Hendy (Town Clerk).

Mariposa departing Sydney

Mariposa departed Sydney on 27 February, the voyage back to California being made by way of Port Moresby, Celebes, Java, Singapore, Bangkok, Manila, Shanghai and Yokohama, returning to Honolulu before berthing in San Francisco on 28 April

The second ship, *Monterey*, was delivered to the Oceanic Line on 29 April 1932 following trials, during which a maximum speed of 23 knots was attained. *Monterey* also went first to New York, where it boarded passengers and left on 12 May, passing through the Panama Canal on its way to California. On 28 May, *Monterey* became the largest vessel yet to enter the port of San Diego, arriving in San Francisco on 29 May.

As had happened with *Mariposa*, the funnels of *Monterey* initially carried a large blue "M" on either side, but these were painted out before the first Pacific voyage, and the funnels remained plain yellow with a blue top until the Government loan was paid off in the late 1930s.

Mariposa and *Monterey* were 632 feet/192.6 m long with a beam of 79 feet/24.2 m. *Mariposa* was 18,017 gross tons, while *Monterey* was slightly larger at 18,170 gross tons. They were powered by a pair of geared turbines driving twin propellers, with a service speed of 20.5 knots.

A major feature of the new liners was air conditioning in the dining room, a first for the trans-Pacific trade. Each vessel cost about US$8,000,000 to build, of which amount US$5,850,000 was provided by the United States Government as a low interest loan.

The interior décor of the staterooms, cabins and public rooms was done in soft colours, evoking a South Sea Islands theme. The emphasis was on simplicity and beauty, there being no ornate decorations. In the first class public rooms the windows did not have curtains, instead being fitted with carved wooden grilles. Much of the furniture was made of bamboo, rattan and cane, but in the library there was more traditional furniture, including upholstered chairs. The floors were covered with rubber tiles in soft colours.

Each ship provided luxurious accommodation for 475 first class passengers in 57 single bed cabins and 209 double occupancy staterooms. There were extremely good cabin class facilities for up to 240 passengers in 67 cabins. Three of these cabins had only two beds, while 33 could accommodate three persons, and 31 four persons, but 11 of the 3-berth cabins were fitted with an extra berth if needed. A particular feature of the first class accommodation was the inclusion of eight "lanai suites", located at the forward end of A Deck, which provided the occupants with a private balcony.

First class quarters comprised 57 single and 209 double occupancy staterooms, all fitted with proper beds. At the forward end of A Deck there were ten deluxe staterooms, eight of which had a private enclosed verandah, or "lanai", which could be converted into sleeping areas if required. The rest of the first class staterooms were on B Deck.

In cabin class there were 67 cabins with beds, but some also had folding upper berths. There were three

Monterey (John Mathieson collection)

cabins for two persons, 33 for three persons and 31 had four berths. However, eleven of the three-berth cabins had an extra fold-out upper berth. All these cabins were located on C and D Decks.

The major first class public rooms were located on A Deck, including a large two-deck high lounge amidships, smoking room, men's club and bar, writing room and the library. Right aft, with windows on three sides, was a dance pavilion and palm garden which at night became a verandah café and night club. The forward deckhouse on the Boat Deck contained the bridge with officers' quarters and the radio room behind it, and a Turkish bath and gymnasium for first class passengers. In another deckhouse towards the stern was the accommodation for the engineer officers and the officers' mess.

The open deck space between the deckhouses was available to first class passengers as an area for promenading or sitting in deck chairs. Right amidships was the Sport Deck over the two-deck high main lounge, which contained deck tennis court and other games.

The first class dining room, which could seat 376, and the 134 seat cabin class dining room were both located midships on E Deck, just above the waterline. Cabin class public rooms were located on C Deck, with a main lounge, and a large smoking room aft with views on either side and over the stern. There were also open promenade areas for cabin class passengers on C Deck.

On the morning of 7 May 1932, *Mariposa* was inducted into the United States Government Naval Reserve during a ceremony held on the flying bridge of the ship, which was followed by a special luncheon. That afternoon 275 passengers embarked, and in the evening *Mariposa* departed on its first sailing from San Francisco on regular service, arriving in Sydney on 26 May. Two days later *Mariposa* left for Melbourne, arriving there for the first time on 30 May, berthing at Station Pier.

Monterey departed San Francisco on its first Pacific voyage on 4 June, arriving in Auckland on 19 June. On the sector between Auckland and Sydney *Monterey* created a new record of 62 hours 35 minutes for the run, berthing in Sydney for the first time on 23 June. *Monterey* also went on to Melbourne, arriving for the first time on 27 June.

A schedule of regular departures every fourth week was established, and the route followed took the liners from San Francisco to Los Angeles, Honolulu, Pago Pago, Suva, Auckland, Sydney and Melbourne. The round trip lasted forty-nine days, with each ship spending a week in San Francisco between trips.

A promotional brochure published at this time proudly trumpeted:

Mariposa at Station Pier, Melbourne on 30 May 1932, with *Oronsay* and *Carthage* (Bobby Brookes Collection)

First class library (Tony Ralph collection)

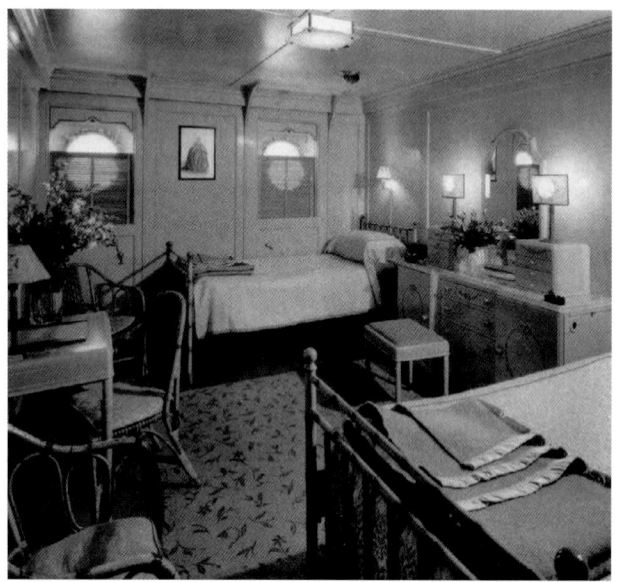

First class stateroom (Tony Ralph collection)

Cabin class cabin (Tony Ralph collection)

Mariposa and Monterey are new sovereigns of the Pacific vested with every attribute of ocean royalty! There is a majesty in their poise, all white against the blue of sea and sky…a royal power in their swift conquest of distance…a queenly graciousness in the atmosphere which pervades throughout. They are nine decks in size…they accommodate over 700 passengers each…their speed is over 20 knots…they run the gamut of sumptuous living at sea. From a byway to a highway, they are transforming the route between California and the Antipodes. Ship life vibrant with the sorcery of the South Seas, yet keyed with perfect harmony to the luxury you always expect on liners like these. Patrician lounge…staterooms spaciously charming…outdoor swimming pools…talkie theatres…night clubs…shops…daily newspapers…every modern facility…and so much more. Tropic sunshine splashing with you in that pool...peacock-colored seas no movie can ever screen…night club gaiety catching its glitter from the Southern Cross! No ocean can boast a finer crossing – in ships, in route, in service.

Meanwhile, the third vessel built for Oceanic had been launched as *Lurline* on 18 July 1932 and was completed in December. Designed to operate on the lucrative service between California and Hawaii, *Lurline* was fitted out with superb accommodation for 475 first class and 240 cabin class passengers. The first class accommodation included several three-room "lanai suites", located midships on the Main Deck. They comprised a bedroom with twin beds, a sitting room with a verandah, and a fully equipped bathroom.

Lurline and her two sisters were the first large liners to have the sides of their hulls insulated with a cork lining, intended to reduce the amount of heat inside the ship in sunny climes. The two restaurants were fitted with air conditioning, then quite new, and there was also a new form of ducting, by which the air in every stateroom in the ship was changed every six minutes.

Lurline was first sent on an extensive cruise, for which only the first class cabins were used. Departing New York on 12 January 1933, the liner went through the Caribbean and Panama Canal to San Francisco. Leaving there on 27 January, and Los Angeles the following day, *Lurline* headed into the South Pacific, with calls at Honolulu and Suva before arriving in Auckland on the morning of 14 February. A short time after *Lurline* berthed, sister ship *Monterey* arrived in Auckland, carrying 296 passengers from Sydney, of whom 159 were disembarking in New Zealand, while 66 would be joining for the voyage to San Francisco.

On the evening of 14 February the *Auckland Star* reported:

The latest addition to the Oceanic lines passenger fleet, and sister ship to the Monterey and Mariposa, the Lurline, with 252 passengers, arrived in Auckland early this morning in the course of a South Seas and Oriental cruise.

She was followed into port not long afterwards by the Monterey, and as the two ships lay alongside the Queen's and Princes wharves, there was no outward difference between them. A display of bunting, however, from the Lurline was an indication that she was on her maiden voyage. Except for a difference in interior colour schemes and minor furnishings they are twin sisters.

Lurline arrived in Sydney on 19 February. Among the passengers on board was the Woolworth heiress, Miss Barbara Hutton, who was accompanied by two friends. They all left the ship in Sydney to spend some time touring Australia. Another notable passenger to disembark in Sydney was the author Alan Villiers, well known for his books and films on sailing ships. The *Sydney Morning Herald* reported:

> Mr Villiers is on his way from New York to South Australia to join the Finnish sailing ship Parma, on which he hopes to travel round Cape Horn to Europe. This will make his seventh - and, he says, his last - voyage around the Horn on a windjammer.
>
> Mr Villiers said that travelling in a luxury liner did not appeal to him after his sailing ship experiences. "It is too monotonous", he said, "you have the feeling that you are a piece of cargo, consigned from one port to another".

Lurline departed Sydney on 21 February, going first to Batavia, then Singapore, Bangkok, Manila and Honolulu, arriving back in San Francisco on 24 April. On 1 May 1933, ownership of *Lurline* was transferred from The Oceanic Steamship Company to Matson Navigation Company, and the blue "M" was painted on the funnels.

A few days later, *Lurline* made its first voyage on the route from San Francisco to Honolulu, operating in conjunction with *Malolo*. *Lurline* became extremely popular on this route, and enjoyed great success.

The advent of the two new liners brought to a close the careers of *Sierra*, *Sonoma* and *Ventura* on the South Pacific trade. *Sierra* was laid up in San Francisco on 22 April 1932, followed by *Sonoma* on 12 May. *Ventura* was the last of the trio to make a trans-Pacific voyage, its final departure from Sydney being on 10 May arriving back in San Francisco on 4 June.

The three vessels were offered for sale, but the only interest came from shipbreakers, and on 18 May 1934 they were sold as a group to a Japanese firm, Yiyikimota, of Osaka. The new owners added the word "Maru" to each of their names, and a crew was sent from Japan to take them across the Pacific under their own steam.

The first to depart San Francisco was *Ventura Maru*, in July 1934, followed by *Sierra Maru* in August and *Sonoma Maru* in September. The three

Lurline berthed and *Monterey* arriving in Auckland on 14 February 1932 (Alexander Turnbull Library)

vessels were anchored out in Osaka Bay until it was their turn to be taken to the scrapping dock, but in October 1934 a typhoon struck the area. Both *Sierra Maru* and *Ventura Maru* were driven aground and wrecked, having to be broken up where they lay. *Sonoma Maru* survived the storm, but was broken up shortly after.

Although the three ships had been replaced by only two vessels which provided a departure every four weeks, with their extra size *Mariposa* and *Monterey* could carry 9,022 passengers each year, compared to 4,056 on the older ships, and there was also an increase in the amount of cargo the new ships could carry.

On the outward voyage the vessels carried supplies to military establishments on Pago Pago, and such items as new cars, lubricating oil, dried fruit and general cargo to Auckland and Sydney. For the return trip the ships loaded large amounts of Australian wool, while in Auckland they took on board frozen lamb and dairy goods.

Unfortunately, the entry into service of *Mariposa* and *Monterey* coincided with a world trade recession, and the Oceanic service only remained economically viable due to the substantial subsidy being provided by the United States Government, which amounted to about US$10 for every mile they travelled.

Monterey in Auckland (Alexander Turnbull Library)

Chapter Eighteen

1934 to 1939

Mariposa and *Monterey* totally outclassed both in size and comfort *Monowai* and *Makura* being operated to San Francisco by the Union Steam Ship Company, but they made no move to build new vessels for their service Although they were receiving subsidies to carry the mail, they were not nearly as generous as the amount being paid to their American rivals.

The Union Line also had a half-share in Canadian-Australasian Line with Canadian Pacific Line, and was operating two liners, *Niagara* and *Aorangi*, on a service from Sydney and Auckland to Vancouver via Suva and Honolulu. While this service was not directly affected by the arrival of the new American liners, there were those who decided to travel on the new American ships, and connect to or from Vancouver by train.

For potential passengers going to or from San Francisco, the lure of the luxurious American liners was too great, and loadings for the Union Line ships declined considerably. *Monowai* had been scheduled to depart Sydney on 29 September 1932, and again on 24 November, but during October the Union Line decided to withdraw *Monowai* from the San Francisco trade, and replace it with *Maunganui*.

Monowai departed San Francisco for the last time on 26 October 1932, arriving back in Sydney on 18 November, and was transferred to the trans-Tasman trades, leaving Sydney on 25 November for Auckland. *Maunganui* departed Sydney on 24 November for San Francisco, becoming the permanent partner for *Makura*.

The withdrawal of *Monowai* from the San Francisco trade in 1932 did not mark the end of trans-Pacific voyages for this vessel, as from time to time over the next six years it would be called upon to make a voyage to Vancouver. The first time this occurred was in May 1933, when *Aorangi* was

Maunganui joined the San Francisco trade in 1932

taken off the Canadian trade for a refit. *Monowai* was brought in to make a round trip to Vancouver, departing Sydney on 11 May, returning on 6 July. *Aorangi* returned to service with a departure on 20 July, and *Monowai* resumed its place on the Tasman trade.

Going into 1934, the Union Steam Ship Company was operating regular four weekly departures from Sydney and Wellington to San Francisco with calls at Rarotonga and Papeete along the way. The Oceanic Steamship Company was also maintaining a regular schedule of departures from San Francisco every four weeks by *Mariposa* and *Monterey*, calling at Honolulu and Pago Pago en route to Auckland, Sydney and Melbourne.

On 23 January 1934, *Lurline* left San Francisco on its second lengthy cruise to the South Pacific and Asia, carrying about 400 passengers. After visiting Auckland, *Lurline* arrived in Sydney on 14 February, departing two days later. Returning to San Francisco on 14 April, *Lurline* resumed its place on the Hawaiian trade.

Apart from passengers, *Mariposa* and *Monterey* also could carry a considerable amount of freight, and on 17 July 1934 *Mariposa* arrived in Sydney with an unusual deck cargo. This was a single engine Lockheed Altair aircraft, which had been bought second-hand in the United States by legendary Australian airman Sir Charles Kingsford Smith. The aircraft had been built in 1929 for a planned 1930 New York to Paris flight by George R Hutchinson which never eventuated.

The aircraft was lifted off *Mariposa*, berthed at Circular Quay East, by the Cockatoo Island Dockyard floating crane, which lowered it onto a barge. This was then towed across Sydney Harbour to Neutral Bay, where the crane lifted the aircraft onto Anderson Park.

Kingsford Smith had planned to leave the aircraft there overnight, but with bad weather forecast, he quickly prepared for take-off. At 4pm, the aircraft rolled down quite a steep hill in the park and lifted into the air, flying out to South Head before following the coastline south for a landing at the Mascot Aerodrome.

Kingsford Smith had bought the aircraft, which he named *Lady Southern Cross*, so he could compete in the upcoming Victoria Centenary Air Race from London to Melbourne, but that plan had to be dropped when modifications to the aircraft could not be completed in time for the start of the race on 20 October 1934. Instead, Kingsford Smith and P G Taylor flew *Lady Southern Cross* from Brisbane to San Francisco in October-November 1934, this being the first west to east trans-Pacific flight in aviation history.

Kingsford Smith tried to sell the aircraft in America, but when this was not achieved it was shipped to England. With J T Pethybridge, he

Lurline berthed in Sydney in February 1934 (John Mathieson collection)

took off from Croydon Aerodrome on 6 November 1935, aiming to make one more record-breaking flight to Australia, but on 8 November the aircraft disappeared in the Bay of Bengal. His memory is perpetuated by Sydney's Kingsford Smith Airport.

The Union Line San Francisco service received a boost from an unexpected source in 1935, when the release of the movie *Mutiny on the Bounty* during 1934 resulted in a huge interest in North America to travel to Tahiti. The Union Line reported that passages to Tahiti increased by almost 50 percent in 1935 over the previous year. However, this was not enough to make the overall service an economic success.

Meanwhile, *Aorangi* and *Niagara* continued to maintain the Canadian service, and on 16 July 1935 *Niagara* departed Vancouver on a voyage back to Sydney, one of the passengers on board being the Prime Minister of Australia, Joseph Lyons, accompanied by his wife and some officials.

Mr Lyons was on a six month trip around the world, having first gone by ship from Australia to London to attend King George V's Silver Jubilee celebrations and hold trade talks with the British Government, then crossed the Atlantic to have talks with American officials in Washington, before heading north to Ottawa for more talks with the Canadian Government. The Prime Minister and his wife travelled across Canada by train, and spent three hours in Vancouver before boarding *Niagara*.

On 17 July *Niagara* called at Victoria, departing at 5pm to continue its voyage south. Only hours after leaving port the liner ran into thick fog while in the Strait of Juan de Fuca, and was involved in a collision with the 4,535 gross ton cargo ship *King Egbert*. The freighter hit *Niagara* on the port side just aft of the bow next to number one hatch, causing buckling to several hull plates and frames.

King Egbert suffered extensive bow damage, it being reported that the forecastle of the cargo ship was demolished, and the hawse pipes and anchors were carried away. Water ballast had to be pumped into the after section of the vessel to prevent it settling too deeply in the water by the bow. Once it was ascertained that neither ship was in immediate danger of sinking both headed for Victoria, where *Niagara* arrived in the early hours of the following morning, and all the passengers disembarked.

Among the Government officials traveling in Prime Minister Lyons' party on board *Niagara* was Mr R I Douglas, a Commonwealth Publicity Officer, who provided an eyewitness account of the collision, stating:

> The collision between the King Egbert and the Niagara on which Mr Lyons and his party were traveling, occurred as most of the passengers were leaving dinner. A dense fog was encountered an hour or so previously and the foghorn was continuously blowing. Hearing the foghorns of other ships, the Niagara had been practically hove-to when the King Egbert loomed out of the fog, striking us a blow which sent a shudder through the ship and tore away most of the superstructure on the bow as far as the bridge on the port side. It also burst the water pipes and dislocated the telegraphs from the bridge to the engine-room.
>
> The King Egbert backed away with water pouring out of her bows. She was, fortunately, lightly loaded. All the passengers on the Niagara were ordered on deck to don lifebelts, and the lifeboats were slung out. There was a complete absence of panic. Mr and Mrs Lyons were in their cabin a few feet from where the King Egbert struck.
>
> As the Niagara was returning to Victoria, the orchestra struck up dance music, while a picture show was put on in the lounge. Mrs Lyons handed chocolates around and shortly afterwards the vessel ran into another fog. The continuous blowing of the siren upset the nerves of many of the women.

In Victoria, arrangements were quickly made for passengers who wished to continue their journey to New Zealand and Australia to be taken by ferry to Seattle, where a special train was organised to transport them to San Francisco, where they would board the American liner *Mariposa*. Prime Minister Lyons and his wife were among those who took advantage of this arrangement, leaving Victoria a few hours after the *Niagara* had limped in. Meanwhile, *Niagara* went to a shipyard at Esquimalt for repairs.

On his arrival at Seattle, Mr Lyons spoke briefly to local reporters, saying "I wish you could meet my wife, but she's asleep. She was rather knocked out, you know, by the steamer collision. She'd been up early in the morning to see the scenery, hoping to have a good sleep that night, and that's the kind of a bally night she had. There wasn't really an awful lot to the collision, though. We are most anxious to get home to see our kiddies. We have eleven, you know."

Mariposa departed San Francisco on Tuesday, 23 July, on a regular voyage to the South Pacific. On the passage from Auckland to Sydney, *Mariposa* set a new record of 58 hours seven minutes, bettering the time set by *Monterey* on its maiden voyage in 1932. Arriving in Sydney on 12 August, Mr and Mrs Lyons and their party disembarked, while *Mariposa* left Sydney on 14 August to continue its voyage to Melbourne.

Niagara finally departed Vancouver again on 1 August, by which time it was running two weeks behind schedule. The vessel was scheduled to leave Sydney on 15 August on its next voyage to Canada, and rather than upset this, it was arranged that passengers and cargo booked on the departure would leave on the same day aboard *Marama*, which was operating a regular service between Sydney and Auckland.

Niagara and *Marama* both arrived in Auckland

Niagara (Vancouver Maritime Museum)

on 19 August, and the passengers bound for Sydney were transferred to *Marama*, while those who had travelled from Sydney on *Marama* were moved to *Niagara*, which left the same evening for Suva, Honolulu and Vancouver, thus being able to maintain the published schedule.

The departure from Sydney for Vancouver on 18 July had been taken by *Aorangi*, and on its voyage back from Canada that arrived in Sydney on Friday, 6 September, *Aorangi* carried over two hundred leading medical professionals, many accompanied by their wives, who were coming to Australia to attend the annual meeting of the British Medical Association, which was being held in Melbourne at the invitation of the Melbourne Centenary Committee. The passengers came not only from Britain and Canada but also numerous other countries within the British Empire, as well as some from the United States.

In an unusual change of routine, *Aorangi* departed Sydney on the evening of 7 September, and carried the medical professionals on to Melbourne, berthing there on 9 September, this being the only time *Aorangi* visited the southern port. The liner arrived back in Sydney on 13 September, berthing at 5 Darling Harbour where it underwent annual maintenance. Once again *Monowai* was taken off the Tasman trade to replace *Aorangi* on the service to Vancouver, with a departure from Sydney on 12 September.

Meanwhile, *Niagara* completed its next trip from Vancouver, passing through Auckland on 1 October and arriving in Sydney four days later. The next voyage to Vancouver was scheduled to depart at noon on Thursday, 10 October, but the seamen in the crew decided not to sign on until certain guarantees had been received regarding the working of cargo in Vancouver, where two rival waterside unions were involved in a protracted dispute.

Only one of these unions was recognised by the Canadian Government, and the Union Line said that it would employ members from this union, but the seamen wanted members of the other union to do the work. As a result the departure of *Niagara* was put back twenty-four hours, and on the morning of 11 October a call for seamen was made, but none signed up. The departure was then rescheduled for 5pm, but another call for seamen was unsuccessful, and the departure was delayed indefinitely. As usual there were quite a few passengers who had booked for the sector from Sydney to Auckland only, while others were going on to Suva, Honolulu and Canada. On Saturday, 12 October the *Sydney Morning Herald* reported:

> The Royal Mail steamer Niagara, whose departure for Vancouver was delayed on Thursday by the job control tactics adopted by the crew, is still held up in Sydney, and her sailing is now indefinite.
>
> The Union Company has decided to take a strong stand in the dispute. The men have been notified by the general manager in Vancouver that, in the event of the trouble continuing, the ship will be placed on Canadian articles, and the Australian seamen replaced by men engaged in Vancouver.
>
> About 70 passengers who had booked to sail by the Niagara transshipped to the Marama, which left for Wellington yesterday evening. Several passengers have

cancelled their passages, and many have transferred to the American mail steamer Mariposa, which will sail for San Francisco on Wednesday.

A special meeting of the seamen decided yesterday not to take the Niagara to sea unless adequate guarantees were given by the Union Company that non-union labour would not be employed in unloading the vessel at Vancouver. The guarantee they demand would enable them to insist that the unofficial body should unload the ship, if the union recognised by the Government was not acceptable to them.

Niagara remained tied up at No 5 Darling Harbour, with the remaining passengers still on board, being looked after by cooks and stewards, who had not joined the dispute. During Saturday the Union Company organised two more crew calls, but still could not sign up any seamen. On Monday, 14 October, the *Sydney Morning Herald* reported:

It is understood that a meeting of seamen will be held today to discuss the situation. If the men do not return to work today the stewards, numbering 132, will be paid off and the Niagara will probably be tied up indefinitely. The vessel will sail at noon today, however, if the men sign on.

All the passengers who had remained on board on Saturday in the hope that a crew would be forthcoming, have now left the Niagara. Throughout Saturday morning numbers of intending passengers called at the Union Company's offices for a refund of their passage money. They were informed that the ship might sail today, but a number insisted on cancelling their tickets and then sought accommodation on the American mail steamer Mariposa, which will sail for San Francisco on Wednesday.

The dispute has cost the Union Company thousands of pounds. Even if the ship sails today there will probably be no more than 80 passengers on board.

With no immediate resolution to the dispute in sight, on the morning of 16 October *Niagara* was moved from No 5 Darling Harbour to No 1 Woolloomooloo. At the time it was stated that it was hoped the vessel would be able to depart in the next two days, and if this occurred it would bypass Auckland and go directly to Suva, to pick up some of the lost days on its schedule.

On Thursday, 17 October, a meeting was held at the Arbitration Court, at which the shipping company and the union were able to reach an agreement, but when the seamen met again on the morning of 18 October the terms of the agreement was rejected. Up to this time thirteen third class passengers had remained on board the ship, but they now gave up and disembarked, leaving the ship completely empty. On the afternoon of 18 October *Niagara* was moved from Woolloomooloo to anchor off Garden Island.

Faced with the rejection of the agreement they had reached with the union, Canadian-Australasian Line decided to go outside the normal system and advertise for volunteers to man the *Niagara*. With hundreds of former seamen out of work, it took only a short time to find enough to fill all the positions available on the ship. It was then arranged that the *Niagara* would depart on Saturday evening. On Monday, 21 October, the *Sydney Morning Herald* reported:

The Canadian-Australasian liner Niagara sailed from Sydney on Saturday evening, for Vancouver, via Suva and Honolulu, manned by a crew of volunteers, mostly ex-naval men.

Scores of capable and experienced men applied at the offices of the Union Company on Saturday morning in response to an advertisement calling for a crew for the Niagara, and little difficulty was experienced in obtaining a thoroughly competent crew.

The Seamen's Union was dismayed when it was learned that the Niagara had sailed. Officials had stated early in the day that negotiations for a settlement were in progress, and that it was probable a special meeting of the union today would decide to man the ship.

Seamen had scouted the suggestion that the company would take a strong stand and dispatch the vessel to sea with a non-union crew, contending that the owners were attempting to intimidate them into manning the steamer, and that they would hold the volunteers in reserve. The departure of the Niagara caused consternation in union circles, and the situation that has arisen is bound to lead to much plain speaking and recrimination at today's meeting.

Long before the Union Company's offices in George Street were opened on Saturday, large numbers of applicants for positions were waiting outside, and by 8.30 more than 30 men had volunteered their services. Throughout the morning numbers of seamen thronged the office. The majority of the applicants were ex-naval men who held excellent discharges, and little difficulty was experienced in securing the requisite number of seamen. Many applicants, however, had no seafaring knowledge whatsoever, but were anxious to secure employment in any capacity.

The police were advised of the company's proposed action on Friday night, and plain-clothed and uniformed police were on duty outside Union House in case a demonstration was attempted. Police were stationed at the corner of Bridge and George Streets, and outside the building entrances. Although several seamen watched the applicants passing in to offer their services, there was no hostile demonstration.

As soon as the men required had been signed on they were told to secure their belongings and report to Fort Macquarie, where launches were waiting to carry them to the Niagara, which was moored off Garden Island.

The cooks who had been employed on the Niagara refused to sail when they learned that there was a possibility of non-union labour being engaged, but the company found no trouble in replacing them. The stewards were willing to sail in the same ship with seamen who were not members of the Seamen's Union.

The Niagara carried one first-class passenger, and three second-class and 18 third-class passengers. By sailing direct for Suva, she will make up three of the days of her schedule lost through the hold-up, and by reducing the normal number of days she usually stays in Vancouver, she will almost pick up her running schedule when she sails on the return journey to Australia.

With the depression continuing to affect the viability of the Union Line services to both Vancouver and San Francisco, in February 1936 the company made an approach to the governments of Australia, New Zealand, Fiji and Canada to provide a combined subsidy to support British passenger liners operating across the Pacific, and enable them to remain competitive with their American rivals. This proposal was rejected by all the governments.

The Canadian-Australasian Line service was suffering a downturn in passenger numbers, and as a result during 1936 both *Niagara* and *Aorangi* underwent refits during which the first class accommodation was reduced on *Niagara* to about 260, while on *Aorangi* it was almost halved to 248, with smaller reductions in second and third class.

On 9 February 1936 the Union Line announced that during June, July and August, which was winter in the South Pacific, they would be offering a 30 percent reduction on first and second class fares from both San Francisco and Vancouver, these being advertised in North America as "summer rates". While this may have resulted in increased patronage, it did not really increase the income being derived from the services, and in May 1936 the Union Line announced they would be withdrawing permanently from the San Francisco service by the end of that year.

On 21 October 1936, *Maunganui* departed San Francisco for the last time, and was then placed on a summer service from Wellington and South Island ports to Melbourne. In winter *Maunganui* began operating occasional cruises to the Pacific Islands from Wellington, and also spent periods laid up.

The final Union Line departure from San Francisco was taken by *Makura* on 18 November 1936, arriving in Sydney on 12 December.

On 15 December *Makura* left Sydney for the last time, on a voyage to Wellington on which passengers were carried. At that time there was no alternative employment for the 28-year old vessel, so it was laid up in Wellington and offered for sale. The only interest came from ship breakers, and at the end of 1936 *Makura* was sold to China Shipbreakers Ltd. On 30 January 1937 *Makura* steamed out of Wellington on its final voyage, going to Shanghai where it was broken up.

However, all was not doom and gloom for the Union Steam Ship Company. In 1934, in a bold move considering the world was gripped by a major depression, they had ordered the construction of a new

Makura made the last Union Line sailing from San Francisco (John Mathieson collection)

liner for the Tasman trade, which would be the finest vessel they ever operated. Launched at the Vickers-Armstrong shipyard at Barrow-in-Furness on 25 February 1936, the new liner was named *Awatea*. On speed trials, and using only four of its six boilers, the vessel attained 22 knots, while with all boilers lit it reached a top speed of 24.5 knots, making *Awatea* the third fastest British liner of that era, surpassed only by *Queen Mary* and *Empress of Britain*.

Awatea offered exceptional comfort to passengers, being capable of carrying 377 in first class, 151 in second and 38 in steerage. There was also 164,000 cubic feet of general cargo space, with an additional 23,500 cubic feet for refrigerated cargo. At 13,482 gross tons *Awatea* was smaller than the two Matson liners, *Mariposa* and *Monterey*, with which it would have to compete on the route between Auckland and Sydney.

On its delivery voyage to New Zealand *Awatea* went first to Liverpool to embark passengers, departing on 5 August 1936, and voyaged by way of the Panama Canal to Wellington. Despite using only three of the six boilers, and traveling at the most economical speed, *Awatea* averaged 17.08 knots, setting a new record for the passage of 28 days 6 hours 33 minutes, beating the previous record by eighteen hours, arriving in Wellington on the morning of 3 September.

Awatea was a truly outstanding liner, and on 3 September *The Dominion* newspaper published an extensive article describing the ship and its features, which included the following :

A masterpiece of British shipbuilding science and art, the Union Steam Ship Company's new trans-Tasman express liner Awatea…has been described by Vickers-Armstrong Ltd who built her at Barrow-in-Furness as the finest ship they have ever turned out, and by Sir Charles Craven, chairman of that firm, as the fastest and most luxurious liner of her tonnage in the world.

The first class dining saloon on B Deck, measuring 80 ft in length by 70 ft breadth, and accommodating 264 persons at a sitting, is superbly appointed. Panelled in bleached Nigerian cherrywood and sapele mahogany bandings, the general effect of which give the room an extremely comfortable appearance…A gallery for the orchestra is at one end and a bow-fronted balcony extends across the other, its handsome front being in a special aluminium alloy. Beautifully decorated glass in sliding grilles which are fitted to each window, and skilfully arranged mirrors, add to the appearance of this great apartment, the fittings and appointments of which add to its magnificence. A children's dining room and playroom adjoins the dining saloon.

The great lounge is a magnificent room panelled in straight-grained ash and black bean with Macassar ebony in narrow strips as relief…Large couches in green and comfortable armchairs in pink and beige are grouped around low tables of pale gold polished wood. Gorgeous carpets and rugs tone in with the appointments of this room, which is said to be one of the most beautiful apartments ever fitted in a ship. A permanent cinema

Awatea at Liverpool, 5 August 1936 (Dallas Hogan collection)

screen is skilfully concealed at the after end of the lounge.

Club rooms are a novel feature of the Awatea. The reserved to the use of the ladies is a delightful apartment in rose and ivory furnishings and fittings with gilt enrichments on natural coloured satinwood panelling. The men's club room is a comfortable apartment in which English brown oak is used in contrasting squares relieved with long panels of rich red leather studded with staybrite steel bosses.

Accommodation is provided in the Awatea for 337 first-class passengers in 164 one, two or three-berth staterooms on the Boat Deck and A, B and C decks. The staterooms represent the very latest ideas in seagoing comfort and luxury and are fitted with telephones and hot and cold running water. There are 25 special staterooms, each with its private bathroom. Fourteen have two berths and 11 single berths. These cabins are panelled by master craftsmen in beautiful woods. The furniture and other fittings in each cabin match the walls...and there are tall mirrors and capacious wardrobes. All these cabins have bedsteads; over each bed is a cleverly screened reading lamp and every cabin has its telephone finished in ivory.

On B and C decks accommodation is provided for 151 tourist-class passengers in 42 beautifully furnished and fitted cabins. Comfortable accommodation for 38 steerage passengers is provided on C Deck aft.

The tourist-class dining saloon on B Deck is a handsome apartment with seating accommodation or 123 persons. A bar and bar lounge is arranged at the fore-end. The tourist lounge and smoking room are on A Deck and there is a cinema-projection room at the after end of the lounge. A promenade and swimming-bath for tourist-class passengers are arranged at the after end of the Promenade Deck.

After being open for public inspection on 13 and 14 September, when thousands of people swarmed aboard to admire the new liner, *Awatea* departed Wellington on 15 September for Auckland, arriving on the morning of 17 September, having made the fastest ever passage between the two ports. At 5pm on Friday, 18 September 1936, *Awatea* departed Auckland on its maiden crossing of the Tasman Sea to Sydney. The vessel was under the command of Captain Arthur H Davey, whose name would always be associated with the ship.

Using only four boilers, *Awatea* completed the voyage in two days 13 hours 40 minutes, and made the return trip to Auckland in a slightly quicker time, carrying 409 passengers. This was achieved despite the ship running into some very bad weather, and also having to reduce speed to 17 knots so it would not arrive before the scheduled time of 8.30am on 29 September. Following the entry into service of *Awatea*, *Monowai* was withdrawn from service and laid up in Auckland.

At the same time the Union Line withdrew from the San Francisco trade, the Oceanic Steamship Company was facing major problems with their service from San Francisco to Auckland and Sydney. For several months in the middle of 1936 the Pacific coast had been the scene of maritime unrest, with the relationship between members of the Maritime Federation of the Pacific and shipowners becoming increasingly acrimonious. The threat of a major strike grew stronger during September and October, and came to a head at the end of the month. At midnight on 29 October 1936, the maritime industry on the Pacific coast of the United States came to a halt as an estimated 40,000 seamen and longshoremen went on strike.

Mariposa had departed Sydney on 14 October, passing through Auckland three days later, and continuing its regular voyage to Honolulu and San Francisco, arriving there on 3 November. By then the maritime strike was on, and the crew of *Mariposa* walked off the ship, which had to be laid up, with the next departure cancelled.

Monterey had departed San Francisco on 13 October on a regular voyage to Auckland, where it arrived on 30 October, and Sydney, berthing there on 2 November. Although the strike had started by then in America, the crew did not leave the ship, which left Sydney as scheduled on 11 November, reaching San Francisco on 30 November, at which time the crew joined the strike, and *Monterey* was also laid up.

As the strike dragged on through December and into January 1937 there was no immediate settlement in sight. With the Union Line having withdrawn from the San Francisco trade, there was no direct connection available between California and New Zealand and Australia, but the Vancouver service was not affected by the strike, and many passengers took advantage of that route to travel across the Pacific, the extra revenue being very welcome for Canadian-Australasian Line.

The Pacific Coast maritime strike lasted ninety-nine days before the strikers were forced into a rather humiliating backdown, and work resumed in early February 1937. It was estimated the strike had cost the maritime and related industries about US$700 million, and many of the strikers ended up leaving the sea permanently.

With the end of the strike, the Oceanic Steamship Company could make arrangements to recommence their service, and the first departure from San Francisco was by *Monterey* on 9 February, calling at Auckland on 26 February and arriving in Sydney on 1 March. *Monterey* left Sydney on 5 March on the return trip, the first departure for San Francisco from the port in four months. *Mariposa* departed San Francisco on 2 March, arriving in Sydney on 22 March, so the regular four-weekly schedule was resumed.

The Union Steam Ship Company had for many years operated a network of passenger services across the Tasman Sea, the main routes being those

Mariposa arriving in Sydney (John Mathieson collection)

between Auckland and Sydney and Wellington and Sydney. For many years the only competition they faced was provided by the Australian company, Huddart Parker Limited, which had introduced a new liner, *Wanganella*, to the trade in January 1933. However, *Mariposa* and *Monterey* were also allowed to carry passengers between Auckland and Sydney, and from the moment they entered service many passengers were attracted to travel on them for the trans-Tasman trip.

Going into 1937, *Aorangi* and *Niagara* were continuing to operate departures every four weeks from Sydney and Vancouver. *Aorangi* left Sydney on 15 April, and was scheduled to leave again on 10 June, but on 26 April the newspaper advertisements suddenly changed to show *Monowai* taking that departure. On its voyage north *Aorangi* had suffered damage to a crankshaft, but was able to complete the trip, calling at Honolulu on 30 April and arriving in Vancouver on 8 May. On the return trip to Sydney, *Aorangi* had to travel at reduced speed, passing through Auckland on 2 June, arriving in Sydney on 6 June, but would miss its next round voyage to enable repairs to be completed.

Since the arrival of *Awatea*, *Monowai* had been laid up at Hobsons Bay in Auckland, and the vessel required several weeks of work, including repainting and drydocking, before it could be reactivated to take over the Vancouver route. *Monowai*, once again commanded by Captain A J Toten, arrived in Sydney on 8 June, carrying a large number of passengers as well as cargo and the mails on the voyage from Auckland.

Monowai left on 10 June 1937 for Canada, passing through Auckland on 14 June, arriving in Vancouver on 4 July. *Monowai* returned to Sydney on 31 July, and on 3 August left Sydney for Wellington, where it was again laid up. Apart from occasional periods on the Tasman trade when *Awatea* was out of action, and a few summer cruises, *Monowai* spent the next two years sitting idle in Wellington Harbour.

With the Vancouver service not doing particularly well, and the Union Line having withdrawn completely from the San Francisco trade, the British Government appointed an Imperial Shipping Committee to scrutinise the situation affecting British shipping in the Pacific. Its report was released on 7 December 1936, after the Union Line had withdrawn from the San Francisco trade, and it blamed the generous subsidy being paid to the Oceanic Company for the demise of the Union Line San Francisco service. The report found that prior to 1931 only one-fifth of passengers to and from Australia had been carried on the old Oceanic ships, but the new ships had been carrying three-fifths of the passengers on the route.

The report also stated that the United States Government had provided a loan of over US$11 million to enable Oceanic to build their two new ships for the South Pacific trade, with more provided to build *Lurline*, and in addition had paid Oceanic a subsidy of US$800,000 a year from 1928 to 1932, this being increased to one million dollars from 1933 on. The Imperial Shipping Committee recommended the construction of two ships at a cost of £2,500,000 for the Canadian service, but with a stop at San Francisco included on the southbound voyage.

Further impetus for the construction of new ships was reported in two items sent from London on 10 June 1937 that appeared in the *Sydney Morning Herald* the next day:

> Speaking at the launching of the new P&O liner Stratheden at Barrow-in-Furness today, the chairman of the company, the Hon Alexander Shaw, said he hoped that his company would soon be able to place two new ships on the Australian-Canadian route.
>
> "I cannot say any more," he added, "but at least there is a good chance that the berth vacated today will be filled by a new ship to keep the British flag flying in the Pacific."
>
> He said that the P&O Company and its associated lines within a few weeks would have 100,000 tons of shipping building, at a cost of £4,250,000.
>
> Although the shipping committee of the Imperial Conference has not yet reached a decision, there is now every hope that an agreement will be arrived at for the construction of two 22,000-ton liners for the trans-Pacific route, costing approximately £3,000,000 compared with the original estimate of £2,500,000.
>
> It is understood that the discussions took a more favourable turn after the delegates had conferred with the chairman of Canadian Pacific Steamships Ltd (Sir Edward Beatty).
>
> The agreement would involve a compromise regarding financial guarantees of the British and dominion Governments to shipping companies, probably necessitating in each case a somewhat higher contribution than that tentatively suggested in Britain's memorandum which was submitted to the dominions as the outcome of the report of the Imperial Shipping Committee.
>
> The new vessels would be financed by the Governments in a manner similar to that adopted in the case of the Atlantic liner Queen Mary, when a bill was passed by the British Parliament authorising the Treasury to advance up to £9,500,000. It is believed that each dominion will have to pass separate legislation.

Not surprisingly, considering the world economic situation, this recommendation was not accepted, and nothing was done to improve the Canadian service, while the San Francisco service was never resumed by a British shipping company.

It was also during 1937 that The Oceanic Steamship Company faced a major problem, when the United States Government launched an investigation into the mail contracts that had been awarded to various companies in 1928, which resulted in all such agreements being cancelled.

The Oceanic company immediately filed a complaint, pointing out that while they had indeed made a profit of over a million dollars in the years 1932 to 1936, they had received a mail subsidy over the same period of just over five million dollars, so without that subsidy they would have incurred a loss of over four million dollars, which would have forced them to abandon the South Pacific trade. As a result a new subsidy scheme was organized, which while not as generous as the previous one, enabled the company to continue its operations.

In May 1937, *Awatea* entered the Cockatoo Island Dockyard in Sydney Harbour for a major overhaul, lasting over two months. It was during this overhaul that the funnels of the *Awatea* were heightened to stop soot falling on the after decks when the liner was at sea. While this change solved the soot problem, it radically altered the streamlined appearance of the ship.

Also during the overhaul, severe damage to the main propulsion reduction gearing was discovered. Repair work involved stripping down the gearing cases so the old gearing could be removed and replaced with new gearing of a different design, which had been manufactured in Britain and shipped to Australia. The turbines were also closely inspected but found to be in good order.

On 27 July 1937, *Awatea* conducted sea trials off the New South Wales coast, and for the first time all six boilers were fired up at the same time. It was reported in the local press that the ship achieved a maximum speed in excess of 26 knots, but the official announcement put the top speed at just over 23 knots.

Despite being restricted by having to maintain a regular schedule of arrival and departure times, *Awatea* had broken all previous records for the Tasman routes within a year of entering service. Departing Sydney on 9 October 1936, *Awatea* averaged 20.45 knots on a voyage to Wellington, setting a new time of 2 days, 12 hours and 33 minutes, which was bettered in early November and again in late December, but on the voyage that departed Sydney on 1 January 1937, *Awatea* reduced the time to 2 days 9 hours and 15 minutes, at an average speed of 21.62 knots.

On the route between Sydney and Wellington *Awatea* faced no serious competition for these records, but on the Auckland service the situation was quite different, as *Awatea* was up against *Mariposa* and *Monterey*. In July 1932, *Mariposa* had beaten the record between Sydney and Auckland previously set by *Maheno* in 1907, and in January 1936 *Monterey* set a new time for the voyage from Auckland to Sydney, 2 days, 10 hours and 12 minutes. In October 1936, *Awatea* was able to set a new record for the voyage between Sydney and Auckland, 2 days, 11 hours and 36 minutes, but the record for the trip from Auckland to Sydney remained with the Americans, a fact that did not please Captain Davey of the *Awatea*.

Awatea returned to the Tasman trade at the end of July, with a voyage from Sydney to Auckland, from where it was due to sail again on Friday, 6 August 1937. By coincidence, one of the Matson liners, *Monterey*, was also due to depart Auckland for Sydney the same day, the first time *Awatea* had been able to directly compete with one of the American liners. *Awatea* left first, followed four hours later by *Monterey*, but the two liners did not sight each other during the crossing.

On the morning of Monday, 9 August 1937 the two liners passed through Sydney Heads, *Awatea* leading the way at 7.30, followed by *Monterey* at 10.18. This meant that *Monterey* had made the crossing about one hour and fifteen minutes faster than *Awatea*, but had not beaten its own record, as both ships had been forced to reduce speed for almost a day when they encountered heavy weather.

Captain Davey was determined that *Awatea* would take the record from the Americans, but needed the right conditions and situation to enable this to be done. The opportunity arose on Friday, 3 September 1937, when both *Awatea* and *Mariposa* were scheduled to depart Auckland for Sydney. Heavy rain during the day delayed the loading of cargo, so *Awatea* was almost six hours late in departing, while *Mariposa* did not get away until the next day.

Encountering favourable weather in the Tasman on Saturday, Captain Davey ordered that a fifth boiler be brought into service, and speed was increased to over 24 knots, but on Sunday the weather deteriorated, and speed had to be reduced. Despite this, *Awatea* arrived off Sydney Heads just before 7am on the Monday morning, having completed the voyage in 2 days, 9 hours and 31 minutes, cutting 41 minutes off the previous record set by *Monterey*.

On its next voyage from Auckland, weather conditions were ideal for *Awatea* to make a concerted effort to create an even better time. Departing Auckland on 1 October 1937, a special speed trial was run over a 24 hour period from noon on Saturday, during which *Awatea* maintained an average speed of 23.35 knots, covering 576 nautical miles. Even then the ship was not utilising its maximum power, but the average speed for the entire trip was 23.1 knots, and the previous record was eclipsed by two hours and four minutes, the new time being 2 days, 7 hours and 28 minutes.

In the opposite direction, on 25 October 1937, *Awatea* arrived in Auckland to complete another record breaking voyage, having taken two days, 10 hours and 52 minutes on the crossing from Sydney, 44 minutes faster than the previous record set a year earlier. This record would not be broken for 24 years, when, in June 1961, the brand new *Oriana* made the trip from Sydney to Auckland in 47½ hours, at an average speed of 27 knots.

On 27 December 1937 *Awatea* completed a record breaking voyage from Sydney to Wellington, 2 days, 7 hours and 49 minutes, at an average speed

Monterey in Port Phillip Bay (WSS Vic)

of 22.19 knots, breaking the record it had set in January 1937 by one hour 46 minutes. *Awatea* also set a new record for the voyage from Wellington to Sydney, 2 days, 12 hours and 26 minutes. This was further eclipsed when the vessel arrived in Sydney on 10 March 1938, having completed the voyage from Wellington Heads to Sydney Heads in 2 days ,11 hours and 11 minutes.

Awatea now held the speed records for all the major routes across the Tasman Sea in both directions, and to celebrate this, the Union Line commissioned Cockatoo Dock to construct a stainless steel greyhound, which was mounted proudly on the fore truck on *Awatea* to symbolise its title of "Queen of the Tasman Sea". When Captain Johanson of the *Monterey* first saw the emblem, he sent a message to Captain Davey, asking him why he had a kangaroo at his masthead.

Mariposa and *Monterey* were not far behind, and striving to reclaim the records between Sydney and Auckland. The Union Line was adamant that *Awatea* was not to become involved in any races with the American liners, and their schedules did not coincide for a lengthy period. This changed on 10 June 1938, when both *Awatea* and *Mariposa* were scheduled to depart Auckland for Sydney.

Awatea left on time at 5pm, but *Mariposa* was an hour late when it pulled away from the dock at 11 pm. Running as usual on only four boilers, *Awatea* rounded North Cape and set course for Sydney, but ran into deteriorating weather. Speed had to be steadily reduced through the first day at sea, until it was down to 15 knots as the liner ploughed through high waves and strong winds. Gradually *Awatea* steamed out of the bad weather, and by midnight was back up to normal speed. A few hours later, the officers on the bridge sighted lights coming up from astern, and Captain Davey correctly assumed it was *Mariposa*, travelling at top speed.

Shortly before dawn *Mariposa* went past *Awatea*, and gradually pulled ahead, then disappeared over the horizon. Captain Davey had watched the American liner steam past his pride and joy with a heavy heart, and eventually could not take it any more. He gave the order for a fifth boiler to be fired up, and as speed increased the *Mariposa* reappeared over the horizon ahead as *Awatea* closed on her rival.

During the afternoon the gap between the two liners slowly closed, and by nightfall *Awatea* had caught up several miles, but was still trailing. Through the night the gap slowly closed further, and by dawn *Awatea* was only a mile behind. With *Mariposa* using full power, and *Awatea* still on only five of her six boilers, the two ships were going at almost identical speed, but *Awatea* continued to chip away at its larger adversary. By 2.30pm *Awatea* and *Mariposa* were side by side, but then *Awatea* commenced to pull away.

Awatea managed to keep its lead through the rest of the afternoon, and as 5pm approached anyone standing on Sydney Heads would have witnessed an amazing sight. Steaming at full speed from almost due east they would have seen *Awatea* and *Mariposa* almost together, while coming from a more southerly direction was *Wanganella*, on a voyage from Wellington, though it had left a full day earlier than the other two.

Awatea passed through Sydney Heads at 5.05 pm, followed at 5.10 by *Wanganella*, then *Mariposa* came through the Heads at 5.15. The three liners proceeded in single file down Sydney Harbour, with *Mariposa* pulling into Woolloomooloo Bay to dock, while *Awatea* and *Wanganella* went to their usual berths in Darling Harbour.

When quizzed later by local newspaper reporters about the voyage, both Captain Davey and Captain William Meyer of the *Mariposa* denied they had been engaged in a race. "There was no race," said Captain Meyer, "but there was no need to loaf about when the weather improved, so we did 21 knots." However, it was revealed that a porthole on *Mariposa* had been smashed by the seas, and a mattress was stuffed into it for the remainder of the voyage.

"What race?" queried Captain Davey. "There was no race. The sea was rough, but I've struck lots worse. The ship behaved splendidly. We suffered no damage. The Matson boat was flat out. I knew she was and I was surprised to see her put on so much speed. She must have been doing 21.5 knots. We were doing 21.7 knots and with just that extra fraction it took me 24 hours to overhaul the 20-mile lead she had on us." Captain Davey went on to point out that he had only been using five boilers, and if he had intended to get involved in a race he would have ordered all six boilers be used.

Almost overlooked in the excitement of the event was *Wanganella*, which had managed to arrive in Sydney at the same time as *Awatea* and *Mariposa*. Asked for his comment, Captain Bates of *Wanganella* replied, "It was just like three horses racing abreast down the straight. It was a wonderful sight. It will probably never happen again." Sadly these last words would prove to be only too true. This was the last time *Awatea* engaged one of the American liners in direct competition, but their friendly rivalry continued over the next two years.

Mariposa and *Monterey* continued providing regular monthly departures from both San Francisco and Los Angeles to Auckland, Sydney and Melbourne. On the Vancouver route, *Aorangi* and *Niagara* also continued to provide a departure each month from Sydney. During the first half of 1939 both these liners were due to be withdrawn for one round trip each to undergo an overhaul, being replaced by *Monowai*, which was laid up in Wellington. *Niagara* had departed Sydney on 16

March 1939, returning on 6 May, and then was withdrawn.

Monowai left Sydney on 11 May, calling at Auckland on 16 May and Honolulu ten days later, arriving in Vancouver on 2 June. *Aorangi* had left Sydney on 13 April for Vancouver, and on returning on 5 June was also taken out of service, with *Niagara* being due to depart Sydney on Thursday, 8 June, but this did not happen, as reported next day in the *Sydney Morning Herald*:

The Canadian-Australasian Royal Mail liner Niagara, with 450 passengers on board, is held up in Sydney Harbour by a dispute with engineers. The vessel was to have sailed for Vancouver at 4pm yesterday. Her departure was delayed until 9pm in the hope that the dispute would be settled, but she had not left the wharf at an early hour this morning.

Early this morning officials of the company said they hoped the vessel would sail at 10 o'clock this morning. The vessel will move to the adjoining wharf, No 4 Darling Harbour, at 6am to allow Awatea, which is due from New Zealand this morning, to berth.

The trouble arose because several junior engineers were dissatisfied with their quarters. The men refused to discuss their grievances, but it is understood that they demanded single-berth cabins instead of the two-berth cabins allocated to them. Members of the crew said that the quarters for the engineers left much to be desired.

"Some of the cabins are like boxes," one man said, "and become unbearable for two men to live in when we reach the tropics." The men allege that they were promised that arrangements would be made for them to obtain single-berth cabins during Niagara's recent lay-up, and when they found that this had not been done they decided to strike.

The liner was scheduled to sail at 4pm, and one gangway had already been removed when eight engineers in street clothes, some of them carrying luggage, hurried off the ship. Half an hour before the Niagara was scheduled to leave, about nine of the engineers sat quietly sipping tea in the engineers mess room, awaiting instructions from officials of the Australian Institute of Marine and Power Engineers. They said that 15 engineers who were key men of the Niagara's crew were involved in the dispute. It was noticed that only seven of the men later left the ship.

In the afternoon, and again at night, large crowds assembled on the wharf to bid farewell to friends on the vessel. Both at 4pm and 9pm, festoons of streamers linked ship to the wharf, only to be despondently thrown away.

The manager for New South Wales of the Union Steamship Co of New Zealand Ltd, Mr A J Soutar, said during the afternoon that the departure of the Niagara has been delayed because of the dissatisfaction of some

Mariposa and *Empress of Britain* berthed in Auckland on 12 April 1938 (Alexander Turnbull Library)

engineers with their quarters on the vessel. Only eleven men were involved in the dispute.

The Institute of Marine Engineers met at 8pm to discuss the matter. At 11.30pm two officials of the company arrived. The meeting adjourned early this morning, but union and company officials refused to divulge the result of the conference.

The Awatea has encountered rough weather on her passage from Auckland, and is not expected to berth until 9.30 o'clock this morning. She was scheduled to arrive at 8am, but a wireless message from Captain Davey stated that, because of the high seas, he expected to arrive at Sydney an hour and a half late.

Under the original schedule, *Niagara* would have left on 8 June, enabling *Awatea* to use the same berth on 9 June. However, with Niagara still alongside, *Awatea* had to go to an alternative berth when it arrived. With the delay to *Niagara*, the arrival of *Awatea* a few hours before *Niagara* departed, and *Aorangi* in port as well undergoing maintenance, this was the only time that these three liners were in Sydney Harbour at the same time.

Fortunately the dispute was settled quickly, and *Niagara* departed at midday on 9 June, with this story appearing in the *Sydney Morning Herald* the following day:

After having been held up in Sydney for 20 hours with 450 passengers on board, because of a dispute with engineers, the Canadian-Australasian Royal Mail liner Niagara sailed for Vancouver, via New Zealand, at 12.10pm yesterday.

The nine engineers and two electricians concerned in the strike had demanded better accommodation for some of the junior engineers, who wanted single-berth cabins instead of the two-berth cabins provided. They claimed that one of these two-berth cabins had no ventilation.

Shortly after 11 o'clock yesterday morning it was announced that company officials and the Institute of Marine Engineers had reached an agreement that first-class accommodation was to be provided for two junior engineers, and that the Niagara would sail without further delay. Union representatives and the men inspected the quarters to make sure that they would be satisfactory. They were in the best part of the ship and were tastefully furnished.

However, one junior engineer refused to sign on after this agreement was reached, and his place will be filled when the Niagara arrives at Auckland. There was then a further wait of three-quarters of an hour while one of the engineers went by taxi to Rosebery for his luggage.

At last, shortly after noon, the Niagara began to draw away from the wharf, while passengers who had already been twice farewelled, and a group of about 300 friends, who had again visited the ship's side cheered ironically.

Nearly all of the 450 passengers remained aboard the ship on Thursday night. Some were inconvenienced by the delay. Sir Charles Marr, a director of Forest products Ltd, of New Zealand, said that he was to have attended a board meeting in Auckland at 9 o'clock on Monday morning. Directors were coming from all parts of New Zealand. The Niagara is not expected to berth at Auckland until early on Tuesday morning.

Monowai returned from Vancouver on 3 July and had a quick turnaround, departing again for Vancouver on 6 July. *Monowai* returned to Sydney on 28 August, ending what was destined to be the last voyage this vessel would make across the Pacific. The following day *Monowai* left for Wellington, and was again laid up, while *Aorangi* resumed its place on the Vancouver route.

*Monowa*i passing under the Sydney Harbour Bridge (John Mathieson collection)

Chapter Nineteen

The Second World War

The outbreak of war in Europe in September 1939 did not have an immediate impact on the trans-Pacific passenger operations. With the United States not becoming involved in the war, the San Francisco service of *Mariposa* and *Monterey* was not affected at all, though each ship had large American flags painted on their sides.

As had happened in the First World War, it was decided that the Canadian-Australasian Line service linking Vancouver to Auckland and Sydney was too important to be curtailed. *Niagara* and *Aorangi* continued to maintain regular departures without interruption, though both vessels were repainted with black hulls and grey upperworks and funnels.

Aorangi had departed Sydney on the afternoon of 3 September, only a matter of hours before the war started, but the voyage continued as usual. On its southbound voyage in November 1939, at a cost of £800, *Aorangi* was diverted to Fanning Island to embark one officer and one sick member of the garrison.

On 13 June 1940, *Niagara*, under the command of Captain W Martin, departed Sydney at the start of what was hoped would be another pleasant voyage to Vancouver. *Niagara* left Auckland at 11.30pm on 18 June, bound for Suva, Honolulu and Vancouver. On board were 146 passengers and a crew numbering 203. Unknown to the captain of the *Niagara* or to local maritime authorities, on the night of 13-14 June the German merchant raider *Orion* had laid 228 mines in the northern and

Niagara in wartime colours (John Bennett collection)

eastern approaches to the Hauraki Gulf. Over the next few days several ships had voyaged through the area, but none had come to grief, and the minefield remained undetected.

At 3.43am on 19 June, when in a position between Bream Head and the Maro Tiri Islands, *Niagara* hit one of the mines, which exploded on the port side of the ship directly under No. 2 hold, blowing the hatch covers off and causing considerable damage to the bridge. Captain William Martin attempted to save the stricken vessel by closing bulkhead doors to prevent the onslaught of water, but *Niagara* had suffered terminal damage. As the ship began to roll to port, Captain Martin, aware of the precious cargo. He ordered "slow ahead engines" in an effort to move toward shore without increasing the rush of water, but it was too late. Captain Martin gave the order to abandon ship, and within twenty minutes of the explosion all passengers and most of the crew had been safely evacuated in lifeboats.

The few men who stayed aboard *Niagara* fought to slow the inrushing water, in the hope that the liner would remain afloat long enough to be beached. However the liner was filling too fast and it was not long before the engines were disabled. Realising their ship was doomed, the last men left aboard took to the lifeboats. At 5.32am, less than two hours after hitting the mine, *Niagara* sank, leaving the survivors bobbing in the lifeboats.

In those pre-dawn hours of 19 June, the Huddart Parker liner *Wanganella* was approaching Auckland on a voyage from Sydney when the distress message was picked up from *Niagara*. Despite the danger of also hitting a mine, *Wanganella* rushed to the scene of the sinking. Also making for the same location was the cruiser HMNZS *Achilles*, which had been berthed in Auckland when the distress message was broadcast. Steaming at full speed, *Achilles* arrived at the site of the sinking shortly after 8am, and a few minutes later it was joined by *Wanganella*, which rescued 340 of the people in lifeboats, being assisted by the small New Zealand coaster *Kapiti* which had also come to help. Once everyone had been saved, *Wanganella* continued its voyage to Auckland.

Among the passengers on board *Niagara* at the time of the sinking were a family, a military officer and two tradesmen bound for Fanning Island, where *Niagara* had been scheduled to stop briefly after leaving Suva. The family comprised an employee of Cable & Wireless, his wife and two children, while the others were Captain B Houston, who was due to take over command of the military post on Fanning Island, but was traveling as a civilian, a carpenter and a plumber, whose services were urgently required on the island. In addition, nine bags of mail and 25 tons of supplies for the Fanning Island garrison had been loaded onto *Niagara* in Sydney.

Among the cargo *Niagara* had been carrying on that fateful voyage was a shipment comprising about half of New Zealand's stock of small arms ammunition, which was being sent to England to help make good the shortage of such ammunition existing there after the evacuation from Dunkirk.

Of even more importance were 295 boxes containing 590 gold ingots, valued at that time at £2,500,000 and weighing about eight tons, which were being sent to the United States by the Bank of England to pay for war materials purchased by the British Government, and had been locked in the strongroom deep down in the ship. Despite the fact that *Niagara* was lying on its side in 438 feet of water, the Bank of England immediately organised a salvage effort. A Melbourne salvage company, United Salvage Proprietary Ltd., was given the contract to recover the gold and commenced operations from Whangarei on 15 December 1940, using the *Claymore*, an old ship of 260 tons purchased for the purpose. It took the *Claymore* approximately two months to locate the wreck, which was done by dragging their anchor along the seabed, and through the minefield. Twice during the locating phase of the operation the vessel fouled unexploded mines and was almost sunk itself.

On 2 February 1941 the wreck of the *Niagara* was located in 438 ft of water, the greatest depth at which salvage operations had ever been carried out up to that time. The operations were directed by Captain JP Williams, managing director of the salvage company, and Captain JW Herd, representing the London Salvage Association. The salvage involved the use of a mushroom-shaped diving bell which was lowered to the wreck with Chief Diver John Johnstone, from Australia, inside. Thick glass viewing ports around the upper portion of the bell allowed the diver to survey the wreck and provide guidance for the ship's mechanical grab which was used to pick up objects and tear away metal.

Weather conditions were frequently impossible, and there was a constant menace from mines. After nine months of blasting and cutting away the structure of the wreck to gain access to the strong room, the first two ingots were recovered. Two days later the *Claymore* steamed into Whangarei Harbour with £84,600 worth of bullion in its hold. When operations finally ceased, on 8 December 1941, 555 ingots, valued at £2,379,000, or 94 per cent of the total shipment, had been salvaged.

It was only the depth at which the *Niagara* lay and the inaccessibility of the strong room that had prevented the *Claymore* expedition from recovering the full amount of bullion, but after the war there were several attempts to recover the final 35 ingots. In 1953 John Johnstone, raised the backing to carry out further salvage, but being aged nearly 60, he was too old to dive personally, and acted purely in an advisory role. One of the factors leading to the eventual resumption of salvage operations was a rise in the price of gold, which had increased the market value of each ingot from £4,300 to nearly £6,000. The salvage party arrived in Whangarei Harbour in April 1953 with the salvage craft *Foremost 17*, and after about five weeks work, nine of the bars of gold had been brought to the surface. When the salvors decided to abandon operations in July, there were only five bars left on the sea floor. The thirty bars that had been recovered were valued at approximately £180,000.

When John Johnstone died in 1976 he believed he knew of the location of the remaining five bars, valued by then at approximately $1.2 million New Zealand dollars. Having obtained this information, Keith Gordon acquired the salvage rights to the *Niagara* in 1988. Using new mixed gas diving techniques and divers, Gordon made numerous attempts to recover the last of *Niagara*'s lost gold, but without success.

In 2008 Keith Gordon and an international team of divers spent two weeks exploring the wreck of the *Niagara*, looking for any worthwhile artifacts. The engine room telegraph from the bridge was recovered, which was set to "stop engines", but the most exciting find was the ship's bell, which was brought to the surface after 67 years underwater. However, the final five missing bars of gold were not found.

Aorangi continued to operate on the Vancouver service, but as *Monowai* had been converted into an armed merchant cruiser, the only suitable vessel to replace *Niagara* on the Canadian trade was *Awatea*. For almost a year after the start of the war *Awatea* had continued to operate across the Tasman Sea, but in July 1940 that liner was taken off the route, being replaced by *Maunganui*.

Awatea arrived in Sydney from Wellington on 1 July, and left the next day on what was destined to be its last voyage on the Tasman trade. However, before *Awatea* entered the Vancouver service the vessel was called upon to make a special voyage to Manila, in the Philippines, to collect a large number of women and children who had been evacuated from Hong Kong aboard *Empress of Japan*, and bring them to Australia. Some of these evacuees were taken on board *Awatea*, which was scheduled to depart Manila on 4 August, though I cannot confirm that it did leave on that date.

Awatea carried the evacuees directly to Brisbane, where it arrived on 13 August and some passengers disembarked, while others were landed in Sydney when the vessel arrived there on 15 August, and the rest left the ship in Melbourne two days later. This were the only time *Awatea* visited Brisbane and Melbourne in its career.

A Mrs Wilson was among those evacuated at this time with her two young boys, and later wrote about the experience:

> On the 29th June 1940, 1,500 women and children received notice to leave Hong Kong. The population at that time, made up of all nationalities, including a large number of Chinese refugees from the mainland, was about 2 million, quite a lot to feed. Furthermore it was just after Dunkirk, there was a large number of Japanese troops on the other side of the border on the Chinese mainland, who might have thought this a good moment to attack. So the evacuation of all (non-essential) women and children was ordered, excepting single and childless married women who were doing special jobs.

Awatea departing Brisbane on 13 August 1940 (John Mathieson collection)

We were told we were to go to the Philippine Islands and that we could take one trunk per adult, one suitcase per child, and a small case for immediate use. It was difficult to know what to pack, the general opinion being that we would probably spend two or three weeks in the Philippines and then return. But there was always a chance that we might go elsewhere so I put in a few warm clothes just in case. How differently I would have packed had I known we were leaving for ever.

However we all got packed somehow and on the 1st July were herded onto a liner called, of all names, "The Empress of Japan". This ship was designed to hold 600 passengers, so with 1,500 on board there was a bit of a crush. Our 4-berth cabin held 9 women and children, but some of the other cabins were even more crowded. There were no stewards or stewardesses and very little in the way of crew and in the dining room it was all help yourself. The heat and smell were terrific down there so during the 2 days and nights we spent aboard I would grab a tray with hunks of bread and greasy stew, or whatever there was, and settle down with the boys on the corridor floor to eat the meal. There was nowhere else to sit as every available space was filled with camp beds. Just to help, there was a small typhoon blowing and many people became sea-sick so the ship was very soon in an awful state.

We reached Manila at last and found quite a crowd assembled to watch our arrival. I felt like something out of a zoo as I struggled off the ship with the trunk, 2 small boys and an assortment of bags, thermos flasks and toy rabbits. Once we got ashore it wasn't so bad as the American Red Cross took charge, relieved us of our burdens, and shepherded us onto waiting buses that took some families into camps in Manila and others to the railway station. We were in the latter group and found a special train waiting to take us up to Baguis, a hill station. There was also a small seaside place available called San Fernando where 36 of us could go, and we were able to go there.

The American Red Cross looked after us very well; they had turned one coach into a sort of HQ-canteen-information bureau. We were all given a packet of sandwiches and there was also milk and Coca-Cola and even whiskey for those in need of it. The train journey lasted about 8 hours and then we were bundled out onto a gloomy platform and into lorries with wooden seats and canvas covers. There followed another journey through the dark and rain till finally the few lights of our destination showed and we could hear and smell the sea.

In this camp there was one main building, an annex and 2 or 3 cottages, in one of which I found myself and the boys together with a friend and her boy. The buildings stood at one end of a lovely bay with mountains to be seen in the distance; a beautiful spot altogether. Being in the middle of the rainy season it was very warm and damp and clothes were rather a problem as we still had only the one small case of necessities. We all looked rather grubby and crumpled by the time the rest of the luggage arrived nearly 2 weeks later. Shoes were another problem as most of us had only the light canvas shoes we'd set out in and there were no paths. So we mostly went barefoot with the mud squelching up between our toes. We bathed most days in the bay in some of the oddest garments as few of us had found room for a bathing suit.

The cottages were built mainly of bamboo with slatted bamboo floors raised a couple of feet above the ground. This made cleaning easy and you'd see a smiling Philippine maiden busily pushing half of a hairy coconut husk up and down the floor with one foot, causing all the dust and rubbish to fall to the earth below. This also made a fine hiding place for mosquitoes. After 2 weeks we were sent up to Baguis where we lived in Camp John Hay, a military holiday camp.

There was nothing very special about the town of Baguis except the market where the local tribe of Igorot Indians displayed their goods for sale: handwoven materials, pottery, leather articles and food. We couldn't afford to buy much as the rate of exchange, 4 pesos to the pound, was very unfavourable; the peso didn't seem to be worth more than 2/6, one eighth of a pound. We soon became used to seeing the young braves walking about town clad in loincloths, feathers and beads. One evening we were even invited to watch some of their dances; this was a great thrill.

It was here that we were told that we'd be going on to Australia as our final destination, and, after a month in Baguis, we went back to Manila to embark. This second sea voyage took 13 days and was quite uneventful and not so crowded as the previous one. Owing to war-time secrecy we never knew quite where we were, but we must have passed between Borneo and New Guinea, over the Equator and onwards until at last Australia hove into sight.

Brisbane was the first stop and a few families who had relatives here disembarked. Two officials from the Tourist Bureau came aboard to arrange accommodation for the rest of us in Sydney, Melbourne and Tasmania. We had a day in Sydney and spent most at a beautiful zoo on one of the harbour islands. Here there was an aquarium, full of weird and wonderful fish as well as, in a pool, an extremely sinister-looking shark.

My friend and I had decided to go on to Tasmania and, as only one other family had decided to go this far, our situation was a lot less crowded than it had been when we were 1,500-strong. We left the ship at Melbourne, transferring to a smaller ship that took us to Launceston.

Following this mercy mission, *Awatea* returned to Sydney from Melbourne on 19 August, and was placed on the Vancouver route to partner *Aorangi*. The first voyage by *Awatea* on the Canadian trade departed Sydney on 5 September, calling at Auckland and Suva before arriving in Vancouver on 27 September.

The outbreak of war in Europe in September 1939 at first had little impact on the service provided by *Mariposa* and *Monterey*, apart from an increase in passenger numbers as most of the British liners

Awatea departing Vancouver (Vancouver Maritime Museum)

serving Australia were taken up for military duty. Going into 1940, though, passenger numbers began to drop off considerably, as the war prevented many people from travelling. The two liners continued their regular scheduled sailings, and in order to boost passenger numbers, the Matson Line organised an unusual two-ship cruise from California to Tahiti and also Australia to Tahiti in July 1940, involving both *Mariposa* and *Monterey*.

Cruise passengers boarded *Mariposa* in San Francisco and Los Angeles for the voyage to Tahiti, arriving there on 3 August. The same day, *Monterey* also arrived in Tahiti on a voyage from Australia. The two ships berthed in line astern, and were to leave the next day, but the cruise passengers asked the company to allow them an extra day in Tahiti, which was granted. The American cruise passengers transferred to *Monterey*, while those from Australia moved to *Mariposa*, and the two ships went their separate ways on 5 August.

While *Mariposa* and *Monterey* were completing their voyages, a new competitor was making its appearance in the South Pacific trade. In December 1937 Pan American Airways had begun operating a flying boat service between San Francisco and Auckland, using Sikorski S-42 aircraft, but it had been restricted to carrying mail only, and the service was rather irregular. In July 1940, using their recently delivered Boeing 314 "Clipper" flying boats, Pan American Airways, had operated several test flights from San Francisco to Auckland carrying only mail, but they were about to commence a passenger service.

The Boeing 314 was the largest flying boat yet built, weighing 84,000 pounds, and it had the most powerful engines yet fitted to any civilian aircraft, four 1,500 hp, 14-cylinder Wright Double Cyclone engines. Cruising speed was 145 miles per hour, with a maximum speed of 180 miles per hour, which gave the aircraft a range of 3,500 miles. A unique feature was a catwalk inside each wing, through which the engineer could crawl to attend to any problems that might develop with the engines during flight. The huge flight deck had space for two pilots, a navigator, a radio operator and the engineer.

The Boeing 314 was the first flying boat to have two decks. The upper deck contained the flight deck and the holds for cargo, mail and baggage. The lower deck was divided into nine compartments, which could be fitted with deeply upholstered seats for up to 74 passengers on daylight flights. However, for overnight flights the number of seats was reduced to about 50, while fold-down berths were provided for 36 persons.

The interior of the aircraft was the height of luxury, among the features being a honeymoon suite in the tail, with large windows on either side. There was also a promenade deck, where passengers could stroll during long flights. There were separate dressing rooms for men and women, each with a toilet, while the men's room contained, for the only time in an aircraft, two urinals. The taps provided both hot and cold water, though in minimal amounts to conserve the supply.

Two stewards were provided to look after the passengers, with seven course meals, prepared in the large galley, being served, complete with wine, in a dining room seating fourteen.

On 10 August 1940 the Boeing 314 *California Clipper* lifted off San Francisco Bay on the first official passenger flight to the South Pacific. The first stop was made at Honolulu, then the flight continued to Canton Island, and a few hours later the flying boat was on its way to Noumea. Due to an accident while taxiing, the aircraft was delayed twenty-four hours, but then continued to Auckland, where it touched down on Friday, 16 August, having taken just over five days from California.

Although almost all the passengers on board were journalists, the flight was seen as a great success, and Pan American announced that it would soon commence operating a schedule of fortnightly departures from San Francisco, but when more of the Boeing 314s were delivered this would be increased to a weekly service. This plan would be totally disrupted when the United States came into the war in December 1941.

Following its successful operation to lay mines in the approaches to Auckland, and also off the east coast of Australia, the German raider *Orion* had not been located, but was known to be still active in the region. On 20 August 1940, at 5 pm, *Orion* came across the New Zealand Shipping Company cargo/passenger vessel *Turakina*, which was voyaging from Wellington to Sydney. Although his vessel was only armed with a single gun at the stern, Captain J B Laird fought the raider for over two hours until his ship was reduced to a blazing hulk. *Orion* then sank *Turakina* with two torpedoes, and 35 persons on the *Turakina*, including Captain Laird, lost their lives, while 73 survivors were taken on board *Orion*.

For a short while after this incident all shipping services across the Tasman Sea were curtailed, and only began operating again when a convoy system was introduced. On future voyages *Aorangi* and *Awatea* would be escorted between Sydney and Auckland, usually by a Royal Australian Navy cruiser. However, as the United States was still neutral *Mariposa* and *Monterey* were not escorted, but their regular service was about to be disrupted.

The deteriorating political situation in China, Korea and Japan was causing concern to the American Government, until in October 1940 they ordered the dependents of American servicemen in the region be evacuated. Five liners were delegated for this mission, including both *Mariposa* and *Monterey*, which had their passenger capacity increased to 776 when several public rooms were converted into dormitories.

Mariposa was on a voyage from Australia to California, but on arrival at Honolulu offloaded all the passengers bound for the mainland. *Mariposa* left Honolulu on 30 October, arriving in Shanghai on 9 November and embarking 100 evacuees, then going on to Chinwangtao to pick up a further 300, and finally Jinsen in Korea, where 200 more American dependents boarded, carrying them to San Francisco.

Monterey had been about to depart San Francisco on a voyage to Australia, but instead headed to China, calling at Shanghai to board 251 American evacuees, and 60 more in Yokohama, where the vessel also took on board a large number of British subjects who wished to leave Japan. They were all carried to Sydney, where the British landed, and then *Monterey* made a regular voyage back to San Francisco. Both ships were diverted to China and other eastern areas on occasion over the next few months, but eventually they were able to resume their regular trade again.

The danger posed by enemy ships in the South Pacific was again graphically illustrated with the loss of another New Zealand liner five months after *Niagara* was sunk. On the afternoon of 24 November 1940, the New Zealand Shipping Company liner *Rangitane* left Auckland for Britain via the Panama Canal, carrying 111 passengers and 200 crew as well as a full cargo. For safety reasons the vessel anchored overnight in the Rangitoto Channel and at dawn continued its voyage. At 3.40 on the morning of 27 November the officers on watch were blinded by a searchlight, followed by an order to stop and not use the radio. Instead the radio officer on *Rangitane* began sending a message that the liner had been stopped by a raider. The enemy ship opened fire on *Rangitane*, but the radio officer sent a message that there were women on board, and the firing ceased.

By then *Rangitane* was on fire and ten persons had been killed, five passengers including three women, three engine room crew and two stewardesses, with many others wounded. The attackers were the German commerce raiders *Orion* and *Komet*, accompanied by the supply ship *Kulmerland*. The survivors were taken on board the raiders, after which a German boarding party opened the sea cocks to sink the liner. To speed up proceedings, *Komet* also fired a torpedo into the ship, and several shells along the waterline.

The sinking of *Rangitane* by German surface raiders caused great concern, and resulted in the movements of British passenger vessels being changed, with varied routes and departure times. Also, the escorting of *Aorangi* and *Awatea* was extended from the Tasman sector to include the voyage to Suva as well. Later the ships would be escorted the entire way from Sydney to Vancouver.

It is worth noting here that another Matson liner, *Maui*, made two voyages to the South Pacific in the war, though only as a cargo carrier. Completed in April 1917 at the Union Iron Works, San Francisco, *Maui* was the last built and largest of a series of five liners of unusual appearance for the Hawaiian trade, all of which had their machinery and funnel at the stern. *Maui* provided accommodation for 240 passengers, but when *Lurline* entered service, *Maui* made its last voyage with passengers in May 1933, then was reduced to cargo ship status.

Maui arrived in Sydney for the first time on 19 December 1940, leaving the next day for Melbourne, returning to Sydney on 28 December, and departing the same day for San Francisco. *Maui* was back in Sydney again on 3 March 1941, departing three days later on the return voyage to San Francisco. The purpose of both these voyages was to load Australian wool, which was taken to San Francisco. Two other Matson cargo vessels to make voyages to Australia to load wool were the cargo steamers *Liloa*, which made two visits, and *Hamakua*, which came once.

After only two round trips to Vancouver, *Awatea* was requisitioned to carry 700 New Zealand troops to the Middle East with convoy US8. However, her luxurious accommodation was not converted in any way, so the troops she carried had probably the most comfortable voyage of any transported to the Middle East. Departing Wellington on 20 December 1940, *Awatea* crossed the Tasman in company with *Dominion Monarch*, entering Sydney Harbour on 23 December, and berthing at Pyrmont.

On 28 December, *Dominion Monarch* and *Awatea* departed Pyrmont, and as they passed under the Sydney Harbour Bridge, *Queen Mary* raised her anchor, and led them out of the harbour, where they joined *Aquitania*, which had left first. Once they had taken up their convoy positions, the four transports, escorted by HMAS *Canberra*, headed south, maintaining an average speed of over 18 knots. As the convoy passed through Bass Strait, it was joined by *Mauretania*, which had boarded troops in Melbourne.

After a stop at Fremantle to take on supplies and bunkers, the convoy went on to Ceylon, arriving in Colombo on 12 January 1941. All the troops disembarked in Ceylon, and transferred to smaller ships to continue their trip to the Middle East, and *Awatea* returned to Australia to resume its place on the Vancouver service partnering *Aorangi*, with a departure every four weeks.

On many voyages *Aorangi* and *Awatea* also carried many Australian and New Zealand airmen who had finished their basic training, and were being sent to Canada to complete their advanced courses before going on to Britain to fly with the Royal Air Force. Airmen were also carried on board *Mariposa* and *Monterey* from Sydney and Auckland to San Francisco, from where they were taken to Canada by train.

Prior to 1939, the British Government had approached Commonwealth countries, including Australia, New Zealand, Canada and South Africa, with regard to the training of airmen for service in the Royal Air Force in the event of war breaking out in Europe. At the 1937 Imperial Conference, Australia agreed to send fifty air force officers to Britain each year for training, while Canada agreed to assist in training British aircrew.

A few weeks after the war started, the British decided that they would prefer it if Australia and New Zealand would assist in a scheme to provide the RAF with fifty thousand aircrew a year drawn from the Empire in general. At a meeting held at Ottawa, Canada, in November 1939, the British proposal was accepted by Australia and New Zealand, and this was developed as the Empire Air Training Scheme. Under this plan, Australian and New Zealand air force recruits would receive their initial flying training in their home countries, then go to Canada for final training before being sent to Britain to join operational squadrons.

The first contingent of RAAF trainees under the Empire Air Training Scheme departed Sydney for Canada on *Awatea* on 5 September 1940, arriving in Vancouver on 27 September. A second contingent was dispatched aboard *Aorangi* on 3 October, and it was also on this voyage that, apart from boarding a group of New Zealand trainee airmen, *Aorangi* also embarked at Auckland the first New Zealand troops to be sent to defend Fiji, which were landed at Suva. A third contingent followed on *Awatea* at the end of October, with the fourth contingent aboard *Aorangi* when it departed Sydney on 29 November 1940. The vessel went first to Auckland, where a draft of New Zealand trainee airmen joined, then continued to Suva and Honolulu.

One of the Australian airmen aboard *Aorangi* on that voyage was William Brew, who wrote home that although the United States was not involved in the war, so technically neutral, the Australian and New Zealand airmen were not allowed to go ashore. However, several of the men tried to swim ashore, but they were quickly rounded up by American Military Police and quickly returned to the ship.

Aorangi arrived in Vancouver on 23 December, having steamed from the warmth of a southern hemisphere summer to the cold of a Canadian winter in just three weeks, William Brew's first impression of Canada being "overcast, cold and wet". on Christmas Eve the airmen boarded a train for the long trip to Toronto, spending a rather miserable Christmas Day on the train.

Some Empire Air Training Scheme men were sent across the Pacific as passengers aboard *Mariposa* and *Monterey*, even though the United States was not involved in the war. An Australian trainee airman, Andy Emmerson, travelled on *Mariposa*, and later recalled, "When we went aboard we were given hammocks down in the lower decks. They wanted people with orderly experience to help, so a mate and I volunteered. It got us out of kitchen duties and other fatigues. One day we found an empty cabin. We managed to get the window open and got in. It was sheer luxury. Even the toilets had electric heaters in them. No one found out about it until we got to Hawaii. Then they seemed to admire our initiative and left us there."

During the period *Awatea* was employed on the Vancouver service the liner carried 3,600 Empire Air Training Scheme men from Australia and New Zealand to Canada. When *Awatea* departed Sydney at 11.15am on 22 February 1941, among the trainee airmen on board was Rawdon Middleton, who would ultimately pay the supreme sacrifice, and be posthumously awarded the Victoria Cross, one of only three awarded to Australian airmen in the war. *Awatea* was escorted by HMAS *Hobart* across the Tasman Sea to Auckland, where they arrived on 25 February. A draft of New Zealand trainee airmen joined the ship, which stopped two days in Auckland, then continued its voyage, now escorted by the armed merchant cruiser HMNZS *Monowai*.

Arriving in Suva on 2 March, *Awatea* departed next day, being escorted by a Canadian armed merchant cruiser, HMCS *Prince Rupert*, all the way to Victoria, on Vancouver Island, where the airmen disembarked on Sunday, 16 March. They marched through the streets to the ferry terminal, to be taken to Vancouver, and the same evening left on a train for their training camps.

On 29 April 1941 *Awatea* departed Auckland on its next voyage to Canada, again carrying a contingent of New Zealand airmen, as well as a group from Australia who had boarded in Sydney several days earlier.

By the middle of 1941 the entire training for airmen was being conducted in their home country, and they were fully qualified by the time they left for Britain, but some still traveled to Canada en route. Among the young fliers to travel on *Awatea* to Canada in August 1941 was Frederick Keck, one of seven brothers, six of whom served in the war, the seventh being too young to enlist. Frederick wanted to be a pilot, but he did not pass the initial testing, and instead became a navigator. Despite his disappointment at not being a pilot, Frederick continued with the scheme, being trained at Evans Head, in New South Wales. As he wrote home on 30 June 1941, "At my passing out parade at Evans Head I was presented with my wing which has been very hard-earned but seems to represent the worthwhile part of it all".

Frederick Keck joined *Awatea*, which departed Sydney on 8 August, escorted by HMAS *Sydney*. On 10 August, crossing the Tasman Sea, Frederick wrote, in a letter home:

Monowai as an armed merchant cruiser (Bob McDougall collection)

The trip across has so far indicated that that part of the sea we are in deserves its bad reputation, and that I am a good sailor although at times I realise that I could without much persuasion become a bad one...We are being treated very well on board. I have a first-class cabin with two others and we eat with the first-class passengers so there are no complaints.

Awatea stopped in Auckland for three days, during which Frederick was able to do some sightseeing and catch up with relatives of his mother. Prior to departure on 14 August a draft of New Zealand trainee airmen embarked, and the voyage continued. Frederick wrote:

We are still having very rough weather and I am still feeling uncertain of my ability to hold everything. This boat is noted for its tendency to upset the hardiest of sailors and as we are travelling at full speed there are many casualties to Neptune. I am trying to fit this in between my duties as Orderly Officer today and night, and two lectures which I have to give daily as well as an hour's wireless duty...We are forced to keep our own studies up to date to be able to lecture to the trainees and together with deck-sports, the work is keeping us out of mischief. I am perfectly fit and doing my best.

During this part of the voyage, *Awatea* was still being escorted by HMAS *Sydney*, and on 23 August, Frederick was writing:

We reached Suva three days after leaving Auckland and spent a day ashore. It was terribly hot and although a most interesting place I have no desire to go there again, much less ever to have to live there or anywhere else so hot. Thank goodness I am headed elsewhere than the tropics.

The two weeks since leaving Sydney have seemed much longer than an ordinary fortnight and taking into regard the fact that we average five hundred miles a day, it is no wonder that home appears very far away. One of the highlights of the voyage was when the *Sydney* left us. The entire ship's companies lined the side of their respective vessels and gave each other three cheers, and up on the bridge we flashed messages of good luck to each other. The Navy looked most impressive in their tropical white uniforms and the *Sydney* made us proud of her as she cut through the water full speed ahead with the flags flying.

As usual, Frederick was not able to be too specific in his letters, but on this voyage *Awatea* did not call at Honolulu. Frederick wrote:

Somewhere at sea is at the moment just north of the equator and well over to the east of Honolulu. Actually we are almost in American patrolled waters so should be quite safe although our escort left us a few days ago. In any case this ship has plenty of pace and if she can't fight very well, she can run pretty fast.

We should reach Vancouver in another six days and on arrival we go straight to the train for our long journey across Canada. It is possible we will have to wait for a convoy then and may not reach England for a month or so after arrival in Montreal. On the other hand, we may get away immediately, in which case I will be there by the time you receive this. One of our escorting officers is returning to Sydney and I am giving him this letter to post there for me. Our trip so far has been absent of anything unusual and there have not even been any rumours.

Appetites are very light these days and my diet consists mostly of fruit, salads, ice cream and lime juice. The ship has an excellent refrigeration plant and summer food is available and fresh.

Two days later, Frederick wrote in another letter:

We are now only a few days from our destination and the weather is treating us more kindly. I think that by tomorrow we will be wearing blue uniforms once more and there will be very few who will not be pleased to get into blue again...It seems a long time already since I had news of home but I must wait until I arrive in England and believe me, that is the only reason I am anxious to get there as quickly as possible.

Also on board for this voyage were Robert Royle and Eldon Beale, who had also completed their initial training as wireless air gunners in Australia. Robert later recalled that he and Eldon were the only fully trained wireless air gunners on board, so they did Aldis Lamp watches on the bridge every day for four hours and were exempt from other duties. The experience was a great help when they had to use the lamp on flying operations when over convoys.

On arrival in Vancouver, Frederick, Robert, Eldon and their fellow flying officers bound for Britain boarded a train, which took them across the country in five days to a Canadian Air Force base in Halifax. It was not until early September that Frederick received news about his trip across the Atlantic to Britain, writing on 7 September:

Our party is being broken up for the Atlantic crossing so once again I am being separated from my friends.

In contrast to our trip so far the meals at this station are the worst ever and the boys just can't eat them.

An RAF officer stationed here advised me to take over as much tea, sugar, razor-blades and cigarettes as possible so I am packing my trunk with same. Fortunately I was able to purchase cigarettes in bulk on the *Awatea* and I already have two thousand in my kit.

Frederick's older brother, Kingwell, who had qualified as a pilot, was killed on 31 March 1942, and just ten days later, on 10 April, Frederick also lost his life. Fortunately for their parents, their four brothers who also served in the war all returned safely to Australia.

At thirty-one, Charlie Williams was older than most recruits when he joined the eleventh intake for the Empire Air Training Scheme in February 1941. Starting in Sydney at No. 2 Initial Training School at Bradfield Park, later training was conducted at Parkes, and completed after six months at Evans Head, with Charlie being commissioned as a Pilot Officer. Having completed his training, in October 1941, Charlie and his fellow fliers were taken to the wharf at Woolloomooloo to board *Mariposa* for the voyage to America.

Once they had boarded the liner, the airmen kept apart from civilian passengers, and, after being shown to their cabins, stood in a cluster on deck as the liner steamed down Sydney Harbour, and out through the Heads. For many, including Charlie Williams, this was to be their last sight of Australia, as they would never return.

On the voyage across the Tasman to Auckland, *Mariposa* was escorted by the cruiser HMAS *Sydney*. It was quite a comfortable journey for Charlie, who had been allocated a berth in a first class cabin. After Auckland, *Mariposa* called at Suva then went on to Pago Pago and Honolulu. The airmen were able to go ashore for the day spent in each of these ports, where they received generous hospitality from local representatives of the American Red Cross.

On their arrival in San Francisco, the airmen boarded a train for Vancouver, then changed to another train, which took them across Canada in five days to Halifax, and within a few days the airmen found themselves on another ship, but this time instead of a comfortable large liner, they were on an ancient, dirty, uncomfortable troop transport, which joined a convoy, and carried them safely to Gourock. From there it was another long train journey, south to Bournemouth, where the reception centre for Empire Air Training Scheme personnel had been established. Charlie Williams later joined the famous "Dam Busters" bomber squadron, and was killed in action on 16 May 1943.

The joint operation of *Aorangi* and *Awatea* on the Canadian-Australasian Line service to Vancouver continued through the first half of 1941. Sometimes military personnel were carried, and on one voyage departing Sydney in late March 1941 a draft of 30 artillery personnel and 42 infantry travelled to Fanning Island in *Aorangi*, which was escorted by HMS *Monowai*, and reached the island on 7 April.

Aorangi and *Awatea* regularly carried airman from Australia and New Zealand to Canada to complete their training. Among the trainees to be transported from New Zealand was Bill Suckling, who had signed up for military duty at the Cambridge Post Office on 24 November 1940, hoping to join the Army. When he was not accepted by the Army, Bill applied for the Air Force, and underwent initial training as a navigator, along with a mate from Cambridge, Martin Byrne. They were among a group of trainee airmen who boarded *Aorangi* at Auckland on 30 January 1941 to be transported to Vancouver, and then by train to the training facility in Ontario.

When *Aorangi* left Sydney on 20 May 1941 no one knew that it would be the last time the vessel would make a voyage to Vancouver for eight years. On the return voyage, No 2 Special Company, comprising five officers and 235 other ranks, boarded *Aorangi* in Auckland on 5 July 1941 for the short trip to Sydney, so they could complete their training in Australia. *Aorangi* arrived in Sydney on 9 July, and on 12 July the vessel was requisitioned by the British Government for conversion into a troopship. The liner left Sydney on 5 September for Britain via South Africa, and was converted into a troopship.

Aorangi was included in convoy WS12ZM which left Britain on 13 November 1941, bound for South Africa. After refuelling at Durban, *Aorangi* and three other ships made up convoy DM1 bound for Singapore, arriving there on 13 January 1942. *Aorangi* was carrying 2,200 troops from the 53rd Infantry Brigade, 232 Squadron RAF, the 6th Heavy and 35th Light Artillery Regiments RA, and the 85th Anti-Tank Regiment RA.

At that time Singapore was under constant aerial bombardment as Japanese troops swept down the Malay Peninsula. The military personnel were disembarked, and all were either dead or prisoners-of-war within weeks. *Aorangi* was then used to evacuate civilians from Singapore and left there on 16 January, arriving in Fremantle on 24 January. *Aorangi* returned to Britain, spending the rest of 1942 transporting British troops, and in 1943 was used to ferry American troops across the Atlantic.

Following the requisitioning of *Aorangi*, *Awatea* continued to operate to Vancouver on its own, but on 8 August 1941 the liner left Sydney for the last time, departing Auckland four days later. The following month *Awatea* was requisitioned by the British Government while in Vancouver. Ordered to proceed immediately to Britain, *Awatea* departed Vancouver on 12 September, but six hours out of port collided with the American tanker *M E Lombardi* when passing through the Strait of Juan de Fuca in fog. *Awatea* suffered numerous tears and holes along the port side of the hull, fortunately above the waterline, and had to return to Vancouver. While repairs were completed the interior was converted to carry troops, and then *Awatea* was prepared for its first military voyage.

Awatea left Vancouver on 27 October, being escorted by HMCS *Prince Robert*, the two ships between them carrying 1,975 troops comprising elements of the Winnipeg Grenadiers and Royal

Rifles of Canada to Hong Kong, One of the soldiers on board *Awatea* was Kenneth Cambon, who later wrote:

> We were a token force, sent over in the hope of giving Japan second thoughts, a bluff that did not work. I was the youngest rifleman (private soldier) in The Royal Rifles of Canada, 1st Battalion from Quebec City, who along with The Winnipeg Grenadiers and some brigade staff, were destined to be the first Canadian soldiers to see action in World War II.
>
> We were crammed below decks in the "MV Awatea", owned by The Canadian-Australasian Shipping Co, that in happier days had been an inter-city ferry in Australasia as well as in the trans-Pacific trade. It had only recently been converted into a troopship. Other ranks were slung in hammocks over the mess tables deep in the bowels of the ship. They bitched about the monotonous diet of mutton and griped about the luxurious quarters of the officers in privileged possession of the exclusive and finely appointed saloons.
>
> There had been a near riot the night before we sailed over the appalling difference in accommodation. Only the genuine desire of most of us to go overseas and into action prevented more serious outbreaks. This seems hard to believe now, but that was the way it was. We wanted to go to war.
>
> One company of the Royal Rifles was on the escort vessel the HMCS Prince Robert. They had much better food, but because of the ship's smaller size and constant roll, most were too seasick to enjoy it. To escape the stale air and dull chatter at night I used to steal up on deck, to lie wrapped in a blanket under the tropical skies. Daybreak brought flying fish, dolphins, the clean swish of the bow cutting through the sea. I remember it as clearly as if it were yesterday.

The troops disembarked on 16 November in Hong Kong, which on 25 December was captured by the Japanese. Another soldier aboard *Awatea*, James MacMillan, wrote:

> The Royal Rifles entrained at Valcartier, Quebec on October 23rd and we arrived at dockside Vancouver on October 27th, 1941. That day we were joined by the Winnipeg Grenadiers and a Headquarters contingent

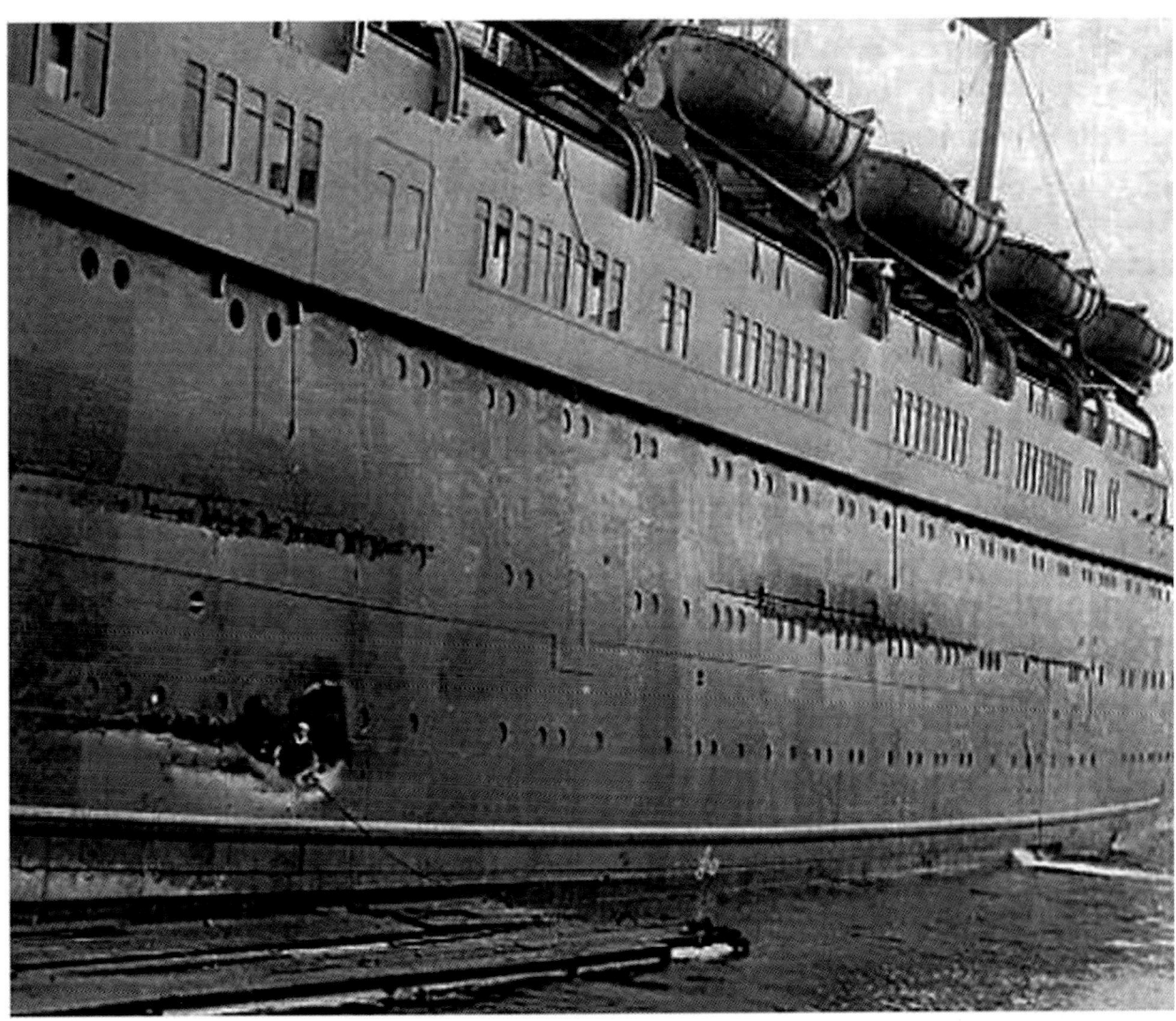

Damage to *Awatea* after collision with tanker *M E Lombardi*

which together became known as "Force C". The sea portion of our trip involved two vessels – the New Zealand Liner Awatea and the converted cruiser HMCS Prince Robert. "C" Company of the Rifles was assigned to the Prince Robert, everyone else boarded the Awatea. We sailed from Vancouver that evening and arrived in Hong Kong on November 16th, having made brief stops enroute at Honolulu and Manila.

At Hong Kong we were stationed at Camp Sham-shui-po which is in Kowloon on the main land, but we were only there two weeks. On December 1st, the regiment moved to the island to take up defensive positions fearing an attack from the sea (shades of Singapore). The Japanese came overland. So the companies became separated.

Awatea proceeded to Britain via Singapore, Colombo, Cape Town and Trinidad. Three days out from Liverpool *Awatea* was fortunate to avoid torpedoes fired by a U-boat. The vessel then made trooping voyages to the Middle East and South Africa.

During 1941 passenger numbers on *Mariposa* and *Monterey* had continued to decline, and the extension of the route from Sydney to Melbourne was dropped, the final departure from Melbourne being taken by Monterey on 3 March 1941. Matson Line also organised another two-ship cruise from San Francisco, which attracted 315 American passengers for the southbound voyage on *Mariposa*, leaving San Francisco on 23 May. This time the two ships met up at Pago Pago, on 3 June, with cruise passengers transferring to *Monterey*, which was on its way from Sydney. While *Mariposa* continued its voyage to Auckland and Sydney, *Monterey* went to Tahiti for a three-day stopover, then Honolulu and San Francisco. In July 1941, *Mariposa* missed one round trip to Australia to make five return trips to Honolulu, mostly carrying contract workers.

By mid-November 1941, the political situation between the United States and Japan had reached crisis point. On 13 November 1941, *Monterey* departed Sydney for what was destined to be its final voyage in peacetime colours, as on 19 November Matson Line was advised that *Monterey* was to be requisitioned to carry troops to Manila on its next trip from San Francisco, due to depart on 8 December, though the plan was that the liner would then continue to Australia and make a regular voyage back to California.

On 24 November 1941, *Monterey* called at English Harbour with the last relief consisting of 41 men, and uplifted 38 who had been on the island for more than a year. *Monterey* arrived in San Francisco on 1 December, being taken over by the United States Maritime Commission two days later. Workmen toiled around the clock to convert the liner to carry 2,950 troops in time for the departure on 8 December, but on 7 December 1941 the Japanese attacked Pearl Harbor. The sudden entry of the United States into the war brought all passenger services across the Pacific to a complete halt.

Monterey was immediately allocated to the Army Transport Service. All the cargo that had been loaded for transporting to Manila, and some to Sydney, was taken off. At the San Francisco yard of Bethlehem Steel the liner underwent further conversion to carry 4,296 troops at one time, and, in order to do so the shipyard had to rip out all her fine accommodation and install multi-tier bunks throughout the vessel. Armaments were also installed, including three-inch guns and a single six-inch gun, as well as anti-aircraft weapons.

With 3,349 troops on board, *Monterey* departed San Francisco on 16 December for Honolulu, in a convoy with two other Matson liners, *Matsonia* and *Lurline*. *Monterey* returned to the mainland, and on 6 January 1942 left San Diego for Pago Pago, returning to San Francisco.

On "Pearl Harbor Day" *Mariposa* was in Sydney, preparing for her return trip to San Francisco scheduled to depart on 11 December, but this was immediately postponed. The vessel was painted grey all over, and the departure date set for 17 December. On that day another contingent of Empire airmen boarded *Mariposa* for the journey to San Francisco, and on to Canada and Britain. The group had completed their training, taken their departure leave, and gathered at the Bradfield Park Embarkation Depot, from where they were taken by bus to the wharf in the morning. After boarding the ship, they were shown to their cabins, had lunch, and waited for the three o'clock departure.

Half an hour before that time, the airmen were ordered to muster on deck with their complete kit, and once gathered there they were marched down the gangplank, and stood on the wharf, from where they watched *Mariposa* depart without them. They were not given any explanation for this sudden turn of events, and all were bewildered, and very disappointed.

Mariposa slipped out of Sydney to follow a circle route across the South Pacific without any stops to reach San Francisco on 30 December, taking 13 days 15 hours and 47 minutes for the voyage at an average speed of 20.42 knots. The next day *Mariposa* was handed over to the United States Maritime Commission, who then allocated the vessel to the Army Transport Service.

Another American liner to carry Australian airmen across the Pacific was the *Mount Vernon*, built in 1933 as the *Washington* for United States Line. It had remained in passenger service until June 1941, then was converted into a troop transport, and renamed. Among those to board the vessel in Sydney in December 1941 was Peter Balderston, who recalled:

The Japs were in the war when we sailed. We embarked in

a ship called the Mount Vernon - an American boat - to Wellington, then straight to San Francisco. There were four to a cabin - comparatively comfortable. The food was good. Before we left Sydney Harbour they opened an ice-cream bar and you could buy a container of ice cream - about a litre - for five cents US - all flavours. I remember I bought one and couldn't finish it so I chucked it overboard.

On arrival in San Francisco, the airmen were immediately put on a train that took them across America to New York, where they were billeted at Fort Hamilton, in Brooklyn, until it was time to join a ship to Britain.

The conversion of *Mariposa* was done in twelve days, and she was capable of carrying 4,272 troops in the same type of accommodation as her sister provided. On 12 January 1942 *Mariposa* left San Francisco with a full complement of troops aboard in a convoy with *President Coolidge* and several other American vessels, bound for Melbourne, arriving on 1 February. From there *Mariposa* went to Brisbane, loaded 14,756 bales of wool, and returned unescorted to San Francisco.

Back in Australian waters, the Matson cargo steamer *Mauna Loa* was seeing considerable action. The vessel had departed Honolulu on 2 December 1941 on a voyage to Port Moresby and Manila, but the latter call had been cancelled and the vessel was instead sent to Darwin, where it remained at anchor for several weeks.

Mauna Loa was then requisitioned to transport Australian troops and supplies from Darwin to Koepeng in Timor, and on 15 February 1942 it was attacked by 27 Japanese bombers. Fragments from several near misses destroyed the port lifeboats and riddled the upper decks, killing one crew member, but the ship survived, landed its troops and cargo, then returned to Darwin, again going to anchor in the harbour.

On the morning of 19 February, *Mauna Loa* was still lying at anchor in Darwin Harbour with numerous other vessels when the Japanese began a major bombing offensive on the town. Dive bombers attacked ships in the harbour, strafing the decks of *Mauna Loa* and putting two bombs into No 5 hold. During a break in the attack all aboard the ship were able to get away in a lifeboat and a harbour work boat, though they were strafed by machine gun fire as they headed for the shore. Fortunately none of the men was injured, but *Mauna Loa* eventually sank. Ironically, in 1959 the wreck was raised and scrapped by a Japanese firm.

Meanwhile, *Monterey* had departed San Francisco on 18 February, carried 3,674 troops to Brisbane, then went on to Melbourne, Adelaide and Fremantle before returning to California. This was followed by a voyage departing San Francisco on 22 April, going to Adelaide, from where the ship was ordered to proceed via the Panama Canal to New York, where it arrived on 20 June.

Mariposa left San Francisco on 19 March with another full load of troops, who were disembarked in Melbourne. The vessel then went to the Dutch East Indies to evacuate 690 Dutch Air Force and Army personnel and their families, who were taken to San Francisco. On 8 May *Mariposa* left San Francisco on a voyage through the Panama Canal to Charleston, South Carolina, to join *Monterey* in transporting American troops across the Atlantic.

In November 1942 *Mariposa*, *Monterey* were both involved in the North African landings, Operation Torch, as was *Awatea*. Prior to this, *Awatea* had been sent to Halifax in August 1942 to bring Canadian troops to Britain. On 22 August 1942 *Awatea* left Halifax in a convoy, but at 10.30 that night an escorting destroyer, USS *Buck*, swung in front of *Awatea*, and the bow of the liner sliced into the warship near its stern, almost cutting it in two. The destroyer sank, while *Awatea* had to return to Halifax for repairs. When these were completed, *Awatea* made a voyage to Britain, and embarked troops for the North African campaign.

Awatea was included in the first wave of landings, landing troops at Algiers on 8 November, then boarding soldiers from a disabled ship and taking them to Jijelli, but high seas prevented them being landed, and they were taken to Bougie and landed on 11 November. *Awatea* left for Gibraltar, but was attacked by waves of German bombers, being hit several times and set on fire. *Awatea* had to be abandoned, and sank during the night of 11 November. It was a very sad end for a fine ship that only survived for six years.

Monterey and *Mariposa* were included in the second wave of the North African operation, with *Monterey* disembarking troops at Casablanca on 18 November, while *Mariposa* landed more at Mers-el-Kebir on 21 November. *Mariposa* was then ordered back to New York, and on 21 December departed Hampton Roads on the longest voyage of her career, lasting 110 days and covering 41,000 miles, taking the vessel via Rio de Janeiro to Suez, Bombay, Cape Town and Glasgow before returning to New York.

Monterey made a further three trips from New York to Casablanca before returning to San Francisco on 15 June 1943, departing on 26 June bound for Brisbane. On returning to San Francisco the vessel was ordered to go to New York, where 6,855 men were embarked and carried to Oran. *Mariposa* was still operating in the Atlantic, mostly carrying American troops from east coast ports to North Africa.

On 9 September, *Mariposa* left New York with 4,277 personnel on board on a voyage to India via Rio de Janeiro and Cape Town, arriving at Bombay on 12 October. *Mariposa* then went on to Fremantle and Sydney, where 2,209 personnel were

Mariposa as a troop transport

embarked and taken to San Francisco. *Mariposa* left San Francisco on 7 December carrying 4,223 Army personnel on a voyage back to Bombay, where 1,000 Italian prisoners-of war were taken on board, along with a large group of New Zealand troops being returned home. *Mariposa* called at Melbourne and Hobart before disembarking the New Zealand troops at Wellington, then continued the voyage to Los Angeles.

On 8 October 1943, *Monterey* departed New York with 6,747 troops on board, bound in convoy for Liverpool. From there the vessel was included in a convoy of 22 ships going to Gibraltar and Palermo. On 6 November, the convoy came under heavy attack from German aircraft off the coast of Algeria. One plane came in very low on the port side of *Monterey*, and had to lift sharply to avoid crashing into the ship. The plane carried away the antenna strung between the masts of *Monterey*, but also exposed its underbelly to the 20mm guns on the ship. The barrage sent up succeeded in causing the plane to crash into the sea.

Two ships in the convoy had been hit and were sinking, one being *Santa Elena*, which was carrying Canadian troops. *Monterey* rescued 1,675 survivors, and as the last men were being lifted from the water, a destroyer reported it was being attacked by a U-boat, so *Monterey* quickly departed the scene, arriving in Philippeville the next morning. After this voyage, *Monterey* returned to the Pacific, making several trips from San Francisco to Honolulu with military personnel, then going to Milne Bay.

On 23 July 1944, *Monterey* was transporting 3,900 troops from Milne Bay to Oro Bay when dust from an exploding volcano in the region turned day into night. As *Monterey* arrived in Oro Bay it was so dark the captain could not get his bearings, and the vessel ran aground on a reef, with a ten degree list to port. The troops were offloaded, but first attempts to refloat the ship were unsuccessful. Two large tugs were brought in next day, but their first attempts to free the liner were thwarted when one of the tugs also went aground.

It was decided to lighten the ship by removing all the oil and water on board, and just before midnight *Monterey* was pulled free. An inspection by divers reported only a few dents in the hull. When the vessel returned to San Francisco it was drydocked for a full inspection of the damage, which proved to be minimal, and *Monterey* was able to resume carrying troops in the Pacific.

Mariposa spent part of 1944 in the Pacific, including a departure from Los Angeles on 3 September on a voyage to Bombay via Fremantle, returning to Melbourne then crossing to the Panama Canal and going to Boston. *Mariposa* spent the rest of 1944 carrying more American troops to Britain, North Africa and Mediterranean ports.

The other two Matson Line passenger ships, *Lurline* and *Matsonia*, remained in the Pacific throughout the war. *Matsonia* was safely berthed in San Francisco on 7 December 1941, while *Lurline* had left Honolulu on 5 December for San Francisco.

When news was received of the attack on Pearl Harbor, *Lurline* was brought up to full speed and was blacked out at night, with passengers wearing their life jackets until the ship arrived in San Francisco at 2am on 10 December.

Both liners were immediately converted into troop transports, and made numerous voyages from San Francisco to various destinations in the South Pacific, including New Zealand and Australia, often unescorted and relying on speed for safety. On 29 July 1942 it was reported that a torpedo was seen passing astern of *Lurline* off Pago Pago.

In September 1943 *Lurline* transported a contingent of troops that would later become famous as "Merrill's Marauders" from San Francisco to Brisbane, where more troops joined the ship, which carried them on to Bombay.

In April 1944, *Lurline* carried Australian Prime Minister John Curtin from Brisbane to San Francisco, from where he travelled to Washington to meet President Roosevelt. The Prime Minister returned to Australia in *Matsonia*, which departed San Francisco on 11 June 1944, also carrying a full complement of troops.

Back in Europe, during the first half of 1944 preparations for the landing of Allied troops at Normandy were being completed, and *Aorangi* was taken off its trooping duty and converted into a depot ship for 150 tugs that would be involved in the invasion, including being able to provide supplies of virtually all kinds, engine repairs, hospital facilities and accommodation for reserve personnel for the tugs.

In May 1944 *Aorangi* arrived in the Solent to begin its new duty, and from D-Day, 6 June, to the end of July, *Aorangi* provided services to 1,200 vessels, and the hospital looked after hundreds of wounded men brought back from the landing beaches. *Aorangi* served in this capacity until late in 1944, then was sent to the Clyde to be converted for duty as a submarine depot ship, which was completed in March 1945.

Aorangi was sent to Trincomalee in Ceylon, but by the time the vessel arrived there the war had moved away from that area. *Aorangi* was sent on to Fremantle, where it remained for three months before proceeding to Sydney to be converted into a Commodore's ship for the fleet train of the British Pacific Fleet for the planned invasion of Japan. *Aorangi* left Sydney in August 1945 for Hong Kong, but by then the war in the Pacific was over. *Aorangi* remained at Hong Kong as an accommodation ship for men released from war service and waiting to go home.

It was estimated that during the war years, *Aorangi* transported 36,000 troops and evacuated 5,500 refugees from war zones.

Chapter Twenty

Post-War Problems

The end of the war did not bring about a quick resumption of passenger services across the Pacific from Australia and New Zealand to San Francisco.

The Matson Line was in the fortunate position that *Mariposa* and *Monterey*, which had been operating the service from San Francisco and Los Angeles to the South Pacific, as well as *Lurline* and *Matsonia* on the Hawaii trade, had all survived the war, but they were still being used by the military.

Monterey had remained in the Pacific until June 1945, then was ordered back to the Atlantic. At Le Havre a full load of American troops embarked who were being rushed to the Pacific. Returning through the Panama Canal, *Monterey* was en route to Manila when the Japanese surrendered, and the voyage was terminated there.

Lurline was also sent to Europe to collect troops that were being redeployed to the Pacific theatre of the war, departing a French port on 29 June. The liner was one day out of Honolulu when the war came to an end, but the troops were still disembarked at their intended destination.

Lurline had been sent to Australia, departing Brisbane on 11 September 1945 for San Francisco, where it arrived on 25 September. On board were 3,560 passengers, of whom 545 were war brides along with 220 young children, the remainder being military personnel returning home.

One of the war brides on board had actually stowed away, and was arrested when the ship arrived in San Francisco. However, she was released into the care of her American husband with instructions to

Lurline departing Brisbane on 11 September 1945

go immediately to Canada, and then effect a lawful entry into the United States.

On 6 October 1945, *Matsonia* left San Francisco bound for Hawaii and then Brisbane, arriving on 22 October. Among the 786 civilian passengers on board were a large number of Canadian war brides of Australian airmen who had trained in Canada. On the return trip to San Francisco, Australian war brides of American servicemen were carried to their new homeland.

Matsonia arrived in San Francisco on her final military voyage on 5 April 1946, and was handed back to Matson Line on 13 April. The liner was then given a very basic refit to commence an austerity service to Hawaii.

With the end of the war in Europe, *Mariposa* had begun carrying American troops home from various European ports. From 7 December 1941 to VJ Day, 2 September 1945, *Mariposa* steamed 414,589 miles, carrying 202,689 passengers, with 10,571,670 meals being served. *Monterey* made 27 trips during the same period, covering 328,490 miles and carrying 170,240 passengers.

On 24 January 1946, *Monterey* left San Francisco for Brisbane, where she boarded 815 war brides and their children to carry them to their new homes in America. Departing on 14 February, *Monterey* docked in San Francisco on 5 March. *Mariposa* was also sent to Australia directly from New York, and the Melbourne newspaper *The Argus* reported on 28 January 1946:

> Fitted out as a floating nursery, the liner and troopship Mariposa sailed from New York bound for Australia to pick up 1,200 wives and 400 children of American servicemen.
>
> The surgery and medical wards have been converted into nurseries with special baby equipment, including 500 toys, 18,000 safety pins, and 20,000 paper diapers. It has playpens, bassinets, and baby bathrobes. The brides and babies will be looked after by the Army until they are delivered right to their husbands.
>
> The Army has created an organisation to handle every detail of transport of dependants of Americans from overseas – estimated to total 50,000 wives and 20,000 children. The first big batch of Australians is expected at San Francisco early in March. The Army will take charge of the girls on arrival, getting their baggage through the Customs, then putting them on special trains under train commanders, with Red Cross girls and medical enlisted men to help. Telegrams at Government expense will be sent to the waiting husbands advising the date and time of wives' arrival. All the husbands have to do will be to meet the train and take delivery of his wife after signing for her.

Mariposa went to Brisbane where 608 wives and 272 children of American soldiers were embarked and carried to San Francisco, arriving on 6 March. *Monterey* also returned to Australia, departing Brisbane on 1 April and arriving in San Francisco on 22 April.

Mariposa made two more voyages to Australia, and also visited New Zealand ports, taking more dependants to America. *Mariposa* departed Brisbane on 11 April with 769 war brides and their children on another trip to San Francisco. One of the war brides to join the ship was Jean Null, formerly Black, who had come up from Melbourne, and later wrote:

> One girl actually got off the ship with her baby, explaining that she had changed her mind and could not leave her family. As we sailed out of Brisbane the dockworkers were yelling, "You'll be sorry," and I think at that time most of us were. Certainly, we were all facing an uncertain and unpredictable future. Many girls were crying. Having lost my parents at an early age, and due to circumstances beyond my control, having been shifted around a lot, it probably wasn't as hard for me as for the others.
>
> I was very fortunate to have gotten a cabin on the top deck of the ship, which I shared with only one other girl. The lower decks had no portholes, and there were ten or twelve girls in each cabin. My cabin mate was very nice, and we became close friends. Many girls were seasick throughout the voyage. My stomach felt queasy, but I was able to retain what I ate. The steward, who attended our cabin, realised the food was foreign to us, and kept fruit in our cabin constantly. It certainly helped, but I still lost fifteen pounds on the trip. Others lost much more.
>
> Our first port of call was Suva in the Fiji Islands, and we were so happy to set foot on land, even if it was only for a day. We found a milk bar that sold ice cream and milk shakes. We'd only been served powdered milk on board ship, which we could not tolerate, so we gorged ourselves on these familiar items. We were permitted to wander anywhere we chose; the natives were very friendly, and seemed pleased to have us there. The following day as we sailed from the harbor, many of the natives stood on the dock and sang, "Now is the Hour" (also known as the Maori's Farewell) to us. It was a song we often sang in Australia, so it was very touching, and many of us were in tears.
>
> Our next port of call was Honolulu, but we were not allowed off the docks. However, the native Hawaiians put on a fabulous show for us, and great food was available. We were there for just one day, and again it was good to be on solid ground. Next we sailed into San Francisco harbor. We were elated to have reached the United States. When we disembarked, one girl with a baby had a telegram waiting for her, which said she was not wanted, and to return home. I have wondered many times what happened to her.
>
> We were then taken to Oakland, and put on different trains, depending on what our final destination was to be. The Red Cross took care of all our arrangements as we traveled across the country. The war brides were dropped off at their individual stations, and the train was not

supposed to leave until the girl had been united with her husband or his family. I do remember one girl was not met by anyone, and the last we saw of her; she was sitting on her luggage, all alone.

As things turned out not all the reunions were successful, and some war brides returned to Australia very quickly, as one report in the *Sydney Morning Herald* indicated:

> More than 50 Australian brides of American Servicemen returned by the Matsonia today, some homesick and others apparently disappointed because they found the United States not always "like the movies or the magazine advertisements."
>
> Among the women were divorcees, widows and some who were "just fed up with America". Some of the women said they felt American women resented their arrival as brides of U S Servicemen. Others found everything in America moving at an exhausting pace. Others simply said they had made a mistake and wanted to forget about it.

As there had been no commercial services across the Pacific since the end of 1941, it was not surprising that there were a large number of passengers wishing to make the journey now that the war was over. The Australian and New Zealand Governments made an appeal to the Matson Line for them to provide an interim passenger service until normal operations could be resumed, and in response to this the company chartered the troopship *Marine Lynx* to operate a voyage from San Francisco to Auckland and Sydney.

Marine Lynx was one of a group of fifteen C4-S-A class troopships built in 1945 for the United States Maritime Commission by the Kaiser Company at their yards in Richmond, California, and Vancouver, Washington, with all except one being given names with the prefix "Marine".

Each vessel took just under a year to be built, the first, *Marine Tiger*, being delivered in June 1945 and the last during November the same year, but by then the war was over. As built the ships could accommodate 3,485 troops, and on completion they were placed under the control of the War Shipping Administration, for whom they were managed by various American shipping companies.

The C4 type had originally been designed in 1941 as a standard cargo ship for American-Hawaiian Lines, having seven holds with the engines, bridge and accommodation block at the stern. When the United States came into the war, the C4 design was extensively revised to enable the ships to be employed in a variety of roles, including transporting troops. In all seventy-five C4 ships were built in various forms, one group of 30, designated the C4-S-A1 type consisting of thirty troopships, being named after American Generals in the First World War. The C4-S-A3 type was a variation of the "General" design, capable of carrying about three hundred more troops.

Work commenced on *Marine Lynx* on 8 December 1944, the vessel being launched on 17 July 1945,

Marine Lynx berthed in Sydney

and being completed on 22 October, following which it entered service as a troop transport. At that time the vessel was managed for the United States Government by Moore-McCormack Line. By the beginning of 1946 *Marine Lynx* was no longer required to transport troops, and was taken on charter by Matson Line.

Refitted to carry about 900 tourist class passengers in rather austere conditions, *Marine Lynx* departed San Francisco on 22 April 1946 on the first post-war commercial voyage across the Pacific. Arriving in Sydney on 5 May, *Marine Lynx* remained in port for nine days before commencing the return trip to San Francisco. *Marine Lynx* called at Auckland on 18 May, berthing at the Western Wharf and staying only a few hours to embark more passengers, leaving at noon.

On 18 May, *Monterey* had also arrived in Auckland, having departed San Francisco on 3 May, calling at Honolulu and Pago Pago en route. The liner was still in troopship configuration, though the maximum capacity had been reduced to 906, with the largest cabins having only six berths. 128 passengers disembarked at Auckland, while before *Monterey* left on 21 May for Sydney some 300 passengers joined the ship, including about 100 New Zealand brides and their children, who were bound for San Francisco. Leaving Sydney on 26 May, *Monterey* proceeded to Suva and Honolulu, arriving back in San Francisco on 9 June.

On returning to San Francisco, *Marine Lynx* was returned to the government, and chartered by American President Line in April 1947 for one voyage around the world via New York and the Mediterranean, but on returning to San Francisco the ship was taken to Suisan Bay and laid up.

Mariposa returned to Brisbane, departing on 31 May 1946 with some 800 war brides and a large number of children. *Mariposa* then made a voyage to New Zealand, embarking New Zealand war brides and children at Auckland, and 16,000 cases of butter, departing on 3 July.

Mariposa was returned to the Matson Line on 1 August 1946, and, still fitted out as a troopship, made two round trips to Honolulu for Matson Line, departing San Francisco on 7 and 21 August. On returning from the second trip the liner was laid up in preparation for conversion back to a luxury liner.

Monterey made two round trips from Seattle to Asian ports in August and September 1946. On 26 September 1946, *Monterey* was handed back to Matson Line, ending a hectic military career. *Lurline* had been handed back to its owners on 26 May 1946, but all three Matson liners were in need of major refits before they could return to commercial service. They were sent to the United Engineering Company yard in Alameda, which was owned by Matson, to be refitted, but none of them was expected to be back in service until late in 1947.

Following the voyage of *Marine Lynx*, Matson Line was encouraged to operate another trip to the South Pacific, and they chartered another C4-S-A3 type troopship, *Marine Falcon*. Launched on 27 April 1945, this vessel had entered service four months later as a troopship. *Marine Falcon* was also refitted to accommodate about 900 tourist class passengers, and on 1 August 1946 departed San Francisco. Passing through Auckland on 19 August, *Marine Falcon* arrived in Sydney on 23 August, but many passengers expressed their dissatisfaction with the facilities provided on the voyage, and the next day the *Sydney Morning Herald* reported:

Passengers who reached Sydney from San Francisco yesterday in the US Army transport Marine Falcon complained of overcrowding, filthy conditions and low-standard food. The ship, they said, could be described only as a "floating slum".

The captain admitted there had been complaints but said the ship was not a passenger liner.

The Marine Falcon will sail for America tomorrow with 750 passengers, including 200 fiancees of American Servicemen and 120 brides and babies.

When the Marine Falcon berthed yesterday a calico sign "SS Floating Flophouse" was draped over her starboard side.

The master of the ship, Captain Robert A Eastman, admitted that the complaints had been made, but said action had been taken where necessary. He pointed out that the Marine Falcon was a troopship, and said passengers could not expect the same luxury of travel as in liners.

The ship left San Francisco with about 700 passengers and a crew of 240, he said. Complaints of serious overcrowding were not justified. It was true the ship had few portholes, but its ventilation system could not be surpassed.

Captain Eastman said complaints of insanitary conditions were not justified. Every day there was a captain's inspection lasting two hours, and no such conditions had been observed. He had heard no complaints of girls being molested or liquor being sold. The crew had not been chosen by the company but was drawn from a labour pool provided by unions.

"When we reached Sydney a number of the passengers called on me to say what a grand voyage they had had," Captain Eastman added.

There were about 530 passengers aboard when the Marine Falcon berthed yesterday. They complained they had been herded into cabins and dormitories, often with no privacy, although some had paid a first-class fare of 345 dollars (about £110 Australian)

Some of the complaints and allegations were:

Mr C Rhodes-Smith, Sydney businessman: "We paid first class fares for third-class accommodation and fifth-class food."

Miss Nola Luxford, a New Zealander resident in New

York, and founder of the Anzac Club there, who, at her own expense, brought home an Australian seaman suffering from advanced tuberculosis: "I travelled to Europe during the war with 5,000 GI's and conditions then were 50 times better. This ship was filthy."

"I was promised a two-berth cabin with porthole and screen for myself and my seaman patient, but the promise was not kept. We were placed in the isolation ward, with no privacy. Nobody was assigned to clean our quarters, and 11 days after leaving San Francisco I was still mopping the floors and cleaning the bathroom with my own disinfectants. I asked the captain to have the isolation ward cleaned. Three days later a coloured boy mopped the floor. Sick children cried during the night in the hospital ward next to our quarters, but the nurses were apparently off duty at night."(Captain Eastman said Miss Luxford later had been given a six-berth room, with private shower, and a room adjoining for herself.)

Miss Ina Starvk, a Canadian girl, traveling to Townsville to be married: "I contracted tinea early in the voyage and after one examination by a doctor was unable to get further treatment for four days. Unable to walk, I called out and attracted the attention of another passenger, who went to the hospital five times, but could not find a doctor. Later, with great difficulty, I went to the hospital and found a doctor, who ordered me to bed."

Mr Paul Jacklin, of radio station 2UE: "While the ship was in port there was plenty of drinking among some members of the crew. Conditions in cabins and washrooms became filthy. Girl passengers were accosted by both white and negro members of the crew."

Mrs Marcia Legg, of Wentworth Place, Point Piper: "There was no privacy in my dormitory."

Mrs Patricia Clarkson Erd, an Australian: "Members of the crew sold liquor illegally."

Mrs Kitty Dillsbough, of Philadelphia: "Conditions during the voyage warrant a Congressional investigation. The American public would be shocked to discover that the War Shipping Administration is charging first-class fares for worse than steerage accommodation."

Mr D G Munro, of Merriwa: "There was no apparent discipline in the crew. No attempt was made to clean up the ship during the stay of two and a half days in Auckland."

Squadron-Leader E B Kraus, who has just been discharged from the RAF: "Women passengers with sick children were treated with callousness. They had to struggle up and down stairs with heavy suitcases, while stewards stood at the rails."

Mr A C Paddison, president of the Australian Federation of Commercial Broadcasting Stations: "The voyage was a blot on the reputation of the American merchant service."

In Sydney a large number of women were preparing to join *Marine Falcon* for the trip back to San Francisco, many being the wives or fiancées of American servicemen they had met during the war. With such bad reports of the outward voyage, the following report also appeared in the *Sydney Morning Herald* on 24 August:

Miss Elva Collins, president of the Wives and Fiancees of US Servicemen Association, said last night that none of her members had baulked at the idea of traveling to America in the Marine Falcon. Some had received notification of passage yesterday and were busy packing. "Some of us have been waiting four years," she said. "It doesn't matter what kind of ship we get now."

Mr Geoff Rampling, formerly of the RAAF, who returned with his American bride in the Marine Falcon, said, "It's a tough break for the Australian girls. I feel sorry for them on the voyage they have ahead of them."

Marine Falcon was scheduled to depart on the night of Sunday, 25 August, and the local Matson Line representative accompanied by reporters made an inspection of the ship, which was reported on 26 August in the *Sydney Morning Herald* as follows:

Passengers who arrived in Sydney by the Marine Falcon on Friday described her as a "slum ship". Before she sailed last night an inspection showed her to be thoroughly clean.

As a result of complaints about conditions aboard by passengers who arrived in Sydney on Friday, the Marine Falcon was inspected at the week-end by the passenger traffic manager for the Matson Line, Mr Earl D Walker, and press representatives. Earlier, Mr S H Richter, Sydney representative of the US War Shipping Administration inspected the vessel, and reported that he was agreeably surprised by the conditions on board.

Mr Richter said he had specifically investigated complaints made by individual passengers from San Francisco. He had not been able, in all cases, to question each passenger, but passengers questioned at random said that their shipmates had exaggerated. Mr Richter said that Mrs J W McDonald, a New Zealander, told him that a few of the passengers had complained about everything, and that many of their complaints were baseless.

Mr Richter said he had paid particular attention to complaints regarding bad food, the molesting of women passengers by members of the crew, and lack of medical facilities. Passengers questioned denied that the complaints were justified. The ship's senior surgeon had shown him the medical stores and facilities aboard, and they were ample to have met with any emergency.

Before leaving yesterday, the ship was in a spotless condition. Floors, decks, bathrooms, toilets and dining rooms were scrupulously clean. Sleeping cabins are similar to those on a troopship, except that the beds are arranged in two tiers, not four, as is usual on Army vessels. The only complaint made by passengers was that children were often separated from their parents.

There were only six cancellations among the 750 passengers booked for the passage to San Francisco. The Australian representative of the Matson Line, Mr E D Walker, said last night four of these were because of sickness and one couple cancelled for personal reasons. Mr Walker said he had visited the Marine Falcon during the afternoon and most of the passengers had spoken in favourable terms of the accommodation and meals.

The master of the Marine Falcon, Captain Robert E Eastman, said he had had numerous apologies concerning "exaggerated reports" from people who had traveled in the ship to Sydney.

It appeared that the problems affecting the ship had been overcome, but shortly before departure time a brawl broke out on board and police had to be called, with this report also appearing in the *Sydney Morning Herald* on 26 August:

Brawls between negro members of the crew occurred last night when the American vessel Marine Falcon, bearing 750 passengers, including about 300 Australian wives and fiancees of US Servicemen, sailed for San Francisco. A detachment of police was rushed to the wharf in response to a call for assistance from the ship and after US military police had threatened to use firearms.

According to the police the trouble started when several of the crew tried to come ashore half an hour before the ship was due to sail. Fellow negroes tried to restrain them and a general brawl developed. There were no serious casualties.

At the height of the brawling US military police threatened to use firearms against the negro crew. "If this spreads there will be no stopping these negroes. If I don't get help I will have to use this," one military policeman said, slapping his holster.

Persons watching the fights from the wharf said that table knives were drawn by some of the negroes.

Passengers' relatives were allowed on to the wharf at 9pm. Hundreds of streamers linked the cheering crowd on the wharf and the girls on board the ship as the vessel prepared to leave at 10 o'clock. As the final whistle blew five young negroes struggled through the crowd, rushed to the ship's side, and asked for ropes to be lowered. Negro sailors shouldered white girls to one side to get to the ship's rails and encourage their climbing comrades. Screams of hysterical laughter from the negroes silenced the cheers of the crowd.

For about 10 minutes nothing happened. White girls continued to embrace negroes leaning from the portholes. Then with all eyes focused on the promenade deck about 10 feet above the heads of the crowd a skirmish occurred between three or four flamboyantly dressed coloured seamen.

Girls farewelling their mothers and fathers and still pathetically clutching forgotten streamers cowered against the rail as the brawl became more violent. From the wharf it could be seen that several of the crew were trying to pacify the negroes, who were struggling in the confined space between the ship's well and the rails.

In a sudden lull a white woman on the wharf diverted the tense interest of the crowd by knocking a man to the ground. She alleged that he had insulted her. She then resisted efforts by the police to lead her away.

Struggling again broke out on deck. A negro clad only in pants had his back to the rail of the ship and could be seen holding off the attacks of several fellow crew members. Once he fell on top of another man. Then half-a-dozen others joined in the fray, swinging blows indiscriminately.

A cry from the side of the vessel attracted a crowd to a row of lighted portholes. Through the portholes, which were in the crew quarters, could be seen struggling negroes. Then the portholes were closed.

As Press photographers' flash-light bulbs lit the scene, voices screamed invective at the crowd. Soon a gangway was lowered and civilian police were taken on board. The appearance of uniform police on the ship quietened the brawling men. The police had no need to take action. The captain, a police officer said, arrested a negro member of the crew who was alleged to have been the ring-leader in the fight, and imprisoned him on board. A few minutes before the ship pulled out into the stream the police returned to the wharf.

The vessel left the wharf at 11.15 and anchored off Bradley's Head to complete agents' formalities. She cleared the Heads at 2.08 this morning.

After the excitement of the departure, the voyage to San Francisco, with calls at Suva and Papeete, seems to have been relatively quiet. Soon after arriving in San Francisco, *Marine Falcon* was handed back to the government. In April 1947 *Marine Falcon* was chartered by United States Line and operated from New York to Southampton, Le Havre and Hamburg until March 1949, then was laid up in the Reserve Fleet.

While the San Francisco service had been recommenced, though only on a relatively small scale, it was enabling people to travel across the Pacific, but there were also demands for passages between Canada and New Zealand and Australia. *Aorangi* was still being refitted by Mort's Dock for commercial service, but this work would take over two years, and until then there would be no regular service to Vancouver.

However, as an interim measure, it was arranged that the Huddart Parker Limited liner *Wanganella* would make a singe return voyage from Sydney to Vancouver at the end of 1946. Built by Harland & Wolff at Belfast as *Achimoto* for Elder Dempster Line, the vessel had been launched on 17 December 1929, but by the time it was completed in September 1931 a financial crisis had prevented Elder Dempster taking delivery of the ship and in 1932 it was offered for sale.

Bought by Huddart Parker and renamed, the liner was placed on the trans-Tasman trade from Sydney to both Auckland and Wellington in January 1933. *Wanganella* had rescued many of the survivors from the *Niagara* when that vessel was sunk in June 1940. In May 1941 *Wanganella* had been requisitioned

Wanganella made one voyage to Vancouver (David Cooper photo)

and converted into a hospital ship, serving in this capacity with great distinction, and being released at the end of 1945.

Refitting *Wanganella* took almost a year, being completed in October 1946, but instead of immediately resuming her place on the trans-Tasman trade, *Wanganella* was dispatched on a round-voyage to Vancouver, on behalf of Canadian-Australasian Line. On Thursday, 31 October 1946 *Wanganella* departed Sydney carrying 432 passengers on the voyage across the Pacific, the longest commercial trip the liner would ever make.

As the liner neared the New Zealand coast it ran into bad weather, as a strong easterly gale developed, but the vessel arrived in Auckland on time on the morning of 4 November. Here 107 passengers disembarked, while 88 joined before *Wanganella* departed at 11am on 5 November, bound for Suva and Honolulu prior to reaching Vancouver on 23 November. Leaving Vancouver on 27 November, *Wanganella* reached Auckland at 3pm on 23 December, leaving at 4pm the next day and arriving in Sydney on Saturday, 28 December.

Wanganella then resumed its place on the Tasman trade, but ran aground at the entrance to Wellington Harbour on its first voyage. Suffering extensive damage, the ship was refloated after seventeen days aground, but then spent almost two years being repaired before it returned to service in December 1948.

Despite the problems that had arisen on the voyages by *Marine Lynx* and *Marine Falcon*, Matson Line arranged the charter of another vessel of the same class, *Marine Phoenix*, this time for three voyages to the South Pacific. The twelfth of the class to be completed, work on building *Marine Phoenix* commenced on 16 December 1944, and it was launched on 9 August 1945, being delivered to the United States Maritime Commission on 9 November, and placed under the management of Moore-McCormack Line.

Marine Phoenix left Seattle on 12 December 1945 on its maiden voyage, going to the Japanese port of Nagoya, departing there on 4 January 1946 to return to Seattle. In February the vessel departed Seattle on a voyage to Inchon, Shanghai and Yokohama, and on 1 May left Seattle again bound for Guam and Saipan.

On being chartered to Matson Line, *Marine Phoenix* was given a more extensive refit than the earlier ships, with accommodation for 520 tourist class passengers being arranged. While conditions were still rather austere, they were better than in the previous ships, with passengers being provided with two lounges and improved dining facilities. The fare from San Francisco to Australia ranged from US$225 to US$370 per person.

On 13 December 1946 *Marine Phoenix* departed San Francisco on its first voyage for Matson Line, with a full complement of passengers, calling at Honolulu, Pago Pago and Suva before arriving in Auckland on 28 December.

Marine Phoenix arriving in Sydney

Apart from many New Zealanders and Australians returning home, and Americans coming to live in either country, there were also some immigrants from Europe, as indicated in the following report sent from Auckland:

> Twenty-one Austrians, Poles and Slovaks, who will settle in Australia, were through passengers on the American liner Marine Phoenix, which arrived to-day from San Francisco. One immigrant, who said Austria was very anti-Russian, stated: "Thousands of people would give anything to get away to Australia or New Zealand; but for most it is impossible to do that with Austrian money."
>
> As a precaution against infantile paralysis infection, children under 18 were not allowed to go ashore from the Marine Phoenix.

Marine Phoenix reached Sydney on 3 January 1947. Departing on 6 January, the vessel retraced the same course back to San Francisco. The second voyage to the South Pacific by *Marine Phoenix* on charter to Matson Line left San Francisco on 31 January 1947. However, on departing Sydney the vessel had one unwitting extra passenger on board, and the *Canberra Times* on Friday 7 March 1947 carried this story, sent from Auckland the previous day:

> A Tivoli Theatre artist, after drinking whisky and beer-chasers from 10am to 3pm at a King's Cross drinking party, recently awoke to find herself and her small son on the liner, Marine Phoenix, on its way to New Zealand. This amazing adventure befell Mrs Terry Littlejohn, a member of a well-known juggling and balancing act in which Mr and Mrs Littlejohn appear.
>
> Mrs Littlejohn is seeking an air passage back to Australia.
>
> She told the police that she attended a party farewelling members of the crew of the Marine Phoenix and she woke up next day on the deck of the vessel, which was at sea. She did not know how she got there. Her small boy was asleep in her arms. She ate in the first class, slept on deck and won 100 dollars at poker, then walked off the ship at Auckland without being questioned because she had no luggage.

Marine Phoenix made a third departure from San Francisco on 22 March, and its arrival in Sydney on 11 April attracted a certain amount of notice in the local press. Next day the *Canberra Times* reported:

> Eight alien immigrants on the steamer Marine Phoenix were not allowed to land owing to their landing permits not being in order. The cases will be referred to the Immigration Department at Canberra for review.
>
> Several are cripples, and one elderly Hungarian woman is reported to be suffering from heart trouble.
>
> The Marine Phoenix brought 100 American ex-servicemen, some with their Australian wives. They will live here because they reckon Australia is a better country.

This was the last voyage under the original charter arrangement. However, as the ship was carrying full loads on every trip, and with no competition there was a continuing demand for passages in both directions, Matson Line arranged to extend the charter for another five voyages. Further impetus to extend the charter came from the Australian Government, which implemented an assisted passage scheme for migrants coming from the United States, particularly aimed at ex-servicemen who had been in the country during the war.

While *Marine Phoenix* was operating across the Pacific, Matson Line was planning for the restoration of regular services by *Mariposa* and *Monterey*, with a departure every four weeks, and a weekly service to Hawaii to be operated by *Lurline*, partnered by the veteran *Matsonia*, previously named *Malolo*. In March 1946 the company had been offered a sum of US$5.6 million dollars per ship by the United States Government for the conversion of *Mariposa*, *Monterey* and *Lurline*, but the projected actual cost of the work was US$9.5 million per ship.

Within weeks of the conversion work commencing serious problems arose, including a lack of skilled labour to do the work, shortage of necessary materials, and constant cost increases. At the end of 1946 the projected cost of converting each vessel had skyrocketed to US$12 million, and by June 1947 the cost was being estimated at $16 million per ship.

Faced with a desperate financial situation, the directors of Matson Line had no alternative but to order that all work on *Mariposa* and *Monterey* cease on 11 July 1947, at which time *Mariposa* was about 50 percent converted, while *Monterey* was only about 30 percent through its conversion. Painted all over in anti-corrosion paint, the two liners were moved to the former Bethlehem shipyard at Alameda, and laid up. All plans for restoring the ships to the South Pacific service were terminated.

Work did continue on the *Lurline*, and was completed at a cost of US$20 million in April 1948. On 15 April, *Lurline*, which had been fitted with accommodation for 484 first class and 238 cabin class passengers, departed San Francisco for Honolulu, where it received a rapturous welcome on 20 April.

On the same day, the veteran *Matsonia* arrived in San Francisco at the end of its final voyage from Hawaii, and was then laid up, as Matson Line had

Mariposa and *Monterey* laid up at Alameda (Vic Scrivens collection)

become aware that the post-war Hawaiian trade would only support one ship, with a departure from San Francisco every second week. In December 1948, *Matsonia* was sold to Mediterranean Lines, which later became Home Lines, and was renamed *Atlantic*. In December 1954 the liner was renamed *Queen Frederica*, and began operating between Piraeus and New York.

On 15 December 1958, *Queen Frederica* departed Naples on a special voyage to Australia, carrying migrants from Italy, Greece and Malta. Reaching Fremantle on 8 January 1959, the liner continued to Melbourne, berthing there on 12 January. *Queen Frederica* then went on to Sydney, docking at 7 Woolloomooloo on the morning of 14 January. On 16 January *Queen Frederica* boarded passengers for Piraeus and Naples, departing Sydney at 6 pm, calling again at Melbourne and Fremantle en route to Europe.

In December 1965, *Queen Frederica* was sold to Chandris Line, and over the next few years became a regular visitor to Australia on voyages from

European ports, and also operated a number of cruises from Australia.

Meanwhile, *Marine Phoenix* continued to provide a connection from San Francisco to Auckland and Sydney. Despite improvements made to the accommodation on the vessel, there were still those who found the voyage less than enjoyable for various reasons. Katie Hargreaves remembered:

> I embarked September 2, 1947 from San Francisco on the Marine Phoenix, operated by Matson Navigation Co and Oceanic Steamship Co in cabin #305 with 20 bunks, mostly occupied by Australian women and their babies. Men were mostly veterans. All together, there were about 200 passengers. It definitely was a troop ship! After stops at Pago Pago and Suva, my parents and I arrived in Auckland, NZ September 18 and Sydney on September 22.

Kathleen (Kitty) Emmanuel said of her trip:

> At the beginning of August 1947 my husband Tony, baby Sally (10 months) and myself left Southampton on board a Holland America Line ship bound for New York, where we stayed for two or three nights. We then caught a train to San Francisco before embarking on the infamous "Marine Phoenix". I, with Sally, was allocated two bunks in a cabin housing 20 or more women. I had to raise Cain, as they say, to get a railing put up at the side of Sally's bunk; otherwise there was a very real danger she would fall out. Tony was given a berth with 11 other men, one of whom disappeared during the voyage. No one ever knew whether he was pushed overboard or just fell, nothing was done for at least a couple of days – far too late to ever find him!
>
> The dining facilities were laughable. Long trestle tables – no tablecloths or napkins, very primitive. The food wasn't much better. Other facilities too were very basic – 4 loos for we women and lots being sick when the sea was rough. To bathe my baby I had to fill a tiny bath and carry it back to the cabin. Not easy with a rolling ship! Another difficulty was the rampant whooping cough that affected most of the children, but thankfully not Sally. Our first stop was an island where the locals came out to the ship in long boats and swarmed up the sides on rope ladders, and then tried to sell their beads and trinkets to the passengers. We would loved to have gone ashore but that apparently was not possible.
>
> On top of this most of the crew were drunk during the whole voyage! And all this for first-class fares!
>
> Our next stop was in Auckland, our destination. We spent three or four nights at a hotel in Symonds Street. Absolute heaven after the "Marine Phoenix".

The last of the five additional voyages departed San Francisco on 12 December 1947, but, with demand still high, the charter of *Marine Phoenix* was then extended into 1948 for a further four voyages. When the ship arrived at Auckland on 4 June 1948 a newspaper report stated:

> More than half of the 460 passengers on the Marine Phoenix, which arrived here to-day from the United States are assisted immigrants for Australia
>
> They are mostly ex servicemen, many of whom have married Australian girls.

The fourth, and last of the voyages under the extended charter departed San Francisco on 19 May, and the next day the *Canberra Times* carried a report sent from San Francisco:

> Carrying more than 500 passengers the Matson liner, Marine Phoenix, sailed yesterday on her last scheduled voyage to Australia. The passengers include 210 ex servicemen and their families, migrating under the Australian Government's scheme.
>
> The total number, who have sailed since the scheme was inaugurated a year ago, is now about 1,000.
>
> An Australian Consular official said there are hundreds more on the waiting list and applications are still pouring in. "The results would be 500 per cent better if only we had the shipping" he said.

With demand for passenger berths to and from Australia still strong, representations were made to the Matson Line to continue the service, and this was agreed, but only for one further trip. On 6 July 1948, *Marine Phoenix* left San Francisco on its final voyage to the South Pacific, terminating in Sydney on 27 July. *Marine Phoenix* departed Sydney on 30 July, passed through Auckland on 3 August, and arrived back in San Francisco on 17 August 1948.

On 26 August *Marine Phoenix* was handed back to the US Maritime Commission, and towed to Suisan Bay to be laid up. Matson Line later claimed that, despite the large passenger numbers carried, they had lost money on the charter arrangement.

With the withdrawal of *Marine Phoenix*, and *Mariposa* and *Monterey* being laid up, Matson Line temporarily ceased their participation in the South Pacific trade, and there was no longer a direct sea connection from Australia and New Zealand to the United States west coast. This situation would continue for almost ten years.

Chapter Twenty-one

Reviving the Vancouver Service

As far as the Canadian-Australasian Line was concerned, the loss of both *Niagara* and *Awatea* during the war meant that they had only *Aorangi* left with which to resume the service to Vancouver. *Aorangi* had remained in Hong Kong until May 1946, when it was released from military control, and handed back to Canadian-Australasian Line, and returned to Sydney, but the vessel had endured a particularly active war, and would need an extensive refit before being able to return to commercial service.

The reconditioning of *Aorangi* was done by Mort's Dock while the ship was berthed alongside 5 Darling Harbour. Due to problems encountered in obtaining necessary supplies and materials which had to be sent from Britain and also constant industrial disputes which often brought work to a complete halt. Hopes to have the ship back in service by the end of 1947 soon evaporated, and the refit would not be completed for another year.

However, during 1948 a new service commenced to connect Australia and New Zealand with Canada. The company involved was Pacific Shipowners Limited, which was based in Fiji, and had purchased two surplus Royal Navy vessels built in Canada to commence their new service.

Originally laid down in 1944 as standard 'Fort' class cargo ships, being included in a group of sixteen such vessels to be built in Canada at this time, they had been redesigned while under construction for duty as landing craft maintenance ship for the British Navy Fleet Train attached to the British Pacific Fleet.

One of these vessels, built by West Coast Shipbuilders at Vancouver, was launched on 15 March 1945 as HMS *Dungeness*, being completed on 2 October 1945. The other vessel was built by Burrard Drydock Company in their North Vancouver yard, being named HMS *Spurn Point* when launched on 8 June 1945, and was completed on 21 December 1945. However, as the war was already over before the ships were completed, neither was required any longer by the Royal Navy, and both vessels were laid up in Vancouver, being offered for sale in 1947.

Spurn Point was purchased by Pacific Shipowners on 10 July 1947, and renamed *Lakemba*, being sent to the Burrard shipyard in Vancouver to be rebuilt as a cargo/passenger liner. In September 1947 the same company purchased *Dungeness*, which was renamed *Levuka* and also rebuilt by Burrards Vancouver shipyard.

Levuka was the first of the two ships to be finished, in early February 1948, having been fitted with accommodation for 60 passengers. *Levuka* went to Coos Bay in British Columbia to load cargo, leaving there on 16 February for Victoria to load more cargo. Leaving there on 25 February, *Levuka* made the short voyage to Vancouver, where the first passengers embarked. Departing Vancouver on 26 February, *Levuka* arrived in Sydney on 24 March and Melbourne two days later.

This was to be the only voyage *Levuka* made for Pacific Shipowners, as a few weeks later the vessel was sold to the British Phosphate Commission, and renamed *Triadic*. On 17 May 1948 the vessel departed Melbourne on a voyage to Ocean Island, and in future the accommodation was only used by company personnel.

Work on converting *Lakemba* was completed in early April 1948. The vessel had been given a raised forecastle, an enclosed bridge and a stumpy motor ship type funnel which reportedly came from a tanker then under conversion at Burrards. Accommodation for 98 passengers had been installed in 49 two-berth cabins. There were also several public rooms, and all passenger areas were air conditioned. The officers and engineers were mostly Australian and accommodated amidships whilst the Fijian crew were housed aft. The original 2,500 ihp triple expansion oil fired machinery, which used about 30 tons of fuel per day, was retained, driving a single propeller, and only capable of a service speed of 11 knots.

Lakemba went first to New Westminster, British Columbia, to load cargo, leaving there on 17 April for Crofton, also in British Columbia. On 28 April *Lakemba* voyaged from Crofton to Vancouver, where passengers were embarked, and on 30 April

Lakemba left on its first voyage across the Pacific. After calling at Suva on 21 May, *Lakemba* arrived in Sydney for the first time on 28 May, and in Melbourne two days later.

Managed on behalf of Pacific Shipowners by W R Carpenter & Co Ltd, of Sydney, *Lakemba* was placed on a regular schedule of trans-Pacific voyages, with a departure from Melbourne and Sydney every about fourteen weeks. On southbound voyages *Lakemba* usually carried a fore and aft deck cargo of timber, with more stowed in the holds along with newsprint, paper pulp and tinned salmon. This cargo would be loaded at various ports in British Columbia, including Vancouver Island, following which the vessel would go to Vancouver to embark passengers.

The route followed depended a bit on where the cargo was to be discharged, but after a regular stop at Honolulu to take on water and bunkers, would usually include calls at Apia, Nukualofa and Suva, where crew changes would also be made. The first port of call in Australia was Sydney, where after landing passengers, *Lakemba* would move to the dolphins in Snails Bay to discharge some of the timber cargo. The vessel would then voyage to Melbourne, usually berthing at South Wharf, and complete discharging its cargo at Adelaide.

Lakemba would then load for the northbound voyage at Adelaide, Melbourne and Sydney, usually taking on grocery items, building materials and general cargo for Fijian ports and any available cargo for Canada. Calls would be made at Lautoka and Suva, and sometimes smaller ports in Fiji, then the vessel would continue to Honolulu, and on to Vancouver, where passengers would disembark, and the cargo would be unloaded.

At the same time *Marine Phoenix* was being withdrawn from the San Francisco trade, *Aorangi* was completing its refit in Sydney, and undergoing final preparations for a return to the service from Sydney and Auckland to Vancouver. During the refit the accommodation had been reduced to 212 first class, 170 cabin class and 104 third class, reflecting the anticipated decrease in demand for passages on the route.

The port of registry was also changed from London to Wellington, making *Aorangi* the largest liner ever to be registered at that port. Sea trials commenced off Sydney on 1 August, and then the vessel was prepared for a return to service.

There was one very noticeable change made to the appearance of *Aorangi*. While retaining the Union Line red and black funnel colours, the hull was repainted white with a thin green band.

On Thursday, 19 August 1948, *Aorangi* departed Sydney on its first post-war voyage to Vancouver, encountering some very bad weather in the Tasman Sea before arriving in Auckland on 23 August. As the liner steamed down Waitemata Harbour it was noticed that the heavy seas had washed some of the white paint off lower sections of the bow, giving her a less than pristine appearance. The *Auckland Star* reported:

Lakemba maiden arrival in Sydney 28 May 1948

Aorangi departing Auckland (Alexander Turnbull Library)

With her new white topsides gleaming and bunting fluttering aloft, the RMS Aorangi arrived in the Waitemata this morning, obviously completely 'rehabilitated,' after honourable wartime service which began in 1940 when she landed the first contingent of New Zealand troops in Fiji. Hooters croaking ashore were Auckland's welcome to an old friend in new dress – a ship which, before the war, was a regular visitor.

Refitting of the Aorangi – a lengthy business carried out in Sydney – involved the rebuilding of all passenger and crew accommodation on the lower decks as well as general reconditioning throughout. The result is an overall impression of genuine comfort catered for in quiet taste.

In the Georgian-style lounge the classical detail of ancient Greek ornamentation has been faithfully reproduced, while covering the parquet dance floor the centre carpet in golden fawn tone-on-tone forms the basic background to the Queen Anne and Georgian furniture, with occasional tables and chairs in mahogany.

The careful attention to restful eye-appeal, combined with comfort, is evident throughout from the Julius Olsson oil of 'Aorangi' (The Cloud Piercer) which takes pride of place above the after staircase, to the white Tudor-Gothic fireplace in the mellow-toned smoke room.

The reconditioning resulted in passenger accommodation being reduced from 636 to 486, which has done away with much of the cramped impression given by quarters on some passenger liners.

Passengers on the present voyage, most of them bound for Vancouver, expressed themselves, in the main, as well satisfied with arrangements.

The reported gale which the Aorangi experienced was not taken seriously by the passengers, some of whom continued to play deck games throughout the heavy weather. Captain W Whitefield, the liner's commander, reported that the voyage had been uneventful.

An official lunch was held aboard the liner today. Other less formal functions are planned before the liner sails from Queen's wharf at 11am tomorrow.

With the withdrawal of *Marine Phoenix*, *Aorangi* was the only passenger liner trading from Australia and New Zealand to North America, while *Lakemba* also provided a passenger service between Sydney and Vancouver.

After only two round voyages it was decided that maintaining the white hull was causing too many problems, so the hull of the liner was repainted in the standard Union Line dark green with a gold band.

During August 1948, the directors of Canadian-Australasian Line, which was still jointly owned by the Union Steam Ship Company of New Zealand

Aorangi at Vancouver (John Mathieson collection)

and Canadian Pacific Railway Company, met in Montreal, and revived the plan to build two new 25,000 ton liners for the service across the Pacific, even though Canadian Pacific had already abandoned their service from Vancouver to Japan and Hong Kong. At the same time the directors stated that the company was seeking a suitable ship to charter to supplement the operation of *Aorangi*. However, nothing further was heard of the building program, nor was any charter organised.

Being a one-ship operation, sailings were infrequent, but passenger loadings on *Aorangi* were quite good, though cargo results were poor. With no mail subsidy being provided by the Australian, New Zealand and Canadian Governments, the service lost money from the start, and in October 1950 Canadian-Australasian Line announced that they were considering withdrawing *Aorangi* from service at the end of the year if the various Governments continued to refuse to provide a subsidy, but none was forthcoming.

As a result, in December 1950 Canadian-Australasian Line announced that *Aorangi* would be withdrawn from service when it returned to Sydney on 31 January 1951. This action prompted the three governments to offer a subsidy of Can$250,000 from 1 April 1951, to keep the ship operating for the next two years. Canada contributed 66.6% of the subsidy, Australia 25% and New Zealand the rest.

With the subsidy secured, *Aorangi* was brought out of layup, and departed Sydney again on 5 April 1951. A schedule of departures every nine weeks was published, future sailings being due on 7 June, 9 August and 9 October. However, by the time the liner returned to Auckland from Vancouver there was a major strike involving waterside workers and seamen affecting all New Zealand ports. *Aorangi* was able to continue its voyage to Sydney, but Australian waterside workers had placed a black ban on all ships registered in New Zealand in support of their Tasman colleagues.

In Sydney all the crew who were members of the seamen's union walked off the ship on 4 June, and none of the cargo was unloaded from the holds. When a call for new crew was made there was no response, and the 6 June departure had to be delayed, and finally postponed. For the next four weeks the liner lay idle in Sydney, but on Thursday, 28 June, the Federal Government stepped in and said that if members of the Seamen's Union had not signed on to the ship by the following week, then ratings from the Royal Australian Navy would be rostered to man the ship, which would leave for Vancouver on 5 July. Despite this threat, the seamen continued to refuse to join the ship, so on 3 July the naval ratings went aboard the ship, as reported next day in the *Sydney Morning Herald*:

Sixty-nine naval ratings went aboard the liner Aorangi yesterday to prepare her for sailing tomorrow. They have taken the place of members of the Seamen's Union who walked off the vessel on June 4 in sympathy with striking New Zealand watersiders.

These seamen, who have since ignored frequent calls to man the ship, again refused to offer for work yesterday.

They knew the Federal Government had announced last Thursday that if the ship was not manned yesterday the Navy would take over, but they remained silent at calls for labour at 9.30am and 11.30am. A spokesmen for the agents said last night that a final call for crew for the liner would be made this morning.

About 160 men were at the pick-up centre yesterday but none offered for the Aorangi. Seamen's Union officials, maintaining the attitude the union has adopted since June 4, said that the union had not banned the liner, that the men had 'the right of free selection,' but were 'just not offering.' Former Aorangi seamen at the pick-up, however, said they were prepared to work the ship, but could not do so 'until union representatives gave the signal.'

The Naval ratings, who went aboard at 2.55pm from Balmoral Naval Base, have replaced the liner's seamen only. The Aorangi's full complement is 280 and more than 200 of these men are members of five unions which have agreed to work alongside the ratings. The Naval ratings, under Lieut-Commander V G Jerram, went aboard from a general-purpose vessel and a launch.

When they boarded the liner 11 of 15 wharf-labourers working the vessel walked off in protest. The Stevedoring Industry Board will decide this morning whether disciplinary action is to be taken against these 11 men.

There was no other demonstration. It was 'smoko' time on the waterfront when the ratings arrived and most of the working members of the Aorangi's crew and waterside workers and seamen on nearby ships watched the operation in silence.

Lieut-Commander Jerram will remain aboard the liner. He will be responsible for the discipline of ratings and will act as liaison officer between them and the ship's officers during the voyage. Many of the ratings have had wartime experience. Some were wearing four rows of Service ribbons.

The Aorangi will sail for Vancouver, by way of Auckland and Pacific ports, tomorrow. Bookings are heavy and she is expected to carry at least 480 passengers.

Security police, plain-clothes and uniformed police have been stationed at the wharf at 5 Darling Harbour, and yesterday only persons with a special pass were allowed to enter the wharf or board the vessel. Waterside workers operated two gangs on the Aorangi yesterday. They were mainly loading ship's supplies and baggage, much of which was left behind by intending passengers who found other means of transport when the vessel's original sailing on June 6 was cancelled.

It was officially estimated last night that the cost of keeping the liner tied up in Sydney for 30 days has exceeded £1,200 a day.

The Naval ratings immediately began working to prepare the ship for departure on Thursday afternoon, and they continued doing this work on the Wednesday morning, but their introduction caused the union to have a sudden change of mind, as was reported on Thursday, 5 July:

Members of the Seamen's Union answered a final call to man the liner Aorangi yesterday, and the Naval men already on board were withdrawn. They were disappointed to have missed the voyage after spending the morning preparing the ship. The ship is due to sail at 4pm today for Vancouver by way of Auckland.

Aorangi repainted with a green hull (John Mathieson collection)

The Naval men were put aboard the ship on Tuesday afternoon after the union seamen had repeatedly ignored calls for labour. Last Thursday the Commonwealth Government told the Union Steam Ship Company, agents for the ship, that it would provide a naval crew. The Seamen's Union knew that Tuesday of this week was the "deadline" for the Naval men to take over, but its members ignored two calls for labour on Tuesday morning.

The Naval men were put aboard the Aorangi on Tuesday afternoon. Yesterday they were preparing the ship for today's sailing when the union seamen answered a call for labour at noon. The seamen had not responded to an earlier call at 9.40am.

Before the second call was made at noon the secretary of the Seamen's Union, Mr E V Elliott, conferred with officers of the Aorangi. Seamen offered for work immediately the second call was made. Forty-five seamen were engaged, leaving a deficit of 11 AB's and four greasers. The ships agents expect to engage these men at the 9am pick-up today. Me Elliott declined to comment on the union's last-minute decision to man the ship.

The men engaged for the ship were obviously excited and pleased as they left the pick-up centre. The Aorangi is regarded as a good ship in which to work. By contrast, the Naval men who were taken off the Aorangi were plainly annoyed. Typical of the remarks they made were, 'They have made a lot of fools of us.' and 'Why did we work so hard this morning.'

A man wearing active service ribbons said, 'It looks as though they used us for political purposes.' He added that the ratings had worked hard yesterday morning, and were looking forward to the voyage. 'They were determined to do their best,' he said.

A Union Steam Ship Company spokesman said last night that the Aorangi would have about 480 passengers. Some would disembark at Auckland.

Eleven wharf-labourers who walked off the Aorangi on Tuesday as a protest against the Naval crew returned to work yesterday.

The Minister for Labour and National Service, Mr H E Holt, said today that a call would be made tomorrow morning for the remaining seamen for the Aorangi. Arrangements had been made for the Naval ratings to stand by until the steamer sailed.

Aorangi completed that round trip, and left for Vancouver again as scheduled in September, but on the return trip ran into a severe storm on its way from Vancouver to Honolulu, and suffered some serious damage. Later in the voyage engine problems developed making the liner two days late arriving in Auckland and Sydney.

Despite the Government assistance, financial returns continued to be poor, with passenger numbers steadily falling, and little cargo being carried. There was also a series of unfortunate incidents that caused further problems for the operation. On 7 June 1952 an engine malfunction when *Aorangi* was berthing at Ogden Point Dock in Victoria caused the liner to come into hard contact with the wharf, causing a 25 foot long gash in the bow. The liner had to go to the Esquimalt Dock Company in Vancouver for repairs. A similar incident, though with much less damage, occurred when *Aorangi* was departing Auckland in October 1952.

With the Government subsidy agreement

Aorangi departing Vancouver (Vancouver Maritime Museum)

due to expire in April 1953, and none of the governments offering to renew the arrangement, on 28 September 1952 an announcement was made by Canadian-Australasian Line that *Aorangi* would be withdrawn from service in June the following year. This decision was also affected by the fact that *Aorangi* had been due for its four-yearly survey in August 1952, and while a one-year extension was granted, there was no guarantee the ship would pass the survey in August 1953 without needing some very expensive work.

On 25 January 1953, the Canadian Pacific liner *Empress of Canada* was destroyed by fire while berthed at Liverpool. This caused a major disruption of Canadian Pacific's trans-Atlantic operation, especially as the ship had been fully booked for several voyage in May and June with Canadians wanting to come to Britain for the coronation of Queen Elizabeth II. At the time it was suggested that, as *Aorangi* was half-owned by Canadian Pacific, it should be taken off the Pacific trade and sent to the Atlantic as a temporary replacement for the lost ship, but this was not done.

On 16 April 1953 *Aorangi* departed Sydney on its final voyage to Canada. The liner left Vancouver for the last time on 14 May, and the arrival of the vessel in Sydney on 8 June marked the end of Canadian-Australasian Line Limited.

Aorangi had already been sold to shipbreakers in Britain, and a skeleton crew was signed on to deliver the ship, but just before departure it was found that the number of crew was just large enough to require the ship to carry a doctor. To overcome this, the purser was paid off.

Aorangi left Sydney on 18 June, being delivered to British Iron & Steel Corporation at their Dalmuir shipbreaking yard on 25 July 1953. It was a sad end for a fine ship that had undergone a lengthy and expensive refit that was completed only five years previously.

Why *Aorangi* was not used to transport British migrants to Australia or New Zealand at a time when liners suited to this trade were in short supply is a question that has no answer.

The withdrawal of *Aorangi* left *Lakemba* as the only passenger vessel operating across the Pacific from Australia to North America.

Lakemba arriving at Adelaide (Jim Freeman photo)

(Above) *Lakemba* berthed in Walsh Bay (Fred Roderick photograph)

(Below) *Aorangi* arriving in Sydney in the early 1950s (Dallas Hogan collection)

(Above) *Aorangi* berthed at 5 Darling Harbour in Sydney in the early 1950s (Ron Knight photograph)

(Below) *Homeric*, formerly *Mariposa*, berthed in New York (Stephen Berry photo)

(Above) *Orcades* berthing at Pyrmont in Sydney (Ron Knight photo)

(Below) *Iberia* arriving in Auckland (Ron Knight photo)

(Above) *Mariposa* berthed in Honolulu (Andy Kilk photograph)

(Below) Monterey in San Francisco Bay (Andy Kilk photograph)

Chapter Twenty-two

Orient Pacific Line

In April 1953, the Orient Line announced that, in view of the pending withdrawal of *Aorangi*, they were proposing to introduce some voyages across the Pacific. While these voyages would not be on a regular basis, they would offer an opportunity to travel to North America by sea.

The Orient Line had been maintaining a regular steamship service between Britain and Australia since 1877, with a few extensions to New Zealand and Pacific island cruises in the 1930s.

The first Orient Line vessel to make a voyage across the Pacific was *Oronsay*, which was built at the Vickers-Armstrong Ltd shipyard at Barrow, being launched on 30 June 1950. While being fitted out with accommodation for 668 first class and 833 tourist class passengers, a fire started in No 1 hold on 28 October 1950, and the local fire brigade pumped so much water into the ship, it began to list towards the wharf, and there were fears it would capsize, so holes were cut in the hull to let the water out. This incident caused only a minor delay in completing *Oronsay*, which left London on 16 May on its maiden voyage to Australia, voyaging in both directions via the Suez Canal.

Oronsay left Tilbury on 26 November 1953 on a regular voyage to Australia, and on 1 January 1954 departed Sydney on an experimental voyage to both Vancouver and San Francisco, from where the liner returned to Australia, with calls at Auckland, Suva and Honolulu in both directions. Although passengers were carried to and from North America, it was also possible to make the round trip, though it was not advertised as a cruise.

Oronsay operated a second voyage on the trans-Pacific route, departing Sydney on 21 May 1954. The third Orient Line trip across the Pacific in 1954 was taken by *Orion*, which departed Sydney on 17 September, reaching San Francisco on 11 October.

Oronsay made the first Orient Line voyage across the Pacific

Built in 1935 by Vickers-Armstrong Ltd at Barrow, *Orion* was the first Orient vessel to be permanently given a corn coloured hull. The 23,696 gross ton vessel operated regular voyages to Australia prior to the war, as well as making numerous cruises, mostly from British ports. Following a hectic war career, *Orion* was handed back to Orient Line in April 1946, and became the first Orient liner to resume commercial service with a departure from London on 25 February 1947, having accommodation for 546 first class and 706 tourist class passengers.

Oronsay made a third voyage across the Pacific in 1954, leaving Sydney on 19 November, while the final trans-Pacific voyage for the Orient Line in 1954 was made by *Orcades*, also built by Vickers-Armstrong Ltd, Barrow, being launched on 14 October 1947. Fitted out with accommodation for 773 first class and 772 tourist class passengers *Orcades* left Tilbury on its maiden voyage on 14 December 1948, becoming the first brand new liner to arrive in Australia after the war. On 17 December 1954, *Orcades* departed Sydney on its first voyage across the Pacific, arriving in San Francisco on 6 January 1955, then returning to Sydney.

The next trip to North America was taken by *Orsova*, which had also been built by Vickers-Armstrong Ltd, Barrow, being launched on 14 May 1953, and achieving a top speed of 26 knots on trials in March 1954. *Orsova* was fitted with accommodation for 681 first class and 813 tourist class passengers, and departed Tilbury on 17 March 1954 on its maiden voyage to Australia. *Orsova* was notable in being the first liner to have an all-welded hull, and also the first large liner to be built without conventional masts.

Orsova left Sydney on 28 January 1955, going to Vancouver and San Francisco. *Orsova* completed the sector from San Francisco to Honolulu in 89 hours at an average speed of 23.39 knots, breaking by three hours a record that had stood since 1921.

The Orient Line also decided to introduce an occasional around-the-world sailing between Britain and Australia, using both the Suez Canal and the Panama Canal. The first of these voyages was the departure of *Orsova* from Tilbury on 27 April 1955, going out to Australia via Suez, then continuing from Sydney to Auckland, Honolulu, Vancouver and San Francisco, and back to Britain through the Panama Canal, arriving in Tilbury on 13 July.

The second of these round-the-world voyages was taken by *Orcades* from Tilbury on 22 August 1955, but in the opposite direction. After passing through the Panama Canal, *Orcades* went up the west coast of North America to Los Angeles, San Francisco and Vancouver, with passengers being able to join the ship at any of these ports for the voyage to Auckland and Sydney. In 1956 *Oronsay* made its first voyage on this route.

Although Orient Line was a subsidiary of P&O, and the two companies operated a joint service from Britain to Australia via Suez, the Orient Line was the only one to operate a service across the Pacific for four years. This service was usually advertised as

Orsova

the Orient-Pacific Line to differentiate it from the regular service to Britain.

It was not until 1958 that the P&O Line introduced their ships to the trans-Pacific trade, the first being *Himalaya*. Like the new Orient Line vessels, *Himalaya* was built at Barrow by Vickers-Armstrong Ltd, being the first new liner to be built for P&O after the war. Launched on 5 October 1948, *Himalaya* provided accommodation for 758 first class and 401 tourist class passengers, and departed Tilbury for the first time on 6 October 1949.

One problem to affect *Himalaya* was smuts from the funnel falling on the after decks, so in 1953 a Thorneycroft top was fitted, which solved the problem and also enhanced the appearance of the liner.

In February 1958 *Himalaya* left Tilbury on a regular voyage to Sydney, from where the vessel departed for Auckland and Honolulu, then on to Vancouver and San Francisco, returning to Sydney and then making a regular voyage back to Britain. In March 1959, *Himalaya* left Sydney on its second voyage across the Pacific, but after leaving San Francisco and Honolulu the liner made the first ever P&O crossing of the North Pacific to Japan, returning to Sydney via Hong Kong.

Late in 1959 two more P&O liners, *Arcadia* and *Iberia*, also made voyages across the Pacific. Although essentially sister ships, these liners came from different shipyards, *Arcadia* being built by John Brown & Co at Clydebank, being launched on 14 May 1953, the same day as *Orsova*. Fitted with accommodation for 675 first class and 735 tourist class passengers, *Arcadia* departed Tilbury on 22 February 1954 on its maiden voyage to Australia.

Iberia came from another famous shipyard, Harland & Wolff at Belfast, being launched on 21 January 1954, and fitted with identical accommodation to *Arcadia*. On 28 September 1954 *Iberia* left Tilbury on its maiden voyage to Australia. The sisters could be distinguished by their funnels, that on *Iberia* being topped by a smoke deflecter while *Arcadia* had a black dome.

On 11 December 1959, *Arcadia* departed Sydney on its first voyage across the Pacific, going to Vancouver and San Francisco, returning to Sydney on 19 January 1960. On 15 December 1959, *Iberia* departed Tilbury on the first P&O around-the-world voyage, going out through the Panama Canal, with calls at San Francisco and Vancouver, then on to Honolulu, Auckland and Sydney, returning to Britain through the Suez Canal.

The last liners that the Orient Line and P&O would place on the trans-Pacific routes would also be the largest and fastest to be built for the Australian trade. Apart from their size and speed, *Oriana* and *Canberra* attracted divided comments on their appearance, which was quite different to any existing liner. Both liners had a service speed of 27 knots, and reduced the passage time from Britain to Sydney by almost a week.

The first to be completed, the 41,915 gross ton *Oriana* was launched at the Vickers-Armstrong

Arcadia

Ltd shipyard at Barrow on 3 November 1959. With accommodation for 638 first class and 1,496 tourist class passengers, *Oriana* departed Southampton on 3 December 1960 on its maiden voyage to Australia, arriving in Sydney on 30 December, having cut a week off the previous scheduled time. *Oriana* then made a ten-day cruise from Sydney to Hobart, Wellington and Auckland.

On 16 January *Oriana* departed Sydney on a voyage across the Pacific via Auckland, Suva and Honolulu to Vancouver. The new liner arrived at San Francisco on 5 February, which was declared '*Oriana* Day' by the city council. After a call at Los Angeles, *Oriana* voyaged back to Sydney, and then returned to Southampton via Suez, having been away for 111 days.

After its second voyage to Australia from Southampton, *Oriana* again headed off across the Pacific, but after calling at Vancouver, San Francisco and Los Angeles continued south to pass through the Panama Canal and head back to Britain.

The 45,270 gross ton *Canberra* was built by Harland & Wolff at Belfast, being launched on 16 March 1960, and departing Southampton on 2 June 1961 on its maiden voyage to Australia. *Canberra* was fitted with accommodation for 548 first class and 1,650 tourist class passengers, and had a top speed of just under 30 knots.

Canberra arrived in Sydney for the first time on 29 June, and after an overnight stay left for Auckland, arriving there on 4 July. Canberra continued to Suva, Honolulu, Vancouver and San Francisco, calling at Los Angeles before going back to Honolulu and back to Sydney, with another call at Auckland on the way.

On one voyage, in December 1962, *Oriana* was scheduled to make a call at Long Beach, the port for Los Angeles, then head back to Sydney. On the voyage south from San Francisco, *Oriana* ran into thick fog, and shortly after 9am on Monday, 3 December, when approaching the breakwater off Long Beach, *Oriana* collided with the aircraft carrier USS *Kearsage*, which was leaving the port. Fortunately no one was injured, and no serious damage was caused to either ship apart from large rips near the bow of *Oriana*. The ships were both moving at slow speed at the time of impact, which was so gentle most passengers on *Oriana* were unaware their ship had hit anything.

Oriana had to undergo repairs to the bow before being allowed to depart, and the liner was sent to the Todd shipyard where workers toiled day and night to complete the job. *Oriana* left Long Beach just on midnight on 6 December, and caught up the lost time on the voyage back to Sydney.

Both *Oriana* and *Canberra* continued to make voyages across the Pacific on an irregular basis over the next few years, as did various other liners of both the P&O and Orient Line.

Canberra

Chapter Twenty-three

The New *Mariposa* and *Monterey*

The Matson Line had resumed a regular passenger service from San Francisco and Los Angeles to Honolulu after the war, using *Lurline*, but they did not resume the passenger trade to the South Pacific, operated by The Oceanic Steamship Company. The two liners they had operated on that trade before the war had been laid up in July 1947. *Mariposa* was sold to Home Line on 18 December 1953 and went on to enjoy a highly successful career under the name *Homeric*, while on 6 August 1952 *Monterey* had been sold to the United States Maritime Commission, and laid up in Suisan Bay in the reserve fleet.

In 1947, a cargo service had been established from California to New Zealand and Australia using three ships built during the war years, which were purchased by The Oceanic Steamship Company and renamed *Alameda*, *Sierra*, and *Sonoma*, thus reviving the names of passenger vessels well known on the route in previous years. These vessels did provide accommodation for a maximum of twelve passengers, but it was a far cry from the magnificent passenger liner service of the 1930s.

Matson Line always hoped to be able to resume the Oceanic Steamship Company passenger service to New Zealand and Australia at some time, and during the early 1950s the Stanford Research Institute was called upon to prepare a feasibility study. The results of this were so positive that preliminary plans were drawn up for the construction of two ships to operate a revived Pacific service.

The renowned firm of Gibbs & Cox, who had been responsible for the design of all the major American liners built since 1927, including the original *Mariposa* and *Monterey*, came up with a design that was very similar to the pair of ships they had designed for the Grace Line, which were named *Santa Paula* and *Santa Rosa*.

On 28 October 1954, Matson Line President Randolph Sevier announced that the Matson subsidiary, Oceanic Steamship Company, would be resuming its service to the South Pacific. However, instead of building new ships, it had been decided that it would be more economical and quicker to purchase two recently built fast cargo ships, *Free State Mariner* and *Pine Tree Mariner*, and have them converted for the trade.

Both these vessels had been built as standard "Mariner" class vessels by the Bethlehem Shipbuilding Corporation, *Free State Mariner* at the Sparrow's Point facility in Maryland, being launched on 29 May 1952, and completed on 8 December. *Pine Tree Mariner* was built Quincy, Massachusetts, where it was launched on 7 November 1952, and completed on 3 April 1953.

As built the ships measured 9,217 gross tons, and they were handed over to the United States Maritime Commission, but only saw a brief period of active service before being laid up, mainly due to high operating costs primarily caused by excessive fuel consumption.

On 28 July 1955 both these ships, which had cost US$17.8 million to build, were purchased by Matson Line for US$9.6 million, and they were sent to the Willamette Iron & Steel Company yard at Portland, Oregon, for a major rebuilding into modern luxury liners to a design supplied by Gibbs & Cox.

The pair was scheduled to enter the trans-Pacific trade at the end of 1956, reviving the names of the pre-war pair, with *Pine Tree Mariner* being renamed *Mariposa* while *Free State Mariner* became *Monterey*.

The cost of the conversion of the two ships was estimated at US$27 million, but only US$15 million of this was paid by Matson, the balance being provided by the U S Government. In exchange the Government had a considerable say in the design process of the ships, to ensure they could be quickly converted to transport troops if the occasion arose.

In the meantime, with *Lurline* operating at an average 97% occupancy rate throughout the year, and in 1955 Matson Line had decided the Hawaiian trade would probably be able to support a second ship. The company had the option of building a new vessel or doing what they had done for the Pacific route and purchase an existing vessel which could be converted.

The fast cargo ships *Pine Tree Mariner* (above) and *Free State Mariner* were rebuilt into the passenger liners *Mariposa* and *Monterey* (below)

In a surprise move, Matson was able to buy back the original *Monterey* from the Government on 3 February 1956. Having been laid up for almost ten years, the vessel was in need of a major refit, and the engines also required an extensive overhaul. *Monterey* was towed from Suisan Bay to San Francisco, and then left that port under tow on 15 March for the Newport News shipyard on the east coast, to undergo conversion into a modern luxury liner.

This meant that during 1956 the Matson organization had three liners undergoing extensive alterations at one time, which was a major allocation of resources.

The work of converting the two freighters into luxury passenger liners included the removal of all but two of the original cargo holds and the entire original deckhouse, and the construction of a new superstructure on the existing hull.

Staterooms, all with a private shower and toilet, for 365 first class passengers were spread over four decks, many having a private sitting room while others had beds that could be converted into sofas during the day.

Public rooms included a large dining room on Main Deck, the Southern Cross Lounge, Polynesian Club and Outrigger Bar on the Promenade Deck, and a theatre on A Deck. An outdoor swimming pool was added on the Boat Deck, with an adjacent Pool Terrace Bar. The entire interior of the ship was air conditioned.

The original double-reduction geared turbine engines were retained, and the ships had only a single propeller, but could maintain a service speed of 20 knots. Two of the cargo holds were also retained, becoming the first United States flag ships to be fitted with quick opening hydraulic hatch covers, providing 200,000 cubic feet of space, of which 28,000 cubic feet was insulated.

A water distilling plant was fitted that could produce 65,000 gallons a day, and they were the first American flag ships to be fitted with Sperry Gyrofin stabilizers.

Matson Line was able to secure an operating subsidy for the two ships from the United States Government, which was described by one United States Senator as being a "fantastic and unjustified waste of taxpayers money." This subsidy would cover about 45% of the cost of each voyage, and without it the company would not have been able to return to the South Pacific trade.

The former *Pine Tree Mariner*, now renamed *Mariposa*, was the first of the pair to be completed, and on trials achieved a maximum speed of 24.6 knots, well in excess of the required service speed of 20 knots. On 16 October 1956 an official naming ceremony was held in San Francisco, and on 26 October, *Mariposa* departed San Francisco on its maiden voyage, witnessed by a large crowd and group of specially invited guests. There were also two kangaroos on the wharf, one of which suddenly attacked a guest, causing considerable chaos for a short time.

Mariposa called at Los Angeles, Honolulu and Papeete before arriving in Wellington on 15 November, Melbourne on 19 November and Sydney two days later. On the return voyage, *Mariposa* went from Sydney to Auckland, Suva, Pago Pago and Honolulu, arriving back in San Francisco on 11 December.

An extensive observation of the *Mariposa* was published in the March 1957 issue of *The Log*, at that time the quarterly magazine of the Australian and New Zealand branches of the World Ship Society, written by their New Zealand correspondent, who inspected the ship on its visit to Wellington. Apart from comparing the American ship with one of the newest British liners, *Southern Cross* of Shaw Savill Line, he gave an interesting description of the new liner.

The Mariposa cannot adequately be compared to any of the new vessels which have been seen on the Australia and New Zealand coast. It has been said that her public rooms are just as large and comfortable as those in the Southern Cross but there any comparison ends. The accommodation in the Southern Cross is more akin to a comprehensive system of rabbit warrens when one has seen the Mariposa.

The design and construction of the new vessel has been largely dominated by two factors - one - the ship was originally a freighter and -two- she was converted to US Navy specifications and therefore her owners had to observe certain rulings in regard to fireproofing the ship, arrangement of watertight bulkheads, and the need for easy conversion to a trooper in time of war or other major crisis.

Fireproofing in this ship is unprecedented and is only rivalled by the liner United States. The only signs of wood are to be seen in the pianos, the small dance floor in the after lounge and the butcher's chopping block. Aluminium has been used in the making of cabin furniture, lounge tables, deck chairs, the upper superstructure, the funnel, life boats and hundreds of other fittings. The fabrics used for drapes, curtains and upholstery are all fire resistant and are made from a chemical fibre of linen-like appearance.

There are no neatly holystoned wooden decks. All the exterior steel decks are coated with a blue-coloured composition which appears to have been spread on like cement. In addition to these materials the latest fire detection and fire prevention equipment has been fitted. Although the extensive use of 'cold' materials may tend to infer that the ship is more utilitarian than homely, this is not so, and public rooms and cabins dispel any such qualms. One can soon obtain a feeling of comfort and glancing through a rack of photographs taken during the voyage, it is even more evident that the steamship's

Mariposa

companies publicity slogan of "Rest, Relax and Recuperate" is pursued to the full on this vessel.

In contrast to British liners, there is no great class distinction either amongst the passengers or the crew. The stewards and waitresses observe a standard of courtesy that does not give an impression of stiffness and the informality of everyone on board must go a long way towards promoting a feeling of friendliness and a 'happy go lucky' atmosphere that must be prevalent for a company to succeed in a competitive run.

The meals are predominantly on American lines and Australians or New Zealanders should have little complaint from the menus offered. They are served, as well as morning and afternoon tea, by waitresses. These ladies are not the very young heady type of girl, but hand picked waitresses, chosen for their cleanliness, tactfulness, experience and general outlook on life.

Every cabin (from the dearest to the cheapest) in the vessel is air conditioned. One only has to turn a knob to alter the temperature of the cabin, remove humidity or ventilate. The air is diffused through very small holes in the roof of the cabins and by this method no draughts are created and even distribution is effected.

While on air conditioning it must be borne in mind by the prospective traveller that the single cabins are highly priced and one plans to share a two or three-berth cabin, he should bear in mind that most Americans like the temperature of the air somewhat higher than the average Kiwi or Aussie. There is also a radio and telephone in each cabin. Windows have replaced portholes and instead of blinds, aluminium slides preclude all light. Kennels provided for eight dogs are also air conditioned.

The main entrance hall, dining room, lounge and theatre, bars and other smaller public rooms are all finished in light pastel colours and motifs of Polynesian origin (also done in metal) are featured in all rooms. The chairs in the lounges are most comfortable and one seems to sink well into the carpets which are laid over sponge rubber.

The exterior design of the ship compared with many of the postwar models is very pleasing. Messrs Gibbs & Cox have done a good job although there will no doubt be criticisms from those who would prefer two smaller funnels, pole masts and the stately appearance that went with ships of a past decade. The funnel is made of aluminium alloy, is 42 feet in height, and is designed to throw the smoke clear of the decks. This it does, without the aid of any Welsh bonnets or other stove pipe additions. Louvred grills on either side of the funnel produce a Venturi effect by allowing air to pass up the inside of the casing thus rapidly drawing the exhaust fumes well clear of the passenger decks. Also the elliptical shape tapered to a thin edge aft causes the air split by the funnel to re-unite and thus prevent any vacuum for the fumes to sweep down.

The swimming pool appears to be the most popular part of the games deck and considering the climate throughout the voyage it would be surprising if it were not the centre of activity.

Another passenger selling aspect of the vessel is the use of stabilizing fins. These are the first of the new Sperry type to be fitted to an American passenger ship and they differ somewhat from the Denny Brown type. The fins feather and fold back into a recess in the hull and do not slide back into the side of the hull as in British ships. They are designed to reduce motion by 90% but this can only be measured by tests under service conditions and on the voyage south they were used for only a short period.

In anticipation of television at sea, all the cabins are wired ready for the installation of viewers. The ship has limited cargo capacity and the hatchcovers for the two holds are opened by push button method. Double sets of derricks are provided for both holds.

The former *Free State Mariner*, which was renamed *Monterey*, had been scheduled to depart San Francisco on its maiden voyage in November 1956, but due to delays in completing the conversion, this voyage was cancelled. *Mariposa* left on its second voyage to the South Pacific in December, and the official naming ceremony for *Monterey* was not held until 31 December 1956. On 8 January 1957, *Monterey* departed San Francisco on its maiden voyage, following the same route as *Mariposa*, arriving in Sydney on 29 January.

Matson Line was keen to show off their new ship to as many people as possible, and among those to inspect *Monterey* was a group from the Sydney branch of the World Ship Society, and the following note appeared in the March 1957 issue of *The Log*:

> In the past month the new Matson liner *Monterey* has entered Sydney port and members had visitors tickets made available by the owners, and a group availed themselves of the opportunity to inspect her. She is very typical of American ship builders efforts. Very obviously a converted cargo ship, luxurious cabins, but to this writers' view just somehow missing in that 'air' necessary to make a 'shiplike' vessel.

This type of comment was rather frequently expressed by those more used to the British type of passenger liner, with its teak decks and large armchairs in the lounges, which made the new American ships seem rather mundane with their metal decks and modern furniture.

The fares charged were quite high by Australian and New Zealand standards, and deterred many potential passengers from those countries. By following a different route in each direction, the 42-day round trip could also be advertised as a cruise from San Francisco, and this became quite popular with wealthy Americans. Although the route was nominally operated by the Oceanic Steamship Company, the service was advertised under Matson Line.

Meanwhile, work had also been proceeding on the conversion of the original *Monterey* into a luxury liner suitable for the Hawaiian trade by including many of the features installed on *Lurline* when it was refitted nine years previously.

The original open promenade deck on B Deck

Restaurant (Tony Ralph collection)

Lanai suite (Tony Ralph collection)

Theatre (Tony Ralph collection)

was plated in, being replaced by new staterooms, though there was only one luxury lanai suite on either side, compared to three on *Lurline*. The existing accommodation was completely rebuilt, with staterooms for 761 first class passengers being installed. The public rooms were all decorated in a Polynesian theme, and air conditioning extended throughout the liner.

The major external alterations were the removal of the mainmast, the addition of a raked section on the upper part of the bow, the forward well deck being filled in, and streamlining of the superstructure and funnels. The changes increased the overall length of the ship to 641 feet/195.5 m, and increased her size to 18,655 gross tons.

As the name *Monterey* had been allocated to one of the two vessels being converted for the Pacific service, the original *Monterey* was renamed *Matsonia* in a ceremony held at Newport News on 17 May 1957, becoming the third ship to carry that name in the Matson fleet.

Matsonia went to New York for a publicity visit, then on 22 May boarded passengers for a special delivery cruise via the Panama Canal to Los Angeles, departing there on 11 June on its first voyage to Honolulu.

Later in 1957 the accommodation on *Lurline* was altered to cater for 722 first class passengers only. Through the rest of 1957 *Lurline* and *Matsonia* offered regular voyages from Los Angeles and San Francisco to Honolulu, and for a while passenger loadings on both liners serving Hawaii remained high.

Matsonia remained on the Hawaiian trade all years, but at the end of 1957 *Lurline* was taken off the route to make a special Christmas cruise to Acapulco, Mexico, which would be repeated each year until 1961. In the first year this cruise was followed by a 73-day jaunt to fifteen ports in the South Pacific and Orient.

Departing San Francisco on 7 January 1958 with 575 passengers on board, *Lurline* called at Papeete, Pago Pago and Suva before visiting Auckland on 25 January and Wellington two days later, arriving in Sydney on 31 January, berthing at Woolloomooloo for two nights.

Departing Sydney on 2 February, *Lurline* went to Port Moresby, Bali and Singapore, continuing to Bangkok, Manila and Hong Kong before visiting the Japanese ports of Kobe and Yokohama, returning to San Francisco on 19 March.

Lurline then returned to the Hawaiian trade alongside *Matsonia*, while *Mariposa* and *Monterey* maintained a regular schedule of sailings to New Zealand and Australia. After only a few voyages the route was modified, with the calls at Wellington and

Matsonia, formerly the first *Monterey*

Lurline berthed in Sydney on 1 February 1958

Melbourne being abandoned. Instead, from June 1957 the southbound route from San Francisco and Los Angeles went to Papeete, Auckland and Sydney, returning via Auckland, Suva, Pago Pago and Honolulu to San Francisco.

A change was made to the southbound route they followed from the departure of *Mariposa* from San Francisco on 16 November 1960, when a stop at Bora Bora was added.

In 1962 the northbound call at Auckland was dropped, being replaced by a call at Noumea, while at the same time a brief stop off Niuafo'ou was also added. Better known as Tin Can Island, it is one of the outlying islands of the Tongan group. The Matson ships were the first liners to include such a call since 1946, when a volcanic eruption caused the island to be evacuated, and the population was now only about 300 persons. The call was done primarily to enable the passengers to witness the unusual way mail was delivered to the island, and collected.

As there is no harbour, the liner would come to a stop some distance from the shore, from where a boat would be rowed out to the side of the ship. The boat would bring out mail in a container, which was hoisted aboard the liner, while letters for the small population, along with some other small items such as cigarettes and confectionary, would be placed in the container and thrown over the side of the ship, to be picked up by the men in the boat and taken ashore. It was also quite usual for passengers to write letters to be included in the container, which would be stamped on Niuafo'ou, then sent on by the next vessel to call there.

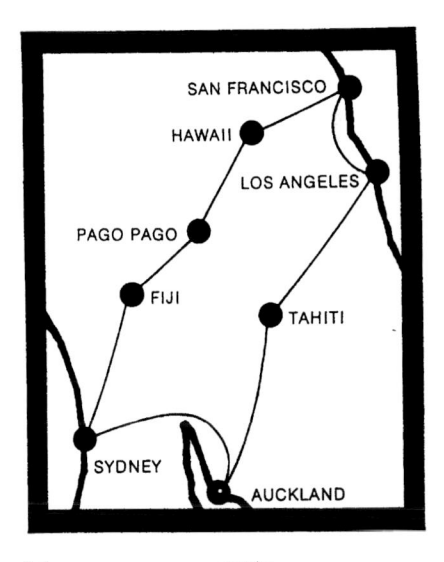

Matson route map 1958

Mariposa berthed at Suva on 16 June 1958, with *Wanganella* ahead and *Beaverbank* astern (The Beacon)

In 1960, *Matsonia* became the first liner in the world to be fitted with Flume Stabilisers, which were also fitted to *Lurline* at a later date.

With four liners in service, Matson Line was a major force in the Pacific passenger trades, but their optimism in adding *Matsonia* to the Hawaiian trade had not been as successful as expected. Going into the 1960s Matson Line still held high hopes for the future of their services to Hawaii and the South Pacific, but the next few years would be increasingly difficult, as the advent of jet airliners began to siphon passengers away from sea travel.

In March 1962, a 27 day national shipping strike caused five voyages by *Lurline* and *Matsonia* to be cancelled. The ships then operated with some uncertainty for the next 71 days until the dispute was settled, but major damage had been done to the passenger services.

As passenger numbers fell away, Matson Line was forced to cut costs, and on 5 September 1962 *Matsonia* was withdrawn from service, being laid up in San Francisco. During 1962, Matson Line lost over US$2.2 million on their service to Hawaii,

On the morning of 3 February 1963, *Lurline* was arriving at Los Angeles on a voyage from Hawaii when the port engine failed. Inspection showed that many of the blades on the rotor rings of the high and intermediate pressure turbines were either broken off or badly damaged, and as repairs would be very expensive, it was decided to withdraw *Lurline* from service when it limped into San Francisco on one engine on 5 February.

Initially it was stated that the damaged turbine would be repaired, and the ship returned to service on 14 June, but instead *Lurline* lay idle while Matson Line considered what to do with her, and in August 1963, it was decided the liner would be offered for sale in its damaged condition.

It was quite a surprise when the liner was purchased by Chandris Line on 3 September 1963, for US$3.4 million. After the engine was repaired the vessel was renamed *Ellinis* and left for Britain to be converted for the Australian migrant trade.

The withdrawal of *Lurline* left *Matsonia*, the former *Monterey*, as the only liner providing a service to Hawaii, and on 6 December 1963 that vessel was renamed *Lurline*. For the next two years *Lurline* operated regular voyages from the mainland to Honolulu, but it continued to suffer from declining patronage.

Monterey was on a regular voyage from San Francisco to Sydney, with 320 passengers on board, when, on the morning of 30 December 1964, it ran aground on a coral reef while departing Bora Bora after an overnight stay. As the tide fell the vessel took a ten degree list, but it was soon apparent that the passengers were in no danger, and they remained on board. It was found that 200 feet of the keel was wedged on the reef, but no water was entering the vessel.

The next day, *Monterey* was refloated, and proceeded to Papeete, where an underwater inspection showed that no damage had been sustained. As a result the voyage continued two days behind schedule, with *Monterey* arriving in Auckland on the morning of Saturday, 9 January 1965. The same day the *Auckland Star* reported:

> The Matson liner Monterey – nicknamed the 'Tiltin' Hilton" by some of the passengers – arrived in Auckland this morning two days late after grounding on a coral reef at Bora Bora on December 30.
>
> The liner took a 10-degree list on the reef and this created some problems for crew members and passengers. Stewardesses serving meals complained of aching back and leg muscles. And passengers found they couldn't get a shower because of the angle at which the water came out.
>
> Mr Morris F Ketay, of Los Angeles, concocted a new cocktail for the occasion, appropriately named 'Monterey on the Rocks.' He declined to give the recipe.
>
> Mrs Abel Levy, of Beverley Hills, California, said most people enjoyed walking about lopsided after they found the ship was not in danger. Breakfast had just been brought in to her when the ship grounded, she said. 'Everything flew off the tray and I still have some bruises from falling against something. We couldn't even use our shower – the water came out at such an odd angle,' she said.
>
> The Monterey sails for Sydney at 7pm today instead of staying the usual 34 hours. A group of 85 passengers is making a hurried trip to the Waitomo Caves.
>
> Only 200 tons of refrigerated cargo will be taken on board instead of the usual 400 tons of refrigerated cargo and 150 tons of general cargo. It is expected the liner will be back on schedule by the time she leaves Sydney on January 14.

During the mid-1960s *Mariposa* and *Monterey* continued to provide a regular service from the west coast of the United States to New Zealand and Australia, but the number of passengers being carried was in a steady decline, as the new jet aircraft then entering service began to take away much of the potential market.

On the Honolulu service, *Lurline* was suffering even more significant reductions in the number of passengers being carried, and in 1966 it was decided to offer an occasional longer trip. These fifteen-day cruises included visits to the islands of Oahu, Kauai, Maui and Hawaii, and soon proved extremely popular.

Monterey

Chapter Twenty-four

Aground and Sunk

Through the 1950s and into the 1960s, *Lakemba* had continued to operate a regular service across the Pacific between Australian ports and Vancouver, with a departure every fourteen weeks. Having had a grey hull since entering service, in the early 1960s this was changed to black, and the ship's port of registry was also changed from Suva to Hong Kong.

In the middle of 1967, Pacific Shipowners announced that *Lakemba* would be withdrawn from service in October that year. The vessel, under the command of Captain J Ward, departed Vancouver for the last time on 14 September, by which time a sale to shipbreakers had already been finalized, with delivery after the final cargo had been unloaded in Melbourne.

As usual the vessel made a call at Suva, arriving there on 3 October, and leaving late the next day for the short trip around Viti Levu Island to Lautoka, but shortly before midnight *Lakemba* ran hard aground on a reef off Vatulele Island.

When the vessel could not be refloated, the 56 passengers and most of the 55 crew members were taken off on 5 October, being transferred to the cable repair ship *Retriever*, which had rushed to the scene from Suva, where it was based. A tug was also sent to the scene, but after initial efforts to refloat *Lakemba* failed, the remaining crew members were taken off, and the tug returned to Suva.

Four days later the tug was sent back to the scene of the grounding, but when it arrived there was no sign of *Lakemba*, which apparently had slipped off the reef by itself and sunk. The full details of how the accident occurred and subsequent events were contained in a report made by Captain John Fant, who had been sent from Melbourne to Fiji to oversee the salvage of the vessel. Captain Fant left Melbourne by plane on the afternoon of 5 October, arriving in Suva early the following morning. The report by Captain Fant stated:

Lakemba departing Sydney on 27 August 1959 (John Mathieson photo)

At a meeting held in Suva at 1130 on the same day, at which the Master, Captain J Ward, was present, he stated that at approximately 2304 hours, 4 October 1967, whilst on passage from Suva to Lautoka, and drawing 23 feet 5 inches forward and 24 feet 3 inches aft, the Lakemba had struck Thakau Leka Leka Reef whilst altering course from 234° to 306° and that at this time the magnetic and gyro compass, as well as the radar were all in use and in working order.

At 2200, a radar fix had given the vessel's position… and at this time the Master had instructed the third officer, A D McEwan, who was on watch to call him before the next alteration of course and had then gone into the chartroom to rest.

At 2220, a further radar fix gave the vessel position… and shortly after this the vessel's position was transferred from one chart to the next one.

When the vessel stranded at approximately 2304 hours, the Master was still in the chartroom. The third officer later admitted that he had not called the Master, as instructed, and when sighting broken water ahead whilst the course was being altered he kept the helm over in the hope of getting clear, with the result that on taking the ground, Lakemba was heading 006°.

Various attempts were made to refloat the ship thereafter by using the engines, but all were unsuccessful. Meanwhile, at about 0400 hours, the wind freshened to force 6/7 in an E S/E direction causing the ship's head to alter to 028°.

In response to the Master's radio message for assistance the cable-laying vessel Retriever left Suva at 0648, 5 October, and arrived at the scene of the casualty at 0930. At this time, Lakemba was listing 10° to starboard. No 1 hold had commenced filling with water and the forepeak tank which had been full prior to stranding, had drained out to external sea level.

During the afternoon all passengers and crew, together with approximately 57 stevedores who had been on board, and the Master, left the casualty and boarded Retriever to return to Suva.

The Salvage Officer, with the Master, flew over the area in a chartered aircraft between 1550 and 1650, 5 October, and noted that *Lakemba* was then heading 50°, that her starboard list had increased to approximately 25° and that the water round her stern was discoloured by pulverized coral, indicating severe pressure on her bottom forward.

Of her deck cargo of timber, that on No 1 appeared to be intact; 15% had been washed off No 2, and approximately 66% had been washed off Nos 4 and 5 hatches; meanwhile, the surrounding sea was covered with pieces of timber all drifting in a northerly to northwesterly direction. On returning to Suva the Salvage Officer received instructions by cable to act on behalf of the Salvage Association, London.

At 0725, 8 October, the MV Ai Sokula of 500 ton gross left Suva with Captain Ward, the Salvage Officer, some European members of Lakemba's crew and a customs officer and the casualty was boarded at 1400 on the same day.

It was noted that the Lakemba had now listed 3° to port with the main deck at sea level on the starboard

Lakemba arriving in Sydney on 6 September 1966 (John Mathieson collection)

side and roughly 2 feet under water on the port side. All compartments appeared to be full of water and No 1 and 2 hatch coamings were full of fuel oil, whilst the engine room was flooded with a layer of oil covering the water. Main deck handrails along the starboard side had been carried away, the main topmast itself and starboard forward main mast swifter were broken, derrick crutches had been carried away, and approximately 75% of the timber cargo was missing. Meanwhile timber stowed under deck was pressing heavily upwards under the deck beams and this was doubtless accentuated by the expansion of bales of waterlogged wood pulp stowed beneath. The rudder quadrant had lifted 7 inches, and the steering flat and after accommodation had flooded to a depth of 1 to 1½ feet, and although the hull was working excessively under the impact of the seas, no buckling or distortion of plating was evident.

In considering Lakemba's condition and the position in which she lay – at the extreme edge of the reef – the Salvage Officer was of the opinion that she could not hope to survive longer than five days before being washed off into deep water and both she and her cargo might therefore be regarded as a constructive total loss.

At 1600 all items of baggage, except four pieces which were in the trunk way of No 3 hatch, the Master, crew and Salvage Officer re-boarded Ai Sokula and arrived in Suva at 2130.

Concurrently with the foregoing, Lakemba's managing agent had been endeavoring to obtain the services of a Japanese salvage tug, Fuji Maru, then believed to be in Auckland, on a Lloyds' Open Form "No Cure, No Pay" salvage agreement but it later transpired the vessel was unavailable.

At 0630, 9 October, the MV Riverton reported to the Harbour Master, Suva, by radiophone that whilst passing Thakau Leka Leka Reef it was noted that Lakemba had disappeared. Riverton berthed in Suva at 1100 and her Master confirmed his radio message. The Salvage Master and Captain Ward, together with the Harbour Master, left Suva in a chartered aircraft at 1426 and searched an area of 25 miles radius around Thakau Leka Leka Reef. The shorelines of a nearby island, Vatu Leile, were littered with pieces of timber and contaminated with fuel oil, whilst the site at which the casualty had stranded was now the point of commencement of an oil slick which extended for some twenty miles.

The depth of the water immediately adjacent to the site of the stranding was some 700 feet and there is little doubt that Lakemba had slipped off the reef and sunk in deep water, some time between 1700 7 October and 0630 9 October.

As Lakemba had been on its last voyage, the sudden loss of the ship did not cause any disruption of services, as they were about to be terminated anyway, and passenger services on the 'All Red Route' between Vancouver and Australia came to an end.

Lakemba aground

(Above) *Lurline*, formerly *Monterey*, arriving in San Francisco Bay (Andy Kilk photo)

(Below) *Lakemba* departing Vancouver on 7 May 1967 (John Mathieson collection)

(Above) *Mariposa* arriving in Sydney in Matson Line colours (Stephen Berry photograph)

(Below) *Monterey* at San Francisco in 1970 (Andy Kilk photograph)

(Above) *Mariposa* at San Francisco in August 1971 in PFEL colours (Andy Kilk photograph)

(Below) *Monterey* off Sydney Heads in PFEL colours (Stephen Berry photograph)

(Above) Jin Jiang, formerly *Mariposa*, anchored in Hong Kong Harbour (Peter Plowman photo)

(Below) *Monterey* after conversion into a cruise ship (Stephen Berry photo)

Chapter Twenty-five

Under New Colours

As the 1960's came to a close the service from San Francisco and Los Angeles to the South Pacific being operated by Matson Line was struggling to attract passengers, especially during the winter months in New Zealand and Australia. As a result, occasional calls at Melbourne, the Bay of Islands and Nuku'alofa were initiated, as well as a stop in the New Hebrides. *Monterey* also included a visit to the Great Barrier Reef on its July 1969 voyage.

The round trip was increasingly advertised as a cruise, and many were given 'special interest' themes, such as golf, photography, bridge and flower arranging, when guest specialist lecturers or participants in the various activities would hold instructional courses during the trip.

In the Hawaiian trade, *Lurline* began operating an increasing number of fifteen-day cruises around the islands, and in 1969 the liner also made a 28-day cruise through the Panama Canal to the Caribbean, while early in 1970 the *Lurline* made a longer cruise around South America.

Mariposa and *Monterey* also began operating cruises at various times during the year. During the northern summer months in 1968 *Mariposa* made three cruises from San Francisco to ports in British Columbia and Alaska, with three more in 1969. During May and June 1969 *Monterey* made an extensive cruise around South America, including a visit to the Galapagos Islands.

An extensive program of cruises was operated by

Mariposa in Alaskan waters (Tony Ralph collection)

Matson Line in 1970. From April 1970, *Monterey* made two eleven-day cruises from San Francisco to Mexican ports, followed by a 20-day cruise around the Hawaiian Islands. *Monterey* then made a second cruise around South America during May and early June, and in late June cruised to Alaska. *Mariposa* also made a further three cruises to Alaska during the northern summer. These trips greatly reduced the number of voyages each ship was making across the Pacific.

In the middle of 1970, Matson Line announced an expanded series of cruises for 1971, the highlight being a 56-day trip by *Monterey* to the Mediterranean, departing San Francisco on 16 April 1971, with calls at Los Angeles and San Diego to embark more passengers, and the ship was very quickly sold out.

In June 1964 Alexander & Baldwin Inc, which already held a 33% interest in Matson, had bought out several other large shareholders, increasing their interest in the company to 74%. By the end of 1964 Alexander & Baldwin had increased their share of ownership of Matson Line to 95%, giving them total control of the company.

Alexander & Baldwin, founded in 1869 by Samuel Alexander and Henry Baldwin, initially owned large tracts of land on the Hawaiian island of Maui, on which sugar was grown. By 1920 the company owned most of the Hawaiian sugar crop, several island railroad systems and a large share of the pineapple business. In the 1960s they had expanded into developing a luxury resort on Maui.

On 26 March 1969, Matson Line became a wholly owned subsidiary of Alexander & Baldwin. Their directors were concerned with several aspects of the Matson operation, in particular the passenger ship side, and on 27 May 1970, it was announced that *Lurline* was to be sold. *Lurline* arrived in San Francisco for the last time on 25 June and was sold to the Chandris Line, by whom it was renamed *Britanis*, and survived a further thirty years.

If the cessation of their Hawaiian passenger service came as a shock, on 13 August 1970 Matson announced that they were negotiating the sale of their entire South Pacific operation. Negotiations had commenced with Pacific Far East Line earlier in the year, a sale agreement being reached on 1 October 1970, approved by the United States Maritime Commission on 15 January 1971, and finalized on 22 January.

For just over twelve million dollars, Pacific Far East Line bought both *Mariposa* and *Monterey*, along with two freighters operating to the South Pacific, *Sonoma* and *Ventura*, as well as two container ships then under construction to replace them on the South Pacific route.

The ships were transferred to their new owners over a period of two months. The first was *Mariposa*, which arrived in San Francisco on 21 January 1971 from a cruise to Mexico, while *Monterey* was handed over on 15 February at San Francisco after arriving there from a regular voyage to the South Pacific.

Ventura was handed over to PFEL on 29 January at Seattle, and *Sonoma* at the same port on 8 March. However, Matson Line had retained the title of The Oceanic Steamship Company, and four cargo ships were transferred to Oceanic from the main fleet, but only operated a service to Hawaii.

The sale of *Mariposa* and *Monterey* by The Oceanic Steamship Company to Pacific Far East Line marked the end of Matson involvement in the South Pacific

Lurline, originally *Monterey*, was sold in 1970 (Stephen Berry photo)

passenger liner trade, but the two liners were destined to spend several more years voyaging from California to New Zealand and Australia, this being the last regular passenger service to be operated across the Pacific.

The purchase of *Mariposa* and *Monterey* at the beginning of 1971 sent Pacific Far East Line in a totally new direction, one for which they were really not adequately prepared. Apart from repainting the funnels in the standard Pacific Far East Line funnel colours, no changes were made to either ship, and they continued to operate a mixture of regular voyages from San Francisco to Auckland and Sydney interspersed with cruises. In addition, PFEL retained the advance schedule of cruises that Matson had organized for the two ships.

Pacific Far East Line had been founded by Thomas E Cuffe at San Francisco in July 1946, and commenced trading with five cargo ships that were bareboat-chartered from the United States Maritime Commission. Three of the vessels were reefers, their holds being fully refrigerated perishable goods, and there was also one Victory type ship and one Liberty type ship to carry general cargo.

In 1947 the new company purchased five C2 type cargo ships, which were renamed *California Bear*, *China Bear*, *Indian Bear*, *Pacific Bear* and *Philippine Bear*, and most of their subsequent vessels were also given names ending with 'Bear'. The company ships had a very distinctive funnel, featuring a large yellow Californian bear between two narrow yellow lines on a blue background.

Pacific Far East Line grew quite quickly into a sizeable operator, and on 1 January 1953 was granted a Government subsidy for the cargo services it was operating from the west coast to Japan, Hong Kong, Korea, the Philippines and other islands in the western Pacific.

PFEL was one of the first companies to operate container ships. In 1968 they purchased two C4 S-A1 type troopships, *General R L Howze* and *General A W Greely*, which were laid up in the United States Reserve Fleet, and both were rebuilt into container ships, entering service in 1969 as *Guam Bear* and *Hawaii Bear*.

Pacific Far East Line also became a major supporter of the 'LASH' (lighter aboard ship) concept, and from July 1971 took delivery of six vessels of this type, the last being completed in March 1973.

For the first three months of 1971 *Mariposa* and *Monterey* operated on their regular route from San Francisco to Auckland and Sydney, but then *Monterey* departed San Francisco on 16 April 1971, Los Angeles the next day, and San Diego on 18 April, on the 56-day cruise to the Mediterranean, which was booked out prior to the ship being sold.

Returning to San Francisco on 11 June, *Monterey* resumed its place on the South Pacific route, while a season of seven 13-day Alaskan cruises previously scheduled for *Mariposa* was operated, the first departing San Francisco on 13 June and it was not until 15 September that *Mariposa* left San Francisco on a voyage to the South Pacific, followed by another departure on 26 October. *Monterey* also made a cruise around the Hawaiian Islands in October, followed by two round trips to the South Pacific, then in January 1972 both *Mariposa* and *Monterey* made a Hawaiian cruise.

During 1972 the two ships made only eight departures from San Francisco on the regular South Pacific route, spending the rest of the year cruising. Mostly these went around the Hawaiian Islands, but

Mariposa in PFEL colours

on 9 March 1972 *Mariposa* departed on a cruise around the world.

After visits to Honolulu, Pago Pago, Suva and Nuku'alofa, *Mariposa* was in Wellington on 31 March, then crossed to Sydney, arriving on 4 April and leaving next day. The voyage then continued to Port Moresby, Bali and Singapore, Madras, Colombo and Bombay, then south to Durban and Cape Town and across the South Atlantic to Rio de Janeiro and other South American ports before passing through the Panama Canal on the way back to San Francisco.

Mariposa then operated four round voyages to the South Pacific while from the end of May *Monterey* made two long cruises around the Pacific, not returning to the South Pacific service until 9 December.

The schedule set down for 1973 followed a similar pattern, though there were more regular voyages on the South Pacific service, the world cruise was not repeated, and more excursions around the Pacific were operated.

Renowned shipping writer Peter Knego reminisced about a visit he made to *Monterey* when it was tied up in San Francisco in 1974:

There was "something" about the *Monterey* and her sister Mariposa that made one feel at home, despite their somewhat subdued, spartan decor. They were cozy and had the feel of a friend's informal living room. I remember the *Monterey*'s linoleum-lined passageways with backlit incandescent lighting and brushed steel railings. Her 1956-designed public rooms were more comfortable than chic in 1974, when they were not old enough to be deemed "classic", nor new enough to be fashionable. The colors were muted, with soft pastels, browns, and gray. The lack of abundant wood paneling gave her an unmistakably American ambiance. The food and service on board were reputedly excellent, but then, anything served on PFEL china with Matson Line's silverplate cutlery in those sunken dining rooms with their smoked glass panels and heart-shaped naugahyde and chrome chairs would probably taste all that much better. For a ship of her relatively modest size, the Monterey had fantastically wide, sheltered promenades and looked especially appealing in Matson and Pacific Far East Line brochure shots, filled with swooning passengers draped in streamers.

The two ships lost money for their new owners, despite the Government subsidy they received, but this would only be provided until the vessels were twenty-five years old, which would be in 1977/78. Without this subsidy there was no possibility that the two liners could continue operating, and it was inevitable that the service would end.

Mariposa departed San Francisco on 1 November 1977 on its last voyage to the South Pacific, being in Auckland on 21 November, and Sydney from 26 to 28 November, returning to San Francisco on 14 December.

Mariposa departing Wellington on 31 March 1972 (V H Young L A Sawyer photo)

The final voyage to the South Pacific commenced on 7 December 1977, when *Monterey* left San Francisco. Calling at Auckland on 27 December, the vessel was in Sydney from 1 January 1978 for three days. Departing on 3 January, *Monterey* called at Suva, Pago Pago and Honolulu before arriving back in San Francisco on 19 January and being laid up. This brought the era of regular sea passages across the Pacific from North America to New Zealand and Australia to an end.

Mariposa operated several cruises from San Francisco and Los Angeles to Hawaii, but on 7 April 1978 the vessel berthed in San Francisco, and then joined *Monterey* in lay up. Both vessels were offered for sale, but for over a year no offers were received. Meanwhile, Pacific Far East Line was suffering a complete financial collapse, and eventually went bankrupt.

On 10 April 1979 *Mariposa* and *Monterey* were offered for sale at auction, being purchased by Edward Daly, then the president of World Airways, for a mere US$2.7 million for the pair.

Unfortunately this sale did not herald a bright new future for the two liners, as they remained idle in San Francisco while the new owner tried to negotiate a sale or charter of the vessels. At one time it was reported that *Monterey* had been sold to a new company, Royal Hawaiian Cruise Lines, but this fell through, then in November 1980 the vessel was sold to a company called American Maritime Holdings Inc, but still nothing more happened, and *Monterey* was destined to spend the next six years idle in San Francisco.

The magazine *New Zealand Marine News* in August 1979 carried a report that it was proposed that *Mariposa* be chartered for use as a floating hotel in Auckland, but the Auckland Harbour Board would not release a berth for this purpose.

In October 1980, *Mariposa* was sold to a company called American World Line, and on 7 November the liner left San Francisco, being towed by the large Dutch tug *Zwartze Zee*, bound for Mihara in Japan, but on arrival there on 6 January 1981 the liner was once again laid up. Later in 1981 the purchasers of the vessel defaulted on their payments, and *Mariposa* was again offered for sale.

In December 1983, *Mariposa* was purchased by China Ocean Shipping Company, the major operator of ships in mainland China. The original engines were removed, being replaced by a pair of Pielstik diesels, which gave a service speed of 17 knots, while the accommodation was revamped to carry 446 passengers, with extra berths being added to many of the cabins. Renamed *Jin Jiang*, in 1984 the vessel began operating a regular service from Hong Kong to Shanghai, and was often seen at anchor in Hong Kong harbour.

Meanwhile *Monterey* remained laid up in San Francisco until the middle of 1986, when it was announced that the liner was to be extensively

Mariposa arriving at Vancouver

refitted for a return to service with a newly formed company, Aloha Pacific Cruises, a subsidiary of American Maritime Holdings.

On 24 June 1986 the liner was towed away from San Francisco to Portland, Oregon, where the hull and superstructure underwent a partial rebuilding at the Tacoma Boatbuilding Company. The most notable change to the ship was a rather ugly extension to the stern section of the liner to provide more open deck space, several new public rooms and extra cabins.

In December 1987 *Monterey* was towed down the west coast of North America, through the Panama Canal, across the Atlantic Ocean and into the Baltic Sea to Turku, in Finland, where the interior was rebuilt by the Wartsila shipyard to provide accommodation for 661 passengers.

On 21 July 1988, *Monterey* departed Finland under its own power, going back across the Atlantic to Baltimore, where it was drydocked at the Bethlehem Steel Corp facility to have stabilizers fitted. Leaving Baltimore on 25 August 1988, *Monterey* went back through the Panama Canal to the Pacific, arriving at San Francisco on 15 September. *Monterey* began operating cruises from San Francisco to Hawaii, but on 7 February 1989 Aloha Pacific Cruises filed for bankruptcy, and on 13 May *Monterey* was laid up in Honolulu.

On 16 March 1990 *Monterey* was repossessed by the Connecticut Bank & Trust Co, and soon after sold to Coral Cruise Lines, of New York, but very quickly changed hands again, the new owner being listed as Cia Naviera Panocean SA, registered in Panama. This company was a subsidiary of Mediterranean Shipping Company, a major operator of container ships, who had entered the passenger business in 1987 by purchasing Star Lauro.

Without being renamed, *Monterey* returned to cruise service, operating mostly in the Mediterranean, for what was probably the most profitable period of its entire career. The accommodation now comprised 2 Royal Suites, 2 Deluxe Suites, 157 Outside Staterooms and 127 Inside Staterooms, all with private facilities, a safe, TV, telephone, refrigerator and balconies off some of the suites.

In 1992 *Jin Jiang*, the former *Mariposa*, was renamed *Queen of Jin Jiang*, which was changed to *Heng Li* in 1993, but the vessel continued to operate out of Hong Kong to Shanghai. In 1995 a fire caused serious damage to the galley, and the liner had to be taken out of service. Instead of being repaired, the vessel was sold to shipbreakers in China in 1996.

Monterey enjoyed a further decade of service, but having passed its fiftieth year since first entering service as a humble freighter, the liner was being superseded by numerous large new liners being built for Mediterranean Shipping Company. At the end of the 2005 Mediterranean summer cruising season *Monterey* was withdrawn from service.

It was reported that MSC was trying to sell the vessel for further trading, but the asking price of US$15 million was too much for a fifty year old vessel, so late in 2006 *Monterey* was sold to Indian shipbreakers. For its final voyage the name of the vessel was shortened to *Monte*, and it arrived at Alang on 3 November 2006. Five days later the vessel was run ashore on the beach, and within a matter of months it had been completely demolished.

Jin Jiang in Hong Kong Harbour (John Mathieson photo)

Rebuilt stern of *Monterey* (Stephen Berry photograph)

Monterey as a cruise liner

Index

Achilles (HMNZS) 210
Aeon 97, 98
Alameda 55–60, 63, 64, 79, 84, 85, 108, 114
Antinous 172
Aorangi (1) 81–83, 93–98, 100, 101, 109–111, 115–119
Aorangi (2) 141–153, 171, 180–183, 188, 189, 195, 198, 200, 203, 209, 211, 213, 215, 216, 218, 219, 223, 234–240, 245
Aotearoa 125, 141
Aparima 94
Aquitania 215
Arawa 71, 72, 75, 79,
Arcadia 247
Atlantic 232
Atrato 15
Australia 48–50, 52–55, 57, 59, 60, 63, 71
Avenger (HMS) 125
Awatea 201–208, 211–213, 215–220, 234

Black Swan 12
Britanis 262
Buck (USS) 221

Canberra 247, 248
Canberra (HMAS) 215
Carriso 169
City of Adelaide 22, 23, 25, 36–38
City of Melbourne 20–23, 26, 30, 31, 34, 35, 38, 40, 42, 44
City of New York 48–52, 54
City of San Francisco 43–46, 48, 50–52
City of Sydney 50, 52–54
Claymore 210
Colima 40–42, 46–48
Colorado 26
Conside 9, 10
Cyphrenes 29, 33, 36–39, 42

Dakota 23, 26–28
Danube 16
Dinornis 12
Dominion Monarch 215
Dungeness (HMS) 234

Ellinis 256
Emeu 12
Empress of Britain 200
Empress of Canada 240
Empress of Japan 211

Foremost 17 211
Free State Mariner 249, 253

Gdansk 137
Golden Age 12, 13
Governor Blackall 30
Governor General 11
Granada 45–47
Greycliffe 163–168

Hamakua 215
Hauraki 141
Hauroto 109
Heng Li 267
Hero 28
Himalaya 247
Hobart (HMAS) 216
Homeric 249

Ibuki 123
Iberia 247
Idaho 21

Jin Jiang 269, 270

Kaikoura 13–18
Kangaroo 12
Kearsage (USS) 248
King Egbert 197
Komet 214
Kulmerland 214

Lakemba 234–236, 240, 258–260
Leipzig (SMS) 120
Levuka 234
Liloa 215
Lord Ashley 13
Lord Worsley 13
Lurline (1) 184, 191–193, 196, 203, 215, 220, 223, 224, 227, 232, 249, 251, 253, 254, 256
Lurline (2) 256, 257, 265, 266

M E Lombardi 218
Macgregor 29–38
Maheno 95, 96, 119, 184, 204
Maitai 96, 100, 110, 112, 114, 116, 121, 123, 126, 127, 129
Maitland 10
Makura 98–100, 102, 103, 107, 117–120, 122, 123, 129, 131–133, 135, 136, 144, 145, 151, 153–156, 161, 163, 171, 172, 195, 200
Malolo 180, 183–185
Manapouri 57, 108, 109
Manuka 94–99, 101, 110, 118, 121,
Marama 96, 97, 100, 102, 103, 107, 117, 119–123, 129, 130, 132–134, 145, 177, 197, 198
Mararoa 56–60, 178
Marine Falcon 227–230
Marine Lynx 226, 227, 230
Marine Phoenix 230–233, 235, 236
Mariposa (1) 55–57, 59–61, 63–65, 72, 73, 79, 84–86, 108–110, 114
Mariposa (2) 183–197, 202, 207, 209, 213, 214–216, 218, 220–225, 232, 233, 249
Mariposa (3) 249–257, 265–270
Mataura 16–18

Matsonia (1) 185, 225, 226, 232
Matsonia (2) 254–256
Maui 215
Mauna Loa 221
Maunganui 103, 121–123, 134, 135, 145, 151, 171, 177–180, 195, 200, 211
Mauretania 215
Menura 12
Mikado 29–32, 36–38, 44, 47
Miowera 68–78, 82, 83, 93, 94, 96, 97, 100, 110
Moana 79–81, 84, 93–98, 100, 102, 116–121, 123, 127–131
Moeraki 94, 109, 134
Mohongo 25
Mokoia 109, 110
Mongol 29, 33–36
Monowai (1) 62–65, 79
Monowai (2) 177–180, 195, 196, 198, 202, 203, 206–208, 211, 216, 218
Monte 270
Monterey (1) 183–185, 190–197, 202–207, 209, 213, 214–216, 220–225, 232, 233, 249, 251, 254, 257
Monterey (2) 249–258, 265–270
Monumental City 10
Moses Taylor 25
Mount Vernon 221

Navua 108
Nebraska 23–28
Nevada 23–28
New Orleans 10
Niagara 104–107, 119–122, 124, 129, 131, 132, 134, 136, 137, 144, 145, 151, 179, 182, 183, 195–200, 203, 208–211, 229, 234

Orcades 246
Oriana 247, 248
Orion (1) 209, 214, 215
Orion (2) 246
Oronsay 245, 246
Orsova 246

Paloona 127, 129, 130
Pearl (HMS) 35
Pelican 12
Penbryn 172
Pine Tree Mariner 249, 251
Port Kingston 110, 112
Portland 10
President Coolidge 221
Prince Alfred 13, 16, 18
Prince Robert (HMCS) 218, 219, 220
Prince Rupert (HMCS) 216

Queen Frederica 232
Queen Mary 200, 215
Queen of Jin Jiang 270

Rakaia 14–18
Rangitane 214

Rapid 11
Razmak 177, 178
Retriever 258
Ruahine 14–18

Santa Elena 223
Santa Paula 249
Santa Rosa 249
Selandia 128
Sierra 84–88, 114, 126–129, 137, 169, 170, 181, 187, 193, 194
Sonoma 84–88, 113–115, 120, 126, 128, 129, 133, 137, 169, 170, 181, 193, 194
Southern Cross 251
Spurn Point (HMS) 234
Strathnaver 188
Strathnevis 76–78
Sydney (HMAS) 217, 218

Tahiti 112–114, 116, 117, 119–123, 129, 131–134, 137–140, 145, 151, 163–168, 170–177
Takapuna 54
Tararua 17
Tarawera 109
Tartar 29–38
Tofua 119, 130–133, 172, 176
Turakina 214

Vasco da Gama 40
Ventura 84–88, 113–115, 120, 126, 128, 129, 133, 137, 138, 169, 170, 172, 174, 175, 177, 181, 187, 193, 194

Wairarapa 79, 108
Wairuna 127, 128
Wandilla 116
Wanganella 203, 206, , 210, 229, 230,
Warilda 116
Warrimoo 67–78, 82, 83, 93
Willochra 116–121, 123, 124
Wodonga 71
Wolf 128
Wonga Wonga 20–23, 26

Zealandia (1875) 46–48, 51–55, 57, 59, 60, 63, 79
Zealandia (1899) 129
Zealandia (1910) 101–103, 106, 107
Zwartz Zee 269